FAMILY ABUSE AND VIOLENCE

W9-ASJ-227

VIOLENCE PREVENTION AND POLICY SERIES

This AltaMira series publishes new books in the multidisciplinary study of violence. Books are designed to support scientifically based violence prevention programs and widely applicable violence prevention policy. Key topics are juvenile and/or adult community reentry programs, community-based addiction and violence programs, prison violence reduction programs with application in community settings, and school culture and climate studies with recommendations for organizational approaches to school violence reduction. Studies may combine quantitative and qualitative methods, may be multidisciplinary, or may feature European research if it has a multinational application. The series publishes highly accessible books that offer violence prevention policy as the outcome of scientifically based research, designed for college undergraduates and graduates, community agency leaders, school and community decision makers, and senior government policymakers.

SERIES EDITOR

Mark S. Fleisher, Director, The Dr. Semi J. and Ruth W. Begun Center for Violence Research Prevention and Education, Case Western Reserve University, 10900 Euclid Avenue, Cleveland, OH 44106-7164, USA, 216-368-2329 or msf10@po.cwru.edu

BOOKS IN THE SERIES

Gang Cop: The Words and Ways of Officer Paco Domingo by Malcolm Klein (2004)
Measuring Prison Performance: Government Privatization and Accountability by Gerald G. Gaes, Scott D. Camp, Julianne B. Nelson, and William G. Saylor (2004)
European Street Gangs and Troublesome Youth Groups edited by Scott H. Decker and Frank M. Weerman (2005)
Violence and Mental Health in Everyday Life: Prevention and Intervention Strategies for Children and Adolescents by Daniel J. Flannery (2005)
Studying Youth Gangs edited by James F. Short, Jr., and Lorine A. Hughes (2006)
Family Abuse and Violence: A Social Problems Perspective by JoAnn Miller and Dean D. Knudsen (2006)

FAMILY ABUSE AND VIOLENCE

A Social Problems Perspective

JoAnn Miller and Dean D. Knudsen

ALTAMIRA
PRESS

A Division of Rowman & Littlefield Publishers, Inc.
Lanham • New York • Toronto • Plymouth, UK

AltaMira Press
A Division of Rowman & Littlefield Publishers, Inc.
A wholly owned subsidary of The Rowman & Littlefield Publishing Group,
Inc.
4501 Forbes Boulevard, Suite 200
Lanham, MD 20706
www.altamirapress.com

Estover Road
Plymouth PL6 7PY
United Kingdom

British Library Cataloguing in Publication Information Available

Library of Congress Cataloging-in-Publication Data

Miller, JoAnn L., 1949–
    Family abuse and violence : a social problems perspective / JoAnn Miller
and Dean D. Knudsen.
        p. cm. — (Violence prevention and policy series)
    Includes bibliographical references and index.
    ISBN-13: 978-0-7591-0800-4 (cloth : alk. paper)
    ISBN-10: 0-7591-0800-5 (cloth : alk. paper)
    ISBN-13: 978-0-7591-0801-1 (pbk. : alk. paper)
    ISBN-10: 0-7591-0801-3 (pbk. : alk. paper)
    1. Family violence—United States. 2. Problem families—United States. I.
Knudsen, Dean D., 1932- II. Title. III. Series.
    HV6626.2.M55 2007
    362.82'92—dc22

                                                           2006011288

This book is dedicated to the wonderful men in my life who, as they celebrate the wonderful women and girls in their lives, encourage my work. This is for Jonathan, Gus, Scott, Bob, Pete, Gary, and Don.

JM

Contents

Acknowledgments

Generous people helped us turn an idea into a book. We especially appreciate the encouragement and advice from Rosalie Robertson and the anonymous reviewers who gave us detailed suggestions for revisions. Two excellent copy editors, Carol Bangert and Annie Belt, improved our drafts. Carol, since 1993, has been the best friend an author can have. She's critical, thorough, and not at all hesitant to tell us when we are not getting our message across. The production editor, Jehanne Schweitzer, and her staff smoothly facilitated the preparation of the final draft. Our spouses, Scott Frankenberger and Lucille Knudsen, as always supported and encouraged our work. Two graduate students at Purdue, Sarah Kenny and Tauna Starbuck Sisco, worked with us on the glossary and the index. Two excellent judges have, over the years, helped us understand the importance of what we try to accomplish. We are inestimably grateful to Judge Johnson and Judge Hand. While they are not responsible for the mistakes that we make, they are indeed responsible for some of the most important lessons we have learned.

Introduction

It is nearly impossible to imagine women and men who do not have some response to reading or hearing about "family violence," "child abuse," "spouse abuse," or "elder neglect." But all too often, well-intentioned persons, informed by the popular media, ask the *wrong* questions:

- Why doesn't he leave his abuser?
- How could she let him *do that* to her own children?
- Why don't they hire better nursing home assistants to prevent elder neglect?

And all too often, well-intentioned persons offer unsolicited and inherently flawed solutions to the persistent social problem of family abuse and violence:

- A woman should develop a strong work ethic and get a good-paying job and day care for her children to prevent domestic violence.
- We need better sex offender registration laws to prevent child sexual abuse.
- If the alcohol abuse problem were solved, the family violence problem also would be solved.

- Increasing a person's self-esteem will prevent family violence victimization.

The wrong questions and many ineffective solutions tend to focus on the victim rather than the perpetrator of family violence. Some of these nonsolutions also are centered on the individual perpetrator, as if the family abuse and violence problem were a personal problem, not a social problem.

Some well-intentioned, albeit incomplete, solutions focus on empowering victims and potential victims. Others take the perspective that victims need protection from threatening circumstances. It is easier to *see* a victim or a potential victim of family violence than it is to understand the causes of the social problem. It is easier to *relate* to the individual social actor, who may be a victim or a perpetrator, than it is to draw connections across social organizations and social institutions to analyze social problems. It is much easier to reduce a complex social problem to what is intuitively plausible based on a first-hand experience or, say, a rumor about what happened to someone in the neighborhood: *Drinking causes people to lose inhibition, so they hit each other. When he was a child, he was abused by his own parents; violence is what he knows. Violence begets violence.*

The *myths* persist.

Since the early 1960s social scientists, legal researchers, and health researchers have studied the family violence problems that afflict social actors throughout the United States, regardless of social status, race, ethnicity, and geographical location. Nowadays it is almost impossible to attend an annual social science, legal or criminal justice, or health-related professional association conference in the United States without seeing sessions on some form of family violence or abuse. And it is impossible to attend an interdisciplinary family violence conference without hearing the usual assorted debates, including those surrounding the following questions:

- How did the 1996 welfare reform law exacerbate the family violence problem in the United States?
- Does the intergenerational transmission hypothesis explain spouse abuse?

- Should a child who witnesses domestic violence be removed from the home and placed in foster care? How important is family reunification?
- How can police encourage women of color and ethnic minorities to report domestic violence, elder abuse, or child neglect?
- Why aren't more jurisdictions adopting innovative prosecution policies for domestic violence cases?
- Are batterer intervention programs effective?
- Should an elder who engages in self-neglecting behavior be institutionalized?
- Should corporal punishment be criminalized?
- Can "family violence" be effectively studied, or is it preferable to analyze child abuse, intimate partner violence, and elder abuse as distinctive social problems?
- How effective are elder abuse prevention programs?
- How can researchers, policymakers, and service providers work together to address the family violence problem in the United States?

This list of issues is not exhaustive or even representative of the abundance of material available in journals, books, and online. Family abuse and violence, once limited to the study of child abuse, and once studied by only a small number of researchers, is a persistent and large-scale social problem in the United States (and in most countries) that now has the attention of government, the popular media, and local community workers in every town and city. Readers can search libraries and online sources and find thousands of items produced each year.[1]

We, as authors, take a social problems perspective to our work. We have spent many years researching the specialized problems of child abuse and intimate partner violence. We have put our ideas together every now and then for the purpose of integrating what we know across distinctive fields of inquiry. In 1989 we organized an international conference on the Purdue University campus, bringing together experts across the fields of child abuse, intimate partner abuse, and elder abuse. We published *Abused and Battered: Social and Legal Responses to Family Violence* (Knudsen and Miller

1991), which sociolegal and social science researchers and practitioners have read and cited over the years. In 1999 we coauthored the "Family Abuse and Violence" chapter that appeared in the second edition of the *Handbook of Marriage and the Family* (Sussman, Steinmetz, and Peterson 1999). Our alliance keeps us alert to how problems and research agendas related to child abuse and intimate partner abuse converge and diverge.

As we began work on this book, we knew full well that some important issues keep us on the same page, while others keep us on different pages. To illustrate: We both have studied social learning perspectives and research on the intergenerational transmission of violence. We are both intellectually curious about the culture of privacy that seems to influence appellate court decisions on family violence problems. The volunteer work that we do in our community illustrates how we differ: One of us has provided pro bono advice to social welfare organizations and family courts; the other has volunteered in domestic violence prevention programs and criminal justice organizations. One of us is somewhat more concerned with family unification policies; the other, with the consequences of domestic violence arrest policies. With this book we hope to achieve another alliance, not a merger. We present a conceptual perspective, some original research,[2] and analyses of relevant studies. Some of the chapters analyze child abuse, partner abuse, and elder abuse as distinctive problems. Other chapters examine them as dimensions of a family abuse and violence problem.

We begin this study of a family-focused social problem by presenting a conceptual framework in chapter 1 that integrates the work produced by specialists in subfields of family violence with that produced by researchers studying child, partner, and elder abuse as dimensions of a single problem. We call this framework the "Family Abuse and Violence Episode" perspective. Our framework does not present a new theory, but it does integrate social science theories and represents a new method for examining *intra*generational and *inter*generational abuse or violence. To illustrate the dimensions of this perspective, we present a case study of a family that has experienced neglect, abuse, and violence within and across generations.

We define "family abuse or violence episodes" here and will return to components of this definition in subsequent chapters:

> Family abuse and violence episodes are usually repeated but always purposeful social behaviors or omissions that tend to be motivated by inappropriate intentions to control or dominate family members or situations that affect family relationships. They may be characterized by an intention to harm or by a deliberate failure to nurture appropriately one or more family members. While members of a family may include intimate partners, spouses, children, siblings, parents, and other kin, FAV episodes refer to family or family-type relationships located in social spaces and places that give social actors opportunities to nurture and support or to harm or injure each other.

The FAV Episode framework is a general one that researchers, social change advocates, policymakers, and lawmakers can use to guide analyses of immediate problems or to propose new ideas for responding to persistent family abuse and violence problems. Our perspective highlights the importance of understanding the social context in which family problems occur. Thus, we use the term "social actor" to refer to persons who perpetrate or are victimized by family abuse and violence. The term "social actor" reflects the premise that what we study is social behavior. Even what appears to be the most individual behavior, we contend, must be examined as social behavior that occurs within the broader context of social relationships. In this book, social actors are the children, women, and men who are somehow affected by family abuse and violence. They are also the social workers, police officers, attorneys, judges, physicians, and other social service providers who respond to family abuse and violence.

Our analysis focuses on the problem of family abuse and violence within the contemporary United States. We look to the past in order to understand the present problem. We borrow studies from England and Canada only when we cannot find parallel research within the United States. Our intention is not to judge the relative severity of a social problem. Nor is it our intention to ignore the excellent cross-cultural work that scholars produce (see, e.g., Welden 2002). Our aim is to examine closely one social problem that federal and state governments respond to within the United States. We account for the social context of violence and abuse, that is, the social structural and cultural factors as well as the social psychological characteristics of FAV, which vary across social places, social spaces, and social time.

Chapter 2 introduces the data sources that are used to estimate the problem of family abuse and violence in the United States. We examine government, agency (or clinical), and social survey data, which are collected for different purposes but purport to produce accurate estimates of the incidence and prevalence of family violence. We identify the data sources we think most accurately portray *intra*generational and *inter*generational forms of family abuse and violence.

In chapter 3 we turn to historical studies to uncover the social institutional factors that have shaped contemporary U.S. understandings of family relationships and abusive family relationships. We study the past to understand how contemporary conceptualizations of child abuse and spouse abuse have emerged. Chapter 4 frames a description of how a private problem—unexplained, severe injuries sustained by children—became a public problem. Most evident in this chapter are two issues addressed by FAV theorists and researchers: First, social problems are continuously redefined in part by powerful social organizations and institutions that make large-scale investments in their efforts to protect victims and to punish or treat perpetrators. Second, family abuse and violence narratives and data represent real acts or omissions that cause tangible, measurable physical and emotional injuries to thousands of persons every year in the United States.

Chapters 5 and 6 examine two types of *inter*generational family abuse and violence. These chapters focus on child abuse, or the abusive behavior that a family member of one generation—a parent or a caretaker—perpetrates against a child, a family member of a younger generation who is dependent upon the adult. These chapters recognize the need to scrutinize distinct forms of family violence, which are defined as parent-child, partner-partner, or adult child–parent relationships. The physical and emotional abuse of children is the subject of chapter 5; thus the research on the contentious issue of corporal punishment or spanking is systematically analyzed. What do we know? We know that physical and emotional child abuse can have long-term, negative social consequences for some. What can we do? While we can identify the social structural factors affecting the likelihood that caretakers will abuse their children, we cannot identify the specific characteristics of social actors who are likely to harm or injure their children.

Chapter 6 considers the medical, legal, and social problems of child sexual abuse and exploitation. The inherent difficulties associated with diagnosing sexual abuse episodes interact with changing definitions of this particular dimension of family abuse and violence. All told, the analysis of the sexual abuse literature reminds the reader that some of the most insidious forms of family abuse are extremely difficult to study systematically. How do we approach victims without causing more harm? Can retrospective accounts accurately summarize children's experiences? Can they be used to develop strategies for preventing the sexual abuse of children?

Chapter 7 examines the process of figuring out who "counts" as a victim or as a perpetrator and what the extant medical and legal responses are to family abuse and violence episodes. Arguably the two most influential professional associations within the United States, the American Medical Association (AMA) and the American Bar Association (ABA), have worked diligently to define family violence problems and to stake claims for how society should respond to victims and perpetrators. The AMA and the ABA work within a culture that highly values privacy and autonomy.

Chapter 8 turns to the general population to see if perceptions of what constitute appropriate social responses to FAV problems correspond to the prevailing practices. We must rely on a Canadian survey to estimate perceptions regarding the overall problem of *intra-* and *inter*generational forms of family abuse and violence. However, we use a telephone survey, which we conducted specifically for the purposes of chapter 8, to answer specific questions: What should happen to first-time or repeat offenders of *intra*generational family violence perpetrators? Should the men and women who perpetrate acts of violence against their intimate partners be sanctioned? Should they be required to participate in therapeutic programs? Or should nothing be done?

Chapter 9 examines *intra*generational forms of family abuse and violence. We begin with an analysis of dating violence studies that have been conducted by researchers in recent decades. We analyze the data from a recent nationwide survey mandated by the Violence Against Women Act[3] for two purposes: First, we compare gender differences in reports of physical assault, rape, and stalking that were disclosed in telephone interviews by 8,000 women and 8,000 men. Second, we develop a typology of intimate partner violence to explain the threats and controlling behaviors women experience within their marital or cohabiting relationships as a function of their childhood experiences with violence.

Chapter 10 presents an overview of the consequences of *intra*generational episodes of family abuse and violence. For victims, consequences range from hurt feelings to emotional scars to death. We listen to narrative accounts of women, men, and children who are victims of family violence and narrative accounts of men who participated in a batterers' counseling program. We return to the national data examined in chapter 9 and continue our analysis to compare gender differences in injuries and lost time from work resulting from *intra*generational family abuse and violence. We conclude the chapter with a content analysis of newspaper reports of a homicide and the criminal trial and sentencing hearing that followed. While some victims of family violence are silenced by murder, readers can become at least somewhat familiar with what the victims experienced by studying the court testimony that journalists report.

Chapter 11 returns to *inter*generational forms of family abuse and violence. We consider dependent children and dependent elders and how the family neglect of each group is similar and different. Because they depend on caretakers—who may be their parents or their children—for their well being, dependents across generations require financial support, medical services, adequate nutrition, and reasonable housing. Children and dependent elders differ, however: Neglected children have always been the subjects of social intervention within the United States. In 2002 more than half of all maltreated children were reported to be victims of neglect. Neglected elders have only recently come to the attention of social service agencies. For young dependents, neglect means the

failure to provide what they need to thrive physically, intellectually, and psychologically. For older dependents, neglect means the
failure to protect them from financial exploitation or the failure to
provide the medicine and food or the connections to social groups
and social organizations that are necessary to survive.

For elders, self-neglect is also a form of abuse that can elicit
state intervention. The elder neglect problem, a new social problem
that is partly a consequence of increased longevity and medical
technologies, reminds us that FAV episodes continue to emerge
and transform as society and families change. Thus we conclude
our study of family abuse and violence with a pair of chapters. In
chapter 12 we discuss some of the persistent and often contentious
controversies and some of the emerging debates that characterize
the field, examining issues across *intra-* and *inter*generational forms
of family abuse and violence. In chapter 13 we summarize what we
know about this persistent social problem in the United States:
How successful has the United States been in reducing family
abuse and violence? What do we need to do?

We end here with some notes on terminology. We use the
phrase "Family Abuse and Violence Episode perspective" to refer
to the conceptual framework that guides our analysis of FAV. We
describe this framework in chapter 1. Our intention is to use one
expression to refer to a cluster of family abuse issues, such as emotional or financial abuse, and a cluster of family violence issues,
such as physical assault or rape. In each chapter we identify specific dimensions of family abuse and violence episodes. We use the
terms "child abuse," "child sexual abuse," "emotional abuse," and
"neglect" to make clear distinctions among the specific behaviors
or omissions to which we refer. We use the term "intimate partner
violence" to refer to what other researchers call "domestic violence," "woman abuse," or "spouse abuse." We chose this term for
the purpose of including marital, cohabiting, and dating couples.
All partnerships to which we refer are romantic or sexual partnerships. Finally, we use the terms "elder abuse" and "neglect" to refer to forms of family abuse and violence that are generally
perpetrated against a dependent and elder social actor. The elder
parent may live with his or her adult child, in a private residence,
or in a residential facility. He or she may be active and healthy or

frail. For the purposes of this study, what makes the elder vulnerable to abuse is a social status that for one reason or another is characterized by a lack of autonomy.

> A note to students and classroom instructors: We insert newspaper reports of specific cases of family abuse and violence throughout the book. Our intention is to encourage readers to think about how this pervasive, national social problem affects our hometowns and our university campuses. In addition, we conclude all but the last chapter with discussion questions and possible research projects. Some of the questions and projects invite library research, others require Internet searches for data and legal cases. We also include some research design projects, which are suitable for graduate and upper-division baccalaureate students.

Notes

1. In the appendix we list some of the best online sources and interdisciplinary professional journals available to researchers and students of family abuse and violence.

2. The case study in chapter 1, the vignette survey in chapter 8, the analysis of Violence Against Women and Men in the United States data presented in chapter 9, some of the consequences of partner violence and the content analysis of news coverage of a domestic homicide presented in chapter 10 are all studies we conducted for this book. They have not been published elsewhere.

3. The federal Violence Against Women Act called for the collection of nationally representative data. Patricia Tjaden and Nancy Thoennes are the principal investigators of the resulting survey. Originally the data set archived for analysis was titled "Violence and Threats of Violence Against Women and Men in the United States, 1994–1996." Subsequently the study has been called the National Violence Against Women survey. We use both titles in this book because we analyze the male and the female data from the survey.

I

A FAMILY ABUSE AND VIOLENCE EPISODE FRAMEWORK

1

Family Abuse and Violence Episodes: A Case Study and a Conceptual Framework

What accounts for family violence? Why are some persons more likely to perpetrate, and others, to become victims of child abuse or neglect, of intimate partner violence, or of elder abuse? How are the different types of family violence related to each other—if at all? In this chapter we begin to address these and other questions in a systematic inquiry designed to summarize what is known and what remains unknown about family violence and what governments and local social service and criminal justice agencies can do to ameliorate the family violence problem in the United States.

We begin with a case study of the intimate partner violence experiences of four sisters. The case study is not fictional, but we use pseudonyms and do not disclose the family members' locations. In telling the four sisters' stories, we include their childhood experiences and examine how their parents became vulnerable to elder abuse. An analysis of the case study, using a conceptual framework we call the Family Abuse and Violence (FAV) episode, follows. The framework helps piece together the social and contextual circumstances and explanations for the abuse and violence the sisters experienced or perpetrated. We conclude this chapter with an overview of the leading social science explanations for family violence. We show how the FAV perspective can be used to integrate existing theories, which offer individual-level, social psychological, and social structural explanations for child abuse, partner abuse, and elder abuse.

Four Sisters

Mary, Bernadette, Rose, and Margaret are sisters, born to the same parents between 1948 and 1962. Their life stories, as told to us by Bernadette in 2002, are used as a case study to show how a family provides the social space for love and sometimes maltreatment, and how young girls who experience degrading punishment and emotional neglect may, as young adults, find themselves in abusive intimate relationships. The sisters' stories illustrate the importance of examining intra- and intergenerational issues to understand family abuse and violence. Thus their stories are useful for articulating the FAV episode conceptual framework, which generates a comprehensive understanding of a social problem. The sisters' life stories also remind us that although women in the United States are usually the victims of intimate partner violence, which ranges in severity from battery and emotional abuse to homicide, men are also victims (U.S. Department of Justice 2004). Male victims cannot be neglected if an analysis of family violence is designed to be comprehensive. One of the most tragic victims in the four sisters' stories is a young man, the victim of a family homicide. The other is his surviving son, recently imprisoned for a felony conviction of elder abuse.

The sisters' stories were communicated to us exclusively by Bernadette, whose voice, we recognize, filters her sisters' life stories. In addition to her account, we reference correspondence, including letters from prison, and newspaper articles.

Three of the sisters are divorced from their first husbands, each having experienced a different form of intimate partner abuse. One was sexually molested during adolescence by a family member. Rose, the only sister who is not divorced, is a widow and one of the two primary suspects in the homicide of her first husband, Billy. Rose's second and current husband, Christopher, is the other suspect. Lieutenant Myrdek, the police officer in charge of investigating the murder, claims that Christopher, on account of his age at the time of the event (he was 15), has "an out" but is unlikely to admit to his involvement or to implicate Rose.[1]

Christopher was 15 and an unofficial foster child to Rose and Billy at the time Billy was killed. Rose, a special education teacher, was asked to consult with teachers and counselors in a small public school about Christopher and his two siblings, whose lives had been severely disrupted by their parents' tragedies and were missing school. While their father experienced a protracted dying process as a consequence of an inoperable tumor, their mother worked as a cocktail waitress and masseuse, leaving the three children at home with their dying father. The children stated that their father locked them in the basement to keep them out of trouble (and out of school) while their mother was away from the home. The parents were investigated for and cleared of child neglect and abuse.

Rose decided she would take the children to her home and become their unofficial foster mother. The two elder children lived with Rose and Billy only for three months, but Christopher's biological mother decided he could remain with Rose and Billy. No local government agency ever approved or sanctioned Rose's arrangements regarding the children. While the three children lived with her, their biological mother paid Rose a monthly stipend to feed and shelter them, and a local public school paid her to tutor them.

Christopher never returned to public school and he never completed the GED or any trade school curriculum. Christopher was employed on a number of occasions, but Rose helped him pursue a disability status, based on drug addictions, that kept him in their home. Rose and Billy's home was located in a rural location and removed from places where social actors gather, such as work, school, church, or leisure groups. Rose continues to work as a special education teacher in the public school system, and she and Christopher live in extreme social and physical isolation.

Rose disclosed to Bernadette that Billy, her deceased husband, was extremely jealous of Christopher, especially after Billy came home earlier than expected from work one day to find the teenager washing Rose's hair over the bathtub while Rose was naked to her waist. When Christopher was 15 years old, Rose gave birth to a child, Paul, who was four months old when Billy was killed. Billy was shot in the head four times, gagged and bound, and set on fire in his car, which was found still smoldering by a hunter and his son on a Sunday morning. His murder, on October 14, 1979, remains one of the unsolved homicides in the state. Police Sergeant David Kelley, who heads the Historic Case Unit for his state, claims this type of unsolved homicide is "the most frustrating," because "you know who did it, but don't have the information to support an indictment or arrest" (Taylor 2000). One of the police officers initially responsible for investigating the homicide claims Rose "is a suspect—from the start—but there was no search of the house . . . because the lawyers came in" (Myrdek 1995).

The four sisters' births were spaced across fourteen years. They completed their elementary education at the same religious school, although each sister attended a different high school. Three graduated from church-affiliated high schools and one from a local public high school. Only the youngest sister, Margaret, was allowed to attend a coed school. Mary, Bernadette, and Rose never sat in a classroom with a boy, from kindergarten through high school.

The sisters' parents both left high school at age 16, during World War II. They met on a military base following the war, where the father was stationed and the mother worked as a civil service typist. They worked full time, providing the girls with a comfortable home, fashionable clothing, art and dance instruction, and the promise of college opportunities—as long as the girls remained unmarried.

Their father was a strict, traditional disciplinarian, especially with the two older girls. Corporal punishment was the expected sanction for infractions ranging from "talking back" to breaking curfew for Mary and Bernadette. A slap across the body was common, a paddle with a wooden board that hung on a kitchen wall occurred somewhat less frequently, and on rare occasions, other objects such as belts, brooms, chairs, and a dishwasher rack were used on the two older sisters. Their mother did not hit or slap. She would report the children's infractions to their father as he entered the home after work. He wasted no time in dispensing the punishments, either with his hand or by reaching for an item in close proximity.

Corporal punishment was therefore a component of the family's ordinary parenting practices (Horn, Joseph, and Cheng 2004;

Paolucci and Violato 2004; Regalado et al. 2004; Turner and Muller 2004). The paddling board, for example, was a Christmas gift from the sisters' maternal aunt. On it, painted in bright red and green letters, were the words "Board of Education." As children the sisters did not think their father mistreated them. To the contrary, Bernadette and Mary often traded stories with their adolescent classmates on Monday mornings to see who got into the most trouble over the weekend. Bernadette likes to tell her own son a particular story: When she was 4, her father tried to teach her the importance of playing on the sidewalk and not on the street. Standing on the curb he told her, "If you put one toe—just one little toe— in the street, I will spank your bottom." Bernadette claims to remember the sting of the spanking, and she also claims the lesson was highly effective.

Margaret, the fourth sister, was an unplanned baby. By the time she was 10 years old, her oldest two sisters were married. By the time she began high school, she was the only sister in the household. Like the two oldest sisters, she experienced relatively severe corporal punishment. But unlike the oldest sisters, she experienced corporal punishment infrequently. The third sister, Rose, seems to have totally escaped her father's assaultive behaviors. She and her sisters recall no hitting, no slapping, and no spankings for Rose.

The older sisters, Bernadette and Mary, wonder why they experienced frequent, somewhat harsh physical punishments that left marks and welts and occasionally some bloody wounds. They were never injured severely enough to require a physician's intervention, but they remember experiencing frequent and sometimes extreme corporal punishment from early childhood through their high school years. Once they had children and grandchildren of their own, they realized the television shows they watched as children, *Father Knows Best* or *Leave It to Beaver*, presented the image of an emotionally distant father but not a father who hit the way they had been hit and occasionally injured. One especially brutal episode left them bruised and injured severely enough to require a few days of bed rest. Their parents had discovered that both girls lied about seeing and talking to Mary's boyfriend while they were at a high school football game on a Saturday afternoon.

The two oldest sisters left home and married as each turned 19, one year after high school graduation. They missed the opportunity to go to college because they married. Unfortunately for both of them, they exchanged marriage vows with men who continued their father's traditions: Their husbands practiced the same religion, expected their wives to have children and to be obedient and supportive, and hit or threatened to hit, sometimes with objects, just as their father had.

Mary's husband, Doug, imposed frequent corporal punishment on their children as well, and it was her attempts to defend the children from his blows that would trigger his assaults on her. Mary and Bernadette did not share their marriage stories with each other until their own children were married, and they worried aloud to each other about how their own family experiences could or would affect their children's marital and parenting relationships.

Rose, the third born, was small and frail compared to her sisters. She was the only daughter with her father's light complexion, blue eyes, and blonde hair. It is possible that her resemblance to her father protected her from his physical punishments (Burch and Gallup 2000). Her father often commented that she was the only "real McCoy" in the family. Rose was a precocious child who, at age 4, won a summer talent contest that was held on the bandstand at the beach. That fall she was placed in a kindergarten class in a private day school for children with special needs, in order to allow her parents to place her in elementary school a year earlier than the minimum age specified by the state. Once Rose was in school, their mother had no need to attend to her children in any physical or nurturing way until she got pregnant with Margaret. Her daughters stayed at their religious-affiliated schools until 5 p.m. daily.

Margaret, the youngest daughter, tells her oldest siblings that they, Mary and Bernadette, took care of her as a young child. They bathed her and took her to the bathroom. They put her to bed at night and helped her dress in the morning. Margaret recalls when her parents went out to dinner on a weekend evening, she would crawl into her parents' bed, knowing they would have to carry her upstairs and to her own bed upon their return. While she does not remember how old she was when she did these things, she does remember that she engaged in this deliberate behavior because she believed there was no other way to get her parents to touch her or hold her.

The older sisters have no clear memory of their mother physically caring for them. They do not remember her fixing their hair or bathing them as toddlers and preschoolers. What they vividly recall is growing up with a live-in housekeeper who slept upstairs with the girls while their parents slept in a downstairs bedroom. The housekeeper was responsible for the girls' bedtime and morning routines. Although their mother rarely came up the stairs, their father occasionally came up to inspect their rooms or to punish them for not being asleep on schedule. When the sisters look at family photos of holidays and other events, they see their mother well-dressed and coiffed but never touching any of them. Bernadette characterizes her mother as distant and not involved emotionally with her or her sisters. To illustrate her position, she recalls at age 11 proudly announcing the onset of menses to her mother, only to be told that Mary would "give her something to use" and tell her what to do.

Mary, the oldest sister, met Doug at a school function when she was 13. She married at age 19 and stayed married to him for fifteen years. He continuously abused her emotionally. He referred to her as "stupid" or "fat" and "lazy" at home, in public settings, and at family gatherings. Less frequently he hit her, and occasionally he took from their home safe a gun that his father had made for him, to remind Mary that he was the head of the household. Mary's account is that Doug never intended to hurt her, but he did chase her around the house with the gun to scare her when she interfered with his intent to hit the children.

Mary dated only Doug. While he was in college, Mary worked full time and lived at home to save money and to collect things for her hope chest. Doug completed a bachelor's degree in business administration at a college in their hometown. In her early thirties Mary decided to begin a college program in elementary education. Doug was employed as a sales manager in a wholesale plumbing supply company. During Mary's second year of college, Doug lost his job and remained unemployed for the rest of their marriage. His verbal and emotional abuse escalated to daily verbal insults and humiliating taunts that were directed at her and at their children in the privacy of their home and in front of their friends and extended family members.

Doug's assertions of having control over Mary began at the start of their relationship. When they were high school students, he often claimed his superiority: He was more physically fit, smarter, less sheltered, more ambitious, more clever, and wiser than Mary. His claims were frequent and never challenged by Mary's parents. His sudden and unexpected unemployment provoked sharp marital discord. He taunted Mary every day, telling her she was ignorant and mocking her college program (in elementary education) because it prepared her to pursue only a low-paid occupation and did not prepare her to face the real world. Doug's verbal abuse typically included a reminder that Mary was wholly dependent on him, incapable of surviving and taking care of their two children without him, and incapable of ever becoming attractive enough to leave their marriage. Mary's parents, too-often witness to Doug's abuse, talked openly about what they saw and heard. They told Bernadette that Mary was shy and suffered from low self-esteem, which prevented her from developing her talents and aspirations. According to them it was Mary, not Doug, who had a problem.

After approximately one year of relentless verbal abuse and threats and occasional episodes of hitting and slapping, Mary fled her home with a suitcase packed with clothing and toiletries, leaving behind her two children. The bitter divorce that followed included court hearings in which Doug claimed Mary was an unfit mother; Doug's claims were backed up by expert testimony from a child psychologist, who contended only an unfit mother would leave her children. Mary prevailed, perhaps because her father financed the divorce proceedings by hiring an attorney—the same attorney who instructed Rose and Christopher not to talk to the police about Billy's homicide. She was eventually granted custody of her children and moved out of state with them.

Bernadette turned 19 in July, one year after high school graduation, and married 20-year-old Tim in August. Bernadette wanted to get married to get out of her father's home. Tim wanted to marry to quiet his mother's accusations that he was gay because he was pursuing a performing arts career. Before they married and until they divorced, Tim pursued other women whom he perceived were interested or willing to get involved with him emotionally or physically. Bernadette gave birth to their only child 15 months after they married. She became pregnant after her physician, who displayed a Papal Blessing in the waiting room, told her she was sinning against God and the Church by taking birth control pills. While she labored in a hospital as a Medicaid patient, Tim was too restless to wait with the other expectant fathers. As he roamed the hospital hallways, he met a nurse who was completing her work shift at 3 p.m. They went out together, and Tim could not be located when his child was born. He returned to the hospital later that evening, several hours after Bernadette birthed her child, and watched the nurses place the infant in an incubator due to breathing problems.

Bernadette was unaware of Tim's extramarital relationships, although she admits she should have suspected them from the beginning of their marriage, when Tim, then a student at a music conservatory, would stay at school to rehearse performances until after midnight five or six nights a week. Bernadette financially supported Tim's education and provided their only source of income until their child was born. At that time Tim took a weekend job as a room service waiter in an upscale hotel. He quit work three months later. To pay the rent and buy food, Bernadette worked three part-time jobs for the balance of the time it took Tim to complete his formal education. From the time they married until their child began elementary school, there was no violence or abuse that Bernadette recalls. She admits that her work schedule and Tim's performance, rehearsal, and school schedule probably protected her from any overt abuse.

When their child was in the first grade, Tim's mother died. A few months before her death, Tim began telling Bernadette about the other women in his life. In response, Bernadette courted Tim, hoping to please him, even taking him on a second honeymoon while her parents cared for their child. Soon after they returned from their trip, Tim disclosed that he was an exhibitionist, using his performing arts interest as an opportunity to exhibit himself for sexual gratification. He told Bernadette that his numerous love affairs were actually a manifestation of his exhibitionism.

Tim began psychotherapy following his disclosures and vowed to remain faithful to the marriage. They moved across the state and Tim began a graduate program while Bernadette worked and attended a local college part time. Shortly after their move, Bernadette spotted one of Tim's girlfriends in town, driving a yellow Volkswagen. Tim and Bernadette argued. Without raising his voice, Tim reached for a carving knife, knocked Bernadette to the floor, knelt on top of her with one knee, and held the knife to her throat, threatening to kill her if she told his girlfriend's husband what she had seen. Bernadette wonders why Tim never yelled and why he never called her names. Her father's angry outbursts always included shouting and name-calling: According to her father, she was a "bitch," a "whore," and a "fucking wench." Why would Tim hurt her when he had never even called her names? Compared to her father, it was clear that Tim respected her.

Bernadette later wondered why she desperately worked to preserve her marriage. The knife incident seemed to light a fuse. It initiated at least twice-weekly episodes of Tim pushing, shoving, and slapping Bernadette for nearly three years. In response, she began drinking heavily each night, hoping it would hurt less if she could get drunk enough. She also focused on begging Tim to stop the physical abuse. Their child, she assumes, heard the fights and was aware that his mother drank herself to sleep every night. Bernadette never thought about leaving or calling the police. Her arms, legs, and trunk were continuously bruised—but never her face—and she never perceived that she needed medical attention.

When Tim's mother died Bernadette knew how to locate him to break the unexpected news. She found him, by phone, at a dance studio where he was naked and being watched by his girlfriend who drove the yellow Volkswagen. Tim stayed in therapy for approximately eighteen months. He moved in and out of their home until he came back one day to announce that he was cured and therefore wanted to leave the marriage. He did, however, give Bernadette one more opportunity to preserve the marriage. She was working part time and had saved enough money to pay state college tuition and had enrolled full time in a public college. Tim told her he would stay if she dropped out of school. If she chose to stay in school, he would leave.

Bernadette chose school and remains convinced that she made a good decision. She does, however, regret the year following Tim's departure. As the sole caretaker for her sixth-grade son, she drank alone each night until passing out, never staying awake long enough to make sure he was asleep, and never waking in time to say hello to him before he left for the school bus. She bragged to her friends that divorce helped her son mature. One friend urged Bernadette to visit a campus mental health office for help with her alcohol problem.

Years following Bernadette's divorce, Margaret, the youngest sister, told Bernadette that Tim had exhibited himself to her. Margaret also disclosed to Bernadette that Rose's first husband, Billy, by then murdered, had molested her. Margaret often spent the night at Rose and Billy's home, usually at Rose's insistence and always to help out with weekend household chores. From the onset of Margaret's puberty and for four years after—until Billy's murder—Billy would wait until Margaret was supposedly sleeping. He would approach Margaret, who was feigning sleep on the living room couch, and would fondle her breasts. During those four years she never told anyone what she was experiencing. By the time she was 16, she was having violent nightmares during which she would thrash about, throwing items from her bedroom furniture. Her father would shout up the stairs to wake her and interrupt the dreams. He took Margaret to a psychologist who was the same man who had treated and supposedly cured Tim of his exhibitionism. The psychologist asked Margaret to tell him what she did to *encourage* Billy to touch her breasts. Margaret told her parents that she did not need psychotherapy and never returned after her first and only meeting with the psychologist.

Margaret married her first husband, Richard, after a series of short-lived, bad relationships. Richard was an abusive drinker, but he only drank at parties or on weekends and holidays, usually drinking beer until he passed out. Margaret was fully aware of his drinking patterns, having met him at a company party when he was drunk. She and a friend had driven the passed-out Richard home. On their wedding day Margaret dreaded the likelihood that

Richard would get drunk and not make it through the reception. She told Bernadette while they were dressing for the wedding ceremony that she feared their parents would discover his drinking problem.

Richard's drinking episodes followed the same pattern: At the beginning, he drank in near silence, sometimes watching television, at other times listening to music. The quiet Richard then transformed into a boisterous and aggressively friendly Richard, who, when perceiving that his overtures were unappreciated, then transformed into an angry Richard who shouted threats and threw objects. Margaret reports that he occasionally hit his target but he usually missed her. When she could, she would escape into a bedroom or the bathroom and lock the door until he became quiet. Wherever he passed out or fell asleep is where he would awaken. Following most of his drinking episodes, he apologized, but sometimes he claimed he had no memory of what had occurred. When their child was nearly 2 years old, Margaret divorced Richard (with her father's financial assistance) because she feared Richard would push her or their child down the stairs and cause serious injury. Once the divorce was finalized, she left the state, afraid that Richard would stalk her.

Why did three of the four sisters marry into abusive relationships? Why did two sisters marry men who abused their younger sister? If Rose killed Billy or participated in his homicide, as the police suspect she did, was Billy's abuse of Margaret a motive? Or was her relationship with her informal foster son, who is now her husband and the father of at least one of her children, the motive for a family homicide? Did four sisters learn how to abuse or how to be abused from their father's physical aggression or from their mother's neglect?

The sisters all finished college as nontraditional students and they all had children. Mary never dated following her divorce from Doug. He was the only boy or man, other than her son, her son-in-law, and her father, whom she ever let into her life. She admits that one frightening marriage was all she cared or dared to experience. Mary's daughter is married and has children. Her son and his wife are childless by choice. Bernadette's only child married his college girlfriend.

Margaret married twice following her divorce from Richard. Each marriage lasted less than one year. Each husband promised a fortune, but one declared personal bankruptcy, leaving her with a portion of his debt, and the other was unemployed throughout the duration of the marriage. Margaret's daughter is a troubled teenager. She is a cutter who carves her wrists as well as her upper arms. She was hospitalized following a possible suicide attempt and was chronically absent from school. As a consequence, at age 16 she dropped out of school and has not progressed beyond the eighth grade.

Margaret had her placed in a three-week intensive outpatient program for drug abusers following an arrest for drug use. While participating in the program, she told Margaret that the counselor helped her recover her supposed "repressed memories." Her father had sexually molested her (sometime before age 2), her girlfriend molested her at age 8, and she had watched a group of her friends commit suicide when she was in the sixth grade.

Margaret expresses pride in her daughter, saying she is beautiful and looks much older than her age. She notices adult men look at her daughter in the shopping mall, interpreting their glances as signals of attraction. She tells Bernadette that she looks forward to the day when her daughter drives and works and will become independent. She is convinced her daughter will become a fashion model.

Rose has two sons. The older son, Paul, is Billy's child according to hospital and health department records. Rose told Bernadette that she had the birth certificate, which listed Billy as the father, legally changed to indicate that Christopher, once Rose's foster child, is Paul's father. When Paul was 6 and 7 years old, Christopher attempted to get trained out of the state for a telephone maintenance job. Rose traveled to Texas and California with him and kept Paul out of school, with strong disapproval from the school, resulting in Paul being held back in the first grade. Paul has been in and out of state prison (mostly in) since 1996 when he was 17. Rose and Christopher allowed Paul to smoke marijuana and to drink beer in their home by the time he was 13 years old, on the premise that he was better off doing these things, which they also do, in front of them rather than outside their home. Rose kicked

Paul out of the home when he was 15—the same age Christopher was when Billy was murdered and Paul was born—only to have the police return Paul and explain to Rose that, as his mother, she was responsible for Paul until he was 18.

Most of Paul's prison time has been served for heroin and burglary offenses. On one occasion he stole a gun and claimed in court to have sold it to the man from whom he bought heroin. In 2003, he was convicted of selling jewelry stolen off the hands of elderly women living in a nursing home. The newspaper reported:

> "A man and a woman are in . . . County Jail in Bangor facing charges they stole expensive and cherished diamond rings off the fingers of elderly patients at a Portland nursing home. The thefts occurred last month, when diamond solitaires were slipped off the fingers of two women in their 80s who are residents at Fallbrook Woods. One of the rings was worth $17,000, the other $1,500, said Portland police Detective Cheryl Holmes. 'One of them, the woman couldn't even get it off her hand because it was so tight' suggesting the thief had to work hard to get the ring off, Holmes said. 'One, her family said it had been on her hand for 52 years'. . . . In one case the woman had moved into the facility the day before the theft, two days after her husband died" (Hench 2003: 9B).

Convicted of a Class B felony, Paul was sentenced to ten years in state prison.

In a 1997 letter from prison, where Paul was serving time for an earlier burglary and theft of a .44 caliber Magnum from a neighbor (*Manchester Union Leader* 1997: A10), Paul had written to Bernadette, saying, "I'd like to be a lawyer. I've learned a lot [about] this system from where I stand. . . . I filed this pro se motion [to be resentenced] but because of the past when I was on bail it was denied." Rose, in November of 1998, sent photos to her sisters of a newborn child—her grandson, and Paul's son, she claimed. She wrote, "He is *beautiful*. The silver lining is . . . I'll get to see great grandchildren in my lifetime. *Never* imagined that it could come to pass" (Personal correspondence November 18, 1998). However, the child was not her grandson. During a six-week period when Paul was not in prison, he thought he had impregnated his girlfriend but had not. While incarcerated in 2003, Paul attempted suicide by swallowing the cap of a ballpoint pen.

Rose's younger son, Tony, left high school in the eleventh grade. At age 18, he moved out of state to live with a former babysitter. When that did not work out, he returned home and stayed for nearly a month before Rose had him committed for observation and evaluation at a state psychiatric hospital. Now in his mid-twenties, he has never been employed. Both of Rose's sons communicate by phone with Margaret's daughter. As Rose and Margaret explain to Bernadette, they are "like brothers and sisters." They are each other's "best friend."

Three of the four sisters experienced sometimes-excessive levels of corporal punishment at the hands of their father. Margaret, while she was an adolescent, was abused sexually by two men, each married to one of her older sisters. No account of the family violence that the four sisters experienced as adults would be sufficient without a focus on both the *inter-* and *intra*generational abuse they experienced.

Three sisters experienced different forms of intimate partner abuse and violence. One was threatened with a knife and recalls a large number of pushing, shoving, and hitting incidents. One was verbally taunted on a continuous basis and on occasion was reminded of her status with a gun. One mastered the art of ducking to avoid injury from flying objects. Each woman's family abuse and violence experience points to different *intra*generational problems. One partnered with a man with a supposed mental illness, one experienced an escalation in abuse that accompanied unemployment, and one married a man with an abusive drinking problem. No explanation of what they experienced would be sufficient without a focus on *intra*generational abuse issues.

Each woman, on her own schedule and on her own terms, figured a way out; however, three depended on their father to finance an attorney for a divorce or to protect against a homicide investigation. One sister, Rose, whose first husband molested her younger sister, remains a suspect in the homicide. Her family life experiences seem odd, at best, and perhaps disgusting. Her story, of course, demonstrates the most tragic outcome of family violence. Billy was killed, and no one has ever been held legally responsible for his brutal homicide. He is survived by his imprisoned son, his elderly parents, his sister and brother, and his nieces and nephews.

While there may be a villain, there are neither heroes nor victims among the four sisters. Collectively their life stories help to illustrate a number of important issues. Similar childhood or family experiences contribute to relatively disparate outcomes, yet family patterns are repeated across generations. Bernadette married a man who abused her as her father had, but she figured out how to get out of the relationship and survive as a single mother, albeit not a good mother, according to her own perceptions. Rose's son Paul, in a letter from prison, communicated that he would like to repeat the relationship his mother had with a boy—the foster child she eventually married. At age 17 Paul wrote: "I need a girl. Actually I'm done with girls. A *woman* is more suitable. . . . I really want to change my life around but can't do it up here without a mature woman" (Personal correspondence April 29, 1997). A year later, Rose wrote to Bernadette, telling her how the family's traditions and values helped to get her and her imprisoned son through difficult moments. She wrote, "I know he'll survive, he is a survivor. . . . [Paul has] that tenacity for holding onto life no matter how badly it kicks you in the face" (Personal correspondence May 11, 1998).

The term "survivor," of course, has different meanings. While Paul may indeed have survived his childhood and adolescent experiences, normative social standards, used to judge issues ranging from an individual's mental health to his contribution to the well-being of a social group or society, suggest that Paul survives outside of prison only by engaging in criminal activity, including criminalized forms of elder abuse. Paul's story illustrates how families can be characterized by widespread *inter-* and *intra*generational forms of family abuse and violence. Because Rose is possibly culpable for the homicide of her first husband, it is possible also that an extreme form of *intra*generational family violence affected Rose's relationship with her son Paul, who was neglected by her from a young age, an *inter*generational problem. By age 6, Paul was continuously absent from school and was held back in the first grade. By age 15, his mother had thrown him out of their home. Since 1997 he has lived most of his days behind bars.[2] There are, however, short periods of time, measured in weeks but not months, when he lives on the outside. During the summer of 2003, when he committed a form of elder abuse, he was awaiting trial in jail. He phoned his 83-year-old maternal grandfather, who manifests forgetfulness, and asked him to mortgage his retirement home to raise bail. Only because Mary and Bernadette found out and convinced their father otherwise did he escape becoming another elder victim, abused by his grandson.

Childhood experiences can put young adults at risk for abusive relationships, but they do not determine who will become a perpetrator and who will become a victim. Moreover, it is imperative to acknowledge two additional factors that the sisters' stories do not address: First, most adults in abusive or violent relationships with their partners were *not* abused or neglected as children (Tjaden and Thoennes 2000). Second, most children who experience troubled or abusive childhoods do *not partner* with abusive spouses or lovers (Gelles 2003).

Integrating Issues: A Family Abuse and Violence Episode Perspective

The four sisters' life stories demonstrate that many family violence episodes can be better understood through a theoretical and empirical lens that considers what happens to family members across and within generations. Parent-child relationships can provide important insights into the dynamics of family abuse, although they also leave many questions unanswered. Indeed, the hypothesis that family violence is transmitted across generations is rejected as often as it is confirmed by clinical and survey data (Kaufman and Zigler 1987; Kwong et al. 2003; Langhinrichsen-Rohling, Hankla, and Stormberg 2004; O'Keefe 1998; Rosen, Bartle-Haring, and Stith 2001; Widom 1989). These inconsistencies lead to two important propositions: First, a child's family experience influences his or her chance of forming relationships that become abusive or violent. Parent-child relationships, however, are not sufficient to account for who is likely to become a perpetrator or a victim. Second, to explain sufficiently family violence, something more than an *inter*generational perspective is needed.

We contend that a combination of within (intra-) and across (inter-) generational factors better explains child abuse, intimate partner abuse, and elder abuse. We also posit that an event of abuse or violence can be understood as a family abuse or violence episode, which can be characterized along ten dimensions of information. Family abuse or violence episodes can be single social acts, such as the murder of Billy. Or they can be ongoing, chained, or connected episodes of abuse, such as Bernadette's experiences with repeated acts of physical violence or Mary's experiences with continuous emotional abuse.

A Conceptual Framework

The conceptual framework we develop and present here to comprehensively examine family abuse and violence is an adaptation of the Meier, Kennedy, and Sacco (2001) theory of the criminal event. We present the Family Abuse and Violence (FAV) episode as a conceptual framework rather than a formal theory. Our intention is to articulate a structure that can be useful to researchers and scholars who describe or attempt to explain family violence. The FAV framework invites an integration of theoretical and empirical perspectives across ten dimensions.

The FAV episode, whether it is a single act, such as a homicide, or reoccurring instances of intimate partner violence, child abuse, or elder abuse, occurs within a social and historical context. An episode can be understood sufficiently only by looking at its past, but its characteristics also predict a possible or probable—but not determinative—trajectory of future events.

The family violence episode helps to account for the victim's experiences, the perpetrator's motivation and behaviors, the circumstances surrounding specific events, and the consequences of family violence. The FAV episode framework thereby integrates explanations of socially deviant family behaviors, victim and perpetrator problems, and the social context of family abuse and violence. All told, it represents the confluence of ten dimensions or characteristics of social actors and social space that help to explain a persistent social problem.

The term "episode," as we use it here, can be understood in terms of a television show. Consider the 1950s classic *The Honeymooners*. An "episode" may depict a one-time event, such as a wedding anniversary celebration. It may also refer to a process that occurs over several years, such as Ralph and Alice Kramden's marital relationship, memorialized by phrases such as "One of these days, Alice . . . POW, right in the kisser!" or "Baby, you're the greatest!"[3]

Likewise, a family violence episode can appear to be a discrete act of aggression or neglect, yet the episode also occurs within a context of ongoing, family relationships. An FAV episode is either perpetrated by a social actor against another of the same generation—an *intra*generational episode—or it is perpetrated by a social actor against another of a younger or older generation—an *inter*generational episode. Intimate partner abuse and violence, including all forms of dating abuse and marital abuse, are *intra*generational family violence episodes. Child neglect perpetrated by a parent, and elder abuse perpetrated by an adult, child, or grandchild are examples of *inter*generational family violence episodes. *Inter-* and *intra*generational forms of family abuse are qualitatively different in many important ways. Nonetheless, they both occur within ongoing, family relationships.

The context for the family violence episode represents an intersection of social structural and cultural and social psychological factors. The episode occurs within a context that includes social structural factors such as perpetrator motivation and opportunity, the mechanics for the socially deviant act, and the social space or location. Social and legal definitions of family violence, or a patriarchal explanation of wife abuse, are also structural-level factors. A woman's religious beliefs that discourage her from leaving an abusive marriage represent cultural factors. A partner's controlling behavior within a household is social psychological–level explanation. We posit that context is a necessary but not a sufficient dimension of information to explain family abuse and violence.

A family abuse and violence episode can cause psychological or physical harm and injury with short-term or long-term consequences. The episode, as it is witnessed or experienced directly or indirectly by social actors, varies in *type*. It can be an episode characterized as sexual abuse or physical assault or negligent behavior.

The episode, quite independent of the short-term or long-term harm that it causes, varies in *severity* or seriousness. Arguably, episodes of child neglect, which may be manifested by a parent's repeated refusals to take responsibility for getting a 7-year-old child to school, are less serious than a single episode of spousal battery that causes a broken bone. The parent held responsible for educational neglect could be warned by a school principal while the adult who injures a spouse faces the possibility of arrest, criminal conviction, and jail time.

It is, however, possible that the child deprived of education experiences long-term, harmful consequences, while the spouse who is the victim of criminal battery recovers emotionally and physically in a short time. All family abuse and violence episodes have consequences for the *primary* victim or offender, and they have possible or probable consequences for other social actors who are *secondary* victims or offenders. The episode causes direct harm to the primary victim as well as measurable but indirect harm to others, such as a child's classmates, extended family members, or neighbors.

The purpose for articulating an FAV episode perspective is to create a framework locating events and connections between events and social actors across time and space. This perspective helps explain why some victims of child abuse, elder abuse, or intimate partner abuse experience isolated or repeated victimizations. It explains variation in the types of events and in the severity of abusive episodes. It also allows us to make sense of the general population's perceptions of the social problem of family violence.

The FAV episode perspective explains a specific but widespread social problem. It contributes to a general theoretical explanation of deviant family behavior and aids in the social and legal responses to social problems. It integrates ten dimensions of information that can be used to comprehensively explain *inter-* or *intra*generational forms of family violence. We illustrate each dimension with examples from the case study of four sisters.

1. Social Actors Internal to the Episode

    The FAV episode includes two types of social actors who are internal to the episode. There are the primary victims and the primary perpetrators. Bernadette is a primary victim of intimate partner violence. Her ex-husband, who threatened her life with a knife, is a primary perpetrator. There also are social actors who may be secondary victims or perpetrators. They may be internal to the family violence episode. Bernadette's child is a secondary victim of ongoing family violence episodes. He was neglected by her as a result of her alcohol abuse, which she claims was a response to intimate partner violence. He also was witness to ongoing intimate partner violence.

Margaret may be considered a secondary victim of Bernadette's abusing husband. She is clearly a primary victim of sexual abuse by him, her brother-in-law. Christopher, who was Rose's foster child and is her current husband, is a secondary perpetrator of the child neglect that Paul experienced when Paul was denied schooling. Paul is a primary victim of neglect.

The sisters' stories illustrate the importance of looking for what in the social science literature is conventionally called "co-occurring family abuse or violence" (Margolin et al. 2003; Margolin and Gordis 2003). Co-occurrences can refer to abused parents who abuse their children or to partners who engage in mutual abuse and violence. The empirical study of co-occurring forms of abuse is made possible with the FAV episode perspective. More importantly, the perspective, while viewing secondary victims and perpetrators as social actors affected by co-occurring violence, implies that social relationships and social actors, rather than individuals,[4] should be the focus of inquiry.

2. Social Actors External to the Episode

Social actors who are not members of a household or a family group are external to the family abuse and violence episode. External actors can help remedy a family abuse problem, or unwittingly they can play a role in maintaining such episodes. When Margaret's nightmares initiated a visit to a clinical psychologist's office, the clinician exacerbated the abuse she experienced. In blaming the victim (Fortune 2001) by asking her to identify what she had done to provoke molestation, he blocked her opportunity to begin to heal, and he increased the likelihood of subsequent acts of abuse.

If Bernadette had seen a physician for treatment of her injuries, a doctor could have helped her understand that what she was experiencing was not normative or acceptable marital behavior (Campbell et al. 2001). A social actor external to the family abuse episode could have directed her to the appropriate exit. Medical personnel, social welfare workers, mental health workers, and criminal justice personnel are the types of social actors external to family abuse and violence episodes who can observe and intervene to alter what the primary victim, the primary perpetrator, and their family member's will experience. Friends, coworkers, and others external to the family violence episode can witness events, hear about episodes, and intervene in productive or counterproductive ways (Black and Weisz 2003; Hirschel and Buzawa 2002; Moffitt and Caspi 1998).

3. Relationships and Connections among Social Actors

While Bernadette experienced physical assaults by Tim, her younger sister Margaret was being molested by Rose's husband, Billy. Margaret also was the victim of Tim's exhibitionist behaviors. All the sisters were aware, as were their parents, that Mary was continuously belittled and berated by Doug. Why were the sisters unaware of what was happening to Margaret and uninformed about each others' intimate partnerships? Only after they experienced divorces and a family homicide did they begin to talk about family violence episodes. The relationships and connections that characterized the families explain this phenomenon.

Each sister was embedded within her own unique family (Farmer and Tiefenthaler 1997). A marriage ceremony signified the first level of each sister's unique family embeddedness. A child born to or brought into the family signified subsequent levels of family embeddedness.

The more embedded each sister became within her own family, the less she was willing to disclose troubling events to her siblings, to extended family members, or to colleagues at work or in college. New connections with spouses and children changed the relationships the sisters had with each other and with their parents. The connections and relationships that characterized their increasingly complex family and social networks ironically protected the abusive partners and made three of the sisters more vulnerable to abuse within their marriages.

Consider, in addition, the social actors external to the episodes, such as social workers, the police, and public health practitioners. They, too, maintain relationships across organizational boundaries and affect family violence episodes and their consequences. Within a community, a legal advocate who works for a domestic violence program routinely interacts with judges and court clerks to request protection orders (Burgess-Proctor 2003; Keilitz, Hannaford, and Efkerman 1996). Teachers and social workers together can show children and adolescents how to prevent dating violence or how to report forms of abuse that they experience (Foshee et al. 2000).

4. Opportunity Structures

Family abuse or violence cannot occur without perpetrator opportunity. At least three of the four sisters lived with husbands who had daily opportunities to harm them emotionally or physically. The sisters did not have or perceive alternative opportunities for living independently from their abusive partners. Their economic circumstances, their relationships with other family members, and their religious beliefs structured opportunities for ongoing and hidden abuse. Moreover, the lack of intervention by a state or local agency (social actors external to the family violence episode) presented Rose with the opportunity to neglect Paul. Rose kept Paul out of school when he was 6 and 7, and she expelled him from his home when he was 15. These are arguably child neglect incidents that cannot be sufficiently explained without an account of opportunity.

Physical proximity, or living together or close to each other, is only one dimension of an opportunity structure.

The opportunity to abuse can also come from physical or social isolation (Logan, Walker, and Leukefeld 2001). Doug wore down Mary's confidence by continuously calling her "fat," "stupid," and "lazy" to the degree that she isolated herself from her sisters and her neighbors for a number of years. Although she lived within a few miles of her parents and one of her sisters, their opportunity to assist her was negated by her social isolation and her social distance from her family. Only after her divorce did she tell Bernadette about the gun episodes and her constant battle to keep Doug from hitting her children. While Doug prevented social actors external to the family violence episodes from intervening, he also established the social opportunities he needed to continue his relentless emotional abuse of Mary.

The opportunity dimension of the family violence episode perspective does not by itself explain who is likely to be a victim of partner abuse, child abuse, or elder abuse. We recognize that women who are separated from their abusive husbands face an increased risk of violence (Hardesty 2002; Walker et al. 2004), although the separated husband supposedly has fewer opportunities to abuse. Further we recognize that cohabiting women face an increased risk over married women in the likelihood of experiencing violence within their relationships (Brownridge 2004). The FAV episode perspective does not ignore these empirical findings, but it does encourage the incorporation of opportunity in an explanation that includes multiple dimensions of information.

5. Perpetrator Motivation

The four sisters illustrate only some of the motivations that need to be examined when researchers study family violence episodes. A parent's practice to control and discipline a child is appropriate and normative social behavior. The too-frequent use of punishment or the excessive use of corporal punishment that causes bruising or bleeding, however, may be motivated by additional factors, including an excessive level of control. Inappropriate control of one adult over a partner as well as the lack of control of an adolescent, as exemplified by Rose permitting Paul to smoke marijuana in their home, are key motivations for family abuse. Jealousy, lack of self-control, alcohol abuse, and a need to reduce the stress accompanying unemployment are additional motivations for the deviant or abusive family behaviors illustrated by the sisters' stories (Burch and Gallup 2004; Del Sol, Margolin, and John 2003; Gover 2004; McCloskey et al. 2002). If Rose and Christopher are indeed responsible for Billy's homicide, as the police investigators believe, whatever motivated them to end a person's life would be important to understand.

6. Victim/Survivor Vulnerability

The sisters more or less successfully survived family violence episodes. One of their husbands, however, may indeed represent the true forgotten and ignored victim. Because his homicide remains uncleared by the police, it cannot be classified for the official police records as a family homicide. The other forgotten victims are Rose's sons. Paul experienced educational deprivations as a very young child. As an adolescent he was permitted to drink alcohol and smoke marijuana. By age 15 he was denied a home by his mother. He is indeed a convicted offender, but he remains a hidden victim of family abuse and violence. It is likely that for however long he lives he will be vulnerable to assaults by prison inmates, the threat of suicide, and dire circumstances, should he ever live for a period of years outside of prison.

The four sisters maintain either somewhat close or cordial relationships with their parents, and three of them survived the termination of their abusive marriages. Three of the sisters talk on the phone to each other at least weekly and visit each other each year. Two of them were, nonetheless, made vulnerable to family violence episodes on account of the excessive corporal punishment they experienced as children and adolescents (Higgins and McCabe 2001; Levendosky, Huth-Bocks, and Semel 2002). They also were made vulnerable with a denied opportunity to attend college and by early or premature/immature marriages that were provoked by the need to get out of their parents' home to avoid the frequent hitting and the occasional beatings they experienced (Collins, Stevens, and Lane 2000; Kaukinen 2004).

7. Survivor's Objective and Subjective Power

The sisters' economic resources and their levels of educational attainment placed them in disadvantageous positions within their marriages. The lack of power Mary had within her marriage to Doug was due in part to the relative amount of objective resources that Doug commanded (Fox et al. 2002; Melzer 2002; Miller 2003). Until he faced unemployment, he was the family's breadwinner, and he enjoyed the privileges of a college education at Mary's expense.

Bernadette's economic or objective circumstances were different. She worked and earned either the family's only income or the largest share of the family's income for most of her marriage. She did not, however, during her marriage to Tim, command the subjective resources or power sufficient to prevent violence. To the contrary, she defied the normative status of wife within her marriage, thereby losing any potential power or autonomy within the relationship (Macmillan and Gartner 1999). In addition, like all other women who lived within abusive relationships at that time, she lacked the legal power she could have today to stop the abuse (Ford 2003; Mills 1998). Police during the 1970s did not generally arrest men who assaulted their partners in their homes. The combination of personal and legal power is necessary for adults who are vulnerable to family violence to escape the violence or minimize the threat of victimization or revictimization (Miller 2003; Mills 1998).

8. Space and Place

As children the four sisters lived in a home on a state road, far removed from neighbors. Mary, Bernadette, Rose, and Margaret all experienced the American dream as adults: Each lived in private homes (rented or owned) with their husbands and their children. The type of residence or the space and place in which the abuse occurred helped keep the family violence episodes private. There were no downstairs neighbors to hear the sounds of violence. No one, except her child, heard Bernadette fall to the floor. No one heard objects crashing into walls when Richard threw them at Margaret.

Rose chose to live in homes located in extremely rural and geographically isolated locations. The place where she lived helps explain why a school district did not intervene when she failed to take her unofficial foster child to school. It also helps explain why the state did nothing when she failed to take Paul to school when he was 6 and 7 years old. The place where she lived explains why no caseworker ever visited her home to see that Christopher was not actually living with her as her foster child. The place also explains why the state police, rather than a local police department, investigated a family homicide. The town in which Rose chose to live does not employ police officers. It has no 911 emergency phone number to call. There are no house numbers to help police or ambulances locate victims, perpetrators, or patients.

Family violence researchers, especially those who study child abuse or intimate partner violence, have documented some important differences in family violence episodes that occur in rural or urban locations (Lee, Thompson, and Mechanic 2002; Logan, Walker and Leukefeld 2001; Smith and Williams 1992; Walsh and Foshee 1998). Space and place—or the distinctions that social science researchers more traditionally examine as rural, suburban, and urban—uncover cultural practices for how families perpetrate or respond to family violence episodes. They also uncover how social actors external to the family violence episode, such as police or clergy or social service agencies, respond or fail to respond to known cases of ongoing abuse.

9. The Mechanics of the Episode

A family abuse or violence episode is characterized in part by its mechanics, or the series of activities or events that occur with or without facilitating objects such as weapons. For example, Billy engaged in a series of related activities that together constitute acts of molestation. Rose and Margaret would go to bed and he would wait for a period of time until he thought they were asleep. He would leave his bedroom, navigate furniture and hallways in the dark to reach the living room, and would find Margaret pretending to be asleep and begin to fondle her.

Some family violence episodes, such as the homicide of Billy, require complex plans, complex activities, and weapons (Halliday-Boykins and Graham 2001; Houry et al. 2002; Mollen et al. 2003; Morgan, Nackerud, and Yegidis 1998). Others, such as Mary's descriptions of Doug chasing her around the house and eventually hitting her as she attempted to keep him from hitting their children, are simple, spontaneous, yet often-repeated chains of events. Each sister's family violence experiences have different mechanics. Collectively their life stories document the need to specify the mechanics, along with the nine additional dimensions of information, to explain family violence episodes. Understanding the mechanics of family violence episodes helps researchers and practitioners propose methods to break the chain of events that can culminate in physical or emotional injury or harm.

10. Situations and Definitions

Social climates generate definitions of appropriate or socially deviant family behavior and, therefore, definitions of violent or abusive family behaviors (Bush 1992; Gagne 1996; Rothenberg 2003). How the law defines a wife's relationship to her husband or the parents' responsibilities to a child is a function of social forces, such as employment opportunities for women or formal educational requirements for children under age 16.

It would be a mistake to conclude that the sisters perceive that they experienced child abuse. What they subjectively experienced was being spanked and punished—just like their friends were punished—during the 1950s and 1960s. Corporal punishment was normative (Paolucci and Violato 2004; Turner and Muller 2004). "Time outs" had not been invented. When we look at the four sisters' life stories, we can also make the mistake of viewing them as helpless victims trapped in bad marriages, unless we account for the social climate. Rather than wonder why Bernadette would court her abusive husband to retain a deviant marriage, we can take account of the religious values that permeated her household, her doctor's office, and her extended family (Fortune 2001). We must also place the marriage in the 1969–1975 time frame. A photograph of Bernadette holding her infant son in her arms is on the front page of the September 5, 1970, issue of *The Phoenix: Boston's Weekly Newspaper*. The caption reads "Women's Rights Day: Stories & Photos." The women's rights demonstration in which she participated as a mother at age 20 featured speeches about the need to obtain birth control information and the need to pursue equal pay for equal work for women. The social climate that defines partner abuse currently is markedly different than the social climate of the early 1970s.

Integrating Explanations with a Family Abuse and Violence Episode Framework

Our study of child abuse, intimate partner violence, and elder neglect and abuse unfolds within a Family Abuse and Violence Episode framework. The excellent theoretical papers, books, and empirical studies that have been published in recent decades, with notable exceptions, tend to focus on one or another form of family violence. The scholarship on each form of violence or abuse has gravitated toward particular fields of study. Child abuse and elder abuse studies are more likely to be found in the social welfare and social work literature than in the criminal justice literature. Intimate partner violence studies, on the other hand, are likely to be located in the criminal justice journals. Studies of family violence are much more likely to appear in interdisciplinary journals than in sociology or psychology journals. All types of family abuse and violence are studied by public health researchers, and all present an interdisciplinary problem. Thus, we find that journals spanning academic disciplines, especially those in the fields of public health, family studies, family therapy, and interpersonal violence, address all forms of family violence episodes.

The multidimensional FAV episode perspective, which we articulate and illustrate with the four sisters' life stories, shows that the framework is useful for studying the problem across types of family relationships, including parent and child, intimate partners, and child and parent. Furthermore, the perspective complements the most informative theories and perspectives. Social structural and social psychological explanations are merged. Feminist perspectives and family systems approaches are blended. In subsequent chapters we look carefully and separately at *inter-* and *intra*generational forms of family violence episodes. We conclude this chapter not with remedies and solutions, but with suggestions for how social scientists may use the FAV episode perspective to piece together different explanations of why some social actors perpetrate family violence and how some victims use power and resources to survive.

A Synopsis of the Dominant Explanations for Family Abuse and Violence

An early overview of the theoretical explanations for child abuse and spouse abuse was prepared by Gelles and Straus (1979). They published a typology of potentially useful perspectives and concluded that individual, social psychological, and social cultural level theories are suitable for studying the occurrence of family violence. When reviewing the hundreds of papers published on child abuse and intimate partner violence during the 1980s and 1990s, we also found that explanations tended to examine phenomena at the individual, social interaction, and social structural or cultural level (Miller and Knudsen 1999). While some explanations integrate multiple perspectives, they tend to be anchored by a single level of analysis.

An FAV episode framework is helpful for explaining a social problem with an integration or a synthesis of theories that moves across levels of analysis. Table 1.1 illustrates levels of analysis, the dimensions of the FAV framework, and exemplars of existing theories or explanatory factors in the field of family violence.

Table 1.1. Using and Integrating Existing Explanations with the Family Abuse and Violence Episode Perspective

Level of Analysis	Dimension of FAV Episode Perspective	Examples of Explanations

INDIVIDUAL	1. Social Actors Internal to the Episode
	  • Primary and Secondary Perpetrators
	  • Primary and Secondary Victims
	  • Self-Control
		• Personality Traits
		• Disorders
		• Addictions

SOCIAL RELATIONSHIPS AND SOCIAL ORGANIZATIONS	2. Social Actors External to the Episode
	  • Physicians and Nurses
	  • Schools
	  • Social Service Agencies
	  • Criminal Justice
		• Rational Choice
		• Deterrence
		• Social Learning

	3. Relationships and Connections
	  • Extended Family Members
	  • Coworkers
	  • Friends and Neighbors
		• Social Control / Social Bonds
		• Social Learning
		• Symbolic Interactionism / Gender Roles

(continued)

Table 1.1. *(continued)*

Level of Analysis	Dimension of FAV Episode Perspective	Examples of Explanations
	4. Opportunity Structure	
	5. Perpetrator Motivation	
	6. Victim / Survivor Vulnerability	
	7. Victim / Survivor Power	
	• Objective	• Resources
	• Subjective	• Social Exchange
	• Personal	• Autonomy
	• Legal	
	8. Space and Place	• Isolation
		• Marital Status
		• Family Embeddedness
		• Weapons
	9. Mechanics	• Alcohol and Drugs
	• Sequenced Behaviors	• Disorganized Neighborhood
	• Objects and Weapons	• Criminal / Therapeutic Responses
	10. Situations and Definitions	
	• Social Climate	• Patriarchy
	• Gender Relations	• Norms, Beliefs, and Values
	• Cultural Values	
CULTURE AND SOCIETY		

Researchers can use the table as a guide to design empirical studies. To illustrate: A researcher guided by the FAV framework could design a study examining how coworkers and friends help terminate family abuse. The researcher could turn to the published papers and books on social control, social learning, and social interaction theories—explanations anchored at the social relationship level of analysis. The midlevel theories can be used to construct research instruments and to develop a research plan. The researcher could also turn to theories about beliefs and values, which are specified at the cultural level of analysis, to make sense of the gender relations and social climate, which explain the persistence of the intimate partner violence problem within the United States. And the researcher could examine theories about addiction and personality traits to study—at the individual level of analysis—how alcohol abuse is empirically related to family abuse and violence.

Individual Level of Analysis Theories

Psychopathology or personality disorders are prominent explanations for behaviors that range from secretive hurting to hitting or battery, and more severely, to homicide of a spouse, partner, parent, or child. Munchausen syndrome by proxy, poor impulse control, drug or alcohol addiction, a violent personality, and antisocial personality disorder are examples that focus on explaining why a perpetrator aggresses against or abuses a family member (Arbuckle et al. 1996; Caetano, Schafer, and Cunradi 2001; Capaldi and Clark 1998; Dube et al. 2001; Feldman and Brown 2002; Thompson et al. 2001). Post-traumatic stress disorder and a state of learned helplessness are examples of explanations that focus on victim vulnerability (Briere et al. 2001; Dutton and Goodman 1994; Fennema-Notestine et al. 2002; Jones, Hughes, and Unterstaller 2001; Kelley and Jennings 2003; Margolin and Gordis 2000; Overmier 2002; Palker-Corell and Marcus 2004; Rotenberg, Shewchuk, and Kimberley 2001). Individual perpetrator or individual victim perspectives are useful for examining *social actors internal to the family violence episode.* Understanding primary and secondary perpetrator and victim characteristics and conditions contributes to a comprehensive explanation of family violence episodes.

Social Interaction Level of Analysis Theories

Perspectives that are based on the process or consequences of social interactions within a social group or family include social exchange and resource or interpersonal power explanations for violence or the resistance of violence (Bird, Stith, and Schladale 1991; Brownridge and Halli 2000; Featherstone 1997; Fineran and Bennett 1999; Foshee et al. 2001; Graham-Bermann and Brescoll 2000; Pittaway, Westhues, and Peressini 1995). At a social psychological or social interaction level of analysis, Gelles specifies an explanation that integrates social exchange and social control theories (Gelles 1983). Gelles argues that the probability of committing abuse or violence within the family increases when the cost or punishment for family violence is insufficient because effective formal or informal controls against violence are missing or weak. Social interaction–level explanations are useful for examining how *social actors external to the family violence episode* can influence the reoccurrence or desistance of family abuse or violence. Schools and health, mental health, social service, and criminal justice organizations can prevent family violence or repeated episodes of family abuse and violence. They also are useful for illustrating how *victims* are more or less *vulnerable* to family abuse and violence or empowered to prevent reoccurring violence. An adolescent or adult victim's objective and subjective power (or disempowerment), whether it is within the family or from her or his connections to legal authorities, is explained by social interaction–level perspectives (Ford 2003; Keilitz, Hannaford, and Efkerman 1996; Miller 2003; Mills 1998).

The theory or perspective that is specified at the social interaction level of analysis, which has been used, tested, and at least partially confirmed most frequently in the field of family violence, is social learning. Bandura's model, initially specified to explain aggressive behaviors (Bandura 1973), is used to test the intergenerational transmission of violence hypothesis and to explain why adolescents or adults who were exposed to violence within their homes are more likely than others to perpetrate intimate partner violence.[5] Social learning perspectives show how *social actors external to the family abuse and violence episode* who respond to family abuse or violence are models or teachers who can perpetuate or discourage violence and aggression. They also are useful for explaining why *relationships among social actors* and *connections among social groups or organizations* can exacerbate or prevent family abuse and violence episodes. They can help explain the perpetrator's *motivations* to engage in family violence episodes. Violence and aggression are socially learned behaviors. The desire and motivation to control and extreme jealousy within intimate relationships are socially learned emotions and psychological states (Hardesty 2002; Walker et al. 2004).

Symbolic interactionist (Birkbeck and Lafree 1993; Goode 2004) and sex or gender role studies (Ammons 1999; Johnson, Adams, and Ashburn 1995) provide additional explanations for victim empowerment or autonomy. The meaning of being a "good wife" and a "good mother" in the twenty-first century can empower a woman to protect herself and her children against any potential abuse. The social identity of a "good husband," which is affected by normative conceptualizations of masculinity, can emerge within nurturing parenting and partnering activities.

An FAV episode framework accounts for the *space and place* where events occur. A family's geographic isolation can preclude home visits from a public health nurse that could prevent child abuse (Eckenrode et al. 2000). The physical isolation associated with some rural locations can preclude alternative places to live in safety for victims of intimate partner violence (Gordon, Burton, and Porter 2004; Logan, Walker, and Leukefeld 2001). The symbolic dimensions of *space and place* are addressed by theorists who address the perplexing observation that cohabiting partners, compared to married partners, experience more violence within their intimate relationships (Brownridge and Halli 1999; Brownridge 2004). The social isolation of cohabiting can result from fewer attachments to extended family members (Ellis 1989). Some social actors are successful in compensating for the familial isolation that is associated with an increased probability of family violence by establishing ties to friends and coworkers (Stets 1999). Marital status is one level of family embeddedness that also can be used to explore the *space and place* dimension of family violence. A married person is more embedded within the family than are daters or cohabiting partners (Farmer and Tiefenthaler 1997). Children embed family members further. The more embedded a woman is within her own nuclear family, the less likely she will be able to prevent repeated acts of intimate partner violence.

The *mechanics* of a family violence episode are important to understand for the purpose of preventing child abuse, partner violence, and elder abuse. If the chain of behaviors that results in an episode of elder abuse is broken, the deviant or criminal act will not occur. If the weapon—a gun or a knife—that could be used to kill a spouse is not available to the perpetrator, the homicide could be prevented (Brantingham and Brantingham 2001). The *mechanics* are connected, according to social scientists studying the consequences of disorganized neighborhoods (Van Wyk et al. 2003), to the physical *spaces and places* that make family violence more or less likely. In disorganized neighborhoods, formal social control processes that inhibit violence are inadequate, and the social supports necessary to protect social actors from violence also are inadequate. As a consequence, victims of family violence within the disorganized urban neighborhood can experience a level of social isolation that increases the probability of reoccurring violence and abuse.

The *situations and definitions* that promote or inhibit all forms of family violence can be studied at the social interaction level of analysis with symbolic interactionist and social constructionist perspectives. They also can be studied at the cultural or societal level. Social movements theorists (Bush 1992; Gagne 1996; Jenness and Grattet 2001; Rothenberg 2003; Schmitt and Martin 1999) show how social change advocates successfully reframe social issues and define social problems that warrant not only appropriate social intervention but also a redefinition of the norms, beliefs, and values that guide and sanction intimate relationships, parent-child relationships, and child–elder parent relationships. The cultural- and structural-level theorists who explain the consequences of family systems and patriarchy examine the effects of material and symbolic resources that can result in family abuse or violence episodes (Dobash and Dobash 2000; Dobash and Dobash 1992; Dobash et al. 1992; Greene and Bogo 2002; Rand and Saltzman 2003; Straus and Gelles 1986).

All told, this synopsis of some of the most prominent explanations of family abuse and violence illustrates three important points: (1) No single theory or perspective is sufficient for explaining the *intra-* and *inter*generational forms of family violence that hurt or injure hundreds of thousands of persons each year in the United States. (2) The research literature in the field of family violence shows that most explanations focus on what occurs as a consequence of social organizations and in the process of social relationships. (3) An FAV episode framework can promote theoretical integration and synthesis across levels of analysis. This synopsis of the current perspectives is illustrative, not definitive. Hundreds of specialized or more general perspectives and theories are not analyzed here. Nonetheless we advance a social science understanding of family abuse and violence with a framework that comprehensively incorporates the known conceptual and theoretical perspectives. To move forward, we must account for what we know. Only then can we imagine a reasonable proposal for what we ought to do to ameliorate a persistent social problem.

Discussion Questions

1. Consider the four sisters' case study. What were the decision points in the family's history where (A) social actors, such as teachers, therapists, or neighbors, and (B) social organizations, such as law enforcement, courts, and social services, failed to act in ways that could have changed the family's experiences and the consequences for the four sisters?
2. Each sister experienced social isolation. Describe the different forms of social isolation each experienced. Illustrate how social isolation facilitated different forms of family abuse and violence.
3. The husband's and the father's power within a family is often bolstered by religious beliefs and traditions, as is evident in this case study. How do such values and beliefs contribute to the problems of family abuse and violence within the United States?

Research Projects

1. Design a survey of the local community to measure perceptions of appropriate punishment for children. Does the general population support the use of corporal punishment? Does it support the use of corporal punishment only to protect children against grave harms or extremely dangerous behaviors? Are there differences across the social classes, race and ethnic groups, and religious groups in the community?
2. Interview a man and a woman who are similar in age. Do not inquire about family abuse or violence. Ask them to tell you about their childhood experiences in their families, in their schools, and in their local communities. How are they similar or different from your own? Did either person disclose events or episodes that you would consider to be episodes of family abuse?

Notes

1. Personal correspondence with State Police Officer Mark Myrdek on 8/1/95.

2. This case study of family abuse was prepared initially while I was a Liberal Arts Fellow at the Harvard Law School (1999–2000). Since then, the four sisters' parents moved into a retirement community. The mother has been hospitalized a number of times for pulmonary problems. In the summer of 2005, the father was interviewed for approximately three hours by Adult Protective Services. An agency representative was notified when the mother, upon hospitalization, was found to be severely bruised. Bruises were on her face, body, and arms and legs. The father explained that while he cares for his elderly wife as best as possible, she falls frequently due to mobility limitations. Although they have a wheelchair in their apartment, the father does not allow the mother to use it. Instead she is allowed to use a walker.

3. Ralph and Alice, portraying a working-class marriage in 1950s Brooklyn, were not displaying socially deviant forms of interaction. "You're going to the moon, Alice!" was a perceived by television viewers as a funny and normative statement. Alice was not the victim of intimate partner abuse. She would get angry, express anger, and move out of the

home on occasion. Similarly, Buck Henry, on *Saturday Night Live* episodes more than a decade later, was considered to be funny when he engaged in behaviors that depicted what today would be defined as child abuse. Such portrayals nowadays, clearly considered depictions of wife abuse or child abuse, illustrate how definitions and constructions of deviance change.

4. Thus we choose to use the term "social actor."

5. The published research on social learning theory, as it is applied to family abuse and violence, is extensive. It includes but is not limited to the following studies: (Anda et al. 2001; Ballif-Spanvill, Clayton, and Hendrix 2003; Bevan and Higgins 2002; Brendgen et al. 2002; Capaldi and Clark 1998; Corvo and Carpenter 2000; De Bellis et al. 2001; Del Sol and Margolin 2004; Eckhardt, Jamison, and Watts 2002; Ehrensaft et al. 2003; Foshee, Bauman, and Linder 1999; Hendy et al. 2003; Hines and Saudina 2002; Hoffman and Edwards 2004; Kaura and Allen 2004; Kwong et al. 2003; Langhinrichsen-Rohling, Hankla, and Stormberg 2004; Margolin et al. 2003; McCloskey and Lichter 2003; O'Keefe 1998; Rosen, Bartle-Haring, and Stith 2001; Sappington 2000; Simons, Lin, and Gordon 1998; Stith et al. 2000; Wolf and Foshee 2003).

2

Measuring and Estimating the Cases: Agency, Government, and Social Survey Data

Richard Gelles identifies three data sources that are useful for estimating and studying family violence episodes (Gelles 2003). We call them "agency," "government," and "social survey" data. Each type of data is collected within a different social context. Some of the data are collected within the context of measuring crime, others in measuring public health or safety issues. Interviews are conducted in homes; case information is recorded at a police station or a child protection agency. The data are collected for various purposes, and the sampling or population issues they address also vary. Table 2.1 highlights the major differences among the three types of data that are gathered to describe and explain family abuse and violence (FAV) episodes.

Agency Data

Agency data, or what Gelles and others call "clinical" data, are collected by treatment providers, such as individual physicians or psychologists, or by employees of treatment programs, such as safe shelters or domestic violence intervention programs. Agency clinicians—social actors external to the family violence episode—are more likely to intervene in or to treat the more severe or chronic cases of family violence. A partner who experiences a

Table 2.1. Three Types of Family Violence Episode Data

	Agency Data	Government Data	Social Survey Data
Place for Data Collection	Social Service or Criminal Justice Agency	Homes or Agencies	Respondent's Home
Context for Data Collection	Crisis	Daily Operations	Day-to-Day Life
Purposes for Data Collection	Describe Needs; Account for Expenditures; Project Future Needs	Accounting; Projecting Need	Measure Prevalence and Incidence; Track Changes; Compare Across Social Spaces
Sample/Population	Clients in Need	All Recipients of Funds or Services	General Population; Representative Samples; Special Populations; Purposive Samples

one-time emotional outburst or a one-time slap by a partner who expresses aggression or frustration over a job loss, for example, is not the typical client who approaches a police officer, a counselor, or a physician for advice and help. A child brought to the attention of a social service agency by teachers concerned about problems at school suggesting abuse at home, however, is a typical client whose case will generate agency data.

Public agencies are more likely than private physicians or counselors to treat clients who have no other place to go. A so-called middle-class employee who experiences recurring episodes of family violence or abuse may turn to a physician covered by his or her health insurance policy, or an employee-assistance program designed to help or make referrals, or to his or her friends or family members to seek advice. Though both a middle-class and a working-class client may face a similar crisis, the middle-class client will likely turn to a private agency whereas the working-class client will more likely rely on a public agency for help.

Public agencies, however, are less likely to treat or respond to clients who fear them or their reprisals. For example, a family member who is in the United States illegally cannot turn to the police department or the courts without a reasonable fear of deportation for himself and his family; the 1994 Violence Against Women Act recognized this dilemma. But the federal law cannot address the fear of reprisal from the criminal justice system that minority women or women of color face for themselves and their partners (Richie 2000).

Agency clinicians collect and analyze family abuse and violence data for specific purposes. They must summarize and describe accurately the needs of the clients they serve. Because all public agencies rely in part on federal, state, or local public funds, a related purpose for collecting data is to account for how these monies are spent: How many clients are served? How many days or hours of service do clients need? How many workers does the agency need to function smoothly and to meet the needs of the community?

Researchers cannot use private or public agency data to accurately estimate or describe the family abuse and violence problem in the general population or across sociodemographic segments of the population. Using agency data to draw conclusions about the general population would greatly exaggerate the number of victims, perpetrators, and families affected by FAV episodes. Similarly, using agency data to generalize about the degree of injury this social problem causes would greatly exaggerate the physical, emotional, and psychological damage resulting from FAV. Imagine the typical albeit hypothetical local domestic violence shelter, operating on a shoestring budget with funds from the United Way, federal STOP (Services, Training, Officers, and Prosectuors) funds, and a handful of small grants. The shelter accepts clients brought in or referred by local police departments. The women, usually with one or more young children, come to the shelter on the advice of the police because they have no place to turn and need to get away from the violence. If alternative places to live safely were available, why would a woman choose to live in the shelter? Imagine the researcher who draws conclusions about the family violence problem by studying only shelter clients. An *absolutely flawed* picture could look something like this:

> Women who experience intimate partner violence or domestic violence are poor, white, and undereducated. They have no jobs and no savings account. They have inadequate medical care and grossly inadequate dental care. They have young children who are exposed to danger and violence, often to weapons and illegal drugs. Their children also lack appropriate medical and dental care and often miss school days. The women were abused as children and if they have older children, the children are abusive toward them. The victims of domestic violence, within a month's time, are likely to lose patience with other women and with their own children. Violence begets violence.

While it would be a grievous error to draw conclusions about the general population from agency data, it also would be a horrible mistake to dismiss the data. Public agency data provide detailed accounts of the women, children, and men who seek out (or are sought after) for intervention and treatment or punishment for a specific event or reoccurring FAV episodes.

Agency data also provide accurate statements of the financial costs of responding to the most serious and most socially visible forms of family abuse and violence. Such data can provide rich descriptions of the problems that some victims and perpetrators face. Observations from workers in child protective services agencies, police and probation departments, and publicly financed treatment and counseling programs provide valuable insight into some of the victims and perpetrators of FAV episodes. Without agency data we could not understand the complexity of the issues encountered by agency workers and their clients as they struggle to prevent recurring violence.

Agency data can also be used to uncover hidden forms of abuse. For example, a woman at a domestic violence shelter may disclose threats or acts of child abuse by the man or the woman who battered her. Or the child removed from her home and placed in foster care in response to a child protective services investigation may disclose that her siblings or her father are also victims of family violence episodes. Agency data are useful for establishing the connections and relationships across social actors affected by FAV episodes.

Finally, agency data inform other groups of social actors about the problems the agency responds to within the community. Without this information, the organization itself could not depend upon staffing or funding.

Government Data: Official Reports

Government data, or what Gelles and others refer to as "official reports," include criminal offense and victimization data and public health reports. Because each federal agency collecting data defines FAV problems from a different perspective—as a crime versus an illness, for instance—comparing data collected by state and federal government agencies can produce sharply different estimates of the amount of family abuse and violence within a society or across social groups. Consider, for example, the National Crime Victimization Surveys (NCVS), which ask respondents to report on criminal violence. Analysis of NCVS data indicates that men and women are not likely to report *most* of the crimes they experience, including violent crime. Thus, relying on government-sponsored crime survey data would generate substantial underestimates of family violence episodes.

Government data can be collected from social actors in their homes: Bureau of the Census employees who collect data for the NCVS conduct interviews with persons over age 12 in the privacy of their homes. The place where an interview occurs can affect the quality of the data. If a person being interviewed is fearful that a family violence perpetrator will overhear what is disclosed, a victim may disguise the event to the interviewer. Conversely, the perceived safety and privacy of one's home may invite a victim to disclose an incident.

Government data also can be supplied by agency workers who compile data and statistics and report them periodically on standardized forms to a central office for data collection. These types of data are gathered and reported in the course of day-to-day operations. They may be required by an administrative agency responsible for implementing a state or federal law pertaining to family violence.

Government data, purportedly measuring the same dimension of a family abuse and violence problem, can generate different estimates of the problem. Public health reports and criminal justice data, for instance, are likely to generate qualitatively different disclosures or reports of family violence. As with criminal justice data, the analysis of data from public health reports will likely lead to inaccurate estimates of the level of the social problem. Incidents that are not reported to health practitioners by victims or by a social actor external to the FAV episode remain hidden. In the United States, physicians are required to report suspected cases of child abuse. Reporting intimate partner violence or elder abuse, however, is not legally mandated in all states.

Government data are important for understanding FAV episodes. The data, in principle, represent all the clients who seek and need services within a particular jurisdiction or location. Thus, they are especially helpful for projecting the near future needs of federal, state, or local agencies to serve clients effectively. One major limitation with some sources of government data is a focus on "the count." The data tend to count people in need, the number of incidents, hospital beds, jail cells, and counseling hours. Counts provide little help to the researcher who attempts to explain FAV episodes.

Social Survey Data

Social survey data, especially those based on nationally representative samples, have the potential for generating accurate estimates of the number of persons affected by FAV episodes and for specifying some of the social structural and social psychological characteristics associated with violent or abusive family relationships. Michael Johnson, however, argues that even national probability sampling, if it does not allow for different types of family violence, tends to be biased, resulting in an under- or overrepresentation of certain types of experiences (Johnson 2004). For example, a survey described as regarding "family violence" or "domestic abuse" may dissuade social actors who fear reprisal from participating. A biased sample can be the result.

The social survey can be conducted in the privacy of a social actor's home (assuming the home is safe) or in other places. Everyday life experiences can be used to frame the research instruments used to measure FAV experiences. For example, an interviewer could say to a potential respondent: "We are interested in the things women and men do when they disagree over important issues in their marriage." Another could say: "We are interested in the things women and men do to protect themselves against the threat of violent crime." The context, especially the words used where the interview is conducted, for asking questions can and will have a dramatic influence on how respondents will answer the same questions: "How many times in the past six months did your partner coerce you?" "How many times did your partner threaten you?" Research questions that are framed in terms of everyday experiences, compared to the questions that are framed in terms of criminality, will provoke respondents to indicate that many more events have occurred. The issue is not which disclosure is more true or real. The issue is how the questions are interpreted once they are contextualized differently. Respondents are less likely to say they have experienced criminal victimization than they are to say they have experienced aggressive responses from their partners when they disagree over important issues within a marriage. Parents are less likely to disclose committing acts of child abuse or neglect than they are to describe abusive methods they use to discipline their children.

Researchers, policymakers, and lawmakers often depend on social surveys to estimate the prevalence (the number of victims) and the incidence (the number of events) that occur within specified periods of time. Changes in prevalence or incidence levels can be tracked with social surveys as can differences across geographical spaces, such as urban versus rural locations, or comparisons among regional locations. For FAV surveys to be useful for studying the causes and consequences of events that occur relatively infrequently, large sample sizes are necessary, making social surveys financially costly. Perhaps the most substantial drawback of this data source is its limited ability to represent certain segments of the general population that face risks of FAV episodes. Elders and children are the most obvious missing voices from social surveys attempting to measure and explain FAV episodes.

In sum, researchers, practitioners, and social change advocates conventionally depend on multiple sources of data to estimate and analyze FAV episodes in the United States. To accurately summarize the degree of the FAV social problem currently requires identifying multiple puzzle pieces and assembling the pieces together carefully to see the entire picture.

Reports *of* Abuse and Disclosures *by* Victims and Perpetrators

Agency or clinical data can be observations *of* the social actors who seek or are required to receive some form of intervention. Physicians, counselors, social workers, and other treatment providers observe women and their children in a safe shelter, children who are placed in foster care by Child Protective Services, teens who seek medical treatment for dating violence injuries, a convicted batterer who completes a counseling program, and elders who are neglected or abused, and generate agency data. Court personnel, teachers, and therapists who deliver services all make observations *of* some of the social actors who are found responsible or who take responsibility for perpetrating family violence episodes. Agency data are based on observations *of* clients and are compiled by social actors external to the FAV episode.

These data are derived from the full range of social science research designs: An experimental study randomly assigned adolescent and young-adult FAV victims who were treated by a trauma center to more treatment that included case management and referrals to health care and social service agencies. Researchers followed participants for six months and found a strong association between case management and the use of services within the community (Zun, Downey, and Rosen 2003). As a result, the research team argues convincingly that the "treat 'em and street 'em" philosophy of the typical medical trauma center misses the opportunity to intervene effectively. Greene and Bogo (2002) used a post hoc examination of family violence social actors that were seen by psychotherapists. They show that at least two qualitatively different types of intimate partner violence are treated, thus requiring therapists to adopt at least two qualitatively different therapeutic approaches. Psychologists used a longitudinal study to follow 534 children over twenty years to measure the relationship among conduct disorders, exposure to family violence, and substance abuse as well as their effect on intimate partner violence (Ehrensaft et al. 2003). Observations of the research subjects found that childhood physical abuse and adolescent conduct disorders predicted a likelihood of intimate partner violence as well as injuries resulting from violence.

Agency data can also be reports *by* social actors who are internal to the FAV episode. Victims or perpetrators disclose their experiences and emotions following some form of treatment or intervention. Empirical studies examining reports *by* social actors also reveal a wide range of research methodologies. For example, an experimental design was used to assign patients seeking emergency medical service for intimate partner violence to a computer-generated health promotion and advice program that invited disclosures of violence. Researchers found that 33 percent of the female patients disclosed emotional abuse and 15 percent disclosed physical abuse by their partners. When comparing the disclosures *by* patients to the observations of patients that physicians recorded on their charts, researchers concluded that a confidential self-disclosure procedure would be a welcome and perhaps necessary supplement to the screening efforts health care providers use to identify FAV victims or perpetrators (Rhodes et al. 2002).

Using a comparative design, social scientists found that women in safe shelters experienced more fear and anger in response to family violence compared to a group of men attending a court-ordered counseling program. The perpetrators were found to exhibit more controlling and dominating behaviors, and they were found to initiate intimate violent episodes more frequently and with more severe consequences for their partners. Compared to those in the shelter, the partners of men who were court-ordered to counseling were less likely to have called the police. If they themselves had experienced violence, they were less likely to try to escape their partner's assaults or attacks (Hamberger and Guse 2002).

Disclosures *by* FAV victims and perpetrators can also be studied by examining social actors who are undergoing clinical care or agency intervention for nonviolent problems. Men and women in treatment for post-traumatic stress disorder (PTSD) or alcohol or cocaine abuse participated in a study to measure correlates of family violence. The study's authors found that substance abuse and PTSD are associated with an increased risk of intimate partner violence (Parrott et al. 2003). Rather than sample cases of adult violence, Bowen surveyed family members associated with cases of children evaluated for potential sexual abuse. She found that domestic violence was occurring within 54 percent of the children's homes. Among the mothers who disclosed violence, 28 percent also reported they had experienced physical violence as children. As a result, the research team concluded that child sexual abuse is a part of a larger pattern of family violence (Bowen 2000). These studies demonstrate the importance of examining relationships and connections among social actors associated with FAV episodes.

The value of agency data, whether the data are reports *of* abuse or violence that service providers observe, or they are disclosures *by* victims and perpetrators, cannot be overestimated. No reasonable understanding of battered women's experiences and aspirations would be possible if we did not have the rich, detailed, and nuanced accounts told by thousands of women who seek help from their community agencies. The long-term consequences of many types of child abuse could not be observed without agency data. The problem of elder abuse could not be appreciated. The more severe examples of FAV episodes would escape comprehension.

The strength of agency data is also its weakness. It is unreasonable to generalize what most victims of FAV episodes experience from agency data. Whether the data come from disclosures *by* social actors internal to the FAV episode or from observations *of* treatment providers who are actors external to the episode, we know that agency data tend to capture the most severe cases, those that got the attention of social actors outside the family. When agency data are misused to represent the pervasiveness and severity of family violence, they can contribute to moral panics, a culture of fear and dread, and desperate and misplaced claims regarding the family in the United States (Best 1990; Jenkins 1995; Johnson 1995).

Research ethics are of special concern for social scientists collecting or analyzing agency data. Therapy or intervention strategies must be distinguished from research observations. If members of a group therapy program are aware the sessions they participate in are being analyzed for research purposes, their disclosures may be self-censored. On the other hand, if the therapist does not disclose the therapy-research connection, research ethics are clearly violated.

Multiple Sources of Government Data

Government data come from as many sources as the laws mandating their collection. Mandatory reporting laws that regulate treatment providers and educators responding to or suspecting child abuse generate "an abundance of official report data on child maltreatment" (Gelles 2003:839). No comparable partner abuse or elder abuse data are collected nationally. We can, therefore, in the United States reach the most reliable and perhaps valid estimates of child abuse, relative to the other types of FAV episodes. However, we see government agencies actively pursuing reports on all forms of family abuse and violence.

The Administration for Children and Families and the Administration on Aging in the U.S. Department of Health and Human Services presented the first national survey of elder abuse in 1998. The survey sampled a nationally representative sample of twenty counties, and two types of data were collected. The Adult Protective Services agency in each of the sampled counties reported the number of physical abuse, sexual abuse, emotional or psychological abuse, financial or material exploitation, abandonment, neglect, and self-neglect cases brought to the attention of their agency over a twelve-month period. Sentinels, or agency workers serving the elderly who are trained to identify elder abuse, also reported cases they were aware of over the same period. The intention was to estimate the number of non-institutionalized social actors who were victims or perpetrators of elder abuse. (The number of persons affected, not the number of incidents experienced, was counted.)

As a result of the survey, researchers estimated that "449,924 elderly persons, aged 60 and over, experienced abuse or neglect in domestic settings. . . . [When also considering unreported cases] one can conclude that over five times as many new incidents of abuse and neglect were unreported" (U.S. Department of Health and Human Services 1998:4).

Table 2.2 shows substantial gender differences across various forms of elder abuse. Men are far more likely than women to be abandoned, usually by a family member; but women are far more likely than men to be the victims of emotional abuse, physical abuse, financial exploitation, and neglect. Most of the perpetrators are men (52.5 percent). In nearly 90 percent of the substantiated cases, family members, generally adult children of the victims, are the perpetrators.

The Centers for Disease Control and Prevention have developed guidelines for describing and monitoring intimate partner violence throughout the United States (CDC 1988). The guidelines, which adopt a public health perspective, are similar to the Uniform Crime Reports (UCR) compiled by the Federal Bureau of Investigation. Their purpose is to collect uniform data, which would allow comparisons across place and time. Thus far the state and federal governments have not decided to use the CDC data collec-

Table 2.2.   Elder Abuse: Results from the National Elder Abuse Incidence
Study

	Percent Women	Percent Men
Victims		
Emotional Abuse	76.3	23.7
Physical Abuse	71.4	28.6
Financial Exploitation	63.0	37.0
Neglect	60.0	40.0
Abandonment	37.8	62.2
Perpetrators		
Emotional Abuse	39.1	60.1
Physical Abuse	37.4	62.6
Financial Exploitation	41.0	59.0
Neglect	52.4	47.6
Abandonment	16.6	83.4

tion system, but it is possible that uniform data will be collected across jurisdictions in the near future.

The CDC initiative calls for uniform definitions of intimate partner violence that would incorporate types of partnerships and types of violence. Data on the following types of partners are proposed: current spouses, current nonmarital partners, dating partners, heterosexual or same-sex partners, former marital partners or common-law spouses, divorced or separated spouses, and former dates or boyfriends/girlfriends. Data on the following types of intimate partner violence are proposed: physical violence, sexual violence, threats of physical or sexual violence, and psychological or emotional abuse that follows prior physical or sexual violence or threats (Desai and Saltzman 2001).

The U.S. Department of Justice makes available the FBI's Uniform Crime Reports (and its more recently formulated National Incident-Based Reporting System data from some states) that include criminalized types of FAV, such as homicide, assault, or rape by a family member. Even the UCR homicide data, measured in detail through its Supplemental Homicide Report data collection system, are limited by substantial missing data problems. Some police departments do not complete the forms, causing a systemic problem of missing data. In other instances, offender-victim relationship information is missing. In general it is safe to conclude that statistics for even the most serious type of FAV episode, tracked by police departments throughout the United States, underestimate the actual number of cases. However, the UCR can be used to roughly estimate the prevalence of homicides, aggravated assaults, and rapes that are committed by family members.

General Population, Public Health, and Criminal Justice Surveys

General population surveys, typically focusing on non-institutionalized adults, are used to estimate the prevalence and incidence of violence and abuse from the perspective of the social actors who are internal to the FAV episode. Most social surveys, designed to measure one or more types of abuse, depend on self-reports of offense[1] or victimization experiences. Survey data, like the other forms of data, are limited. Researchers do not go into homes and ask a parent or caretaker: "How often have you abused or neglected your children?" Likewise, they cannot ask the toddlers and young children: "How often have your parents or caretakers abused or neglect you?"

Adult social actors who are internal to the FAV episode may fail to disclose experiences purposefully or as a consequence of forgetfulness. Others may disclose experiences that fit their own interpretations of the questions, but not the researcher's interpretations. When social scientists attempt to measure certain social problems, such as family abuse and violence, prevalence levels are low enough either to require large sample sizes or specific sampling strategies for segments of the population known to face a higher probability of FAV. For example, DeKeseredy's study of intimate partner violence among college students, which surveyed 1,835 women (DeKeseredy et al. 1997), was based on an adequate sample size because of the high prevalence of partner violence among young adults and college students. The second National Family Violence Survey conducted telephone interviews with persons in 6,002 households (Straus and Gelles 1986). This survey used a much larger sample than the original survey (N = 2,143) partly because researchers determined the prevalence level of intimate partner violence with the first survey. The National Violence Against Women Survey, the national probability survey that has most recently been conducted, completed telephone interviews with 8,000 women and 8,000 men (Tjaden and Thoennes 2000).

Some survey estimates of FAV episodes report the number of persons affected by family violence as a prevalence level, which represents the number of social actors or families who experience a form of FAV over a lifetime or with a specific time frame, such as the most recent year. Other estimates are based on the number of events, or incidence levels, that occur. Incidence estimates are much higher than prevalence estimates because each family or individual social actor is likely to experience more than a single event. Indeed, a single, unrepeated family violence event is unlikely to be disclosed to interviewers.

If "prevalence" refers to the total number of persons affected by FAV within a specified period of time, and "incidence" represents the total number of events that social actors experience within a specified period of time, which is the preferred measure to summarize the FAV problem? The distinction is based on the number of social actors and the number of social events. If a social program is designed to prevent recurring intimate partner violence, the preferred measure is likely "incidence." If the program is designed to make educational resources available to at-risk families, the preferred measure is likely "prevalence."

For three decades (beginning in the 1970s), social scientists have compared prevalence and incidence estimates, which are based on various social surveys of family violence, and have reported dramatic differences. Compare the number of women estimated to be victims of violence in the United States, summarized in table 2.3.

Telephone interviews were used in all three studies and similar items, based on the revised Conflict Tactics Scale instrument, were used to measure what women experienced. Researchers have scrutinized the sampling strategies used in all three studies and found them well-designed to represent women within the general population of the United States. Based on these noteworthy studies, what should a policymaker or a social scientist conclude? Are less

Table 2.3. Estimated Annual Prevalence of Violence toward Women in the United States

Source / Study Name and Date	Description	Estimated Annual Prevalence Level
National Family Violence Survey	6,002 Households Telephone Interviews	6,250,000 women experienced any violence 1,800,000 women experienced severe violence
Commonwealth Fund Survey	1,324 Women Telephone Interviews	4,400,000 women experienced physical abuse
National Violence Against Women Survey[a]	8,000 Women and 8,000 Men Telephone Interviews	3,020,910 women experienced any violence 1,913,243 women experienced physical assault

Source: Gelles et al. 2000

[a] The National Violence Against Women Survey (NVAW) is also known as the Violence and Threats of Violence Against Women and Men in the United States (VAWM). We use both titles because we analyze data from the survey that pertain to men and women in some instances and we analyze only the women's data in others.

than two million or more than six million women the victims of abuse each year? Had the annual prevalence of violence against women in 1996 dropped by 48.3 percent from its 1985 level?

It is reasonable to conclude that the annual prevalence of FAV episodes, like the annual prevalence of all forms of interpersonal criminal violence, has indeed decreased, partly as a function of social intervention and prevention programs, and partly as a function of changing demographic characteristics of the general population. Yet no community has experienced a marked decrease in the number of women or men, or the number of children, or the number elders who need FAV intervention or treatment over the recent decade. We continue to think, based on public health, criminal justice, and social service agency reports, that family abuse and violence remains a serious and widespread social problem in the United States. Much abuse and violence remains hidden, and many cases remain unreported and uncounted.

The Conflict Tactics Scale and the Conflict Tactics Scale 2

No other research instrument has been used more than the Conflict Tactics Scale (CTS) to measure or summarize different types of family abuse and violence. Murray Straus and his colleagues, who initiated the empirical study of family violence within the United States, designed CTS. Two sample surveys, the National Family Violence Survey and the National Family Violence Resurvey, were conducted in 1975–1976 and 1985 (Straus 1990). Both surveys aimed to measure the annual prevalence of family violence. The instruments used, the CTS and the revised CTS 2, were created by Straus and Richard Gelles following exploratory research they conducted in the early 1970s. Because the CTS, and modified or adapted versions of it, have been used widely to measure intimate partner violence across institutionalized and non-institutionalized populations in the United States and elsewhere, we discuss the instrument in detail, acknowledging its key advantages and some of its weaknesses.

The original CTS consisted of two forms. One was designed to be self-administered, and it was used to measure family abuse among a sample of university students in 1971–1972. The second was designed for face-to-face interviews. It was employed in the first national survey, conducted in 1975. The resurvey, in 1985, adapted the CTS for a telephone interview survey.

The original CTS asked nineteen items. The revised instrument, CTS 2, includes items to measure sexual coercion and injury. When the respondent completes the CTS 2, he or she is asked, "If you ever slapped, grabbed, shoved, or hit your partner, or if your partner has ever slapped, grabbed, shoved, or hit you, who was the first one to do this the last time it happened?" Responses are "I hit first," "My partner hit first," or "This never happened." The CTS format asks the respondent "how many times you did each of these things in the past year, and how many times your partner did them in the past year." Each item is paired. For example, the respondent is asked to indicate the number of times "I threw something at my partner that could hurt" and is then asked how many times "My partner did this to me."

To administer the CTS or CTS 2, the interviewer begins with an introductory paragraph:

> No matter how well a couple gets along, there are times when they disagree, get annoyed with the other person, or just have spats or fights because they're in a bad mood or tired or for some other reason. They also use many different ways of trying to settle their differences. I'm going to read some things that you and your (spouse/partner) might do when you have an argument. I would like you to tell me how many times . . . in the past 12 months you . . .

The CTS 2 items are

- I showed my partner I cared even though we disagreed.
- I showed respect for my partner's feelings about an issue.
- I said I was sure we could work out a problem.
- I explained my side of a disagreement to my partner.
- I suggested a compromise to a disagreement.
- I agreed to try a solution to a disagreement my partner suggested.
- I insulted or swore at my partner.

- I shouted or yelled at my partner.
- I stomped out of the room or house or yard during a disagreement.
- I did something to spite my partner.
- I called my partner fat or ugly.
- I destroyed something belonging to my partner.
- I accused my partner of being a lousy lover.
- I threatened to hit or throw something at my partner.
- I threw something at my partner that could hurt.
- I twisted my partner's arm or hair.
- I pushed or shoved my partner.
- I grabbed my partner.
- I slapped my partner.
- I kicked my partner.
- I punched or hit my partner with something that could hurt.
- I choked my partner.
- I slammed my partner against a wall.
- I beat up my partner.
- I burned or scalded my partner on purpose.
- I used a knife or gun on my partner.
- I insisted on sex when my partner did not want to (but did not use physical force).
- I made my partner have sex without a condom.
- I insisted my partner have oral or anal sex (but did not use physical force).
- I used threats to make my partner have sex.
- I used threats to make my partner have oral or anal sex.
- I used force (like hitting, holding down, or using a weapon) to make my partner have sex with me.
- I used force to make my partner have oral or anal sex with me.
- I had a sprain, bruise, or small cut because of a fight with my partner.
- I felt physical pain that still hurt the next day because of a fight with my partner.
- I passed out from being hit on the head by my partner in a fight.
- I needed to see a doctor because of a fight with my partner, but I didn't.
- I had a broken bone from a fight with my partner.

The original items (not reproduced here)[2] were intended to summarize three dimensions of family conflict resolution: verbal reasoning, verbal aggression, and physical aggression. Some researchers who use the instrument distinguish items that measure "emotional abuse" from "physical abuse." Others distinguish among "any violence," "less severe violence," and "severe violence" that marital or intimate partners experience.

Straus (1990) and others report that a large number of studies show the CTS to be reliable (a measure of the items' internal consistency) and valid, in terms of concurrent validity, content validity, and construct validity. The CTS in its entirety, or clusters of questions from the CTS or CTS 2, have been used and often adapted, by researchers as well as clinicians, to measure the abuse experienced by adolescents, college students, state prison inmates, men and women in the general population, and the elderly. In a recent study (Dietz and Jasinski forthcoming) researchers used an experimental design to shuffle the order of questions in the CTS 2 to determine if the order of the items affected what men and women are willing to disclose. They found the items can be reordered without losing reliability. Respondents do not need to be walked gently through the more socially desirable methods for resolving interpersonal disputes before telling researchers how often they threw items or hit a partner.

Estimating the prevalence and incidence of FAV episodes (child abuse, intimate partner abuse, and elder abuse as distinct but related forms of a social problem) was pioneered by Murray Straus and his colleagues (especially Richard Gelles, David Finkelhor, and Suzanne Steinmetz). While the CTS and its variants continue to be the subject of reliability and validity tests (Archer 2000; Boris et al. 2002; Cascardi et al. 1999), criticism and controversy (Johnson 2004) stemming from the use of the instrument also continue. Nonetheless, CTS-derived instruments are used to measure the severity and chronicity of intimate partner violence experienced by incarcerated women (Jones et al. 2002) or perpetrated by violent men (Julian and McKenry 1993). Such an instrument is used to examine variation in intimate partner violence across race and ethnic groups and across time (Billingham, Bland, and Leary 1999; Field and Caetano 2003). Items from the instrument are scaled and used as predictor or as independent variables in studies to describe and explain some of the consequences of intimate partner violence, such as alcohol abuse, depression, and post-traumatic stress syndrome (Parrott et al. 2003; Scholle, Rost, and Golding 1998). Some of the "Spouse Abuse Replication Program" studies (Sherman et al. 1991) used modified CTS items to measure domestic violence following police intervention.

Although slightly different versions of the CTS are used to measure FAV episodes in different and specialized populations and within a phone, mail, or in-person interview or survey, the definition of the violence and the items used to measure it within the family are the same. The definition used by Gelles and Straus (1979) is "An act carried out with the intention or perceived intention of physically hurting another person." Gelles points out that "the 'hurt' can range from the slight pain caused by a slap or a spanking to harm that results in severe injury or even death" (Gelles 1992:21).

Obviously missing from the CTS and the CTS 2 instruments are items measuring other forms of FAV episodes, such as elder neglect and abuse, and especially the stalking and rape that tend to co-occur in intimate partner relationships characterized by severe or chronic forms of physical violence (Brecklin and Ullman 2002; Coker et al. 2002; Hegarty, Sheehan, and Schonfeld 1999; Rand and Saltzman 2003). In addition, threatening behaviors are embedded with other items that are designed to measure violence on a continuum of severity that ranges from threats to harm to the use of a weapon.

The verbal cues that guide respondents, that is, the introductory paragraph noting that "spats" or being "in a bad mood" can result in a list of behaviors, may elicit responses that do not accurately distinguish behaviors and events that are merely annoying from those that merit intervention. While researchers today modify the CTS items to suit specific research questions, the Straus team never intended to measure the prevalence or incidence of intimate partner violence that can affect gay or lesbian relationships.

The most persistent controversy generated by the CTS-based surveys of family violence concerns gender symmetry in intimate partner violence. Disagreements stem from the conceptual or theoretical perspective—family systems theory—that guided the development and use of the CTS. Should we expect FAV episodes to occur when couples have "spats" or when someone is in a "bad mood?" Or is the commission of a violent act against a partner (or a dependent child or elder) an egregious form of deviance and a consequence of patriarchal control and domination?

If one counts the number of persons who tell researchers they "threatened to hit or throw something" at their partner, a gender symmetry pattern becomes obvious. Women are no more or less likely than men, according to empirical counts, to respond to a "spat" with aggression. But if one examines severe violence, any violence that causes injury, or the controlling pattern of violence that is generally initiated and sustained by men in heterosexual relationships, no hint of gender symmetry appears (Anderson 2002; Beach et al. 2004; Das Dasgupta 2002; Johnson 2004; Kimmel 2002). Thus to estimate the prevalence of intimate partner violence within the United States, based on social survey data, it is better to turn to a different type of instrument, one though adapted from the CTS, that clearly distinguishes types of violence, aggression, and threats while also measuring the controlling behaviors that affect intimate relationships.

The Violence Against Women and Men Survey or the National Violence Against Women Survey

Probably the most accurate intimate partner violence data from a general population, nationwide survey are derived from the Violence and Threats of Violence Against Men and Women in the United States (VAWM) survey (Tjaden and Thoennes 1999), also called the National Violence Against Women Survey (NVAW). We use the titles interchangeably.

The data from the survey are used to distinguish types of FAV episodes that women and men, including elder partners, experience. The sample survey study was mandated by the initial Violence Against Women Act to obtain baseline data. When federal lawmakers defined crimes and appropriate punishments in the Act, they also made funds available to create programs—mostly criminal justice programs—to ameliorate the intimate partner violence problem in the United States. Sensibly, the Violence Against

Women Act calls for the collection and analysis of baseline data to measure the prevalence and incidence of stalking, assault, and rape that men and women perpetrate against their intimate partners. The baseline data, in future years, can be compared to the VAWM/NVAW data to judge the progress being made within the United States to diminish family abuse and violence.

The data collection and analysis project was funded jointly by the National Institute of Justice and the Centers for Disease Control and Prevention. Telephone interviews were conducted with a random sample of 8,000 women and 8,000 men for the purpose of measuring different forms of interpersonal violence. A random-digit dialing method was used to select households within census regional strata. In households with more than one eligible respondent, a most-recent-birthday method was used to designate the adult to be interviewed. Only women conducted the survey for the female sample. Both men and women surveyed the male sample. Spanish interviews were conducted when requested.

Patricia Tjaden and Nancy Thoennes (2000), the study's principal investigators, compared sociodemographic characteristics of the sample to the general population of the United States based on the 1995 Census Current Population Survey. The sample resembled the general population with a handful of notable exceptions: The sample underrepresented older social actors, African American and Latino men, and persons who have completed less than a high school education. For example, the NVAW sample consisted of 6.8 percent of women who are between the ages of 70 and 79, whereas this age group of women constituted 8.9 percent of the general population in 1995. The female sample consisted of 10.5 percent African Americans, whereas 12.0 percent of the women in the 1995 general population were African American.

The VAWM/NVAW study generated prevalence data to measure the types of violent and abusive events that occur and co-occur within intimate relationships. These data have important advantages, as well as some limitations, for the systematic study of FAV episodes. The social actors who participated in the study were a representative sample of adults in the general population in 1995. They reported on the many different and distinctive forms of violence and abuse, as well as the threats of violence, that victimized them. Unlike most of the other general population domestic violence studies, VAWM/NVAW did not exclude gay or lesbian persons from their sampling design.

VAWM/NVAW provides a source of nationwide survey data that, when considered along with other measures, makes estimates of abuse and violence more reliable and valid. The data advance the quality of general population survey data on FAV episodes in at least five important ways. First, the data are not limited to acts of abuse or violence that result from interpersonal conflict or "spats." The context for the telephone survey is the behavior social actors engage in to protect their personal safety. The research is designed to measure the motivation for violent episodes, especially the violence that occurs as a result of power or control within relationships. It also is designed to measure violence that occurs for reasons that are not apparent to victims.

Second, the data are not based on the notion that violence occurs in normative family relationships. Sets of questions ask each respondent to disclose violence or abuse incidents. Subsequent question-sets ask respondents to specify their relationship with the offender. This approach permits analysis of FAV episodes that may be motivated by interpersonal power and control or as a consequence of patriarchal social relationships.[3]

Third, VAWM/NVAW data do not measure violence on a linear continuum of severity that ranges from verbal abuse to life-threatening events. An interview question focuses on threats. Separate clusters of questions focus on (a) physical assault, (b) rape or sexual assault, and (c) stalking. The interview ends with questions about violence and abuse within a woman's or a man's current intimate relationship.

Fourth, VAWM/NVAW comprehensively measures the consequences of violence—including physical injuries—and the treatments provided by social actors external to the family violence episode, such as physicians, dentists, mental health workers, and hospitals. It also documents some of the social consequences of violence, such as the amount of time lost from work, social activities, and family activities; and, some of the emotional consequences of domestic violence, especially depression and emotional trauma.[4]

Fifth, VAWM/NVAW measures the respondent's childhood corporal punishment experiences. It allows researchers to examine the *intra-* and *inter*generational factors that together explain FAV episodes.

The data, like all sample survey data, are limited. They measure reports of behaviors and perceptions of behavioral antecedents and consequences. On account of the data collection method used, the study cannot measure accurately, or with sufficient detail, what many social actors experience in ongoing, abusive relationships. Most of the survey instrument is comprised of close-ended survey questions, precluding a detailed understanding of women's and men's experiences from their subjective perspectives. The study is exclusively respondent-focused, thereby producing no information useful for understanding the motivations of partners who abuse, assault, rape, and batter.

Physical Assault, Rape, and Stalking Measures

Their limitations notwithstanding, the VAWM/NVAW data deserve close examination. They summarize what women and men in the general population disclose. The data provide a comprehensive overview of intimate partner violence—an *intra*generational form of family abuse and violence.

Physical violence is measured with a series of twelve items. Respondents are asked:

After you became an adult did any other adult, male or female . . . ever

- throw something that could hurt you?
- push, grab or shove you?
- pull your hair?
- slap or hit you?
- kick or bite you?
- choke or attempt to drown you?
- hit you with some object?
- beat you up?

- threaten you with a gun?
- threaten you with a knife or other weapon besides a gun?
- use a gun on you?
- use a knife or other weapon on you besides a gun? (Tjaden and Thoennes 2000a)

Rather than construct scales and subscales to measure intimate partner violence, any physical assault that a woman or man reports is counted. The respondents also report whether violent acts were perpetrated by a current or former adult partner. For each separate incident reported, the social actor is subsequently asked to indicate the relationship to the abuser: a spouse or an ex-spouse, a male or a female live-in partner, a relative, someone she or he knew, or a stranger. A composite offender grid is composed by the principal investigators and used to identify acts of intimate partner physical violence. In other words, acts of interpersonal violence committed by strangers or relatives can be excluded for analysis of FAV episodes.

The second type of intimate partner violence measured is rape, that is, the prevalence of attempted or completed rape incidents that were committed by partners or other persons known by the women or men. We use the term "rape" because the survey questions ask respondents if they have experienced forced vaginal, oral, or anal intercourse. (No questions in the survey instrument ask about any other forms of sexual assault.) NVAW researchers measure where the rape occurred; additional violent acts that were associated with the rape; the physical, emotional, and social injuries that resulted; and whether the offender used weapons.

The third type of intimate partner abuse is stalking, measured with two sets of questions. The first set asks respondents if they have experienced a stalking incident:

- Did someone follow you or spy on you?
- Send you unsolicited letters or written correspondence?
- Make unsolicited phone calls to you?
- Stand outside your home, school or workplace?
- Show up at places you were, even though he or she had no business being there?
- Leave unwanted items for you to find?
- Try to communicate with you in other ways against your will?

- Vandalize your property or destroy something you loved? (Tjaden and Thoennes 2000a)

The second set of questions measure how frightened respondents were by the incident, and if they believed that someone close to them would be killed or seriously harmed by the stalker. Only those cases of stalking that resulted in "very frightened" perceptions or the belief that someone would be harmed seriously or killed are counted.

Replications of VAWM/NVAW Findings

Researchers have replicated the findings from the VAWM/NVAW survey and compared them to other national sources of domestic violence data. Bachman (2000) compares the data to National Crime Victimization Survey data in her study of rape and physical assault. Gelles (2000) compares the data to other national data systems to estimate the amount of domestic violence. DeKeseredy (2001) examines the VAWM/NVAW data in a study that is designed to recommend definitions of violence against women. Social scientists have independently reproduced the essential findings from the survey. Their studies help convince us that the survey is ideal for understanding some forms of FAV episodes. Its sample characteristics, that is, its sampling design and sample size, make it a representative sample survey that permits generalizations about the major types of *intra*generational FAV episodes that affect women and men in the general population. The participation rate for female respondents is 72 percent and for male respondents, 69 percent (Tjaden and Thoennes 1999; 2000a). Whereas the sampling design permits generalizations, the sample size is large enough to isolate for analysis distinctive types, as well as the co-occurring types, of FAV episodes that are experienced by a small percentage of women and men in the United States. Stalking, a form of intimate partner violence that has been criminalized only since 1990, is covered by no other national survey.

The context for the interview encouraged respondents to participate in a survey on personal safety, minimizing any potential predisposition to report abusive behaviors that do not constitute intimate or family violence episodes. The first interview question measured perceptions of "safety for women in this country" (Tjaden and Thoennes 2000). This makes VAWM/NVAW the only national survey that does not lead respondents to report behaviors that are based on the premise that acts of interpersonal violence are common among marital or cohabiting couples when they "fight" or "argue" (Straus and Gelles 1986). The study's context allows social science researchers to reexamine previous estimates of the prevalence of the most typical forms of intragenerational FAV episodes.

Women's self-reports tend to converge with legal definitions, according to one analysis of the VAWM/NVAW data. In a study focused on stalking, self-defined stalking experiences are compared to legally defined stalking, based on a model anti-stalking law that was developed by the National Criminal Justice Association in 1993. Reported experiences that met the legal definition of stalking converged with self-defined stalking in 93.4 percent of the cases (Tjaden and Thoennes 2000b:13). Moreover, 4.4 percent of the female respondents self-defined as stalking victims, although their experiences did not meet the legal requirements, most frequently because they did not feel very frightened for their own or another's safety. Thus, the survey measures accurately what constitutes the legally defined forms of stalking, a prevalent type of abusive behavior that has been ignored by all other national surveys of family violence episodes.

The VAWM/NVAW instruments that are used to measure intimate partner violence are reliable. They were adapted from instruments, including the CTS, used in earlier general population surveys of family violence that have been subjected to tests of reliability and construct validity (Straus 1990). Initial screening questions ask respondents to report if they have experienced (a) childhood violence, (b) physical assaults since becoming an adult, (c) sexual assaults, and (d) stalking. Affirmative responses are followed by detailed questions regarding the perpetrator's behaviors, the victim's injuries, and the relationship between the perpetrator and victim.

Tjaden and Thoennes estimate, as shown in table 2.4, that 22.1 percent of women and 7.4 percent of men have been physically as-

Table 2.4. Women and Men Physically Assaulted by Their Intimate Partners

Type of Assault Victimization	Percent of Women Reporting Assault	Percent of Men Reporting Assault
Threw Something that Could Hurt	8.1	4.4
Pushed, Grabbed, or Shoved	18.1	5.4
Pulled Hair	9.1	2.3
Slapped or Hit	16.0	5.5
Kicked or Bit	5.5	2.6
Choked or Tried to Drown	6.1	0.5
Hit with Object	5.0	3.2
Beat Up	8.5	0.6
Threatened with Gun	3.5	0.4
Threatened with Knife	2.8	1.6
A Gun Was Used	0.7	0.1
A Knife Was Used	0.9	0.8
Total (Any Assault)	22.1 %	7.4 %

Source: Tjaden and Thoennes, Exhibit 11, 2000a.

saulted by their partners. Typical assault experiences are being pushed, grabbed, or shoved by a partner (18.1 percent of women and 5.4 percent of men), or being slapped or hit (16 percent of women and 5.5 percent of men). Whereas 6.1 percent of women report a choking episode, 0.5 percent of men do. More than 8 percent of women report being beat up by a partner and 0.6 percent of men do. Substantial gender differences are found, regardless of the specific type of assault measured.

Some social scientists and social change advocates argue that life-threatening events, which show the greatest gender differences, should be the focus of intervention programs. Others argue that all forms of physical assault show a gender pattern that must be addressed by any law or social program designed to ameliorate the problem of family abuse and violence in the United States.

The VAWM/NVAW survey measures distinctive types of intragenerational FAV episodes: physical assault, stalking, and rape. Among the women surveyed, 4.8 percent reported a stalking experience, compared to 0.6 percent of the men. Perhaps most important to note are the 24.8 percent of women and 7.6 percent of men who disclosed they had been the victims of physical assaults *and* rape by their current or ex-spouses or partners. In the following chapters on *intra*generational forms of FAV, we examine these data further. In chapter 9 we analyze the VAWM/NVAW data to explore how childhood experiences and controlling partners explain variation in the severity of FAV episodes that women experience. In chapter 10 we analyze the data further to examine gender differences in the consequences of family abuse and violence for intimate partners in the United States.

Discussion Questions

1. Which types of data are most reliable or valid for understanding the scope of family abuse and violence in the United States?
2. Why does the federal government mandate the collection of data pertaining to some—but not all—types of FAV in the United States?

Library Research Projects

1. Compare two newspaper articles on some type of family abuse or violence. Use an article from a local newspaper and an article from the *New York Times* published in the same month. How do they differ? What do they focus on?
2. Find an article from a contemporary professional journal and from a popular magazine that address a specific type of FAV. Compare the articles. Who are the intended audiences for each article? Which article was more or less convincing? Summarize the criteria you used to evaluate the articles.

Notes

1. We use "offense" and "victimization" as generic terms, not legally defined incidents of criminal offense or victimization.

2. Researchers who intend to use any version of the CTS should contact the Family Research Laboratory, at the University of New Hampshire for instructions and permission. There is no charge. The contact information is shown in the appendix.

3. Analysis of the consequences of patriarchy with cross-sectional survey data that characterize U.S. women is not possible. We argue that one consequence of patriarchal relations is intimate partner violence.

4. In this chapter we do not present analysis of the consequences of family abuse and violence. We summarize consequences in chapter 10.

II

A HISTORY OF FAMILY ABUSE AND VIOLENCE IN THE UNITED STATES

3

Interpreting the Past

Contemporary social actors in the United States recognize that abuse and violence are common occurrences, both within families and in the larger context of social life. The images that are presented daily on television allow us to view and experience, at least in a symbolic way, many violent actions, injuries, and deaths almost at the moment they occur. The descriptions of war, criminal activities, and personal attacks generated by oral and written media offer additional evidence that violence has personal and social consequences. Court records, books, and other sources document the violence perpetrated by family members against spouses or intimate partners, children, parents, or elders.

Today's parents and children face issues and problems unique to our times, such as cyber crime, domestic and international terrorism, a world economy affecting job opportunities, frantic work schedules and long commutes that subtract from family time, and other daily challenges. The significance of these and other issues typically is intensified by the dissolution of families through separation and divorce, a dissolution that often occurs because of an inability to resolve the inevitable conflicts associated with marriage, children, and living intimately with others. Not surprisingly, anger, frustration, the lack of resources to meet needs or desires, and ignorance or inexperience with parenting frequently result in violence or abuse within families.

Are the issues that increase the likelihood of family abuse and violence (FAV) episodes today more severe and difficult than those faced by families of past generations? Do the photographs representing happy, traditional, and often multigenerational families of earlier years accurately portray life in the past, or do they disguise hidden abuse and violence? These and other questions regarding the current state of our understanding of family abuse and violence are the primary focus of this chapter.

To address these questions scholars must depend on incomplete data and their necessarily limited understanding of the social context within which earlier generations lived. The record of the past is fragmentary and at best unclear regarding FAV episodes. Some argue that violence was so common in most historical eras that it appears to have been accepted as normative or appropriate, at least by large proportions of the population. Others suggest the evidence does not justify such interpretations. Why are discrepant claims common? Authors use different sources of information and subscribe to differing perspectives. To study the behavior of parents toward their children, for example, one scholar may emphasize texts offering parenting advice while another will privilege empirical reports. In addition, the blurring of time periods, geographic areas, or general social contexts and the preferred theories of the writers may contribute to different judgments and conclusions.

Clearly there was great variation by historical era and geographic region, but for large numbers of social actors prior to the nineteenth century, the context of daily life involved threats to their survival, such as uncontrollable diseases, malnutrition, unsanitary living conditions, inadequate and overcrowded housing, and dangerous work that could bring illness, injury, or death. In many societies, a new child born to a family that was already struggling, if not overwhelmed, with difficult economic circumstances, threatened the existence of the family. Given such conditions, infanticide and abandonment were among the means families used to limit the number of persons to feed, shelter, and clothe and thereby manage to survive (Schwartz and Isser 2000).

Observations or generalizations about family abuse and violence must be examined critically with some understanding of the living conditions and of what was seen as appropriate social behavior for specific historical periods. As Ross notes, "Our ancestors' views of children were deeply entwined in how rational or nurturant the world appeared to them, and in the practical circumstances that shaped their environment" (1980:64), just as our views of children and family relationships today reflect contemporary knowledge and values.

Interpreting the Past before 1850

Can we understand violence among family members in the past, given the limited information available about most historical eras? Are the documents, diaries, journals, and other materials, which in most societies nearly always were written by a small, literate elite, valid descriptions and indicators of behavior and actions for most people, or do these documents primarily reflect the perspectives of the privileged and wealthy when describing themselves and the masses?

Pollock states that the available "sources used for the history of childhood are overwhelmingly secondary: moral and medical tracts, religious sermons and the views of contemporary 'experts,'" and these sources are supplemented with evidence from paintings, fictional literature, travelers' accounts, newspaper reports, biographies, legislation, and diaries, memoirs, and letters (1983:22–23). All of this information was created for personal reasons or official purposes, rather than for historians and social scientists in later generations. Consequently, historical documents (and contemporary documents) must be interpreted as reflections of the social context in which they were written, a significant condition because of the numerous decisions influencing interpretation.

Before the late nineteenth century, public and private documents and records were handwritten by a relatively small group of literate citizens, whose descriptions and insights reflect their values and attitudes. Thus, the social standing of the persons who wrote the diaries and journals, the validity of their descriptions of themselves and others, and the relevance of these materials to gaining an understanding of FAV issues are important to consider for reconstructing and interpreting past behavior (Pollock 1983). In addition, a writer's personal views and theoretical perspectives about several issues, such as the way and extent to which culture affects individual behavior, or the model of social development and change used in the study, or the assumptions made about human nature, also influence conclusions regarding the level and severity of violence in families of the past.

An illustration from the social science literature on childhood demonstrates how the perspectives of writers may be reflected in their interpretations of data: Aries concludes that the concept of childhood was unknown until the seventeenth century, and its so-called invention brought parental concern and constant involvement, leading to stricter punishment and harsher treatment of children. Before then, children generally had been largely ignored or were a source of amusement to adults and were happier and benefited from exposure to a wider range of experiences and people (1962). The opposite view is expressed by deMause: "The further back in history one goes, the lower the level of child care, and the more likely children are to be killed, abandoned, beaten, terrorized, and sexually abused" (1974:1). Others provide additional, and sometimes divergent, insights and conclusions, especially noting varying patterns of child care at differing times and locations (Bakan 1971; Pollock 1983; Radbill 1968; Schorsch 1979). The fact that these interpretations are drawn from many of the same sources indicates any conclusions regarding life in the past are not final and must be viewed as subject to revision and reevaluation by others.

Considering these qualifications about the historical record, what can we say about the behavior of parents toward children and of intimate partners toward each other? Information regarding family behaviors is fragmentary and barely adequate for the nineteenth century, and as we move back into history, information becomes scarcer approaching the 1500s and before that time it is virtually nonexistent (Pollock 1983). While we cannot be sure that child-rearing practices matched the advice and words of philosophers and others whose documents are available, it is clear that children who were born prior to the development of scientific medicine in any society faced an uncertain future. Survival itself was problematic, even if the child was wanted.

Undoubtedly most parents of new children cared for them with love and tenderness, but the conditions of life often were beyond their control. Despite the best efforts of parents, survival for many infants was compromised by disease, poor nutrition, parental ignorance, or socially accepted care that endangered the infant, such as swaddling and wet nursing. The widespread practice of wet nursing, in which a nursing woman hired out to breast-feed another woman's infant for the convenience of the biological mother or due to illness or lactation problems, was common from the time of imperial Rome to eighteenth-century London. In most historical periods neither legal regulations nor government supervision existed that might have guaranteed even a minimal level of care and feeding, with the result that untold numbers of infants died of starvation and disease through what might be called benign neglect. Foster homes for unwanted children often were called "baby farms" and were operated by people who were not only naïve about diseases, nutrition, and sanitation, but at times motivated by such greed that they did not provide the care for which they had been compensated. Not surprisingly, many or perhaps most of the children placed in such homes did not survive.

Prior to the 1500s, it is possible that the general circumstances of life that parents could not control but that threatened all children forced other decisions. An unwanted child, especially a girl with physical abnormalities or disfiguration, who was born to an unmarried woman or whose presence threatened the fragile economic condition of the family, often faced an early death. Infanticide was by strangling, drowning, or some other form of intentional killing. If the unwanted child was not killed, she or he could be abandoned and left where exposure to elements, animals, or exploiters would lead to death. Those whose lives were spared were likely to be enslaved or to endure a life of hard labor.

Abandonment appears to have been so common that it raised special concern among community leaders. Large numbers of abandoned children led community leaders in Milan, Italy, to found the first asylum for such infants in A.D. 787 (deMause 1974). Other homes for abandoned infants were established throughout the continent, but the practice of deserting an infant continued in all societies (Schwartz and Isser 2000).

In response to this problem, the "turning box" was created. A rotating cylinder was placed in an asylum wall with an opening on one side in which a child could be placed. When a nearby bell was rung by the person leaving a child, the cylinder could be turned and the child could be received inside. This device was "fashioned to conceal the identity of the mother and spare her from shame and harassment" (Radbill 1968:10), but unwanted infants continued to be abandoned or left in public places until well into the eighteenth century. Thomas Coram established the London Foundling Hospital in 1741 because his walks "afforded him frequent occasions of seeing young children exposed, sometimes alive, sometimes dead, and sometimes dying, which affected him extremely" (Stone 1977:298).

For some children, severe physical punishment was explained as "necessary either to maintain discipline, to transmit educational ideas, to please certain gods, or to expel evil spirits" (Radbill 1968:3). Beatings by fists, rods, whips, boards, straps, and other instruments appear to have been common, though Pollock concludes the limited evidence available for the sixteenth century does not support the idea that "severe whipping was the normal mode of punishment" (1983:148). Unfortunately, records that would allow an assessment of general patterns of parental behavior are not available for most eras. It is clear, however, that parents were often exhorted to use physical punishment to control their children, as is reflected in the religious and traditional views of childhood and in the adage "spare the rod and spoil the child," which has been passed down through generations.

The use of children for sexual purposes also appears to have been common, often beginning when the child was aged 4 or 5 (deMause 1974). Young girls were victims of rape, an act encouraged by the belief, which continued to exist at least until the late nineteenth century, that gonorrhea and syphilis could be cured by sexual intercourse with a virgin (Bullough 1990). Temple prostitutes, often young boys and girls, were available in Greek and Roman periods, and children were sometimes prostituted by their parents for money. Castration of males to enhance their singing abilities and other forms of mutilation of girls and boys were done to make them more attractive as prostitutes, beggars, or slaves.

Based on the earliest written records, we know that governmental leaders and citizens expressed grave concern about infanticide, abandonment, severe physical treatment, and sexual exploitation of children, but for much of the past these efforts and the laws enacted to protect children produced modest and only temporary effects. The Code of Hammurabi contains one of the oldest statements about the treatment of children and specified punishment for a nurse who allowed a nursing infant to die while in her care. The existence of these rules suggests infanticide was a serious problem, but neither the code nor the punishment eliminated the killing of children.

Children also have been viewed as legal property, subject to disposal or to whatever care or use a father might choose. In ancient Athens, a father who wished to dispose of his child could do so legally before a consecration ceremony, usually on the fifth day after birth; and early Roman law gave a father complete rights to sell, mutilate, or even kill his offspring, though infanticide apparently was rare (Radbill 1968). As deMause notes, "Until the fourth century A.D., neither law nor public opinion found infanticide wrong in either Greece or Rome" (1974:26), and as late as the eighteenth and nineteenth centuries in Scandinavian countries, a father legally had the power of life and death over his newborn child (Zigler and Hall 1989).

For many centuries, in spite of efforts to assist parents in dealing with an unwanted child by what we now would call social services, and in spite of the severe punishments that often included death for those found guilty of killing infants, the deaths continued. In the late eighteenth century, Frederick the Great issued edicts against killing of children, abolished church penance for unmarried women because he felt it contributed to the problem, and changed the form of execution for those guilty of infanticide from "sacking," in which the guilty person was placed in a sack with rocks and thrown into a river, to decapitation, as a more humane approach (Bakan 1971).

Based on the fragmentary records, we may conclude that many children, especially those whose parents were poor, illiterate, and for whom survival was a daily challenge, lived with many forms of violence before the Renaissance and Reformation. Infanticide appears to have been common. The sexual use and exploitation of children by adults occurred with the permission of parents in some cases, and without parental knowledge in others. Physical violence in the form of beatings, whippings, and punishment for alleged misbehavior probably was the most common form of violence for children. Economic abuse, in which children were used as security for loans, as payments for debts, or for labor, was extensive. Given the circumstances in which children were born and reared, combined with intentional acts of violence (killing, abandonment, exposure, beatings, and enslavement), it is not surprising that one-third to one-half of all children failed to live beyond their first five years, even as late as the eighteenth century.

During the sixteenth and seventeenth centuries, the feudal system waned. The development of cottage industries, machines, and finally factories and the growth of urban areas emerged. All of these developments led to significant change in views toward children and childhood and disrupted the traditional patterns of family life (Demos 1970; Lantz et al. 1977; Laslett and Wall 1972; Mintz and Kellogg 1988; Mitterauer and Sieder 1982; Warner and Griller 2003).

Families, shaped by past behaviors and traditions in which male elders dominated decision making, were transformed. Instead of marriages based primarily on considerations of economic or political benefits, partner selection and family relationships became based on sentiment and affection (Shorter 1975; Stone 1977). A type of family emerged, described by Goode (1963) as the "conjugal family"—smaller, and with a marriage based on love and affection between individuals. The moral, political, and economic influence that traditional families had exercised to ensure marital stability and social continuity lessened. While freed from many constraints of the past, conjugal families were expected to deal with conflicts by themselves, setting the stage for potential abuse or violence toward spouses or their children.

These developments affected normative perspectives of children as well. For centuries traditional religious views held that infants were inherently sinful or wicked and must be disciplined severely to make them useful, obedient citizens. As early as the sixteenth century, however, diary and journal entries indicate that some parents expressed ambivalence about children. New concepts about children and their care developed, many reflecting the ideas put forth by Locke and Rousseau, who challenged the traditional assumptions regarding human nature.

By 1800, several distinct views about the human nature of a newborn child had emerged, "the adoption of each of which profoundly affects the way he is treated" (Stone 1977:254–255). The traditional Christian view at the time held that a child was born with the taint of original sin and was willfully disobedient; this view had also received strong support from the religious leaders of the Reformation. To make the child obedient, it was necessary to "break the will of the child," which was accomplished by a variety of methods, such as harsh physical treatment and or an emphasis on guilt and shame. A second view rested on the concept of a blank slate—tabula rasa—on which experience and the environment shaped the child. A third perspective assumed the character of the child was genetically determined, with only minor changes possible through child-rearing. A fourth approach, the utopian view, posited that a child is born good and is corrupted by experience in society, similar to the romantic view identified by Synott (1983). Each of these views held implications for child-rearing, and each was, and is, reflected in the various ways that parents attempt to guide their children.

Historical research into marital relationships is limited by the same issues that pertain to data regarding children. The journals, diaries, and other documents that do exist offer little insight into behavior between husbands and wives for the majority of the population, which was poor, illiterate, and without property. However, the dynamics of change affected husband and wife relations as well, though rarely in a manner favorable for women. Patriarchy and violence by husbands was not only common, but also defined as acceptable and normal. Greek and Roman laws gave husbands authority to control, judge, and punish their wives, a tradition that appears to have continued largely unchanged and unchallenged for centuries in Europe. Biblical writings often were used to support the obedience of wives to their husbands, and when Emperor Constantine established Christianity as the official religion of the Roman Empire, the power of the state became aligned with the husband and remained so for centuries.

During the Renaissance and the Reformation, the view of human nature that previously justified severe physical punishment for children was challenged, but the authority of husbands within marital relationships was reinforced. The writings of Reformation leaders, including Martin Luther, John Calvin, and John Knox, strongly supported the absolute authority of the husband. By tradition and according to legal codes, husbands had near complete control over their wives. Blackstone's *Commentaries on the Laws of England*, published in 1765, declared that women had by marriage been merged with their husbands into a single entity, in which most rights and power rested with the husband. The degree to which near absolute authority was translated into physical violence is unknown, but it is unlikely that violence directed against wives would have been seen as inappropriate and recorded if it had occurred, even if a wife were to dare such a charge. In 1783, English Judge Buller purportedly asserted "the rule of the thumb" that permitted a husband to beat his wife with a stick no thicker than his thumb (Pleck 1989).

The Colonial Period

The traditions of English common law and the religious fervor of the Reformation were evident in the development of the early American colonies, particularly in New England. Among the Puritans and Calvinists, discipline was directed toward breaking the will of the child, who was seen as innately sinful with a need for godly training. In the early years of the Massachusetts Bay Colony, most punishment of children, and of servants, who were to be treated like children, included some form of physical beating, which was widely accepted and practiced (Demos 1986; Pleck 1987), and nearly anything that did not permanently maim or injure the child appears to have been acceptable.

Infanticide was most likely a problem in the early years for most colonies of the New World. In New England laws were passed against infanticide during the 1680s, indicating that informal social controls were inadequate. In the dispositions of the known cases against twenty-eight women accused of killing their infants, Pleck notes, "fourteen mothers were hanged, ten were acquitted, three were whipped, and one was flogged and sent to prison" (1987: 32).

Various forms of family abuse and violence were found in the Plymouth colony, despite laws prohibiting child abuse and wife abuse. "Wife beating" was the most common case that appeared in court records. Premised on the notion that few religious and political leaders were willing to become involved in what were seen as private troubles, these cases underscore the seriousness of the problem.

Perhaps the most important aspect of the English legal tradition that came with the settlers to North America was the body of law addressing the poor. In the wake of the economic and technological change that brought the end of feudalism while creating free labor and urbanization, the failure of some people to find work created so many needy people that churches, which historically had helped the poor, no longer could provide assistance to all in need. In response, the Elizabethan Poor Law was enacted in 1601, making local governments responsible for providing work and aid for unemployed persons, and especially for children and the aged. With the passage of this law, the poor became classified into two general categories: the "deserving poor" and "undeserving poor."

The deserving poor included those who could not earn enough to survive because of age, injury, blindness, or similar conditions and could be cared for through poor houses or in their homes, while children could be apprenticed or trained for work. The undeserving poor were considered to be the able-bodied but lazy and unwilling persons who had no legitimate claim to public support (Van Wormer 1997). Communities struggled with how to deal with the children of "undeserving" parents.

As the Industrial Revolution swept urban England, wage earners included the adult poor and their children, who often worked from dawn to dark six days a week in dangerous conditions for wages that, when combined with the earnings of other household members, were barely enough to maintain families. The working conditions in the mills and factories of the time as well as the attitudes of the owners involved were the focus of Charles Dickens's writings, especially *Oliver Twist* and *A Christmas Carol*. In response to concern that poor relief was responsible for permanent poverty, the New Poor Law of 1834 established the principle of "less eligibility." People receiving aid could not receive more than the lowest-paid worker; it was also an effort to make the poor accept any type of labor available. It was this social and cultural context from which the English colonists came, and the efforts to deal with the poor in the New World imitated the English tradition in the actions taken toward families, and especially toward children, who were often seen as neglected and unsupervised.

A More Recent Past

Many who came to Massachusetts were not Puritans, and not all of the children in Puritan families had the conversion experience that was the basis for membership in the colony. In other colonies as well, the varied religious, social, economic, and cultural backgrounds of those who arrived in the eighteenth and nineteenth centuries brought concern and efforts on behalf of both women and children. Wife abuse, especially by drunken husbands among the new immigrants, became a concern in the period before the Civil War. Despite the reticence of community leaders to become involved in domestic problems, new laws and moral reform efforts emerged. However, no real challenge to male dominance occurred until the decades following the Civil War.

For children, the eighteenth and nineteenth centuries brought changes that can be seen in children's books and magazine articles about child-rearing, most of which encouraged discipline but reserved physical punishment as a last resort (Pleck 1987). Sunley identified three different perspectives regarding the needs of children and their training that were commonly found in books and magazines in the early nineteenth century, often leading to conflicting advice to parents. The first view held that the child was tainted with original sin, with willfulness and disobedience that must be broken, thereby "freeing him from the hold of his evil nature" (1955:163); this view was held by most parents. A second rested on the idea that children faced a dangerous world, and they needed discipline to prepare them for life. A third perspective saw the child as a flower bud, "ignorant of right rather than bent to wrong" (1955:161).

By the 1820s, many articles and books in the United States considered child-rearing to be a rational process, in which parents could, by following the supposedly correct methods, produce the type of child they wanted. These methods included deliberate routines regarding meals, but opposed swaddling or corporal punishment. One parent, Francis Wayland, president of Brown University, through an anonymous letter signed "A Plain Man," told of his dealing with his 15-month-old "self willed" son. When the boy resisted his father's efforts to calm him, Wayland locked the boy alone in a room and visited him frequently, but kept him there without food for thirty-six hours until the boy became obedient. Wayland concluded that he had performed his duty to the child, to God, and to society by training him and breaking his will early (Wayland 1831).

Not all parents used harsh methods to deal with their children. Greven (1977) concluded that a genteel form of child-rearing based on love, reverence, and duty developed, especially among the educated and middle classes, wherein children were perceived to be psychological, not economic, assets. The fear that the unsupervised children of the poor would grow up to be idle, unskilled, unemployable workers led to laws allowing their removal for neglect if necessary. In 1824, New York passed legislation declaring it "a public duty to remove from the streets minor children under the age of 15 who were permitted to beg . . . or were vagrants or convicted of criminal offenses and other disturbances," and soon thereafter, New York City gave officials the authority to remove children "who were neglected or suffering because of the actions or inactions of their parents" (Watkins 1990:500–501). These concerns began to extend to children whose parents mistreated them as well, and in the 1820s, a Tennessee couple was accused of striking their daughter with fists, pushing her head against the wall, striking her with a stick, tying her to a bedpost with a rope, and then beating her with a cow skin (cited in Ross 1980). Clearly a new understanding of children and childhood was developing, one that allowed intervention into families in which parents were seen as neglecting their children or treating them with cruelty. However, it would be another century before the concept of "child abuse" emerged.

Given the limited information available about the past, it may be impossible to answer our initial questions, posed at the beginning of this chapter. The history of family abuse and violence before 1850 clearly is a poorly documented record, but it is obvious that for many families, the daily struggle for sufficient food, adequate shelter, and strength to fight diseases precluded great energy and emotional investment in their children. However, important differences existed within and among families that lived in various geographic areas, across time periods, and with different cultural traditions. Before and after the intellectual developments of the Renaissance and the Reformation, and the impact of the Industrial Revolution on Europe, the authority of the husband or father was absolute in nearly all aspects of life. As economic conditions changed, benefits were not distributed evenly. The poor became community problems. This led to the creation of poor laws designed to eliminate charity except for those unable to work. While children of the poor were seen as neglected, and some efforts were made to assist them, most violence was accepted as a private family matter. The different conceptions of children that had developed are reflected in the books and articles that were written to give advice to parents about child-rearing. Advice ranged from firm physical discipline to punishment that involved guilt and shame but no physical force to love, support, and protection (Miller and Swanson 1958). Before the Civil War, some efforts were made on behalf of children and wives to protect them from family abuse and violence, though children's vulnerability had become a concern that signaled changes in the future.

These interpretations are based on fragmentary evidence and lack the extensive empirical documentation that current resources such as survey research, demographic data, and epidemiological studies can provide, as well as the insights gained from skilled observers. Nevertheless, it is clear that the written documents, official records, legal codes, personal essays or diaries, or other recorded observations of human behavior that are available allow us to create a general history of the persistent and changing patterns of abuse and violence within families, and the responses that have been undertaken on behalf of victims. Changing conceptions of children, the emergence of conjugal families based on sentiment, and the economic and social changes that occurred in the eighteenth and nineteenth centuries created a context for living and brought community responsibility for children who were seen as victims of inadequate parents.

Documenting Change:
Family Violence, 1850–1960

Can the recent history of family abuse and violence provide a valid picture of its past extent and significance? What do we actually know about historical abuse or violence against children and other family members?

In 1849 in Seneca Falls, New York, a group of women and men drafted a Declaration of Human Sentiments, focused primarily on recognizing rights for women in marriage and divorce, and citing the traditional dominance of men in framing and interpreting the laws concerning such matters. They achieved some success in their efforts toward temperance and abolition. But an emerging women's rights movement following the Civil War focused on a wide variety of issues, such as the exploitation of young girls and single women, and the lack of protection against domestic violence. The movement also posed a challenge to the patriarchal family: Laws that gave husbands power in families, those that limited the grounds for divorce to adultery, and laws that denied women property rights in most states received the most attention. But attempts to reform the traditional family were largely unsuccessful for another half century, undermined by the focus on cruelty to children that emerged during the last half of the nineteenth century.

The emphasis on children as psychological assets and on mothers as nurturers, which began before the 1850s among middle-class parents, continued, and the attack on corporal punishment intensified following the Civil War. Violence against children was questioned, and parents sometimes faced prosecution, despite the continuing reluctance of officials to become involved in domestic affairs. In 1868, the Illinois Supreme Court held that parental authority must be exercised "within the bounds of reason and humanity" in the case of a stepmother and stepfather who were prosecuted for wanton and needless cruelty when they locked their blind son in an unheated cellar, then poured kerosene over the boy and lit it with a match to rid the boy of vermin (Pleck 1987). The Mary Ellen Wilson case, however, brought violence against children to the attention of the public—perhaps because of the ties some of those involved had to the press—and led to the founding of the New York Society for the Prevention of Cruelty to Children (NYSPCC).

On May 21, 1864, a woman who said she did not know the parents or how to contact them and had stopped receiving support left a young child named Mary Ellen Wilson at the New York Department of Charities. Mary Ellen was born to a recent immigrant from London and her soldier husband, who died in the Civil War. In January 1866, at age 2, Mary Ellen was turned over to a married couple, Thomas and Mary McCormack. Soon after, Thomas died, and his widow, Mary, married Francis Connolly. Now stepparents of a child neither wanted, the Connollys locked her in their apartment and mistreated her severely. She was left without food, given no shoes or stockings for winter, forced to sleep on a piece of carpet, regularly beaten with a rawhide whip, and at least once attacked with a pair of scissors. When a church worker, Mrs. Etta Wheeler from St. Luke's Methodist Mission, received a complaint from a dying woman about a young child being whipped and often left locked alone in a nearby apartment, she sought help from the police, benevolent societies, and charitable gentlemen, but could not obtain their assistance. After several months of futile efforts, she approached Henry Bergh, president of the New York Society for the Prevention of Cruelty to Animals. Bergh sent a worker to investigate, posing as a census worker. Mary Ellen's stepparents were forcibly removed the following day and prosecuted. At the trial Mary Connolly reported that she knew her deceased husband (Thomas McCormack) had at least three children with another woman, and she was sure Mary Ellen was another one. The court ordered Mary Ellen transferred to a home for grown children who were being trained for service work. When Mrs. Wheeler protested, she was granted custody of Mary Ellen, who was placed with Mrs. Wheeler's relatives. At age 24 Mary Ellen married and later gave birth to two daughters. In 1956 Mary Ellen died at age 92 (Ross 1980; Watkins 1990).

Given the unwillingness of public officials and the police to become involved in what were seen as private family matters, the NYSPCC assumed responsibility, at times with financial support from government and at times acting alone to enforce existing laws to protect children against cruelty and neglect. Within twenty years the society claimed to have been involved with "over 230,000 little outcasts, most of whom but for the interference of the Society would today be mature criminals" (Watkins 1990:501). In developing legal grounds for interventions, NYSPCC attorney Elbridge Gerry cited humanitarian concerns by claiming it necessary to intervene in the private affairs of the family to protect innocent victims of neglect and violence. At the same time Elbridge reassured those who opposed such intervention that "parents had the right to beat a child, so long as it was done for the proper reasons and in a moderate manner" (Pleck 1987:76). Numerous cities and states followed the lead of the NYSPCC with laws permitting the removal of children from homes for a variety of reasons, such as physical violence, neglect, poverty, vagrancy, truancy, and disorderly conduct (Ross 1980). Protective societies also emerged to intervene on behalf of individual children who were seen as being in need of assistance.

Whatever the humanitarian motives behind such actions, Costin, Karger, and Stoesz note that the strategies of the NYSPCC "called for a coercive application of social control: rescue the child, place the child in a controlled environment, and punish the cruelest as a convincing deterrent to others who would cruelly treat and shamefully neglect children" (1996:66). Nowhere is the control strategy more clearly demonstrated than in the work of the "child savers," whose efforts in the second half of the nineteenth century reflected the belief that children could be changed by providing a different social environment than that provided by the families struggling with poverty.

Manhattan's Lower East Side had 250,000 people per square mile in 1850, more than twice the density of the most crowded areas of London. The appalling poverty and crowded conditions were characteristic of most industrial cities (Sokoloff 1993). In addition, the immigration of large numbers of persons who lacked education and job skills, and whose languages, family customs, religious traditions, and cultural backgrounds were different from those established in the communities, created a population not easily assimilated into society, which generated resentment. Many children and adolescents who wandered the streets without parental supervision and at times harassed adults were from poor or working-class homes. They were defined by fellow citizens as neglected, truants, or criminals (Baldwin 2002). Many were homeless. One study estimated 10,000 children were homeless in the mid-1800s in New York City (Fry 1974).

Poverty was pervasive in most urban areas, and infanticide and neglect were among the tragic ways many parents dealt with children who were either unwanted or for whom they were unable to provide. In late-nineteenth-century Philadelphia, "hundreds of dead infants were found in cesspools and streets; 483 were found in one 4 year period" (Schwartz and Isser 2000:31–32).

It is likely that many of the children and adolescents who were defined as homeless or neglected had parents working in factories and sweatshops who lacked the resources to pay someone to care for their children, did not feel their children needed supervision, or could not arrange for child care. Desertion and changing relationships were common among recent immigrants and the poor (Schwartzberg 2004), and family violence and substance abuse were very serious problems in many households. Children were often left to fend for themselves or were forced from their homes temporarily when parents became violent or drunk. Other children were left without parents or homes when their parents died after cholera and diphtheria raged through their poor neighborhoods (O'Connor 2001).

The children who were employed in sweatshops became the focus of many efforts to change working conditions, in recognition of the long hours children had to work, their physical and emotional immaturity, and their vulnerability to exploitation. After bitter disputes, a resolution focused primarily on the age of employability, which was raised from 10 to 12 and finally to 16, and on the number of hours a child could work was introduced; but federal legislation outlawing child labor was not completed until the 1920s, when compulsory education was accepted in most areas. Children and adolescents who worked for their parents in family shops, stores, or on farms, however, were not considered a part of the problem.

Legal actions to protect children working in factories, mines, and mills primarily targeted structural rather than individual reform. The creation of educational institutions, residential homes, and foster care reflected concern about children and adolescents by attempting to control their behavior (Hanawalt 1992) and to protect them from danger. The age of consent laws were also a part of the effort to protect young adolescent women (Robertson 2002), who were frequently subject to sexual exploitation by employers and older men.

So-called child-saving groups and organizations emerged to deal with the problem of orphans, homeless, and vagrant children who supposedly needed to be saved from wasted lives of sloth, bad habits, laziness, and other behaviors that made their parents poor (Bellingham 1988). Given the optimism of the era, as reflected in the popularity of novels of the day—Finley's *Elsie Dinsmore*, Alcott's *Little Women*, and Alger's *Bound to Rise*—(Wishy 1968) and the environmentalist view of children and child-rearing, combined with concern about high birth rates among Catholic immigrants, who were seen as neglectful of their children, adoption emerged as an option for dealing with the children and adolescents roaming the streets. In 1851, Massachusetts was the first state to pass an adoption law, which became a model for other states (Carp 1998).

Child-saving agencies in many urban areas sometimes took drastic action. One such organization was the New York Children's Aid Society, whose founder, Charles Loring Brace, authored *The Dangerous Classes of New York*, published in 1872, which described his experiences working with poor children. Brace's society developed a program for children of the "unworthy poor" that ultimately transported 100,000 children via "Orphan Trains" (O'-Connor 2001) to rural communities in the Midwest. Some of the children were neither orphaned nor neglected. They were to be given fresh air and taught the Protestant virtue of hard work through an informal indenture system, and sometimes adoption, which would save them from the evils of urban life (Costin et al.

1996). The irony of children seen as too immature to work in factories or mills being taught the value of hard work on farms was largely ignored, in part perhaps because there was no adoption market, even for babies, in cities in the post–Civil War period (Zelizer 1985). These child-saving organizations were diverse, with no consistent focus for their actions, but by the end of the nineteenth century, hundreds of these groups were devoted to preventing intergenerational patterns of poverty by saving the children from the habits and behaviors of their parents.

The first juvenile court in the United States was established in Illinois in 1899, but the roots of this action can be traced to ideas and actions that emerged decades earlier: the invention (or "discovery") of adolescence, the recognition that children and adolescents were not adults, concern about the humane treatment of young offenders who might be placed with hardened criminals, and a belief that environmental factors were significant contributors to deviance and delinquency. The juvenile court represented a concern for children whose families, by failing to supervise them or teach them proper values, contributed to their deviance and delinquency. But unlike the punitive character of the Poor Law tradition, the juvenile court often used social workers to intervene, and if that failed, foster care and other types of services might be used with the hope of keeping the family intact (Costin et al. 1996). The family the court sought to preserve was a patriarchal one, in which "the father was seen to be the primary (if not sole) breadwinner, children went to school full time, and mothers remained at home, devoting themselves to housekeeping and care of their children" (Pleck 1987). The cases appearing before the court and the decisions made by judges often reflected a desire to maintain the patriarchal and traditional model. Given the context within which these courts emerged, it is not surprising that cases involving neglect rather than violence became the major concern of juvenile courts. The children were homeless, abandoned beggars and guilty of failing to live up to the expectations of the community.

Similarly the domestic courts, which were extensions of the juvenile court that had legal authority over family crime such as domestic violence, enforcement of divorce settlements, and disputes between parents and their children, were guided by the principle that separation and divorce should be avoided if possible. Women often were seen as dependent housekeepers, whose battering may have been a response to a dirty house, late meals, and disputes over finances. Despite the emphasis on the traditional and patriarchal family, caseworkers were provided with resources and could offer aid to victims of battering, allowing many wives to live independently of their husbands, an outcome that was the opposite of the intended goal of the court. One important consequence of the establishment of juvenile and domestic courts was an increase in the discretionary power of the judge and other court personnel. As a result, intervention was facilitated, but the objectives of the intervention were not achieved in most cases (Pleck 1987).

By the end of the nineteenth century, the private agencies, the juvenile court, and the social service programs that focused on children began to decline in influence and public attention, a trend that was to last through the end of the Progressive Era and World War I. By the 1920s "the cruelty movement had lost its momentum, changed its purpose, and become less visible" (Costin et al. 1996:82). As it became clear that much of the cruelty did not involve physical violence but rather the failure of parents to supervise the behavior of their children and adolescents, allowing vagrancy, delinquency, or unfamiliar actions that reflected their ethnic and cultural traditions, the issue of cruelty toward children was largely redefined into an issue of child neglect.

Neglect was often disputed by those involved, and it was often due to a parental inability to care for children adequately rather than an intent to harm. Conflicts developed between various child-saving organizations, and the organizations' sometimes arbitrary and often discriminatory actions became a focus for attacks on their activities. Disagreements arose about appropriate responses to violence against children, whether legislative action involving structural reform, therapeutic intervention for parents and children, a change of social environment or circumstances through foster or institutional care, or prosecution of parents combined with services to those involved. In addition, the continued reluctance of police and other officials to intervene in families and the lack of clear definitions for cruelty also contributed to a lack of attention to family abuse and violence.

Despite some promising legal activity targeting family abuse and violence in the late nineteenth century, "(t)here was virtually no public discussion of wife beating from the turn of the century until the mid-1970s" (Pleck 1987:182). Instead, most of the attention focused on family abuse concerned the development of public policy regarding children. The 1909 Conference on the Care of Dependent Children and establishment of the U.S. Children's Bureau signaled the beginning of federal involvement in the lives of children.

The emphasis child-saving institutions placed on coercive intervention stood in sharp contrast to the reform emphasis of the federal legislation and programs that followed, which aimed to prevent the removal of children from their families. These programs included pensions for widows to enable them to care for children at home as well as publications to assist parents in dealing with children. Books and magazine articles were mostly for middle-class parents seeking assistance. The pamphlets "Infant Care" were published by the Children's Bureau, representing the first effort by the federal government to provide all interested parents with information about the nurture and care of their children. A review of the early issues indicates that perceptions of children changed over several decades. In 1914 the infant was thought to have strong and dangerous impulses, such as masturbation and thumb-sucking, that should be controlled by restraints if necessary; but by 1945, the child was seen as harmless, with natural impulses or interests. The distinction between needs and wants that was important in 1914 had been eliminated, and play was viewed as a positive activity (Wolfenstein 1951). The child care recommendations in "Infant Care" clearly reflected society's changing views of the child.

Other governmental actions emphasizing the prevention of violence toward children produced significant accomplishments. Despite the continued resistance by social actors who believed that individuals were responsible for their own economic and social condition, the Maternity and Infancy Protection Act in 1921, the Social Security Act of 1935, which included Aid to Dependent Children, later to become Aid to Families with Dependent Children (AFDC), were actions by the federal government to address the poverty and unemployment that threatened both society and families. These acts were significant in that they rested on the recognition that unemployment and poverty were results of economic conditions, including the Great Depression, rather than of individual character or personal attributes. While women won the right to vote in 1920, the focus of a vigorous feminist movement tended to be on children rather than on intimate partner violence.

While some efforts at child saving continued through the Progressive Era and after World War I, there was continued conflict about who should be responsible for protecting children from neglect and violence—the juvenile court, private agencies, or local child welfare units—and how it should be done (Costin et al. 1996). In the public arena, the issues that dominated were survival, both social and familial. By the end of the 1950s, the high rates of marriage and childbirth for veterans of World War II, in addition to a renewed emphasis on family privacy, largely eliminated attention from social service and public agendas to violence directed at children. It would take another decade before child abuse was constructed as a social problem requiring public attention, and at least two decades before violence and abuse against women and other family members entered the public arena.

Discussion Questions

1. Children and women appear to be treated very differently across different historical periods or eras. Consider the Reformation: What are the social, legal, and cultural factors that affected the treatment (or mistreatment) of children and women during the Reformation?
2. Why did intimate partner violence, or what was once called domestic violence or wife abuse, seem to largely disappear from the public agenda in the early twentieth century? Why did concern about wife abuse emerge only after child abuse had become a major focus of public concern?

Library Research Projects

1. Identify a book and a research article on Orphan Trains. Search the Internet to see how Orphan Trains are described. How could you find out if a particular community transported or received children from Orphan Trains?
2. Search the library and the Internet to see how the state in which you live first supported poor women, men, and poor children.

4

From Violence to Abuse: Defining a Social Problem

Before World War II, family abuse and violence was defined as a private family problem, despite the fact that all of the elements of a public child protection system were in place by 1900 (Giovannoni and Becerra 1979). The economic boom of the first decade of the twentieth century was followed by World War I and the 1920s, a period characterized by the expansion of personal freedom, the widespread use of the cars, a so-called sexual revolution, and the movement of rural poor and African Americans to northern cities in search of work and improved living conditions. The massive disruptions initiated by the Great Depression in the 1930s brought the federal government's first extensive welfare programs. World War II followed, with subsequent high marriage, birth, and divorce rates, along with the renewal of civil rights movements among African Americans and women, whose wartime experiences had created new expectations for personal growth and achievements.

By the 1960s, Aid to Families with Dependent Children (AFDC) had become the major source of funding for foster care and other child welfare services for neglected children and youth, drawn primarily from poverty and minority homes. Partly due to its enormous growth, the program was plagued by poor record keeping and other problems and demonstrated "a particular ineptitude for forging a coherent response to child abuse" (Costin et al. 1996:111). Several other developments during the 1950s and 1960s created the context out of which child abuse emerged. In response to "the specter of violent teenagers menacing the public" (Pleck 1987:164), a small group of officials in public and private institutions and professions persuaded their organizations and colleagues that neglect of children would create serious problems for society. These organizations became a driving force for the development of social work services and for the broadening of child welfare concerns. Among the organizations pushing for aggressive social work in dealing with families of neglected and injured children was the American Humane Association, whose children's division was headed by Vincent DeFrancis, former director of the New York Society for the Prevention of Cruelty to Children.

Social workers and some medical personnel had been involved for many years with families that mistreated their children (Lynch 1985). But relatively few members of the medical profession were actively involved in diagnosing such cases, perhaps because they had not been trained to look for parental involvement in child injuries, they could not believe parents could harm their children, they feared libel suits, or they did not want to testify in court. Beginning in the mid 1940s, however, some medical personnel, particularly radiologists, began to notice on X-rays fractures in various stages of healing and other unexplained injuries (Caffey 1946, 1957; Barmeyer et al. 1951; Silverman 1953). An article titled "The Battered Child Syndrome," by Kempe and his associates, published in the *Journal of the American Medical Association* in 1962, attributes the unexplained injuries to intentional actions of parents. The article attracted media coverage and subsequently focused public attention directly on the issue of violence toward children. Perhaps more than any other single event, that specific publication redefined abuse and violence toward children. Under the label of "discipline," violence was acceptable, but as it became "abuse" violence became unacceptable.

After reviewing the results of a survey of hospitals, the authors described the problem of the battered child as one involving parental actions ranging from murder to fantasies of hurting the child, and noted that beating of children "is not confined to people with a psychopathic personality or of borderline socioeconomic status. It also occurs among people with a good education and a stable financial and social background" (Kempe et al. 1962:18). The causal factors that were identified included a character defect that does not inhibit the expression of aggressive impulses, a background of abuse as a child, an unwanted pregnancy or birth, as well as immaturity, impulsiveness, or hypersensitivity. Significantly, the authors focused on inconsistencies, or the injuries in which the severity and type of injury did not involve direct intent by the parent or other perpetrator, but left unexplained injuries.

The 1950s and 1960s provided a receptive social context for concern about child abuse, and child abuse joined civil rights and other issues on the public agenda. When Kempe's article was published in 1962, no state had a mandatory reporting law regarding suspected maltreatment of children, but the response was rapid: "Between 1963 and 1967 every state and the District of Columbia passed some form of child abuse reporting law"—dramatic speed for public policy innovations (Nelson 1984:76). In addition, these laws not only created a new social problem, but also generated demands for services, and within a decade the federal government had developed programs to address this issue. Why did child abuse become a national issue so quickly?

For many years social workers and others had been directing attention to the neglect and injury of children, but it was the combination of several factors that placed the issue on the national agenda. As Pfohl (1977) notes, the "battered child" was identified and introduced by a high status group—the medical profession—at a time when child-saving efforts were being challenged and a children's rights movement was emerging. In addition, the image of a "battered child" was easily adapted for attention by the media, and many magazines and newspapers were quick to publish pictures of child victims, often in vivid colors. Finally, the abusing population, despite the cautions by Kempe and his colleagues, were identified and described, far too easily and superficially, as persons with pathological problems and those living in poverty.

The laws that required reporting of suspected abuse differed across the states. Many questions had to be addressed: Who should be mandated to report: medical personnel, educators, child care workers, or everyone? Should reports focus only on physical abuse, presumably the most severe cases, or also include neglect?

To whom should the reports be made: to police or to social services? What response is required when a report is made: make sure the child is examined and treated, remove the child to safety, arrest the perpetrators, or refer the family to therapy or treatment? What should be done if parents are not cooperative?

Unfortunately, little adequate data existed regarding the scope of the child abuse problem, and estimates of the number of children affected were based on information from selective populations, hearsay, and unreliable methods of research. In 1962 the American Humane Association surveyed newspaper reports of child abuse in forty-eight states and Washington, D.C., and found reports for 662 children, 178 of whom died from the injuries. In addition, a questionnaire sent to a national sample of adults asked if they knew of families who had injured a child (De Francis 1963). The results provided an estimate of more than 2.5 million adults who knew of an abusive family. A reanalysis of the data provided a revised figure of 500,000 families that abused children in 1965. In 1971, De Francis reports that a survey in 1967 found about 12,000 suspected cases of physical abuse and 6,500 confirmed cases and claimed, "If only one child were physically abused it would be a problem, and a serious problem. But, when as many as 6,500 were identified as confirmed abuse cases for the year 1967, we have a problem of national dimensions" (De Francis 1972:8). Child abuse registries received 9,563 reports in 1967, and 10,931 in 1968, but the increase was attributed largely to legal, administrative, and professional activities rather than an increase in abuse (Gil 1979). While the Children's Bureau continued to encourage action to protect children, there were few, if any, reliable data to document the scope of the problem with any degree of confidence.

Federal legislators were reticent to act, particularly in the midst of budget issues created by the economic demands of the War on Poverty and the Vietnam War, as well as the expanding claims associated with AFDC and other social welfare programs. More than ten years after Kempe and his associates identified the battered child, the first federal legislation was passed. Child abuse continued to be a major focus of media attention during the 1960s, but the efforts of some legislators and administrators to involve the federal government in intervention and treatment or prevention programs were thwarted by those who objected to the invasion of family privacy and by disputes about what should be defined as abuse in reporting statutes.

The first successful child abuse bill was introduced by Senator Walter Mondale of Minnesota, chair of the Senate Subcommittee on Children and Youth, with similar legislation introduced in the House by Representative Patricia Schroeder of Colorado. Mondale was successful in describing child abuse as a problem that affected all social classes, rather than an issue associated only with poverty. Two issues that generated controversy during the hearings were the definition of abuse—what is normal and acceptable physical punishment—and when social service agencies have the responsibility and the right to intervene in families and remove children.

On January 31, 1974, the Child Abuse Prevention and Treatment Act (CAPTA) became Public Law 93-247. CAPTA defined child abuse, established a National Center on Child Abuse and Neglect, established requirements for state reporting laws to be eligible for federal grant funding, and created demonstration projects (Nelson 1984). Child abuse and neglect had been recognized as a national problem, but the definition remained imprecise and tenuous: "physical or mental injury, sexual abuse, negligent treatment, or maltreatment of a child under the age of 18 by a person who is responsible for the child's welfare under circumstances which indicate that the child's health or welfare is harmed or threatened thereby" (Child Abuse Prevention and Treatment Act 1974). As explanations and elaborations of the law developed, what had been unexplained injuries became nonaccidental. The Department of Health, Education and Welfare, in 1978, defined child abuse as a nonaccidental act committed by a parent or caretaker who harms or threatens to harm the child's physical or mental health.

The definition represented a compromise between a broad definition that would include any actions or lack of actions that might keep children from reaching their potential (an approach proposed by some) and a much narrower view that focused on documentable injuries, an approach generally supported by those who were opposed to federal intervention. Perhaps more important, this law offered the promise of providing resources to address the problem, but by the late 1970s it was obvious that solutions remained as remote as they had been before the legislation was enacted. Instead of solutions, three professions that had been involved with families and children now offered different theories of causality and different approaches to deal with the issue, and each temporarily held sway in response to the issue of child maltreatment.

The Medical Model: Mental Illness and the Cycle of Violence

The medical profession's involvement in describing child abuse as a serious social problem that needed to be addressed allowed doctors and others in the medical community to outline the problem, its causes, and possible solutions. The article by Kempe and associates on the "battered child syndrome" delineated the medical paradigm for understanding child abuse. Physical abuse is defined by physical injuries "where the degree and type of injury is at variance with the history given regarding the occurrence of the trauma" (Kempe et al. 1962). This perspective assumes an abuser has no intention of causing injuries or harm to the child, but instead that the adult is uniquely motivated by various internal factors—psychopathology, mental illness, depression—that are largely beyond his or her control, comparable to the explanations provided for other diseases (Parton 1985).

Early research was quick to document these characteristics, describing abusers as sick, having uncontrolled psychotic or passive-aggressive tendencies, displacing aggression or other forms of psychopathology (Fontana 1968; Steele and Pollock 1968).

Most of the studies that supported these interpretations were based on samples inappropriate for making generalizations, such as clinical cases, hospital populations, or nonrandom samples, and the validity of these findings soon faced challenges.

In a review of the literature portraying the child abuser as psychopathic, Gelles (1973) found that some authors contradicted themselves by stating that the abuser is psychopathic and then stating that the abuser is no different from the rest of society. In addition, he noted that there was little agreement about the personality traits that made up the psychopathology. Few studies attempted to test hypotheses but instead used ex post facto designs, and only rarely did studies compare the abusers to a control group. A few years later, D. R. Henry reviewed available research and concluded there is some evidence that the broad category of "mental illness may be a contributing factor to child abuse," but "no consistent and homogeneous personality profile of an abusive person has been identified" (1978:217). Studies have consistently confirmed these conclusions, and the search for the factors that cause a person to abuse children is ongoing (Wolfe 1985).

In addition to psychopathology, the medical model proposed a cycle of violence, in which abused children become abusive parents as adults. Prominent authors claimed that the "most consistent feature of the histories of abusive families is the repetition, from one generation to the next, of a pattern of abuse, neglect, and parental loss or deprivation" (Kempe and Kempe 1978:12). The theory of violence as a disease postulates that the experience of being beaten creates a personality or pathology that may be similar to a virus, lying dormant for extended periods of time, but under conditions of stress emerging with violent acts (Antler 1978), often through an individual, psychological response of the abuser identifying with his or her aggressor. Despite studies that claimed to document the cycle of abuse and claims that the cycle of abuse is the dominant factor in child abuse, there is a large, consistent literature that disputes definitive conclusions.

The limitations of clinical data for generalizations and the ex post facto nature of most studies brought challenges to the medical interpretation, particularly as the abusive parent population expanded and more inclusive conceptualizations of abuse were considered. One researcher concluded that while abusive parents "often were themselves the victims of abuse in their childhood, this is . . . neither a necessary nor sufficient cause for abuse. Not all who abuse were abused and not all who were abused, abuse" (Henry 1978:217). The idea that there is a cycle of violence persists, however, and many prevention efforts seek public support with a focus on "ending the cycle of violence."[1]

Proponents of the medical or disease model reinforce the idea that child abuse is not associated with social class. They claim it is as likely to be found in middle-class families as among the poor.

Given the reticence of legislators and others in the 1960s to support programs primarily designed for the poor, the idea that poor, middle, and upper classes were equally likely to be involved in abusive behavior undoubtedly was helpful in gaining and retaining public support for research and treatment programs. As Conrad and Schneider have noted, there are several other benefits from applying a medical definition to any social problem. In the case of child abusers, a medical response leads to the creation of humanitarian and nonpunitive sanctions, care and treatment by the medical profession, and, by applying the "sick" label to abusive parents, a reduction of personal responsibility, blame, and stigma (1982). However effective it may have been in developing public concern and support, most empirical studies of abusers that have been published over the past two decades do not support the view that all social classes are equally plagued by abuse.

The significance of the contribution made by the medical profession both to the development of information about nonaccidental child injuries and to the emerging public concern cannot be overemphasized. The focus placed by the medical community on injury or harm to the child—a physical basis for diagnosis—inevitably results in a concern with treatment and intervention rather than prevention or punishment of the abuser.

The Legal Model: Child Abusers as Criminals and Deviants

By 1967, laws regulating the reporting of suspected abuse existed in the fifty states and the District of Columbia, Guam, and the Virgin Islands, but there was little if any consistency among them. Some jurisdictions had mandatory reporting for medical personnel, a few had permissive reporting, and three states required a report from any person having knowledge or reason to suspect child abuse. Agencies designated to receive reports in some states were protective services, law enforcement and prosecutors only in other states, and both protective services and the justice system in a few jurisdictions (American Humane Association 1967). The inclusion of law enforcement and prosecutors indicated a redefinition of violent actions toward children from a mental illness to a criminal offense that was assumed to be intentional, rather than unexplained as suggested by the medical model.

The legal response took a punitive approach to the problems of child abuse and neglect. Punitive justice is based on the premise that violence by a parent or caretaker toward a child is a criminal act and should be punished, just as a case of interpersonal violence that does not involve family members should result in punishment for the perpetrator. The arrest and prosecution of those who abuse children were seen as necessary deterrents both to continued violence by parents or perpetrators and to possible future abuse by those affected. Successful prosecution of cases tended to rely on clear medical evidence of harm provided by medical personnel or eyewitnesses to the abuse, conditions that were rarely met, especially for those cases that were reported by those who suspected abuse as required by law, but were based on secondhand reports or vague indicators of abuse.

It soon became obvious that prosecution would be difficult in all but the most serious cases of extreme violence and severe injury. The lack of a clear, precise distinction between abuse and appropriate discipline made minor injuries acceptable to many in the legal system. Unless it was an extremely serious case, medical personnel often were unwilling to provide testimony about abuse. The time required to testify interrupted their work, and they had concerns about disrupting their relationship and continued contact with parents and their patients.

In most criminal cases, the injured party can provide testimony of the events, but for child abuse the age and dependency of the child often hinder successful prosecution. Abuse typically involves only two people, both eyewitnesses: the perpetrator and the child. Even if a spouse or a sibling is present, it still may be impossible to obtain a conviction. Few intimate partners will testify against each other,[2] and the perpetrator is older and seen as more credible than a child. In most state courts, children age 8 or younger are routinely excluded from testifying, but most physical abuse reports pertain to children of that age or younger. As a result, many cases cannot be prosecuted. Even an injured child over age 8 may be reluctant to testify against a parent or caretaker because of emotional ties and possible fears of retaliation, or an uncertain home life after the trial. If there is a trial but no conviction, the child may fear that the parent will behave in an even more brutal fashion in the future.

If a parent is convicted, who benefits? From an economic perspective, few children are better off with a parent serving time in a prison or correctional setting, leaving a disrupted (if not destroyed) family. Even fewer children are likely to benefit when they are removed from their home and placed elsewhere, such as in a residential facility or in foster care, even if appropriate new behaviors are learned. In the face of such real and potential consequences, by the end of the 1970s, prosecutions tended to be limited to cases of child sexual abuse, serious physical injury, or the death of a child (Davidson et al. 1981).

Criminal justice approaches to perpetrators of child abuse had limited value as a means of dealing with the problem. It was the juvenile or family court that emerged to respond to deviant family behaviors. Juvenile courts had been established at the beginning of the twentieth century to remove children and adolescents from adult courts and prisons in order to prevent them from being enticed into a life of crime. Premised on the need to apply the best interests of the child standard, the courts shifted focus from the prosecution of parents to the protection of the child. Parents of neglected and delinquent children might be abusive or neglectful without intent due to their immaturity, lack of discipline, or personal inadequacy, but only rarely were they prosecuted. Instead they faced the prospect of losing custody of their children. Suspected parental neglect became the grounds for judicial intervention.

Judges in juvenile or family courts were given great discretion in their interpretation of the facts and in their potential judgments. There were always at least three parties involved—the justice system, the parents or custodians of the child, and the child or a social worker representing the very young child, each of whom brought a unique perspective to the court. Many judges found themselves in situations where a decision was required, but each party brought different evidence and offered different interpretations of the situation. Not surprisingly, justice under such circumstances was highly unpredictable, and varied by geographic locale, the time of day, the training or perspective of the individual judge, and the type of evidence brought to the court. Though some efforts were made to reduce both the vagueness in legal definitions and the many inconsistencies among judges, numerous legal concepts such as substantial risk, inadequate supervision, and emotional harm remained subject to arbitrary interpretation (Institute of Judicial Administration 1977).

Those opposed to the use of juvenile or family courts to deal with child abuse cited the inconsistency in judicial decisions. Others objected to the outcome of court decisions. Children removed from their homes and placed in foster care as a means of protecting them from neglectful and abusive parents often languished there for years, with little prospect of reuniting with their families. Many of these children came from poor families whose child-rearing behaviors often were in conflict with the expectations of social workers and judges. One legal scholar forcefully argued that many foster homes were no better than those from which children had been removed and that parental rights were often ignored in these cases (Wald 1975, 1976). Others challenged the identity difficulties young children often face when removed from their families and shifted among different foster care settings (Goldstein et al. 1979).

Due to not only the lack of empirical evidence that removal of the child from the family is beneficial, the inconsistency in judicial decisions, and the failure of foster care to provide significant modifications in child behavior, the effectiveness of the justice system also was challenged by the sizeable numbers of repeat offenders— parents whose behavior toward their children was not sufficiently modified by prosecution and incarceration to eliminate abusive actions. While methodological and conceptual issues make it extremely difficult to determine the precise level of recidivism for parents who have been prosecuted for abusing their children, estimates for re-abuse among families receiving social services range from zero for low-risk cases (those least likely to be prosecuted) to 85 percent for high-risk families (those most likely to be prosecuted) who were followed for ten years (Herrenkohl et al. 1984). Lack of confidence in the court's abilities to solve problems shifted the general public's focus to the social service agencies that could help families deal with the problems and crises in their lives.

The Social Services Model: Victims of Abuse as Children and Victims of Poverty

Social services have long been a part of the response to parental neglect and abuse, but the Child Abuse Treatment and Prevention Act gave new focus, legitimacy, and more financial support to these services. Based on general social science principles, in particular psychology and sociology, family intervention by social services is deemed to be justified as a means of preventing future parental abuse. As was the case with medical and legal approaches, intervention rests on assumptions and theories about the causes of abusive behavior and how parental behaviors may be altered.

A social science perspective assumes that social actors reflect the cultural context in which they live. Individuals respond to social situations or circumstances, including poverty, stress, isolation, and crises in interpersonal relationships. As children mature, they learn the content of a particular cultural context, shaped in part by social status, income, education, religious and cultural traditions, and family relationships; they learn how to act through the experiences they have as children and adolescents. Perceptions of social situations, assessments of the motives and intentions of others, understanding of the behavioral options available, and decisions about how and when to act are responses to what persons have learned through social interactions with parents, siblings, peers, and friends.

The social science perspective parallels the "cycle of violence" notion that can be attributed to everyday observations, theoretical statements, and a great deal of empirical research. One premise is that there is a significant degree of continuity in attitudes and behaviors between parents and children. The cycle of violence became an explanation for child abuse and a cry for action: "Break the Cycle of Violence!"

Resting on the commonsense idea that children learn how to behave from their parents, the social science perspective argues that children who are subjected to violence will become violent in their relationships because they learned how to behave violently or aggressively by modeling their parents' behavior (Chen and Kaplan 2001). Children, according to the argument, either adopt the attitudes and values of their parents, which justified and legitimated the use of violence, or become violent because the patterns of interaction and general context within the family are conducive to the continuity of violence (Bevan and Higgins 2002; Brook et al. 2002; Markowitz 2001; Straus 1994; Wilkes 2002). Similarly, neglected children will become neglectful of their own children either because they were deprived of the opportunity to learn basic skills regarding parenting, health, and nutrition or because desperate economic conditions overwhelm those facing conditions associated with poverty, such as physical disabilities, poor health, social isolation, depression, and other psychological issues.

According to a social learning perspective, family abuse and violence (FAV) episodes occur because the social actor models behavior that she or he learned as a child or adolescent. Despite its elegant simplicity and appeal, this idea does not provide adequate answers to the questions: Is there an intergenerational cycle of violence? Does violence beget violence?

Skeptics examine at least three assumptions upon which a simplistic version of the social learning perspective rests: First, early experiences of children are irreversible in later life. Second, antecedent experience dominates and has primary causality over proximate events. Third, the cause and effect relationship is unidirectional. Parents are the cause of abuse, and children are the victims who, as adults, become the perpetrators. None of these assumptions is well-supported conceptually or empirically. First, the public educational system rests on empirical evidence that shows later learning and knowledge gained can and does reverse early learning. Second, research consistently demonstrates that situational or proximate events are more likely to lead to abusive behavior by adults than their childhood experiences or events in the past. Third, data from cases of abuse strongly suggest that children or adolescents can and do precipitate abuse or create conditions to which parents respond with abusive behavior.

In addition, some of the research cited to support the cycle of violence perspective is limited by important theoretical and methodological deficiencies (Newcomb and Locke 2001). Many of the studies that claim to document the intergenerational continuity of abuse are based on samples of parents and children who were receiving social services or medical care to address the problem of abuse or neglect, without including matched or comparison groups. Similarly, samples drawn from Child Protective Services, which typically include only reported cases rather than a more inclusive population, exclude from study those parents who were abused as children but do not abuse their children, and rely on the sometimes inconsistent judgments of child protection workers.

An exception to some of these criticisms is Starr's work, which compares families who had a child admitted to the hospital and that had been reported to social services in Michigan for suspected or actual abuse to non-abusive families that had a hospitalized child of the same age and sex. Samples were matched on race and social class. Starr's analysis found that "much of the existing literature describing the causes and correlates of child abuse is not supported" (1982b:129). He concludes that poverty is the primary issue for the abusive families. His findings have not influenced many studies or the popular literature about child abuse.

Another problem with the simple social learning perspective concerns the use of retrospective data in which people are asked to recall and describe events in childhood and adolescence. This approach is a common practice in FAV research. When parents are asked about their childhoods, after being identified as abusive parents, should their claim to have been treated in the same way when they were children be seen as a valid response? Undoubtedly some parents who were not abused will claim to have been abused, and vice versa. Several studies have reported that persons may provide details of violent behaviors directed at them as children or adolescents, but that as adults many of these persons do not view themselves as abused, even if the level of violence was severe and very likely would have been considered physical abuse by Child Protective Services had it been reported (Berger et al. 1988; Bower-Russa et al. 2001; Bower and Knutson 1996; Prescott et al. 2000; Rodriguez and Price 2004).

Clearly, recall may offer some unique insights into the conditions associated with family violence (Dube et al. 2004; Kendall-Tackett and Becker-Blease 2004), but concerns about the validity and reliability of retrospective data remain. These concerns cannot be eliminated entirely when dealing with intergenerational forms of family abuse and violence. As Rutter (1998) claims, there are numerous considerations that are usually ignored that also may affect or influence interpretations of intergenerational abuse. These include whether there are two parents, the changing rates of psychosocial disorder in society, nonfamilial factors such as social class and ethnicity, gender differences, personal traits, and even the level of caution exercised in interpreting statistical data.

Widom (1989; Widom, Raphael, and DuMont 2004) attempted to address problems of retrospective data and the lack of matching samples by collecting information from a sample of children in a metropolitan area of the Midwest whose physical or sexual abuse or neglect were documented through juvenile court records from 1967 through 1971. A control group was selected from hospital and school records in which individuals were matched on sex, race, and week of birth for preschool children and the same class in the same elementary school for those in school. Using arrest records to measure delinquency and criminality in 1988, and again in 1994, her analysis indicated the consequence of "being abused or neglected as a child increased the likelihood of arrest as a juvenile by 59% and as an adult by 28%, and for a violent crime by 30%." Widom and Maxfield concluded that "abused and neglected females were at increased risk of arrest for a violent crime as a juvenile or adult . . . (but the same) pattern was not evident for males." They also suggest that neglect is a major concern, "potentially more damaging to the development of a child than physical abuse" (2001:4).

Several additional longitudinal studies document continuity or intergenerational forms of family abuse and violence. Some of the social processes associated with the transmission of violence are examined, such as the specific types of parental maltreatment that can affect both attitudes toward violence and abusive behaviors. The research has elaborated some effects on children observing parent-to-parent violence when they become adults and have children and spouses or partners. Most research in this tradition seeks to identify the degree to which parenting practices experienced in childhood predict parenting practices in adulthood, and what factors or conditions are responsible for breaking the cycle of abuse.

Data from three geographic areas (Oregon, Iowa, and Rochester, New York) were collected to provide empirical evidence of the factors leading to intergenerational forms of family violence and abuse. The Oregon Youth Study (Capaldi and Clark 1998; Pears and Capaldi 2001; Capaldi et al. 2003; Hops et al. 2003) used a prospective model of parenting and externalizing behavior spanning three generations and reported findings that suggest a direct effect and some mediated effects of poor parenting practices between the generations. Data from the longitudinal Iowa Youth and Family Project (Conger et al. 2003) indicated a direct connection between aggressive parenting by the first generation and aggressive parenting by the second generation. The Rochester Youth Development Study (Thornberry et al. 2003) examined aggressive parenting and antisocial behavior across generations and reported modest support for continuity, though effects vary by gender. Each study provided some support for some aspect of the cycle of violence, suggesting that a child who has been exposed to abuse and has witnessed parent-to-parent violence is more likely, as an adult, to use violence against a child and against a spouse. In addition, he or she is more likely to be victimized by intimate partner violence or an intragenerational form of family abuse and violence.

Among the early efforts to evaluate the intergenerational continuity of abuse was a literature review about two decades ago by Kaufman and Zigler, who concluded that about 30 percent of parents who were abused as children become abusive parents and suggested that the appropriate question to ask is not whether there is intergenerational continuity of abusive behavior but rather "Under what conditions is transmission of abuse most likely to occur?" (1987:191). A few years later, after a similar review of the literature, Oliver concluded that one-third of child victims "grow up to continue a pattern of seriously inept, neglectful, or abusive rearing as parents" (1993:1315), while one-third do not become abusive, and about one-third remain vulnerable to the effects of social stress. Clearly, if at least two-thirds of abused children do not become abusive parents, the cycle of violence is not adequate as a definitive explanation for most family abuse and violence episodes. In order for the number of abused children to persist year after year at present levels, as has been reported for more than a decade, parents who have not been abused as children must be part of the abuser population. An important question remains: What conditions produce parental violence, whether or not the parent experienced a violent childhood?

A concern among social scientists is the effect of poverty and various social conditions associated with poverty, such as social isolation, stress, depression, and trauma, which become a part of the learning context and therefore can affect violence among intimates and against children. Some perceive higher rates of violent behavior in high-poverty neighborhoods as evidence for the proposition that frustration and a lack of financial and personal resources can generate anger and other emotions that lead to family abuse and violence. The supposed tolerance of abuse by families, their neighbors, and the community at large may contribute to a culture of violence (if one indeed exists) in which such actions may not be seen as inappropriate.

In consideration of the significance of poverty, it is important to recognize that most parents who live in poverty do not abuse their children, and most intimate couples who live in poverty are not violent toward each other. Thus, in spite of the intuitively plausible relationship between poverty and family abuse and violence, poverty per se is not sufficient to explain FAV episodes.

Protecting Children: The Development of Child Protective Services

Following the enactment of CAPTA, Child Protective Services (CPS) was created to respond to a perceived epidemic of child abuse. In some ways, this only formalized many of the procedures that developed during the late nineteenth or early twentieth centuries (Myers 2004). These services typically were lodged within the public welfare system, and it was not surprising that confusion about the role of CPS developed among the public, clients, and welfare agencies themselves. Historically, the public welfare system had provided financial and other assistance primarily to poor persons and families and rested on well-defined procedures. Assistance was voluntarily sought by application, with a thorough documentation of need required to meet well-defined criteria governing eligibility for aid (though these rules often were interpreted and implemented in ways that had negative consequences, particularly for African Americans (Lawrence-Webb 1997). In addition, access for persons applying for assistance was limited by time and location—often occurring in a very noisy public area with the potential client paying time and travel costs. In contrast, new child protective services were involuntary, provided without eligibility restrictions, and CPS personnel were available every hour of every day of the year, usually in the privacy of the alleged perpetrator's home, with time and travel costs assigned to the CPS agency (Knudsen 1988). As might be expected, investigation of reports of alleged abuse or neglect often was seen as another intrusion of government into families.

In most states, the responsibilities of CPS include several discretionary decisions. As the increase in reports overtook the resources of CPS agencies, it became necessary to carefully consider the complaint, in order to offer services to children and families deemed to have the greatest need. Consequently, at intake a decision is made whether to screen out or to investigate the report of alleged abuse, based on its appropriateness, previous contacts with the family, and the urgency and seriousness of the alleged maltreatment. Following intake and the investigation of a suspected case, CPS workers decide whether to verify maltreatment based on the evidence obtained in the investigation. This might include an assessment of whether the danger or injury justifies removal of the children. Decisions are made regarding the services needed and offered to the family to make the home safe for the children, as well as to which agencies are best able to provide these services. Finally, after a review of the effectiveness of the services and the progress of the family, a decision is made about whether to continue or to close the case (Schene 1998). Each of these decisions requires extensive information and constant review.

Nationally in 2001, about 870,000 or nearly one-third of the 2,670,000 reports of maltreatment were screened out and not investigated because they were duplicate reports, lacked sufficient information, were prompted by custody disputes, involved children already known to CPS, were the responsibility of another agency, or were in some other way considered inappropriate for investigation (U.S. Department of Health and Human Services 2004a). However, the threshold has been raised for the investigation of even serious or dangerous circumstances and many complaints are routinely screened out, in part because of the inability of CPS staff to handle the large number of reports (Wells 1985; Wells et al. 1989).

When the investigator perceives children to be in some immediate danger, emergency action may involve removal and placement of the children in a foster home or an institution until they can return safely to their parental home. Ultimately juvenile or family courts make the decisions regarding custody, returning the child, or the termination of parental rights. Courts rely in most cases on the reports and recommendations of child protection workers and Court Appointed Special Advocates volunteers. Like CPS, the courts often are overwhelmed by cases pertaining to child abuse and violence.

Many parents do not succeed in meeting the expectations of social service agencies for creating a safe environment for their children. Some parents whose problems are relatively minor may have their children returned despite their failure to comply with the expectations, simply by making minimal adjustments and outlasting the system. For others, failure means permanent loss of custody of their children. The children remain in foster care until the parental rights are terminated and then await a permanency plan that may include adoption. This period often extends to several years. Federal legislation, specifically the 1980 Adoption Assistance and Child Welfare Act, the 1997 Adoption and Safe Families Act, and the 2003 Adoption Promotion Act, provides financial incentives to states and requires agencies to make reasonable efforts to reunify families, but also to make accelerated decisions about permanent homes for dependent children (Collins 2004). Clearly decisions are made more quickly, but among the negative consequences of time limits is that parental rights can be terminated without stable options for the children, such as adoption, permanent foster care, or independent living—especially for children of color—despite the fact that African American parents adopt children from foster care at a rate twice as high whites (Lindsey and Schwartz 2004).

Despite efforts spanning forty years, CPS agencies have not eliminated or even lowered the level of child maltreatment, nor have they received the acceptance and recognition by other professionals or the public that had been hoped and expected when they were created. According to CPS reports, in 1990, the number of victims per 1,000 children in the United States was 13.4. Since that time, it has fluctuated from a high of 15.3 in 1993 to a low of 11.8 in 1999, and in 2002 was 12.3 (U.S. Department of Health and Human Services 2004b). While it is clear that the definitions of abuse and neglect have changed and expanded, it is impossible to determine the effect that changing definitions have had on these rates.

Perhaps more important, there were an estimated 1,300 child deaths due to neglect or abuse in 2001, an indication of lack of reporting, inadequate investigations, or ineffective services. Nearly 10 percent of these children were in families that had received services within the prior five years (U.S. Department of Health and Human Services 2004a). Such statistics are typical for recent years but probably understate the actual deaths because an unknown number of children die of maltreatment who are not so classified (Herman-Giddens et al. 1999).

Many factors contribute to the continued maltreatment of children in spite of the creation of CPS. First, although most states have mandated reporting, especially for medical personnel, police, social services, and educators, a large number (two-thirds or more) of suspected cases in the United States are not reported (Sedlak and Broadhurst 1996). The failure to report may be due to uncertainty as to what constitutes abuse, a lack of confidence in CPS, a belief that no benefits to the child will result from a report, fear of breaking a trusted or confidential relationship, or actual ignorance of the legal requirement (Kalichman and Brosig 1993; Steinberg et al. 1997; Zellman and Antler 1990).

The effects of different interpretations of reporting laws, the media's attention to extreme cases, and the efforts of organized groups to combat abuse are reflected in the data for various states, inflating the level of alleged maltreatment in some states and minimizing it in others. Thus, in 1985 the reporting rate of suspected maltreatment per 1,000 children ranged from a low of 7.29 in Pennsylvania to a high of 57.24 in Missouri. In 1995, the rates ranged from 8.29 in Pennsylvania to 107.64 in the District of Columbia (U.S. Department of Health and Human Services 1997). For 2001, reporting rates varied from a high of 90.9 in Alaska to a low of 18.2

in Illinois, with the U.S. average at 36.6 per 1,000. This means that a report had been made for nearly 4 percent of all children, though the chances of being reported for maltreatment are much greater in some states than others.

Reports that are screened in and investigated require some judgment by CPS regarding the validity of the report. First investigations by CPS inevitably are snapshots of the situation, based on one point in time, so only limited assessments of the parent-child relationships can be made, with little if any knowledge about the process precipitating the incident, or past abuse or neglect unless the family has had prior investigations (Munro 1996; Rossi, Schuerman, and Budde 1999). Numerous studies have documented the problems this situation presents for CPS workers: making decisions based on partial or inadequate information due to poor risk assessment or overreliance on standardized approaches, and dealing with the conflict inherent in the desire to protect the child while also preserving families (Doueck, Levine, and Bronson 1993; English and Pecora 1994; Giovannoni 1991; Kaufman et al. 1994; Lyons, Doueck, and Wodarski 1996; Munro 1996; Rossi, Schuerman, and Budde 1999; Smith, Sullivan, and Cohen 1995). Not surprisingly, these circumstances often result in delayed, inconsistent, and inappropriate judgments or incorrect assessments (Kolko 1998). These assessments either substantiate a report when no maltreatment occurred (overinclusion) or fail to protect a child who has been abused, a case of underinclusion (English et al. 2000). In addition, the confidentiality of records, originally designed to protect the privacy of persons involved with CPS, limits collaboration among agencies. This often leads to claims that nothing was done, that CPS was ineffective, or that CPS interferes in parent-child relationships within normal families.

Both critics and supporters of CPS have suggested that inadequate funding for overwhelming case loads leads to caseworker burnout and is a major reason for CPS problems (Anderson 2000). The psychological impact of working with child victims and unresponsive or hostile parents, whose behavior is often unaffected by services offered, combined with low salaries and little preparation, leads to high turnover. This results in discontinuity in services, low morale, and frustration among CPS workers (General Accounting

Office 2003). Despite the development of Guardian-at-Litem programs, now called Court Appointed Special Advocates, which has reduced the level and intensity of involvement with some clients, and reduced placements and accelerated permanency planning, problems remain (Calkins and Millar 1999). This had led child advocates and those who support CPS activities to suggest our society must make a genuine commitment to child protection and provide greater financial resources to improve and expand CPS work (Kammerman and Kahn 1993). However, other researchers and critics have suggested that the child protection system itself is flawed, directed toward inappropriate goals, and incapable of protecting children or preventing child abuse.

Whether and how CPS can protect children and prevent future abuse is a question that has led to little consensus. While many researchers and child advocates agree that problems exist, some suggest the needed reforms can be made within the existing system. These reforms include: clarifying reporting laws, expanded public education about reporting, providing feedback to those who report, modifying liability laws, and improving and extending services (Besharov 1998). Other suggestions include more legal action to provide focus and sustained pressure on the system or greater involvement of community residents to reduce a crisis orientation and expand services without changing the basic organization of CPS.

In contrast to such proposals, Pelton suggests that "The fundamental structure of the public child welfare system is that of a coercive apparatus wrapped in a helping orientation" (1998:126–129). Combining the roles of judge, in which attention is directed to child protection and safety, with that of helper, in which family preservation is the goal, is arguably contradictory and ineffective. The current system, he argues, is based on simplistic assumptions that parents alone are to blame for injuries to their children. This is a focus maintained through an alliance between those seeking protection of children and those who support coercive approaches to maltreating families. This is despite evidence that numerous social factors are major contributors to the problem and that most families reported for both abuse and neglect are poor (Pelton 1978; Sedlak and Broadhurst 1996). This criticism is echoed by Terling-Watt, whose study of 1,515 cases in Houston found serious inadequacies in risk assessment and available services. Thirty-eight percent of the family reunification cases reappeared. The author notes that a major problem is that both CPS services and the legal system are focused on individuals and their rights, despite the current emphasis on family preservation, so that the basic conditions surrounding child abuse and neglect tend to be ignored (Terling-Watt 2000).

Other critiques have focused on funding, misdirected goals, and the breakdown of the child protection system: "There is little doubt that the child protection system has become a 'nonsystem'" (Costin et al. 1996), and "Although the child welfare system has been transformed into a child protective service . . . there is virtually no evidence that the change reduced child abuse fatalities or even increased safety for children" (Lindsey 2004:157). These critiques suggest the failure to protect children, the primary goal of CPS, is due to the agency's organization and procedures. *The Book of David* (Gelles 1996) delineates this tragedy. It is the story of a child lost in a system committed to family preservation; a child who died, due to human miscalculations and a system that placed more emphasis, and money, on family preservation than on the welfare of children.

Few critics fault the intentions or efforts of CPS workers, but many note that effective child protection requires much more than may be possible, given the problems surrounding many abusive parents. Critics contend that offering the maltreating parent the opportunity to participate in parent education classes, mental health and addiction treatment programs, individual or group counseling sessions, or other interventions that do not address the issue of economic self-sufficiency can only fail.

Discussion Question

1. Nearly all parents claim to love and care deeply for their own children. What are the indicators that suggest the United States, as a country, values children? What are the indicators to suggest that the United States does not value children highly enough to prevent child abuse and neglect?

Research Project

Design a study to measure how the local community defines and prioritizes its most important social problems.

Notes

1. The "cycle of violence" is one of those popular phrases that is (mis)used to explain two separate phenomena in the family abuse and violence literature. Some use the phrase to refer to children who, as adults, abuse their intimate partners supposedly because they were abused as children. Others use the same phrase to refer to the cycle of violence that battered women experience in abusive relationships that are characterized by repeated and sequenced episodes of violence and nonviolent behaviors. In this chapter we are referring only to the cycle of violence that refers to the abused child who becomes an abusive adult.

2. In criminal cases spousal privilege may be exercised allowing a wife or husband to avoid testifying against a marital partner.

III

*INTER*GENERATIONAL FORMS OF FAMILY ABUSE AND VIOLENCE

5

Physical Abuse of Children

In the United States, with the 1974 enactment of the Child Abuse Prevention and Treatment Act (CAPTA:PL 93-247), the physical abuse of children became the major focus of many social services. But there was and there still is no specific definition that could be applied to all reports of physical maltreatment. Congressional hearings included testimony from those who wanted an inclusive definition, such as any act of a parent or custodian that prevented a child from achieving full potential, to those who wanted a narrow definition that focused on serious, documented injury. The definition of physical abuse that emerged specified that some act resulting in physical injury, such as fractures, burns, bruises, welts, cuts, and/or internal injuries, occurred. Child abuse could have been perpetrated in the name of discipline or punishment; and it may have involved a slap of the hand or the use of straps, belts, or other instruments.

CAPTA also required that each state create a system of Child Protective Services (CPS) to investigate reports of suspected maltreatment and to provide services designed to protect the child. All states enacted laws mandating reporting by medical personnel, and a number of states required reporting by other types of social actors who work with children. However, definitions were interpreted in different ways by CPS workers. In addition, many did not report suspected abuse, and when they did, the services that were available tended to be inappropriate or inadequate to deal with the problem. As a result, children and their families were confronted with inconsistencies in the legal codes, in the definitions of abuse used to diagnose and substantiate, and in the ways law enforcement, medical personnel, or social service agencies dealt with children and with perpetrators suspected or found guilty of abuse.

The scope of behavior that should be included in a definition of physical abuse has been debated over the past four decades. These debates reflect genuine differences in opinion about which methods of child-rearing are appropriate and the role of the state in family decisions. "Spare the rod and spoil the child" represents one view that justifies and encourages parental use of physical punishment in training and disciplining children, though this proverb is not adequate for explaining the linkage between punishment and abusive behavior (Carey 1994). This perspective has been fueled by efforts of some religiously oriented organizations and individuals whose books, written in response to the perceived permissiveness of the 1960s, are designed to assist parents in child-rearing (Christenson 1970; Dobson 1970, 1987). In addition, arguments over definitions of what constitutes abuse and what is appropriate in child-rearing tend to focus on whether the parent or the state should define appropriate physical punishment. Many parents believe they have an obligation to punish the self-centered behaviors of young children, based on the belief that human nature is inherently sinful and self-centered and that such actions are necessary to make children responsible adults.

What is inappropriate physical punishment? As defined by Straus, physical or corporal punishment is "the use of physical force with the intention of causing the child to experience pain, but not injury, for the purpose of correction or control of the child's behavior" (1994:4). Teaching the child is undoubtedly the objective of many, if not most, parents when they spank, even if carried to such an extreme that it results in injury. The level of appropriate pain necessary to teach or discipline, however, is subjective and defined by the social actors involved, that is, the child and the parent or caretaker, whose perspectives may differ considerably, particularly in an abusive family. Younger children are spanked or hit more frequently, and not surprisingly, the rate of hitting declines as the child's age increases, though adolescents also are subjected to physical punishment in many families (Straus 1994:29). Can we identify the point that physical discipline crosses the line and becomes an episode of family abuse and violence (FAV)?

Child Protective Service workers, who for many parents represent an unwelcome and unneeded intrusion of the state into their families, act primarily in response to the real or presumed effects of the parental actions—both physical and emotional, in an effort to protect the child from future abuse. A number of other factors also influence whether CPS takes action, such as the availability of services for parents, the perceived severity of the abuse, judgments about parental intention and remorse, and attitudes toward the social status of the family. It must be recognized that there is an implicit standard of care in the assessment of physical abuse, which reflects beliefs about appropriate behaviors of parents toward their children, the use of corporal punishment, the effectiveness of available services and treatment, and the likely response of the parents to services and prevention programs.

Defining and Measuring Physical Abuse of Children

How someone defines physical abuse has a major influence on the way episodes are recorded, measured, and reported. Physical abuse involves an act by a parent or caretaker, often done in the name of discipline, which results in physical injury, in the form of fractures, burns, bruises, welts, cuts, and/or internal injuries. How that definition is applied frequently appears to be arbitrary, in part due to the different perspectives of medical, legal, and social service professionals.

Assumptions about children and parenting, though often unstated and unexamined, have important consequences. For example, how human nature is defined—as basically "bad," "good," or a "blank slate" to be inscribed by experience—is a significant factor in parental approaches to discipline. In addition, the attitudes and behavior of parents toward their children, which reflect their ethnicity, social class, location, and religious or cultural background, differ greatly. How much consensus or agreement exists regarding the definition of physical abuse?

Researchers often have relied on surveys of professionals, such as police, attorneys, pediatricians, and social workers, both to identify what is considered abuse and to identify attitudes toward reporting events to Child Protective Services. Other studies have examined the definitions of child abuse within the general population (Ashton 2001; Brooks et al. 1994; Kalichman, Craig, and Follingstad 1988). In a recent review of ten studies, Korbin and associates found minor differences in how community members define physical discipline resulting in bruises, neglect (especially the lack of supervision), and sexual behaviors. In their study of 400 families in Cleveland, African Americans were more likely to focus on neglect and whites on physical abuse, but there was "a basic congruence in definitions of child maltreatment" among professional groups and socioeconomic groups within the larger population (Korbin et al. 2000:1523). Despite agreement on the basic conditions of child maltreatment in the population at large, numerous factors are involved in which actions, conditions, or injuries are subsequently reported as abuse in CPS investigations. Data drawn from CPS investigations are one of the major sources of information about the amount and types of abuse in the United States and are often cited as official data in media reports.

Some states mandate that anyone suspecting child abuse must report it, but in most states, required reporting is limited to social services, schools, medical personnel, and other social actors who work with children. While these reports implicitly rely on the reporter's conception of maltreatment, the investigation of cases rests primarily with CPS personnel, whose decisions constitute an operational definition of physical abuse. However, in the United States and other countries, many of the social actors who are required to report suspected cases of abuse do not do so. Some studies show that as few as half report suspected cases to CPS (Brosig and Kalichman 1992; Crenshaw, Crenshaw, and Lichtenberg 1995; Delaronde et al. 2000; Hazzard and Rupp 1986; Kenny 2001; King et al. 1998; Sundell 1997; Tite 1993; Van Haeringen, Dadds, and Armstrong 1998; Zellman 1990).

In an effort to overcome some of the deficiencies of CPS data, especially the lack of reporting, three National Incidence Studies (NIS) sponsored by the U.S. Department of Health and Human Services were undertaken.[1] Non-CPS sentinels were asked to report suspected abuse and neglect to a central collection agency, which compared birth dates and sex to eliminate duplications. The sentinels were from law enforcement, medical services, education, and other services that had direct contact with children and families in counties selected to represent the general population of the United States. This method of data collection resulted in the identification of a large number of maltreated children, more than 70 percent of whom in the NIS 3 study were *not* reported to CPS (Sedlak and Broadhurst 1996:7–16). In all three NIS studies, abuse was defined as acts "constituting physical abuse include hitting with a hand, stick, strap, or other object; punching; kicking; shaking; throwing; burning; stabbing; or choking a child" leading to moderate harm (the harm standard) and similar acts that did not cause harm (the endangerment standard) (Sedlak and Broadhurst 1996:2–10).

The most recent NIS study found, based on the harm standard, that an estimated 381,700 children in the United States were victims of physical abuse. An estimated 614,100 children were victims based on the endangerment standard (Sedlak and Broadhurst 1996:3–3, 3–18). These figures represent significant increases over the 1986 estimates.

Critics of the NIS studies point to selection bias in reporting of suspected maltreatment by ignoring family, friends, and neighbors as potential reporters, particularly within African American neighborhoods, where people are less likely to approach the agencies in which sentinels were located. This bias is reflected in the differences between the NIS studies and CPS data (Ards, Chung, and Myers 1998; Morton 1999; Ards, Chung, and Myers 1999; Ards, Chung, and Myers 2001). Such bias lowers the estimated number of children abused and neglected. Thus, the NIS figures must be considered conservative estimates of child physical abuse.

A third estimate of the level of abuse and neglect is based on responses by parents or caretakers themselves regarding their behaviors toward their children. The National Family Violence Surveys, undertaken in 1976, 1986, and 1996, used the Conflict Tactics Scale

(CTS) to measure behaviors with face-to-face interviews in 1976 and telephone surveys in the later studies. The three studies used national probability sampling of married or cohabiting persons with children aged 3–17.

In the first two studies, the CTS included eight possible behaviors by parents toward children within two time frames, during the past year and over the child's lifetime, to measure prevalence. The number of times each act was committed measured chronicity. Parents were asked if they

1. threw something
2. pushed, grabbed, or shoved
3. slapped or spanked
4. kicked, bit, or hit with fist
5. hit or tried to hit with something
6. beat up
7. threatened with a gun or knife
8. used a gun or knife.

Items one through three were defined as "minor violence acts," while items four through eight were seen as "severe violence acts." Items four, six, and eight were defined as "very severe violence" against children.

In the third study, the questions were more specific. Parents were asked to identify where on the body the child was hit (on the hand, arm, or leg, or on the bare bottom), and if they used any type of item or object, such as a belt, hairbrush, or a stick to hit the child. Several additional items were also included: shaking, hitting with fist, kicking, throwing or knocking down, and choking.

Overall rates computed on all eight items were 630 per 1,000 children in 1975; 620 per 1,000 in 1985; and 615 per 1,000 in 1995. Using only the "very severe violence" items, and including hitting with fist, kicking, knocking down, and choking, the figures were 36, 19, and 3, respectively (Straus and Gelles 1986; Straus et al. 1998).

Numerous studies have documented that many persons who experience what legally is defined as abuse do not consider themselves to be victims of family abuse and violence (FAV) episodes.

Berger and associates asked nearly 4,700 students at a midwestern university to indicate what types of physical punishment they had experienced during childhood. Thirty-five percent reported being hit with objects, about 6 percent were punched, 5 percent kicked, 3 percent choked, and 12.1 percent injured. When asked about abuse in their families, however, only 3 percent of the respondents indicated they had been abused (Berger et al. 1988). Similarly, parents in pediatric clinic waiting rooms were questioned about their own childhood experiences and current approval of those types of punishment. Of the 449 responding, nearly one-fourth reported they had been victims of uncommon violence, such as having broken bones, being burned, strangled, or choked. Yet more than 44 percent had been pinched, had their hair pulled, or were shaken. More than 50 percent had been hit with an object or a belt (Buntain-Ricklefs et al. 1994). One ten-year study of students found that of those whose injuries from abuse were serious enough to require medical attention, less than one-fourth defined themselves as abused (Knutson and Selner 1994). Fewer than half of the women in a family medicine clinic who had been abused, according to objective measures, perceived themselves to have been abused (Carlin et al. 1994).

How an individual defines physical abuse is shaped by many factors, including personal experiences of abuse as a child, religious beliefs, social class, and ethnic background (Flynn 1998; Grasmick, Bursik, and Kimpel 1991). As a result, nearly all episodes of intergenerational FAV that result in legal action against the perpetrator involve physical harm or injury to the child that can be seen or is diagnosed by medical personnel. Less easily documented are the psychological consequences of physical punishment, which may (or may not) appear at any stage of the life course. Given that more than 90 percent of U.S. parents or caretakers with children under 4 in one recent study use some form of physical punishment in disciplining their children, can physical abuse be defined in a way that does not include appropriate physical punishment?

One attempt to create an operational definition distinguishing physical discipline from abuse used data from five studies of spanking. Using the frequency of spanking as a measure of abuse, the logic of the normal curve was applied to identify normative from deviant or abusive parents. The average number of spanking episodes was 2.47 for nonabusive families. Families, whose frequency of spanking was two more standard deviations from the 2.47 average (i.e., six or more times per day) were considered to be abusive (Whipple and Richey 1997). Other aspects of spanking, such as the age of a child, the intensity of the blows, the context of the punishment, and its duration, were not included in the calculations.

Benjet and Kazdin (2003), citing methodological limitations and the narrow focus of much research, suggest that studies should address the processes that produce spanking, the influences that maintain its use, the goals of parental discipline, and the effects of its use. The widespread acceptance of spanking in the United States, especially for control and correction of a child's behavior, suggests that it is a part of the cultural tradition associated with parenting, despite an apparent decline in approval of corporal punishment (Straus and Mathur 1996).

Spanking has been associated with several factors contributing to stress, such as socioeconomic status, young parenthood or single parenthood, depression and marital conflict (Eamon 2001). However, a study of college-educated mothers of 3-year-old children found that 77 percent reported they spanked an average of 2.5 times per week (Holden, Coleman, and Schmidt 1995). In a related study, single African American mothers were reported to be less likely to use spanking if they were employed (Jackson et al. 1999). Other studies have documented the importance of community context, personal experience with corporal punishment as a child, and geographic region in shaping the acceptability of spanking (Buntain-Ricklefs et al. 1994; Muller, Hunter, and Stollak 1995; Flynn 1996).

Perhaps the most important and the most consistent finding regarding the use of spanking is the parents' or caretakers' belief that spanking is effective and necessary; this is especially important when the belief is derived from religious or cultural traditions (Day, Peterson, and McCracken 1998; Ellison and Sherkat 1993; Holden, Coleman, and Schmidt 1995). Some studies suggest that these beliefs influence not only the selection of information sources about spanking, but also how parents choose to interpret the information to justify their behaviors. Nonetheless, two empirical questions remain:

1. Does physical punishment work, and if so, under what circumstances?
2. What are the short- and long-term consequences of physical punishment?

Some researchers suggest that corporal punishment not only has the desired effect but also can have positive consequences, notably when used in conjunction with reasoning for small children (Larzelere 1996, 2000; Larzelere et al. 1998), or as one element in a rational-authoritative child-rearing style (Baumrind 1994, 1996). The emphasis on strict discipline and the use of physical punishment by some is often justified as necessary to prepare their children for the hostile experiences they will face as adults (McLoyd 1990). Others have suggested that when children are disobedient, disrespectful, aggressive, or acting in ways that are unacceptable to their parents, physical discipline may be effective (Danso, Hunsberger, and Pratt 1997; Gershoff, Miller, and Holden 1999).

An extensive literature that documents the negative aspects of corporal punishment provides three basic and interwoven arguments against its use:

1. Violence is inappropriate, particularly when age differences are significant. (A moral position.)
2. Spanking does not change behavior, it only stops the immediate act. (A practical approach.)
3. All violence has negative effects, often long-lasting. (A consequences view.)

A review of the research used to support these positions offers no conclusive evidence.[2] Positions on these questions are often supported with anecdotal evidence provided by the caretaker and the child. While it is obvious that sufficient pain will prevent a social actor from continuing undesirable behaviors, the level at which pain is effective is both specific to individuals and not measurable in most contexts within which discipline takes place. However, laboratory studies of animals and people suggest that the effectiveness of punishment depends on administering sufficient pain to stop the undesired behavior, especially if it is administered without warning, immediately, and consistently. These conditions are impossible to replicate in a typical family setting.

Research that attempts to document the consequences of physical punishment faces serious problems due to the necessity of recall and imprecise measures. These limitations preclude detailed analyses regarding which type of parental punishment leads to specific adult behaviors, but several strands of longitudinal data offer insights regarding this issue. However, in an analysis of data from the National Survey of Families and Households, Amato and Fowler found a core cluster of parental practices that are documented to benefit children and other practices that harm children regardless of ethnicity, educational level, single or dual parents, or gender of parent. They conclude, when "parents spend time with children, help with homework, talk about problems, provide encouragement, and show affection, children do well." Conversely, "when parents rely on hitting and yelling as frequent methods of responding to children's misbehavior, children's well-being declines" (2002:714).

An analysis of data from the same project, focusing on the context in which corporal punishment occurs, suggests that when parents develop a warm, expressive style of interaction, which includes hugs and praise, that is combined with strict punishment, the negative effects of spanking are mitigated (Wilcox 1998). A study of families in Iowa found the effects of persistent corporal punishment were negated by the effects of parental support and involvement (Simons, Johnson, and Conger 1994).

These studies notwithstanding, many writers have referred to the negative effects associated with the use of physical punishment at any level. Not only may there be short-term negative consequences, such as increased anger or hostility, but the effects appear to become more apparent as the age of the child increases. That severe physical punishment is related to psychological problems, increased delinquency, and crime is not a new insight, as police and social workers can attest, though only relatively recently has the relationship been supported by formal research (Widom 1989; Wolfe 1987). Data from the National Youth Victimization Prevention Study, focused on 2,000 boys and girls aged 10–16, provide evidence that any experience of corporal punishment as a youth is associated with psychological distress and depression, and these problems intensified as the frequency of corporal punishment increases (Turner and Finkelhor 1996).

Data from the National Family Violence Surveys indicate a significant association between spanking and an increased probability of juvenile delinquency, adult violence including violence toward spouses, and other crime; as well as depression, suicidal thoughts, and alienation (Straus 1991; Straus and Yodanis 1996; Straus 1994). Other studies support these findings regarding inter- and intragenerational forms of family abuse and violence (Alexander, Moore, and Alexander 1991; Simons et al. 1993; Simons, Lin, and Gordon 1998; Swinford et al. 2000). In short, there is strong evidence that physical punishment slightly increases the probability a child will become a delinquent or suffer from psychological problems in later life. Unfortunately, no measures currently are available to allow exact identification of those most likely to be so affected, thereby precluding early intervention at the individual level.

How, then, can the apparent link between corporal punishment and negative consequences be broken? One alternative is to encourage social programs that are designed to reduce parental anger, which often accompanies physical punishment. Parental anger management can be achieved through education or cognitive-based therapeutic programs emphasizing the importance of being emotionally involved with a child. A more comprehensive and controversial approach is the banning of all forms of corporal punishment, even within families, as was done in Sweden in 1979, followed by similar bans in Finland, Denmark, Norway, Austria, Cyprus, Latvia, and Croatia, with actions pending in several other countries (Durrant 2000). Despite some claims to the contrary, careful analysis of Sweden's ban indicates public support for corporal punishment has declined, and youth theft, narcotics trafficking, rape, alcohol use, drug use, and suicide rates have declined as well over the past twenty-five years (Durrant 2000). Clearly the greater acceptance of governmental intervention and activities and the range of social services available in Sweden preclude a direct comparison to the United States.

The active interventions that occur in the United States in most cases are initiated by Child Protective Services. An investigation resulting in confirmation of some level of maltreatment leads to the referral of the child, and perhaps the perpetrator and other family members, to services. Intervention[3] may include individual or group counseling, home visits designed to teach appropriate ways to care for the child, parenting and anger management classes, and other education or cognitive-based activities that address the causes or correlates of family problems leading to abuse and violence.

The causes of intergenerational forms of family abuse and violence are obscure, complex, and may involve several interrelated factors. Though there are several models of causality that offer partial explanations for physical abuse, none are adequate to account for abusive behavior. Much of the research focuses on the characteristics of perpetrators, in order to identify risk factors that are associated with physical abuse. Thus, the characteristics of abusive parents or caretakers that distinguish them from non-abusers are the focus of intervention and services. At the individual level, numerous risk factors have been identified, such as low intellectual ability; lack of anger control; unrealistic expectations regarding the demands of parenthood; harsh physical punishment or abusive experiences as a child; and disciplinary attitudes. Interactions that involve real or attributed child noncompliance, defiance, or other behaviors may lead to an escalation of conflict into abuse or violence, especially in families in which other forms of abuse are common. Poverty, young parenthood, inadequate social support from parents, and other conditions that create high levels of stress may also generate or trigger aggressive responses by parents.

While social scientists work to advance explanations of the possible causes and consequences of physically abused children, newspaper reports highlight explicit examples of social actors who perpetrate unambiguous and horrific acts of physical abuse and violence against children. In some cases the media reports a crime. In other cases the media helps bring intergenerational family abuse and violence episodes to the attention of lawmakers and policy-makers.

The FAV episode perspective can advance an explanation of the physical abuse of children. Multiple dimensions of information must be examined to explain comprehensively a social problem that injures or threatens hundreds of thousands of children each year within the United States. The FAV perspective can be used to analyze cases of physical abuse, such as those reported by the media, and it can be used by social actors within organizations that strive to prevent events and episodes that harm too many children.

Discussion Questions

1. If a 10-year-old child is found to be a victim of physical maltreatment, but the child does not consider the acts to be abusive, is it abuse? Which perspective—an objective or a subjective perspective—do you consider to be more important for determining if a child has been physically abused?
2. Why would it be difficult if not impossible to eliminate the physical abuse of children in the near future within the United States?

Research Projects

1. In the United States, which state governments currently allow public schools to administer corporal punishment? What are the rules and regulations that school officials must follow to administer corporal punishment? Do the states that allow corporal punishment in public schools, compared to the states that do not permit it, have higher or lower rates of child physical abuse?
2. Use credible Internet resources to determine the risk factors associated with the physical abuse of children. Determine how the child abuse prevention programs that exist in the local community are based on the known risk factors.

Notes

1. NIS 1 was conducted in 1979–1980, NIS 2 in 1986–1987, and NIS 3 in 1993–1995.

2. Murray Straus, the country's most highly regarded expert on the causes and consequences of spanking, would disagree with this conclusion. For a complete discussion of the issues, the reader is encouraged to consult his published work.

3. These are commonly called tertiary intervention strategies. Primary intervention or prevention programs tend to be public education programs, whereas secondary intervention or prevention programs target high-risk families with strategies designed to prevent the occurrence or reoccurrence of physical abuse.

6

Sexual Abuse of Children

Concern about the physical abuse of children prompted the development of legal codes in the 1960s that led to family intervention, but sexual abuse did not become a major social concern in the United States until the mid-1970s. Since then, the increased interest in identifying victims and in determining the effects of child sexual abuse is reflected in the fact that more articles are published each year about sexual abuse and responses to it than all other forms of child maltreatment (Behl, Conyngham, and May 2001). Yet little precise information exists regarding the actual extent of child sexual abuse in the United States, perhaps due to the secrecy associated with this form of family abuse and violence, as well as the stigma that is often placed on the victims, variations in definitions, and difficulties in identifying victims (Bensley et al. 2004).

Defining Sexual Abuse

Laws regulating sexual behavior distinguish between children and adults, and rest on the premise that young children lack the information and the ability to consent to sexual behavior. Informed consent assumes awareness of the social meanings, whether subtle or direct, of the social acceptability and of the consequences or risks associated with sexual behavior, as well as the right to make the decision to engage in sexual activity. Children are incapable of truly consenting to sex with adults, so such acts inevitably involve coercion, trickery, force, or threats.

Prohibitions of child sexual abuse are represented in three different forms of law regarding sexual behavior: (1) those governing certain sexual offenses, whether directed toward children or adults; (2) those that concern incest; and (3) those that are designed specifically to protect children. Sexual offense laws address rape or attempted rape, sodomy, unwanted touching or fondling, indecent exposure, and exploitation. Laws define these coerced, nonconsensual contact or noncontact acts as crimes—regardless of the victim's age.

Incest prohibitions were once based on the perception that physical problems or abnormalities would result from inbreeding (Kuper 2002). In recent years incest has been expanded to include all legally defined family members, such as stepparents, half-siblings, in-laws, or other relatives specified by marriage and family law. Incest laws typically specify that all forms of sexual activity are prohibited.

Child protection laws are designed to protect children, usually up to age 18, from maltreatment involving sexual activities, whether or not coercion is involved. However, as the age of the child increases, some activities are ignored by law enforcement, child protection service workers, and parents. For example, consensual sexual intercourse between a pregnant 16-year-old girl and a 19-year-old boy who have been dating regularly might be ignored by the county prosecutor who learns of the sexual activity when the couple applies for a marriage license. Nonetheless, in most states, the young couple's sexual relationship is legally defined as child sexual abuse and is subject to state intervention.

The 1974 CAPTA legislation included sexual abuse as one form of maltreatment, defined as "any act of a sexual nature upon or with a child" (U.S. Department of Health, Education, and Welfare 1978:9). But what is included as an act of a sexual nature, and who decides when an act is sexual—the adult, the child, or a third party such as police or child protective services—is unspecified by the legislation. Is the adult's sexual gratification intent essential for establishing sexual abuse? Does the adult's sexual gratification intent make a noncontact offense an act of child sexual abuse? Where does the line between "appropriate" and "inappropriate" sexual activity fall? Can an 8-year-old child be a perpetrator?

In efforts to identify the range of behaviors that can be labeled appropriate or normative, surveys of professionals and college students have been conducted to develop some understanding of the normal yet sexually oriented behaviors of children. One study, focusing on activities that could be defined as normal sex play with peers, found that playing doctor, showing one's body, rehearsing sexual intercourse through simulation with physical contact, and kissing games were defined to be normal by most of the college undergraduates. Eighty-four percent indicated that no coercion was involved (Lamb and Coakley 1993). An early study focused on responses to vignettes describing sexual activities in which the age and the sex of the child and the adult were varied. Researchers found that the age of the child was the most important factor in defining sexual activities between an adult and a child as abusive. The younger the child, the more likely the event was seen as abuse. The older the child, the greater the blame was assigned to the child, due to a supposed greater ability to resist sexual advances (Maynard and Wiederman 1997). Other studies of students suggest that a core cluster of attitudes against the sexual exploitation of children is shared by most social actors. The core attitudes are largely unaffected by age, family income, or abuse history (Briere, Henschel, and Smiljanich 1992), although women appear to have stronger negative attitudes regarding child sexual abuse episodes than men (O'Donohue et al. 1992; Wellman 1993).

Researchers attempted to identify what professionals consider normal or abnormal childhood behavior by asking four groups of professionals to rate twenty different vignettes describing adults and children who were under the age of 13. Twenty-eight of the professionals were child sexual abuse experts, 35 were therapists in a child sexual abuse training program, 210 were medical students attending a human sexuality program, and 35 were facilitators of human sexuality programs. Analysis of the data showed agreement or consensus in definitions of what constitutes normative and abnormal behaviors. Young children "playing doctor" and an 8-year-old boy peeking in a window to see a teenage girl undress were defined by the respondents to be normal. A 6-year-old boy fondling a 3-year-old girl and a 12-year-old boy penetrating an 8-year-old girl were defined to be abnormal. There was much less agreement about other behaviors, such as a 12-year-old boy pressuring a 13-year-old girl for intercourse (Heiman and Meston 1998).

Similar attitudes about extreme forms of activities were found in a survey of 54 defense attorneys and 100 prosecuting attorneys regarding sexual behaviors of adults and teenagers. The most serious event was a description of an adult fondling the genitalia of a same or opposite sex 6-year-old child. Some behaviors were more likely to be seen as abuse if they occurred with regularity, but sexual activities such as kissing or penetration by someone of a similar age was typically defined as inappropriate but not abuse (Hartman, Karlson, and Hibbard 1994).

Incidence and Prevalence of Sexual Abuse

As with physical abuse, data measuring child sexual abuse reflect the definitions the researcher uses, the type of research methods used to gather data, and the researchers' sources of information. Numerous surveys of college students, community samples, and agency samples were initiated during the 1980s. They have provided considerable evidence that sexual abuse, often defined in terms of unwanted sexual experiences (Kellogg and Hoffman 1995; Whealin 2002), is a common experience for children, especially girls. However, the findings do not present a consistent picture, in part because there are great variations in definitions and in the way data are collected, resulting in major differences in rates of child sexual abuse (Roosa et al. 1998).

The reports from criminal justice agencies and the reports by child protective services rely on statistics gathered from the organizations responsible for investigating suspected crimes or abuse, but student and community surveys are based on responses from individuals and rely on recall, idiosyncratic definitions, and broader definitions. Acknowledging the problems that such conditions create, Finkelhor analyzed the different types of available research in order to estimate the sexual abuse prevalence rate, that is, the proportion of social actors in the general population who have experienced sexual abuse. He concluded that the prevalence rate is at least 20 percent for women and 5 percent to 10 percent for men (Finkelhor 1994a). Two additional literature reviews, one of community and college student research and the other of agency-based research, reported that prevalence rates vary widely in both types of studies, depending on the range of activities included in the definition and methods of data collection (Pilkington and Kremer 1995a, 1995b).

Official statistics, drawn from CPS records, suggest there has been a consistent decline in substantiated cases of child sexual abuse in the United States, from an estimated 150,000 cases in 1992 to about 89,500 in 2000, to about 86,800 in 2001, for a rate of 1.2 cases per 1,000 (U.S. Department of Health and Human Services 2004a, 2004b).

In an effort to explain this unexpected trend, Finkelhor and Jones (2004) examined its following potential causes:

1. an increasing conservatism within CPS, leading to rejection of those cases with weak evidence or those involving custody disputes
2. exclusion of cases that do not involve caretakers
3. changes in data collection methods or definitions
4. less reporting due to sexual abuse backlash
5. a diminishing reservoir of older cases, that is, those previously undisclosed
6. an actual decline in the incidence of abuse due to prevention efforts or other factors.

After careful consideration of the evidence for each potential explanation, Finkelhor and Jones conclude that several programs designed to prevent child sexual abuse and to prosecute perpetrators are somewhat effective and led to the declining number of cases. Similar conclusions were reached in an Australian study (Dunne et al. 2003). Research on the patterns of sexual abuse in Los Angeles suggests that ethnicity and victim age are two factors that stabilize the prevalence rate (Wyatt et al. 1999).

A telephone survey of parents from 1,000 randomly chosen households in August and September of 1995 found that 1.9 percent of children had been sexually abused within the previous year. This is a prevalence rate of 19 per 1,000 persons at risk, with 5.7 percent of children ever having been sexually abused, or a lifetime prevalence rate of 57 per 1,000 persons (Finkelhor et al. 1997).

A self-report survey of sexual abuse victimization experiences covered a geographically stratified, random sample of the general population. Questionnaires were sent to 935 persons, and researchers obtained a 65 percent return rate. Among the respondents who completed the research instrument, 14.2 percent of the men and 32.2 percent of the women disclosed childhood experiences that could be classified as child sexual abuse (Briere and Elliott 2003). The degree to which this sample actually represents the general population is not known.

Despite the lack of authoritative information, it is apparent that child sexual abuse occurs with considerable frequency. The strongest correlate of abuse is victim sex, as girls are approximately three times more likely than boys to be victims of child sexual abuse. The rate for girls is 4.9 per 1,000 girls and the rate for boys is 1.6 per 1,000 boys, based on the harm standard specified by the third National Incident Study, that is, NIS 3 (Sedlak and Broadhurst 1966). How real are the gender differences?

Some research suggests that a substantial portion of male victims of family or acquaintance abuse are reluctant to define their experiences as abusive or negative (Fromuth and Burkhart 1987; Haugaard and Emery 1989; Reed and Kenning 1987; Wurtele and Miller 1987). A review of the early research literature suggests that male victims, compared to female victims, are more likely to experience force; are less willing to tell; and, they are the victims of more repetitive abuse, with the perpetrator more likely to be a stranger or a person outside the family (Watkins and Bentovim 1992). In more recent research, Holmes and Slap (1998) report that male victims, compared to female victims, were older when sexual abuse began. Also, boys were more likely than girls to have been victimized by women.

The age of sexual abuse victims is often not reported, and even when considered may not reflect the age when the abuse occurred, in part because much abuse is not disclosed for weeks or months after it begins. In addition, the type of sexual abuse appears to change as age increases. Nearly all sexual abuse of younger children involves fondling, while coercive abuse, especially rape, is more likely to victimize older children and adolescents. NIS 3 reported that children two years and younger experience the lowest rate of sexual abuse, significantly lower than those aged 12 and older, but using the endangerment standard, the risk of sexual abuse was relatively constant from age 3 to age 18 (Sedlak and Broadhurst 1996).

Public information campaigns in the past often warned children, particularly girls and their parents, about the friendly stranger lurking in the shadows who might molest children. Though it is clear that some sexual abuse is perpetrated by strangers, it is more likely to be perpetrated by a family member.

CPS reports in 2001 found that parents were the perpetrators in 4.7 percent of the sexual abuse cases, other relatives in 31.5 percent, foster parents in 9.5 percent, and an unmarried partner of a parent in 14.7 percent of the cases. These data indicate that more than 60 percent of all sexual abuse is committed by a relative or close acquaintance. Similar findings appear in the NIS 3 study, with slightly more than half (54 percent) of the child sexual abuse reported being perpetrated by biological parents or other caretakers (Sedlak and Broadhurst 1996). One consistent finding is that parents, other relatives, and people known by the child are perpetrators of sexual abuse in a large majority, perhaps 90 percent or more, of all the cases, despite the attention paid to lurking strangers as possible abusers. One important caveat is necessary, however: As Finkelhor (1994a) points out, all substantiated cases of child sexual abuse investigated by Child Protective Services are perpetrated by family members or relatives because CPS is not responsible for investigating allegations of child sexual abuse perpetrated by strangers.

Diagnosing, Detecting, and Disclosing Sexual Abuse

No form of family abuse and violence is less obvious and more difficult to establish than child sexual abuse. How is sexual abuse verified? Nearly all sexual abuse takes place with only the child and the perpetrator present, with great differences in their social status, especially their age, knowledge, credibility, and power. Most sexual contact, especially with young children, is fondling rather than violent acts, leaving no physical evidence (Muram 2003). Because the perpetrator often denies allegations of sexual abuse made by a child, evidence to document the episode must be obtained from the child who may have been threatened or confused. In addition, a child's young age at the time of the abuse, the perpetrator being a family member, continuing abuse, and the shame or guilt an abused child often feels hinder or delay disclosures (Goodman-Brown et al. 2003; Smith et al. 2000), requiring special sensitivity and skills among interviewers evaluating allegations of suspected abuse.

For many years disclosure and diagnosis were handicapped by a lack of understanding of the dynamics of disclosure. Even among those specially trained for dealing with trauma and stress, disagreements persisted regarding children's statements of abuse, especially when projective techniques or anatomically detailed dolls were used to evaluate young children with limited language ability.

The use of dolls became popular, but it soon became apparent that there were serious problems associated with their use. Neither children nor raters of children's behaviors respond consistently. It is not always clear what "play with the doll" means to the child; there is a lack of standardized protocol for their use and a lack of normative standards. Furthermore, the research evidence suggests not all children react in similar ways to the dolls (Aldridge 1998; Boat and Everson 1994; Dawson, Geddie, and Wagner 1966; Elliot, O'Donahue, and Nickerson 1993; Everson and Boat 1994; Simkins and Renier 1996). The misuse of the dolls, suggestive questions, multiple interviews, and interviewer bias, combined with zealous prosecutors, therapists, and child advocates who emphasized the slogan "believe the children," have had significant consequences. Reports based on information obtained with the use of techniques that did not meet standards of objectivity or validity (Bruck, Ceci, and Hembrooke 1998; Ceci and Bruck 1993) resulted in accusations of sexual abuse by those responsible for investigating the allegations, leading to considerable controversy as the accused were arrested, charged, tried, and found guilty on the basis of statements made by children in interviews and from the observations made of the children playing with dolls.

Controversy over such methods intensified as several cases that had been tried on the basis of such information were challenged in legal proceedings. These cases included the Kelly Michaels case, whose prison sentence was overturned on appeal; the trials of several workers from the McMartin day care center in Los Angeles (which failed to produce a single guilty verdict); the trials of workers at the Little Rascals day care center in North Carolina, who received guilty verdicts and prison sentences; and, on the basis of one child's statements, accusations of sexual abuse against more than twenty-five citizens in Wenatchee, Washington.

While some investigators and researchers may continue to use this type of evidence, a recent study found that inferential data, such as those derived from observations of children playing with dolls, have no significant effect on ratings of sexual abuse by either experts or laypersons (Peters 2001). Nevertheless, many researchers and therapists recommend that dolls not be used for diagnosis. They should be used only for corroboration of the evidence gained from other sources or methods, and strict guidelines should be followed (Boat and Everson 1996; Lamb et al. 1996). Other projective techniques, such as human figure drawings, the Thematic Apperception Test, and the house-tree-person exercise continue to be used, apparently with some success and without major controversy (West 1998).

Even among those professionals trained to deal with trauma and stress, however, there are sharp disagreements about the meaning of a child's behavior. A study of 340 members of the International Society for Traumatic Stress Studies found that regional differences existed, with Southerners attributing less credibility to the child than those from other areas. Women and professionals were more likely to believe the child than men or nonprofessionals (Kovera et al. 1993).

In another study, forty-eight mental health specialists, primarily social workers and clinical psychologists who were experienced in dealing with sexual abuse, were presented with a clinical evaluation of a case that included the mother's allegations of the father's molestation, four prior pediatric examinations, and results of police and protective services investigations, including video-taped child-parent interaction. The participants were asked to offer one of six recommendations for contact with the father, ranging from "none" to "custody granted to him," followed by an extended discussion, after which they resubmitted a recommendation regarding contact with the father. Social workers, as a group, were significantly more likely than others to believe the child had been molested and to recommend supervised visits. Consensus on the issues was rare, and the authors concluded that "In cases of alleged sexual abuse, clinical experts have yet to demonstrate that they possess any unique ability to find truth, to determine the credibility of persons giving testimony, or to divine either the past or future from immediate clinical observations and facts" (Horner, Guyer, and Kalter 1993:930).

Recent research offers additional insight into the various ways children disclose abuse. Alaggia (2004) finds the type of abuse, a fear of negative consequences, and the child's perceived responsibility are factors that partly explain delayed disclosure of child sexual abuse (see also Goodman-Brown et al. 2003). Techniques designed to establish accuracy and completeness of the information given by the child (Orbach and Lamb 1999) appear to provide significant and convincing data about the abuse. In addition, understanding the importance of timing, child development, age-inappropriate sexual knowledge and behaviors as indicators of abuse are especially important for cases of younger children (Brilleslijper, Friedrich, and Corwin 2004). Coordination between protective services and police in investigations is imperative in order to eliminate the multiple and often biased interviews with children that too-often result in assessment errors, both false negatives and false positives.

Efforts to develop standardized procedures and objective measures depending on symptoms or behaviors continue, though with mixed results. One problem is that such behavioral measures lead to high levels of error (Wells et al. 1997), partly due to inconsistent behavioral patterns. Children who have not been sexually abused may behave in a sexual manner, and those who have been abused may not act out sexually. Apart from a confession by the perpetrator, no simple approach is adequate to establish that sexual abuse has occurred.

If there is no perpetrator confession, establishing responsibility is problematic, especially if the perpetrator is a family member or an acquaintance. Even those who are identified may not be prosecuted. Consider the following funneling of cases:

- 451 allegations from police and hospital files in Chicago result in the identification of the perpetrator in only 269 cases. Among those 269 cases:
  - 179 are arrested, of whom 136 are charged.
    - Among those charged, 77 are charged with a felony offense.
    - Among those charged with a felony offense, only 66 are indicted.
      - A total of 48 suspects plead guilty or are found guilty.
        - Among those found guilty, 43 serve jail or prison time.

All told, among the 451 suspected cases, 9.5 percent result in jail or prison time (Martone, Jaudes, and Cavins 1996).[1] Police and CPS interviews must provide most evidence regarding perpetrators, a difficult problem in child sexual abuse cases. Results of polygraph examinations, even if they were admissible as evidence in most court proceedings, are at best unreliable and at worst fail to discriminate between non-abusers and abusers, leaving investigators to seek other sources of corroboration.

Causes, Conditions, and Contexts

Why do some social actors seek sexual gratification with a child? The focus for this question can only be on the perpetrator. The perpetrator is usually a man who often is a relative, friend, or acquaintance of the victim, whose experience in his family of origin often included parental rejection and harsh punishment. Most are not pedophiles, if the term "pedophile" is used to indicate a long-term and exclusive interest in children, as suggested by *Diagnostic and Statistical Manual of Mental Disorders, Fourth Edition (DSM IV)*.

Many explanations of child sex abusers have defined the perpetrators as sick or pathological, with a variety of factors in their family backgrounds and in the social context associated with their pathology (Maker, Kemmelmeier, and Peterson 1999). For some abusers, this pathology may take the form of cognitive distortions or erroneous presumptions about children, who are perceived by the perpetrator to be flirtatious, sexually provocative, or enjoying the contact. Some perpetrators focus on their victims merely as objects for their pleasure (Neidigh and Krop 1992; Ward and Keenan 1999). One study found that child sex offenders attributed their behavior and arousal to internal, stable, and uncontrollable causes, all consistent with psychopathology, in contrast to those who had been convicted of property offenses and violent offenses, who attributed their behavior to external, controllable causes (McKay, Chapman, and Long 1996).

Noninvolved parents (or parents who have not bonded with their children) also may have problems that prevent them from protecting their vulnerable children. A study comparing the Minnesota Multiphasic Personality Inventory (MMPI) scores of mothers of sexually abused children with those of mothers whose children had not been abused reported that "these data suggest that there are some personality features of parents of sexually abused children that may contribute to mate selection and parenting problems" (Friedrich 1991). Other studies have identified intimacy deficits, fear of intimacy, and loneliness among some abusers (Bumby and Hansen 1997; Marshall, Anderson, and Champagne 1996, Marshall et al. 1997, 1999; Okami and Goldberg 1992), but there appear to be no consistently identifiable personality differences between abusers and non-abusers, especially in family abuse cases (Hanson, Lipovsky, and Saunders 1994; Serin et al. 1994).

One explanation of child sexual abuse, resting on assumptions about the confluence of biological and social factors, suggests that persons have an aversion to sex with those raised in close proximity. This perspective is consistent with findings that report a higher rate of abuse by stepfathers than natural fathers and lower rates for those who were involved early in the physical care of their child. In an effort to evaluate this perspective, information about family histories was gathered in face-to-face interviews with 55 U.S. Navy and 63 civilian incestuous fathers, matched with 116 control-group fathers. Analysis of the data indicated that incestuous fathers were more likely to have been physically and sexually abused. They perceived rejection and neglect by their fathers, and they had higher levels of marital dissatisfaction.

Family dysfunction or disorganization has been recognized as one of the social contexts within which perpetrators of child sexual abuse emerge, whether they are aggressive or bullies as children or violent as adults. Such families are sometimes characterized by several deviant conditions, such as intergenerational or intimate partner violence, physical and emotional child abuse, poor bonding between the child and parent, low levels of social support, emotional disinterest or ignoring the child by the parents, and parents who have high levels of mental health problems (Burton, Miller, and Shill 2002; Craissati, Clurg, and Browne 2002; Deblinger et al. 1993; Fromuth, Burkhart, and Jones 1991; Gibson and Hartshorne 1996; Lee, Jackson, Pattison, and Ward 2002; Long and Jackson 1994). It is important, however, to recognize that although deviant family characteristics increase the likelihood that an adult or a child may abuse, they do not explain why most individuals in these types of families do not become sexual abusers (Ryan 2002).

Some writers suggest that child sexual abuse is due to cognitive distortions or attribution error, or facilitated by situational opportunities (Simon et al. 1992) such as marital discord and the availability of a young victim with whom there is emotional congruence. Inappropriate or deviant sexual arousal, in some instances due to inadequate moral development or the loss of inhibitions, personality factors, stress, or drugs and alcohol, may lead to abuse (Finkelhor and Araji 1986).

Research on the effects of religion on child sexual abuse has been inconsistent. Some studies suggest there is no association between religious affiliation or religiosity and sexual abuse, but others find that religious beliefs and practices may provide a buffer for some psychological problems. Still other studies report that some beliefs may actually increase the risk of child sexual abuse (Elliott 1994).

The consequences of child sexual abuse may be severe and long-lasting and may include physical injury and emotional consequences although few direct linkages are easily drawn. In one study, nine years after experiencing sexual abuse, victims were compared to a non-abused group of similar age and gender. The results document the negative effects of abuse in depression, self-esteem, anxiety, behavioral problems, and binging, as well as substance abuse (Swanston et al. 2003). Similar findings were reported from a study of children from various sites in the United States comparing 759 sexually abused children with 2,720 non-abused children. Researchers reported significant differences in a large number of psychosocial characteristics and behaviors (Walrath et al. 2003).

Age and gender appear to be important factors or considerations in identifying the effects of sexual abuse. Older boys, especially teenagers, who engage in sexual activities that are legally defined as abuse but which they view as pleasurable or evidence of their masculinity or maturity and attractiveness, may not experience the trauma, guilt, or the shame that more often is experienced by younger boys and by girls. If the child takes some responsibility for the abuse, or has blame attributed by parents or other adults, guilt and shame and the increased likelihood of long-term problems may result (Feiring, Taska, and Lewis 1996; Hazzard et al. 1995).

Negative consequences associated with the experience of sexual abuse have been reported for more than twenty years. But many early studies relied on clinical information without the use of comparison groups and ignored those victims who resolved the experience without therapy or other assistance (Green 1993). More recent research, both with and without comparison groups, continues to report serious effects for both girls and boys, including higher levels of post-traumatic stress disorder (Ackerman et al. 1998; Briggs and Joyce 1997; Epstein et al. 1998; Rudd and Herzberger 1999), and general psychological and social maladjustment (Conway et al. 2004; Everill and Waller 1995; Steel et al. 2004). Increased rates of depression (Gladstone et al. 1999; Miller, Monson, and Norton 1995; Whiffen and Clark 1997), lower self-esteem, cutting or self-mutilation (Briere and Gil 1998), and substance abuse (Moran, Vuchinich, and Hall 2004) also have been reported among child sexual abuse victims. Suicidal thoughts, plans, and efforts appear to be directly related to sexual abuse for boys, but mediated through depression and distress for girls (Martin et al. 2004).

Consequences for sexually abused girls may be pregnancy (Roosa et al. 1998), higher levels of bulimia or purging behavior (Andrews 1997; Jones and Emerson 1994; Perkins and Luster 1999), and suicide ideation and behavior (Bryant and Range 1995). Some studies have found a high probability of revictimization, although the relationship may be more complex, mediated by family functioning (Messman-Moore and Brown 2004). For sexually abused boys, there is an increased rate of delinquency, especially illicit drug use and crimes against persons (Dembo et al. 1992); higher levels of depression, anxiety, and behavioral problems (Wells et al. 1997); increased alcohol abuse; and suicide attempts.

It is important to note, however, that while the empirical studies show an increased probability of negative and long-term consequences for those who have experienced child sexual abuse, they do not indicate that such consequences are inevitable or that sexual abuse is their direct cause (Gladstone et al. 1999). A highly controversial meta-analysis of seven studies concluded the evidence does not support the view that child sexual abuse causes pervasive and intensive harm: "The self-reported effects data imply that only a small proportion of persons with CSA [child sexual abuse] experiences are permanently harmed" and "data on confounding variables imply that this small relation cannot safely be assumed to reflect causal effects of the CSA" (Rind and Tromovitch 1994:253).

It is also important to note that the meta-analysis conducted by Rind and Tromovitch has been replicated and scrutinized by other social scientists. Researchers, for example, have concluded that the Rind study overgeneralized the empirical findings and failed to report that the relationship between sexual abuse and negative consequences is as strong as the relationship between smoking and lung cancer (Ondersma et al. 2001). Dallam et al. (2001) concluded three crucial problems and limitations apply to the Rind report:

1. The report used inappropriate statistics to detect effect size.
2. The report misreports crucial information, such as the percentage of research subjects who disclosed negative consequences of sexual abuse.

3. The report fails to disclose the criteria used to include or exclude studies in the meta-analysis.

Some research on the effects of child sexual abuse show the importance of examining how the consequences of sexual abuse are mediated by a number of important factors. There is empirical evidence to support the claim that a significant number of victims, perhaps at least half, demonstrate the ability, through peer and family relationships that provide protective factors, to avoid nearly all of the long-term negative consequences (Lynskey and Fergusson 1997). For other victims, personal resilience and supportive relationships reduce, but do not negate, the consequences of sexual abuse (Heller et al. 1999; Liem et al. 1997; Luster and Small 1997; Lynskey and Fergusson 1997; Tremblay, Hebert, and Piche 1999; Valentine and Feinauer 1993). One study, comparing female victims from dysfunctional families with those from functional families, reported that those from dysfunctional families scored significantly higher on measures of depression, anxiety, and interpersonal problems (Brock and Mintz 1997), lending additional evidence to the notion that social support is critically important for victims of child sexual abuse to heal.

Numerous studies focus on the intergenerational patterns of sexual abuse, especially for young boys who were abused and then become abusers as adults, with most of the empirical studies showing a strong causal effect (Hunter and Figueredo 2000; Romano and De Luca 1997; Sipe, Jensen, and Everett 1998). Other studies, however, do not corroborate the findings (Benoit and Kennedy 1992).

These findings, regarding the effects of child sexual abuse, stand in sharp contrast to a perspective that emerged from the bitter debate revolving around the issue of recovered or repressed memories of sexual abuse. Experimental therapeutic methods often were used to encourage the recovery of memories of sexual abuse, theoretically as a result of disassociation, amnesia, or supposed multiple personalities (popularized by the films *Three Faces of Eve* and *Sybil*). During the years 1985–1995, approximately 40,000 new cases of multiple personalities were discovered, and in 1980 *DSM III* gave multiple personality disorder (MPD) a primary listing, later changed to dissociative identity disorder in *DSM IV*. Parents were sued for alleged sexual abuse based on recovered memories during therapy, initially with some success.

Many books and articles were published, encouraging women and some men to recognize that many of the problems they were experiencing had their roots in unremembered sexual abuse during childhood, which had been so traumatic it was repressed, only to be recovered by new and different therapeutic approaches. Professionals took opposite sides, some severely critiquing these methods and others accusing the critics of being part of a backlash (Bloom 1995; Briere and Conte 1993; Gleaves 1996; Goldstein 1997; Hyman and Loftus 1998; Lindsay and Briere 1997; Loftus and Ketcham 1994; Ofshe 1994; Robbins 1998; Zola 1998). Opposing authors wrote joint articles in an effort to resolve the dispute (Berliner and Loftus 1992).

By the beginning of the twenty-first century, the repressed memory issue was no longer a significant controversy. Research challenged both the assumptions and the approach of many therapists. Little support remains for the therapeutic methods used to allegedly recover memories, and many professional associations have written or rewritten ethical and procedural guidelines, typically excluding hypnosis or an induced trancelike state as an acceptable approach for most therapeutic settings. In addition, lawsuits against therapists and the organizations that used them became common. Many lawsuits that were successful were encouraged by the False Memory Foundation, which was created by parents and others who claimed they had been falsely accused. Large financial awards resulted as researchers and courts found sufficient evidence to conclude the therapy had created rather than recovered memories of sexual abuse.

There are some significant consequences for victims of child sexual abuse that researchers, practitioners, and policymakers cannot ignore. Interventions in families where sexual abuse has occurred may include both the prosecution of the perpetrator and individual and group treatment for the primary and secondary victims of this form of intergenerational family abuse and violence. Many treatment programs for victims and their families are focused on mental health and mediating the effects of sexual abuse for individuals, such as individual therapy for depression, anxiety disorders, or programs to reduce guilt and shame, to enhance self-esteem, or to deal with substance abuse.

Perpetrator programs have also been created and studied. A twenty-five-year follow-up study was conducted of 7,275 sexual offenders who entered cognitive-behavioral therapy programs. Researchers found that among the 62 percent of offenders they were able to contact, child molesters and exhibitionists had better success rates at five years—and in each successive five-year period—than did pedophiles or rapists (Maletzky and Steinhauser 2002). This large study offers some promise for future treatments.

The intersection of treatment and prevention of subsequent sexual abuse is the focus of nearly all interventions. Responding to the problems that abused children present may prevent them from abusing as adults and eliminate some of the negative effects of sexual abuse. There are too few resources available to address causal factors. Some of the conditions that have been identified may have existed prior to child sexual abuse and also have contributed to it. There currently is no reliable way, if we are concerned about the consequences of false positives and false negatives, to predict who will become a sexual abuser, leaving primary prevention the only viable option for addressing this problem.

Unfortunately, given the secrecy and conditions under which most child sexual abuse takes place, the victim becomes the person responsible for her or his own safety to a degree not found with other types of child abuse or neglect. Programs such as Good Touch–Bad Touch are designed to empower, by giving the child the right and the ability to say no, clearly a laudable objective. However, for a small child to respond to a parent or a friend by saying no requires great courage (or greater maturity than most young children have). Nevertheless, the education of children in schools, aware and sensitive teachers, and supportive family and friends still may offer the best prevention program.

Discussion Questions

1. Researchers have paid much more attention to the sexual abuse of girls than to the sexual abuse of boys. Explain what accounts for this difference.

2. If sexual abuse constitutes less than 25 percent of child mal-treatment cases, why is most of the published research focused on this particular type of child abuse?

Research Projects

1. Examine print and television advertisements for (a) clothing, (b) music and movies, and (c) cell phones. How are adolescent boys and girls—appearing to be under age 20—presented as sexualized persons in the ads? Distinguish between the explicit and the more subtle presentations of sexuality within the ads. Who are the target audiences of the ads? Who are the unintended audiences of the ads?
2. Retrieve library resources summarizing the types of therapy and treatment programs available for (a) victims and (b) perpetrators of child sexual abuse. Which types of therapy are more or less effective?
3. Obtain a copy of chapter 4, "The Making of a Whore" by Diana E. H. Russell, from the book *Issues in Intimate Violence*, edited by Raquel Kennedy Bergen (1998). Respond to one of the questions presented at the end of the chapter: What are the long-term effects associated with childhood sexual abuse? Describe the reasons why incest survivors are hesitant to report their experiences.

Note

1. The percentage of child sexual abuse cases that result in incarceration (9.5 percent) is indeed low. It is, however, high when compared to the cases processed through the criminal justice system in the United States. In general we can conclude that for every 1,000 felony offenses committed, 11 cases or 1.1 percent result in jail or prison time.

IV

CHANGING DEFINITIONS AND PERCEPTIONS OF A SOCIAL PROBLEM

7

Implications of Family Abuse and Violence Definitions

We recently eavesdropped on a conversation between two women, an assistant probation officer and a mental health counselor (both about 30 years old), while waiting for a court session to begin. Each woman told the other that she would probably be comfortable working with "child abusers" but certainly not with "pedophiles." Child abusers, according to their definitions, included offenders who psychologically, physically, or sexually abused children or teens. The abusers and the victims are usually family members or somehow related to each other. Pedophiles, according to the young women, are different. "Pedophiles" are sick, but they are incurable. They are psychopaths. Worse yet, they cannot be helped or deterred by the criminal justice system. Counselors could not hope to understand what was going on in their disturbed minds that would motivate pedophiles or drive them to constantly be on the lookout for their next victim.

Are those *really* the definitions of child sexual abusers and pedophiles? Clearly distinguishing between the two terms was important for the social actors who may have been anticipating their work assignments would likely soon bring them face to face with a "child abuser" or a "pedophile." Are there *real* or objective definitions of family violence and abuse that social scientists, government workers, and practitioners can use to identify and treat victims, to prevent family violence episodes from occurring, and to stop and punish wrongdoers? Legal definitions seem authentic because they can take on an objective quality, representing official definitions of the problem. Legal definitions distinguish perpetrators from victims and determine when social control activities can be initiated. Legal definitions tell the experts how to respond to episodes of family abuse and violence (FAV). Consider Indiana's definition of domestic violence:

> "Domestic or family violence" means . . . the occurrence of at least one of the following acts committed by a family or household member:
> (1) Attempting to cause, threatening to cause, or causing physical harm to another family or household member.
> (2) Placing a family or household member in fear of physical harm.
> (3) Causing a family or household member to involuntarily engage in sexual activity by force, threat of force, or duress (Burns Ind. Code Ann. § 34-6-2-34.5, 2004)

The statutorily defined event specifies a behavior, a state of mind, a perpetrator, and a victim. It does not, however, specify what constitutes harm, and it does tell the experts or the general population within a community how to treat and help victims and how to prevent domestic violence.

The state's statutory definitions of domestic violence, or how it defines dimensions of family abuse and violence (FAV) episodes, are important because they are used in endless ways. In Indiana, for example, they are invoked to certify a victim's voting eligibility, to determine if a victim is qualified for an address confidentiality program, to initiate an order of protection, to remove a dependent child witnessing ongoing violence from the home,[1] or to bring social or human services into a family's home. While the state's definitions are important, and they have real consequences, they are anything but objective.

Like beauty, family abuse and violence can be and is subjectively perceived. No expert—defined as a social actor external to the FAV episode—can tell a woman or a teenage boy or a dependent parent if they have been *real* victims of family abuse and violence. However, the victim's perceptions alone are not sufficient to define the episodes. For the victim or the perpetrator to qualify for services or for punishment, the behaviors, whether physical, sexual, verbal, or neglectful, are only those that the government, the social service agency, or the health provider identifies and has deemed egregious enough to deserve its valuable resources. The government or the local community agency determines the value or disvalue of behaviors and intentions that can be protected, guaranteed, or sanctioned.

Some Prevailing Definitions

Social science researchers, federal and state governments, and professions and professional associations articulate definitions of the various forms of family abuse and violence. The definitions can be broad, and they can be used to measure and analyze the victims and perpetrators of FAV episodes. They may also be highly specific and focused on particular dimensions of FAV problems. It is likely that all the definitions social scientists and agencies use to study family violence have the same limitations:

1. They are not likely to be adequate for depicting the subjective experiences of victims and perpetrators.
2. They are either not inclusive enough or they are too broad to specify appropriately the problem and the issue that researchers attempt to observe and explain.

In 1978, the federal government defined child abuse and neglect with Public Law 93-247:

> [Child abuse and neglect is] the physical or mental injury, sexual abuse, negligent treatment or maltreatment of a child under the age of eighteen by a person who is responsible for the child's welfare under circumstances which indicate that the child's health or welfare is harmed or threatened thereby.

Health, social welfare, and criminal justice agencies at the federal, state, and local levels add layers of specificity to the broad definition in order to identify victims and perpetrators and determine appropriate responses to child abuse or neglect episodes.

For three decades social scientists have defined and redefined terms, such as "intimate partner violence" and "woman abuse." Some researchers recognize that no universally accepted definition of woman abuse is possible, but they offer the following for researchers and social change advocates to consider:

> Woman abuse is the misuse of power by a husband, intimate partner (whether male or female), ex-husband, or ex-partner against a women resulting in a loss of dignity, control, and safety as well as a feeling of powerlessness and entrapment experienced by the woman who is the direct victim of ongoing or repeated physical, psychological, economic, sexual, verbal, and/or spiritual abuse. Woman abuse also includes persistent threats or forcing women to witness violence against their children, other relatives, friends, pets, and /or cherished possessions by their husbands, partners, ex-husbands, or ex-partners. (DeKeseredy and MacLeod 1997)

While DeKeseredy and MacLeod's definition is general and inclusive, taking account of many different types of experiences, it does not distinguish ongoing or reoccurring violence and abuse that is motivated by attempts to control women from the isolated or sporadic outbursts of violence or aggression that have different consequences for victims as well as for perpetrators and other social actors internal to the FAV episode. Moreover, their definition of woman abuse cannot be applied to female perpetrators and male victims who may be the social actors internal to the family violence episode.

Johnson and Ferraro (2000) contend that it is imperative to distinguish types of intimate partner violence that women and men experience. They claim that feminist researchers and social science or criminological researchers tend to use very different definitions. Further, they argue that it is necessary for service providers to distinguish among the types of abuse and violence that women and men experience within their intimate relationships. Counseling and therapy may be useful to remedy some forms or types of family violence episodes but not others.

Johnson and Ferraro studied the domestic and intimate partner violence literature published during the 1990s. They identify four patterns or types of violence, distinguishing isolated or infrequent events from reoccurring episodes of intimate partner violence. They use the term "situational couple violence" (SCV) to refer to an outburst of violent behavior that is perpetrated by a woman or a man in an ongoing relationship. SCV can have tragic or lethal consequences, but it is likely to be a relatively less severe form of intimate partner violence that results from frustration or that may be the culmination of a heated argument. Typically, SCV behaviors are hitting or slapping. Women are not any less likely than men to perpetrate an isolated event of SCV.

"Intimate terrorism" (IT) is a form of chronic, controlling, aggressive, and violent behavior. It typically escalates in severity and frequency. IT is almost exclusively a type of intimate partner violence perpetrated by a man against a woman within an ongoing, marital, or cohabiting relationship. The more unusual type of intimate partner violence, termed "mutual violent control" (MVC), refers to both partners engaging in what can be a fatal or extremely harmful dance of control, characterized by chronic, aggressive, and violent behaviors. "Violence resistance" (VR) is the only type of intimate partner violence that women may be more likely than men to perpetrate. An act of VR is not motivated by a desire to control a partner or spouse. To the contrary, it is provoked by a need to defend the self against violent acts that are initiated by a partner (Johnson and Ferraro 2000).

Levine (2003) acknowledges that elder abuse takes many forms and defines the problem by the type of residence or facility in which an elder family member lives. The behaviors or omissions that are defined to be abusive vary by birth cohorts, cultural backgrounds, ethnicity, and religious affiliation. In the most general terms:

> [Elder] neglect is the intentional or unintentional withholding of food, medication, or other necessities that result in the older person's failure to thrive. Self neglect is behavior that threatens the person's own health or safety. Physical [elder] abuse is any violence—including hitting, striking with objects, slapping, grabbing, or otherwise causing bodily injury. Psychological or emotional abuse is the infliction of anguish or distress through

threats, verbal aggression, intimidation, humiliation, harsh orders, or other forms of verbal harassment. Sexual abuse is nonconsensual sexual contact of any kind. It may be included as physical abuse. Medical abuse is the intentional withholding or improper administration of medications or other necessary treatments. Financial or material abuse includes theft (cash, Social Security checks, personal property), misappropriation of funds, coercion (such as forced amendment of wills or deeds), or other misuse of the person's income or other financial resources. Violation of rights is the deprivation of any inalienable right, such as personal liberty, assembly, speech, privacy, or the right to vote. (Levine 2003:37–38)

These examples of definitions reflect how recently each specific type of family abuse and violence was discovered or made problematic in the United States. The more recently recognized problems are defined with greater specificity. Child abuse was the first form of FAV episode to be recognized. Intimate partner abuse, a problem that was initially called "wife abuse" or "domestic violence" and is sometimes called "woman abuse," followed. Most recently, the various forms of elder abuse have been recognized. The definitions also reflect how different stakeholders represent the social problems. Federal lawmakers, when defining child abuse, formulate in very general terms a conceptualization of child abuse and neglect that could assist local jurisdictions and social service agencies to identify children at risk for surviving or failing to thrive. To define woman abuse, social scientists imply that social structural–level gendered relationships are the cause of a problem that results in injuries and substantial emotional costs for individual women or victims. Different types of elder abuse are defined by physicians specializing in geriatric medicine.

Lawmakers, social scientists, physicians and other health care practitioners have different interests in *how* to define the problem. Lawmakers define problems in ways that allow social control agencies to enforce regulations, identify and protect victims, and identify and punish perpetrators or offenders. Social scientists define problems to empirically study them and to offer generalizations or explanations. Health care providers define problems to identify a condition or illness to treat, cure, or prevent.

Defining Family Abuse and Violence Episodes

The examples of child abuse, partner abuse, and elder abuse definitions may suggest that FAV episodes cannot be defined. Though each form of *intra-* and *inter*generational family violence has unique characteristics to consider, we use a definition that is derived from the FAV Episode framework:

> Family abuse and violence episodes are usually repeated and always purposeful social behaviors or purposeful omissions of behaviors that tend to be motivated by inappropriate intentions to control or dominate family members or situations that affect family relationships. They may be characterized by a care worker's intention to harm or by a deliberate failure to nurture appropriately one or more family members. While members of a family may include intimate partners, spouses, children, siblings, parents, and other kin, family violence episodes refer to family or the family-type relationships that are located in spaces and places that give social actors opportunities to nurture and support or to harm or injure each other.

In today's world, family members need not live under the same roof to support or harm each other. Emotional and financial nurturance can readily be communicated across geographical boundaries. The financial exploitation of elder parents by their children who reside thousands of miles away from them is possible. Similarly, an emotionally controlling and aggressive person can continue to abuse a partner who is away from home on business.

Social and emotional proximity, and not geographical or physical proximity, give some perpetrators of family violence episodes the opportunity to harm and hurt. Physical distance, nonetheless, may give some victims the opportunity to disrupt the mechanics of family violence episodes, to stop the violence, or to terminate the familial relationship. Some adolescents and teens *do* run away to escape physical and sexual assaults that victimize them within their homes. Adult men and women *do* seek alternative places to live, and they change their phone numbers and Social Security numbers to escape the violence that occurs within their marital or intimate relationships.

How FAV perpetrators and victims maintain physical and social proximity or distance from each other varies quite dramatically across social groupings in American society. Adults are supposed to be autonomous partners and children are, by law and by custom, dependent upon their caretakers until they reach a minimum age. Elder parents who are dependent upon their adult child or children do not represent a new phenomenon in American society, but the abuse or neglect of them does represent a relatively new social problem.

Personal and household income, the employment status of autonomous adults, the age and health status of dependent children or elders, the religious affiliation or religiosity level that filters the meaning of experiences, race and ethnicity, and educational attainment levels represent an incomplete list of the factors that vary across family relationships. These factors affect the social proximity or distance among family members and the social actors' definitions of family violence and abuse.

An Illustration of the Consequences of Definitions: The Battered Wife Syndrome

Groups of social actors or social organizations have various interests or agendas and therefore define the problem of FAV differently. A community-based domestic violence intervention program has a recognizable and important agenda: Help some of the victims of partner violence to assemble the economic and interpersonal resources they need to support their dependent children and leave their abusing intimate partners. A community-based police department has a different agenda: Arrest perpetrators of misdemeanor or felony offenses and help the state prosecute and punish criminals. Concepts and definitions, terms and labels, imply "who counts," "what should be done," and set the priority for various social problems. We illustrate this point with a discussion of the "battered wife syndrome" (BWS).

Defining social phenomena as FAV episodes conveys to the victims and the perpetrators, to the social service providers and other actors external to the events, and to social change advocates who and what *counts* and what can or will happen when specific examples of the problem occur. Consider the BWS, a proposed label for chronic woman abuse, a phenomenon that can, according to its proponents, lead victims to a state of learned helplessness. BWS makes women, who are the primary victims of chronic episodes of family violence, become like caged animals, either incapable of escaping abusive relationships, or, under specific circumstances, sufficiently motivated to kill (Rothenberg 2002).

Lenore Walker is a well-known advocate, whose work, albeit controversial, identified a syndrome and its causes that policymakers and service providers subscribed to, especially during the 1980s, in their well-intentioned efforts to ameliorate a widespread social problem. A cluster of pathologies, including ongoing violence within an intimate relationship that is characterized by extreme jealously, physical or social isolation, threats of death, and violence against others, typifies the development of BWS (Mahoney, Williams, and West 2001). A woman suffering from BWS is not capable of making decisions for herself or for her children. She suffers from post-traumatic stress syndrome and faces a future characterized by futility, dependency, and depression (Downs 1996). The BWS continues to be a focus in some social science research on family violence (Serra 1993; Rotenberg, Shewchuk, and Kimberley 2001; Palker-Corell and Marcus 2004). It has not, however, provided the legal defense for battered women who kill or injure their partners, which the identification of the syndrome was intended to provide (Downs 1996). To the contrary, it has been a misunderstood and misused conceptualization of psychosomatic vulnerability (Overmier 2002). Moreover, when it is widely accepted within social service or legal organizations, it can become a schema for simplifying complex circumstances that social actors can use to identify who the *real* domestic violence victim is and what the *real* solution is. The other victims *do not count*: They do not suffer real battered women's problems.

The prosecuting attorney has an agenda, which is to protect public safety and to gain criminal convictions. With the intention of helping a victim, a prosecuting attorney who claims to understand the BWS can argue with a judge for a no-contact or protection order that can result in more harm than good. A victim who does not present the symptoms of BWS who seeks a no-contact order, however, may be denied by a legal advocate or by a judge who is insistent on distinguishing the *real* cases of family violence from the ones that do not merit social intervention. How often do we hear "this is a typical case of domestic violence—the victim is not capable of refusing the perpetrator's demands." Or how often do we hear "the children may hear the family fights, but this is not a 'real' case of family violence. We don't think the court should interfere."

The unintended consequences of subscribing to a concept, such as BWS, to define and figure out who counts as a victim or survivor of family violence are exquisitely problematic. On the one hand, the concept allows well-intentioned social actors who are external to family violence episodes to avoid recognizing most victims and survivors. All the women who are hit repeatedly or raped by their partners, and who do not manifest the passivity or the helplessness necessary to count as battered women under the rubric of BWS, will not get the responses they request from the social actors external to the family violence episode, who claim to know a *real* battered woman when they encounter one. Flip the coin and imagine how it allows social actors, convinced that they know who the real victims are, to intervene in extraordinarily harmful ways. Mothers can lose custody of their children, families can be stigmatized within their communities, adults can lose their jobs, and collectively the social actors hoping to help can worsen the family violence problem (Mills 1998; Horvath, Logan et al. 2002; Ford 2003; Lewis 2003).

We use BWS, not to denigrate a particular conceptualization, but to make two important points. First, regardless of what the prevailing definitions of FAV are within a community or society, they tell social change advocates, social scientists, policymakers, and legal and social service practitioners who the *real* victims and survivors are, and who the *real* perpetrators are. They tell the social actors external to family violence episodes how to recognize symptoms and syndromes, how to propose solutions, and when to invoke the power of the law or other formal mechanisms of social control and come into the family—a private social space in the United States—and convert or transform a private problem into a public problem. We do not claim to have an ideal definition of child abuse, intimate partner violence, or elder abuse to propose. Like other researchers, we recognize the need for a cultural compromise in defining family abuse and violence episodes that allows social actors to work with somewhat limiting or flawed definitions to approach social problems in ways that can help (Rothenberg 2002). That is, we take the position that while some definitions, such as those derived from the Battered Woman Syndrome, are inherently flawed and misleading, it is more important to understand FAV episodes than to analyze their labels or terms. We do not dispute the social facts: Labeling is a social and political process that names problems. Social groups or organizations have a vested interest in labeling. We contend, therefore, that it is more important to do something about family violence episodes than it is to point out the problems with past efforts.

While a cultural compromise is necessary to move forward on FAV problems, the compromise does not imply that, as social scientists, we can afford to be uncritical. To the contrary, it is the unique responsibility of the academic and research community to understand the causes and consequences of a social problem. It is the researcher, not the practitioner, who is responsible for identifying the unintended consequences of social programs or the widespread acceptance of certain definitions for social problems. It is the researcher or the academic who needs to understand the interests of the social organizations that define victims and perpetrators and respond to family abuse and violence problems.

Second, we examine the BWS conceptualization to show how definitions of FAV problems can and even should vary, depending on who is experiencing the problem, who is causing the problem, and who is held responsible for addressing the problem. An adult woman can tell a survey researcher, according to her personal definition of what constitutes abuse, whether or not she has been victimized. A 4-year-old child or a 94-year-old parent suffering from dementia is not likely to have the cognitive ability or the autonomy or agency associated with adult status to define and report abuse (Ferris, Norton et al. 1997; Lewis 2003; Lingler 2003).

A domestic violence shelter worker, who likely sees poor and undereducated women who cannot flee abuse by turning to family or friends, does *not* need to learn any new or different definitions of family abuse and violence. The definitions subscribed to *by* the shelter are useful for helping shelter workers assist the women who need shelter services. The social scientists who study FAV episodes, however, have the responsibility to distinguish among definitions, which are strongly influenced by the interests of the social organizations constructing and refining them. Social scientists must understand the perspectives from which the definitions emerge, and they must also appreciate the implications of subscribing to particular definitions for empirical studies intended to measure, describe, or explain FAV episodes.

The Role of the American Medical Association and the American Bar Association in Defining Family Violence

To comprehend the variety of FAV definitions, we contend it is necessary to peer through the lens of two professional associations that are key stakeholders as they conceptualize FAV. Though it would be ideal to make sense out of a problem that can affect family members (however "family" is defined) across countries and cultures, we take the position that the problem of family abuse and violence episodes can be well-enough understood only when the researcher or analyst recognizes the cultural and social contexts in which social problems definitions emerge. Thus we examine the process of defining family violence episodes in the United States by the American Medical Association (AMA) and the American Bar Association (ABA).

Professional associations represent different service providers, and they have vested interests in family violence definitions. The associations are stakeholders participating in institution-building or what is sometimes called the social problems industry. Associations define what constitutes a problem that needs attention from the state and the workers they represent according to how they think social resources ought to be directed. We examine how two professional associations define and respond to family violence episodes and how, in so doing, these associations shape the FAV problem.

We focus on the AMA and the ABA because they are the most obvious contributors to the lawmaking and social policymaking process. We also compare them to uncover contrasting approaches to determining appropriate social responses. While the AMA has a clear interest in defining problems as public health problems, the ABA has a clear interest in defining problems as criminal justice problems. If a social actor is "ill," she or he (or the family) needs treatment, therapy, and healing. If a social actor is an "offender" or a "victim," the appropriate response is punishment or protection. Hospitals and courts or clinics and jails are social organizations with remarkably different goals, yet sometimes their missions overlap. For example: An emergency room physician is required to report a suspected case of child abuse to legal authorities. A police officer, responding to a suicidal domestic violence perpetrator, may take the offender to a hospital instead of a jail.

When we examine how the AMA and ABA define FAV problems, we do not need to search for differences in behaviors or acts or consequences. We need to understand the differences, implied by the definitions, in how social actors internal to the FAV episode are expected to be treated. We need to understand how social actors external to the FAV episode are expected to respond.

The American Medical Association

The American Medical Association has an interest in defining FAV episodes in ways that bring the primary and secondary victims into medical and health organizations. The AMA, when defining elder abuse, for example, calls for public health agencies and physicians to respond. The medical services provided, the records kept about the case, the reports required by a governmental organization, and numerous other activities result in the hiring of medical and clerical staff, as well as the creation of specialized offices to meet the needs of abused elders.

According to the American Medical Association, the earliest reports of elder abuse and neglect came from the United Kingdom in the 1970s. The U.S. Department of Health and Human Services created the first elder abuse task force in 1990. Because the primary purpose of the AMA's *Diagnostic and Treatment Guidelines* for elder abuse is to help physicians respond to injurious acts or neglect, some forms of elder maltreatment include self-neglect.

The AMA defines physical abuse of elders as "acts of violence that may result in pain, injury, impairment, or disease" (AMA 1992). Examples include force-feeding; sexual coercion; or pushing, slapping, or striking. Physical neglect is the "failure of the caregiver to provide the goods or services that are necessary for optimal functioning or to avoid harm" (AMA 1992:10); the withdrawal of meals or the failure to provide eyeglasses or safety devices are examples. Psychological abuse is "conduct that causes mental anguish" such as "treating the older person like an infant" or "isolating the older person from family, friends, or activities." Psychological neglect, however, is the "failure to provide a dependent elderly individual with social stimulation," such as "leaving the older person alone for long periods of time" (AMA 1992:10). Unlike other forms of FAV episodes, such as intimate partner abuse, the AMA recognizes that the elder's dependent status makes the social actor vulnerable to abuse or neglect that can threaten their physical, psychological, or emotional well-being.

The AMA recognizes that forms of child abuse and neglect, like elder abuse, are partly a result of the child's dependent status on caretakers. It distinguishes child physical abuse and neglect from child sexual abuse. "Physical abuse is defined as inflicted injury to a child and can range from minor bruises and lacerations to severe neurologic trauma and death." Such physical abuse may be indicated by bruises or welts, burns, lacerations or abrasions, fractures, abdominal injuries, central nervous system injuries, or other symptoms, such as those associated with suffocation or chemical abuse. The AMA labels neglect "deprivational syndromes" and considers the lack of appropriate nutrition, clothing, shelter, emotional support, love and nurturing, education, safety, and medical and dental care to be indicators of deprivations (AMA 1992:9).

Child sexual abuse is defined as the "engagement of a child in sexual activities for which the child is developmentally unprepared and cannot give informed consent. . . . The sexual activities may include genital or anal contact by or to the child or nontouching abuses, such as exhibitionism, voyeurism or using the child in the production of pornography" (1992:5). Sexual abuse may co-occur with one or more forms of physical abuse or neglect.

Domestic violence, or adult partner abuse, according to the AMA, is "characterized as a pattern of coercive behaviors that may include repeated battering and injury, psychological abuse, sexual assault, progressive social isolation, and intimidation." Focusing on the patient, as it does when addressing any form of FAV episode, the AMA acknowledges that "(r)esearch has failed to demonstrate a psychological or cultural profile of battered women" (1992:5). The AMA appears to refute the claim that most domestic violence victims tend to suffer from a battered wife syndrome.

When advising physicians on the diagnosis and treatment of domestic violence victims, the AMA clearly identifies women as the victims and intimate terrorism as the type of violence that it seeks to treat (Johnson and Ferraro 2000). Its guidelines note that victims may experience physical, emotional or psychological, or sexual abuse within their intimate relationships. Physical abuse is generally "recurrent and escalates in both frequency and severity" (1992:7). It may include pushing or kicking or choking; assault with a weapon; restraining the victim; and refusing to help the victim when she is sick or injured. The AMA considers threats, deprivations, intimidations, and false accusations to be examples of emotional or psychological abuse, which may "precede or accompany physical violence as a means of controlling through fear and degradation" (1992:7). Sexual abuse "may include any form of forced sex or sexual degradation . . . such as hurting her physically during sex . . . or trying to make her perform sexual acts against her will" (1992:7). The AMA also urges physicians to assess mental health symptoms and indicators that a woman is trapped within a controlling relationship.

The AMA is strongly opposed to mandatory reporting laws for physicians who treat victims of intimate partner violence. The AMA takes the position that mandatory reporting laws would violate medical ethics, which include confidentiality, and undermine the autonomy of patients seeking medical intervention (Mordini 2004).

The Coalitions Against Domestic Violence sponsored a survey of 316 women who were residing in safe shelters in a number of different states. The research, designed to measure perceptions of mandatory physician-reporting laws, appears to support the AMA position. The study found perceptions "concerning mandatory medical reporting laws vary and in many ways are complex. . . . Contrary to the intended consequences the laws are not perceived as beneficial and are not more likely to encourage the assistance of medical professionals by all victims" (Smith 2004).

The AMA strongly supports the existing mandatory reporting laws regarding child abuse and neglect. A compilation of state reporting agencies concludes the AMA's *Diagnostic and Treatment Guidelines* for child physical abuse and child sexual abuse. The AMA also concludes its elder abuse guidelines with a section on "Resources for Physicians," which encourages doctors to become familiar with their state laws, hotlines, and service providers. Complete contact information for adult protective services in each state is provided. The comprehensive information for reporting elder abuse could be one consequence of the AMA (and other professional associations) discovering this abuse decades after it resolved to identify and treat the other types of FAV episodes affecting children and adult intimate partners.

The American Bar Association

The American Bar Association has an interest in defining family abuse and violence episodes in ways that will bring the primary or secondary perpetrators into legal organizations and begin a process of imposing formal social control practices. It defines FAV, as it defines other social problems, in ways that allow the courts or legal agents, including police officers, attorneys, and mediators, to settle these interpersonal conflicts.

The ABA has an interest in defining and identifying both the primary and the secondary victims of FAV. The ABA guides attorneys and legal clinics providing legal advice to parents faced with losing custody of their children. A child who witnesses a partner abuse event may be considered a secondary victim who is also affected by the law. The ABA provides instruction to attorneys representing clients in divorce cases that dissolve marriages character-ized by domestic violence.

The ABA also addresses issues that intersect legal and medical arenas, such as Title II of the federal Health Insurance Portability and Accountability Act (HIPAA), which regulates the privacy and security of health data and information (Sullivan 2004). The ABA instructs attorneys working for Child Protective Services and other social service agencies. It tells them which sections of HIPAA ad-dress situations that help keep medical records "out the hands of an abusive parent" and which sections explain when information disclosures are permitted "to prevent serious harm to [domestic vi-olence] or other potential victims" (Davidson 2003).

The ABA strongly and actively promotes the creation of uni-fied family courts throughout the United States. The court is the place and the space that the ABA sees as appropriate for resolv-ing family abuse and violence conflicts. The unified family court, in principle, integrates the social and legal services addressing family problems, including child custody, intimate partner vio-lence, and elder abuse. Its authority "encompasses matrimonial, domestic violence, juvenile delinquency, substance abuse, child protection, and family crisis cases" (ABA 2004). The ideal unified family court uses a single judge to handle all legal matters per-taining to a troubled family. It also directs court clients to relevant services, such as counseling, mediation, education, and medical treatment, which the judge may order to help prevent FAV episodes from reoccurring. If it orders services, the court also monitors the client's compliance and the completion of therapeu-tic programs.

The ABA defines separate types of FAV episodes. It defines do-mestic violence as a "pattern of behavior in which one intimate partner uses physical violence, coercion, threats, intimidation, isola-tion, and emotional, sexual, or economic abuse to control and change the behavior of the other partner" (ABA 2003). The ABA def-inition, like feminist definitions of intimate partner abuse, clearly identifies control over the other as the issue defining and motivat-ing domestic violence. In doing so it acknowledges that adults within intimate relationships in the United States are autonomous social actors who should not be controlled by their marital or cohabiting partners.

The ABA recognizes that "elder abuse" is a generic term referring to a wide range of behaviors incorporating neglect or exploitation. It calls elder abuse "the hidden crime" that is likely to increase in number as the general population ages. The ABA claims victims of elder abuse have "less ability to recover" from financial exploitation and "fewer options for . . . avoiding the abusive situation due to . . . age, health, or limited resources" (ABA 2002). Elder abuse includes physical abuse, psychological or emotional abuse, sexual abuse, abandonment, and self-neglect. All told, elder abuse is characterized by the elder's lack of autonomy and dependence on other social actors and social organizations.

The ABA strongly endorses the federal Child Abuse Prevention and Treatment Act as amended by the Keeping Children and Families Safe Act of 2003. The act distinguishes the many types of child abuse and neglect that are defined and disseminated by the National Clearinghouse for Information Relating to Child Abuse. It also appropriates funds to prevention and intervention programs that aim to facilitate children's health and growth and to protect them from harm. Similar to definitions of elder abuse, ABA definitions of child abuse and neglect address the child's dependence on caregivers.

The AMA and the ABA recognize a similar set of acts and omissions as defining different types of intra- and intergenerational FAV episodes. The act of hitting a partner, with the intention to control her or him, is similarly defined as wrong by the two professional associations. The failure to provide education for a child and the failure to provide adequate nutrition for a dependent elder are both counted in ABA and AMA definitions of child abuse and elder abuse. The associations differ, however, in their endorsement of policies and practices to lessen these harms and the injuries. The differences attend to how social actors internal to the FAV episode, that is, the primary perpetrators and victims, ought to be handled. The differences also attend to how social actors external to the FAV episode, that is, the medical and legal social agents, ought to respond. The associations clearly differ in identifying the social places and spaces that should be used to lessen family violence problems.

Autonomy and Privacy

Autonomy and privacy are two culturally constructed components of law and medicine that, within the United States and in other countries, shape definitions of family abuse and violence. The ABA and the AMA have strongly influenced[2] the development and implementation of laws and social programs pertaining to FAV. While the two professional associations depart in important ways in their approach to the problem, they both address the issue of autonomy when defining various dimensions of FAV episodes. The AMA supports mandatory reporting of abusive or neglectful behavior toward children, and it encourages the reporting of elder abuse incidents. However, it strongly opposes mandating physicians to report partner abuse to investigating authorities. The AMA position on mandatory reporting reflects the cultural value of autonomy in the United States.

The ABA, in its definitions of various forms of FAV episodes, takes the position that controlling an adult partner is abusive, and that elders and children who lack the resources necessary for autonomy or independence need to be protected. In the United States, adults are supposed to live in noncontrolling, autonomous relationships with each other. Children and unemployed or frail elders are supposed to be able to depend on caretakers. Parent are supposed to control what their dependent children wear, where they go to school or church, and who their friends are. Parents are supposed to control when children go to bed and what they eat. The caretakers who fail to control nutrition, education, recreation, and medical services for their dependent children or elders can be charged with neglect or abuse.

Adults with adequate resources for living independent lives are not supposed to control each other. They cannot force each other to engage in sexual activities, they cannot control access to the family's financial resources, or access to friends and other family members. If an adult partner controls the other, she or he engages in deviant, abusive, and arguably illegal behavior. Many definitions of partner abuse, including those of the AMA, ABA, and social science and feminist fields, are premised on the notion that a controlling partner is an abusive partner. The United States is not unique in valuing autonomy within adult and intimate partnerships. Nonetheless, it is important to recognize that custom, as well as law, defines who is entitled to relative and absolute autonomy within interpersonal relationships. Nineteenth-century women in the United States argued passionately for autonomy within marriage. Ironically, many 17-year-olds of the same era enjoyed more autonomy than they do nowadays.

Social science researchers who study family violence in the contemporary United States argue that it is crucial to consider the importance of autonomy in defining and identifying victims of child abuse, elder abuse, and intimate partner violence (Bergen 2001; Daly, Jogerst et al. 2003). Legal scholars focus on the autonomy of women when they are victims of partner violence and choose not to pursue arrest or prosecution (Coker 1999; Ford 2003).

Privacy, like autonomy, is an American value that lawmakers and health and social service providers must account for when defining family violence episodes. Marital abuse and violence, contrary to some misinformed claims, was (like child abuse) never condoned within the United States. Because some socially deviant or criminal behaviors occur in the private domain of home and family life, some violent episodes, as well as the perpetrators and their victims, are undetected by social control agents and unprotected by law. On the street, if a child or an adult of any age screams, other social actors will not necessarily take action, but they will hear and witness events that they may define to be criminal or bad. In an apartment, a neighbor could listen to the same sounds but not necessarily hear them as criminal or deviant or bad. A neighbor could conclude it is a private matter when it occurs within the privacy of a home or within the private social space of family life.

Whereas the value of autonomy defines the individual's entitlement, the value of privacy defines spaces for social behaviors to take place among social actors. Privacy is, most importantly, about social relationships. In the privacy of the family space a parent may discipline a child in a manner that is inappropriate for a public space. In the privacy of family life, partners engage in sexual activities that would be criminal if conducted in public spaces.

In the United States, unless the government has a compelling interest to serve or protect the community's interests, the social actor's rights to privacy and private property are protected and revered. The American dream for many means ownership of a private home. Children's public school records are private, and their contents cannot be released to the media or to social scientists without explicit consent from parents. Our medical records are private. Physicians and drugstores must remind us they are protecting the privacy of our health status. We may privately own our intellectual products and sell the rights to them to the highest bidder. In the privacy of their homes, adults are free to express their most personal fantasies. The state is not supposed to control or regulate the private choices that social actors make when selecting what to watch on television, view on the Internet, read in books, listen to on the radio, or communicate with others.

The public's interest, however, permits the state to take privately owned property in order to construct a highway, create a park, or allocate a parcel of land for the storage of toxic waste. It is the public's interest that allows the state to enter private homes to remove a child who is endangered by a parent or a sibling, or to arrest a spouse who has assaulted a partner. The public has an interest in the well-being of family members, whether that involves preventing harm or promoting health.

Privacy rights are often discussed as if they are guaranteed to individuals, yet they are often, if not always, expressed within social relationships. Privacy in a marriage, for example, refers to the privacy of a relationship. The U.S. Supreme Court, invoking the Ninth Amendment to the Constitution, has ruled that adult sexual preferences and expressions and women's decision whether to procreate are private matters. The Court would not have heard *Lawrence v. Texas* or *Griswold v. Connecticut* if privacy rights pertained to all characteristics of an individual's behavior. If a legal researcher studied every legal case and statute throughout the United States that addresses masturbation, the researcher would find the person's right to masturbate in private has never been challenged by the state. What is at stake, and what is regulated by the laws controlling or prohibiting masturbation, is its effect on other social actors. Exhibitionism, illicit pornography, and child abuse incidents are not illegal because an adult person masturbates. They are illegal because an individual's behavior affects another social actor who is unwittingly or nonvoluntarily brought into a social relationship with that individual. The relationship may be defined as perpetrator-victim or actor-consumer. Laurence Tribe's analysis of the *Lawrence* decision argues persuasively that our privacy rights are fundamentally situated within social relationships:

> Lawrence, more than any other decision in the Supreme Court's history, both presupposed and advanced an explicitly equality-based and relationally situated theory of substantive liberty. . . . the Court left no doubt that it was protecting the equal liberty and dignity not of atomistic individuals torn from their social contexts, but of people as they relate to, and interact with, one another. (Tribe 2004)

The notion of privacy in family relations is indeed problematic and highly political (Kelly 2003). While social work agencies and public schools have long been the watchful guardians of children, adult marital relationships, and to a lesser extent cohabiting relationships, provide a private domain for social interaction. The privacy of one's home, however, does not trump the public's interest in preventing harm and injury to children, adults, and elders who live together as family.

Beyond Professional Associations

Since the 1970s, the AMA and the ABA have shaped and redefined conceptualizations of family abuse and violence. They have distinctive agendas for how to respond to a widespread social problem. The AMA focuses on treating, healing, and curing ill persons, and the ABA focuses on protecting potential victims and sanctioning wrongdoers. The AMA has an interest in bringing health and public health problems into medical spaces, such as hospitals and mental health clinics; the ABA has an interest in bringing personal and public safety problems into legal spaces, especially the courts. These two professional associations are powerful lobbyists that influence state and federal legislation.

The role of the professional associations in defining FAV problems is clear. It is also clear that the story of an individual social actor's tragic experience or collectively experienced tragedies can initiate or fuel grassroots movements at the local, societal, or transnational level. These movements also define, identify, and name social problems. A process of social institutionalization can then take the movement's agenda through a policymaking and policy-implementation process that can transform the meaning of the social problem, expand its boundaries to include more types of social actors, and establish agencies to deliver the services that represent proposed remedies (Jenness and Grattet 2001).

Some expressions of outrage or some of the more successful demonstrations and protests that are planned to spotlight central problems and issues are covered by news reporters and featured by filmmakers. Media coverage can make audiences aware of a dire need for social change, or media attention can remind audiences of persistent social problems, or what we call mature social problems. Consider two particular films that feature family violence episodes. One is a 1991 PBS documentary for *Frontline* titled "Who Killed Adam Mann?" It tells the story of a 5-year-old boy who slipped through the cracks of the local Child Protection Services agency and died at the hands of his stepfather and his mother. Among the more than one hundred injuries that caused Adam Mann's death were a broken skull and a split liver. By the time he died, according to the autopsy report, almost every bone in his young body had been broken. Adam's mother, Michelle, had completed a program designed to increase her self-esteem by teaching her (among other things) how to apply makeup, on the premise that increased self-esteem would help her to improve her parenting skills. Overworked child protective services employees failed to permanently remove Adam from his home in order to save his life.

Domestic Violence, directed by the legendary filmmaker Frederick Wiseman, follows a number of women who, with their children, approach The Spring, which is a comprehensive and established domestic violence shelter in Tampa, in an effort to survive family violence. Wiseman features visibly battered and bruised women experiencing the intake process. He documents children expressing their problems and group therapy sessions characterized by frustration and disclosures of desperate feelings.[3]

"Who Killed Adam Mann?" was released in 1991, nearly thirty years after the child abuse problem had been discovered in the United States. It provoked Congress to ask the U.S. Advisory Board on Child Abuse and Neglect to study existing problems and programs in order to recommend

- a national policy to reduce and ultimately prevent such fatalities;
- changes needed to achieve an effective federal role in the implementation of policy; and
- changes needed to improve data collection about child abuse and neglect fatalities.

The advisory board produced a report that identified the scope and nature of fatal child abuse and neglect, the most appropriate investigation and prosecution practices, and the most promising intervention and prevention programs. Though fatalities resulting from child abuse were tragedies recognized for decades before 1991, "Who Killed Adam Mann?" brought increased federal attention to some of the most severe forms of child abuse and some of the worst inadequacies in social services, resulting in recommendations for more comprehensive intervention and prevention programs. The child abuse problem in the United States was not getting the necessary legislative response, program funds, and services, according to the report. The film highlighted the need to devote more attention and more research not only to a social problem affecting vulnerable children but also to the problem of not addressing child abuse with resources adequate to prevent fatalities. The film provoked the U.S. Department of Health and Human Services to recognize that the federal and state governments had not yet done enough for a vulnerable and dependent segment of the general population.

Domestic Violence, distributed more than a decade later, was an unlikely candidate to provoke a similar response by any federal agency. The federal Violence Against Women Act, enacted in 1994 with strong bipartisan support, was expanded and reauthorized in 1998, directing almost a billion dollars to local antiviolence programs. The two-part film *Domestic Violence* documents what social movement actors and policymakers had already verified through empirical study and federally sponsored evaluations of programs: Domestic violence, or intimate partner violence, tragically injures too many women and their children. Therapeutic intervention for all family members, including the children who witness violence, is important. Recovering from FAV episodes is a long and demanding process that depends on multiple social services. Perhaps, however, this particular social problem, which affects adults as the primary victims, is not newsworthy and does not warrant increased resources to help supposedly autonomous social actors survive. David Ford, when reviewing the film, claims: "Critical viewers . . . may find *Domestic Violence* disappointing as a latecomer to the popular media on domestic violence. . . . It has less value for documenting a problem already acknowledged in popular culture and academic research" (Ford 2003:429).

This pair of films helps us understand that media and legal attention, sometimes in response to horrific cases of abuse and violence, are a *necessary* but not a *sufficient* condition for understanding how FAV becomes institutionalized as an important social problem in the United States. Social actors within social service organizations, especially physicians and social workers, teachers and mental health workers, and legislators, judges, and policymakers organize activities and initiatives to address emerging and changing social problems. Understanding how family abuse and violence episodes are recognized, identified, and institutionalized as a social problem within and across social organizations helps the social scientist understand the process of defining and redefining child abuse, intimate partner violence, and elder abuse, which together make up inter- and intragenerational forms of family abuse and violence.

The process of defining FAV and identifying appropriate responses is a continuous one. When the problem is a mature social problem, as FAV is in the United States, for example, it is difficult to separate out the components involved in defining and responding to family violence. Nonetheless we can identify and discuss the role of professional associations, the role of social movements, and the role of the media in this process. Organizations of social actors that are external to FAV episodes define the problem and what ought to be done to help or punish the primary and secondary victims and perpetrators. These organizations attempt to address the motivations and opportunities for FAV and to distinguish levels of vulnerability that make certain types of victims more or less deserving of social resources. Professional associations, especially those that influence lawmakers and policymakers, and the media can affect the objective and the subjective power that social actors experience within and outside the family, power that can be used to prevent initial or repeated family abuse and violence episodes.

Discussion Questions

1. How do the various dimensions of family abuse and violence influence your own perceptions of the severity of FAV in the United States?
2. How is the Battered Woman Syndrome a useful or a dangerous concept for understanding and responding to intimate partner violence?
3. What are the behaviors—which may or may not be considered FAV events or episodes—that you consider to be "private" and therefore should not be subjected to state regulation or intervention?

Research Projects

1. Design a questionnaire to measure the importance of autonomy for persons in the general population.
2. Study the film or the book *Mystic River* to identify the themes of family abuse and violence that affect most of the social actors in the story.

Notes

1. If domestic violence has been determined to have occurred, civil courts, domestic violence courts, or unified family courts can make various decisions regarding children or other family members. We use the In-

diana statutory definition solely to illustrate how the legal process can begin with a definition of domestic violence.

2. Other professional associations have also been tremendously influential. Consider, for example, the American Psychological Association or any of the law enforcement, marriage therapy, or social work associations.

3. In *Domestic Violence 2* Wiseman shows the criminal justice response to domestic violence perpetrators and victims.

8

General Population Perceptions of Family Abuse and Violence Problems

The Family Violence Prevention Fund is a nonprofit organization located in San Francisco, which produces and distributes public service announcements and develops education programs and products. It supported *Ending Domestic Violence: Changing Public Perceptions—Halting the Epidemic,* one of the few books (albeit out of print) on family abuse and violence opinion research in the United States (Klein et al. 1997). The authors review surveys that were conducted between 1992 and 1996 and connected opinions and perceptions to what the media can do, in the form of public education, to prevent family abuse and violence (FAV) and especially *intra*-generational forms of FAV episodes.

Surprisingly, few opinion surveys focus on the family violence problems in the contemporary United States. How does the general population define intra- and intergenerational forms of FAV? Child abuse? Intimate partner violence? Elder abuse? What are the prevailing perceptions regarding what social organizations and public agencies should or should not do in response to family abuse or violence episodes?

Although the prevention of family violence episodes is a necessary, laudable public health goal, life-threatening and life-ending events continue to occur. Perpetrators need to be identified and either punished or treated. Primary and secondary victims need health and social service interventions to recover. Until there is no

FAV within the United States, there will be a need to measure and analyze general population perceptions of how serious the problem is and what ought to be done in response to the social problem. Without survey research, policymakers and lawmakers cannot be guided by public perceptions of appropriate responses to FAV episodes. Yet within the United States, there is no contemporary and nationwide survey to inform policymakers, service providers, or the government how local agencies should respond to all types of FAV episodes. No systematic, recent study tells us which types of FAV cases ought to result in jail time for the perpetrators. Should first-time intimate partner violence perpetrators be arrested and jailed? Which particular social institutions do we hold responsible for preventing FAV episodes? How do we, as a society, expect social actors external to the FAV episode to respond when they witness or become aware of family abuse or violence?

Whether a punitive criminal justice or a therapeutic, rehabilitative response to family violence episodes is preferred by the general population is an important issue to address (McGuire 2004; Scott 2004). Public opinion and public policy, as designed and as implemented, are supposed to align. Public and private agencies are *supposed* to meet the family needs that are defined by family members, not only the needs that are defined by agencies or by the state.

The perceptions of the general population in the United States of what constitutes appropriate responses to FAV episodes have not been systematically measured for four distinctive reasons. First, the public opinion and social science research regarding family violence tends to study preferences for how agencies ought to respond to specific types of FAV episodes, rather than how government and social institutions could respond more comprehensively to FAV episodes generally. Second, researchers attempt to understand what the response ought to be either for the victims or for the perpetrators. Research, sponsored by a private foundation or a federal agency, also tends to look either at problems within generations or problems across generations. The child abuse specialist is not expected to know the details of partner abuse studies. Elder abuse researchers are not presumed to understand the dynamics of child neglect.

Third, social scientists do not often collaborate with practitioners or social change advocates. Employees of the local Child Protective Services office, the local police department, and the local domestic violence prevention programs read materials produced specifically *for* them—not for or by social science researchers. They do not consume the basic social science research, which, by design, is produced to measure and explain family violence problems, while saying nothing about what local agencies should do.

To illustrate: Facilitators teaching FAV perpetrators the well-known "Thinking for a Change" program may be trained at the county probation office. The twenty-two-lesson program, which was developed, tested, and refined by the National Institute of Corrections (Bush, Glick, and Taymans 2001) integrates the development of critical social skills with cognitive restructuring and problem-solving techniques. Probation and community corrections agencies throughout the United States, since 1997, have sent key personnel to seminars to learn how to teach the Thinking for a Change program to local probation officers, social workers, or volunteers. Staff and volunteers who teach the program eventually learn the Thinking for a Change program materials. They are not expected to be aware of the extant social science research on family violence. Conversely, researchers in the family violence field, whether they are employed by universities, private research firms, or state or federal government agencies, are not expected to master the Thinking for a Change curriculum.

Fourth, researchers (with notable exceptions)—including survey or public opinion researchers—tend to study specific types of social relationships within specific academic disciplines. While a sociologist or a social welfare survey researcher may be an expert in elder abuse, a psychologist or a criminal justice researcher is more likely to be an expert in intimate partner violence. Trusting relationships, which are exemplified by an elder who is dependent on an adult child for daily care, or by a child who is dependent on a parent, are not likely to be studied by the research program that is sponsored to explain the deterrent effects of arrest on recidivistic domestic violence. Deborah Daro and her colleagues summarize the problem: "This historical variation [across the related fields of domestic violence, youth violence, and child abuse] is manifested in how each problem has been defined, the type of research that has been valued, the partnerships that have been forged (or not forged) between research and practice, and the nature of prevention efforts" (Daro et al. 2004).

In this chapter we attempt to synthesize what the general population thinks the governments and related public agencies should do in response to the varied problems of FAV. Some social scientists contend the public thinks relatively harsh and punitive responses to FAV episodes are appropriate (Johnson and Sigler 2000). Others argue that general population perceptions favor a more therapeutic response (Stalans 1996). To respond systematically to this important debate, we first examine three specific studies. We examine a recent Canadian study[1] that was designed explicitly to measure general population perceptions of family violence episodes and the possible range of social responses to the episodes. We discuss what a U.S. survey of victimization experiences reports on perceptions of the seriousness of intimate partner violence. And we describe findings from a vignette survey that we conducted to measure the public's perceptions of how the state should respond to one intragenerational form of FAV episode.

We then look carefully at a particular research program conducted in one community to observe changing attitudes over the span of a decade. We conclude with a discussion of existing practices in response to FAV in order to ask the question: Is it time to consider a radically different proposal for how social actors and organizations external to the FAV episode ought to respond?

A Canadian Survey of Family Violence

Researchers associated with the Family Violence Initiative, the Department of Justice, the Canadian Council on Social Development, the Royal Canadian Mounted Police, and the University of Toronto conducted a nationwide Canadian study (EKOS 2002) by surveying 2,000 adults in the general population and conducting focus-group interviews across the country to measure perceptions and opinions about child abuse, domestic violence, and elder maltreatment. The purpose of the study was to establish baseline data that would address the following research questions:

- How do citizens understand and define family violence?
- Do adults in the general population accept or tolerate family violence?
- How willing are they to intervene if and when they witness family violence events?
- How should the governments and public agencies respond to family violence?

Canadian researchers found a great deal of consensus on relatively expansive definitions of family violence. The concept "family violence" includes many different types of behaviors, including verbal and emotional abuse that affects intra- and intergenerational familial relationships. The general population also thinks that a child who witnesses violence within the home, whether it is perpetrated by a spouse against his or her partner or by a parent against another child, is a victim of child abuse.

Immediate family members, as well as social relationships based on trust, are included in the definition of "family" by most respondents. There is somewhat less consensus within the general population over whether dating partners and elder parents can be victims of "family violence," but there is nearly unanimous agreement that children and adult partners can be victims of family abuse and violence.

Violent behaviors are defined broadly, including threats with weapons, forced or inappropriate sexual activity, physical acts of aggression, and throwing objects at victims. Most all of the social actors who participated in the survey believed that forms of verbal abuse, such as yelling at a child or making humiliating comments, constitute a dimension of family abuse. In addition, the failure to provide adequate food or shelter or appropriate medical services is generally considered a type of family violence. While there is only moderate agreement over whether or not denying an adult access to information about income or financial resources constitutes abuse, most of the social actors surveyed linked acts of financial abuse to forms of emotional abuse.

Researchers find that the greatest concern within the Canadian general population is for child abuse, followed by a concern for elder abuse and spouse abuse. The vulnerable or dependent family member, rather than siblings or partners within intimate adult relationships, elicits the greater concern. Family violence, in all its forms, has negative consequences, according to the survey. Children who are abused, for example, are thought to suffer from psychological problems and may act out as bullies in school. All victims, according to respondents, can experience health and mental health problems as a consequence of family violence episodes.[2]

When responding to survey questions, social actors expressed the belief that family violence can affect any type of household—those that range from low- to high-income, and those characterized by all ethnicities and races. Moreover, they think that the problem of family violence nowadays is more serious than it was a decade earlier. It is not a social problem that women's groups or the media tend to exaggerate.

What should be done? The general population in Canada thinks the federal and local governments should treat family violence as an urgent social problem that needs to be addressed. They hold social institutions, especially education and health providers, responsible for identifying and responding appropriately to family violence episodes. And they believe that when necessary, as individual social actors, they would intervene and assist a victim by offering advice or by calling the appropriate agency or the police.

Seventy-five percent of the general population thinks that a parent who kicks or hits a child with a fist ought to receive counseling and treatment. Twelve percent think jail time is the more appropriate response. Those who prefer jail to counseling tend to be parents of young children. Regardless of the variation in perceptions of appropriate types of responses, the Canadian population favors a compulsory or mandatory response to a child assault event of family violence. They want to see state authorities—social actors external to the family violence episodes—involved. Even if mandatory counseling is not effective, the general population thinks it can do no harm to the child, parent, or caretaker.

Seventy-eight percent of the men and 73 percent of the women who participated in the study claim that as individual social actors external to a family violence episode, they are willing to approach a friend who they believe to be abusing an adult partner. Slightly fewer male and female respondents indicate a willingness to approach the other social actor internal to the family violence episode—the victim. Nonetheless it is clear that most adults perceive they are capable of and responsible for responding to family violence episodes.

Sixty-seven percent of the general population perceives that a spouse or intimate partner who hits his or her partner should be removed from the home and be required to undergo treatment or counseling. Younger adults are among the minority of respondents who perceive jail time as the appropriate response for an episode of intimate partner violence.

The Canadian general population perceives that dependent elders, like children, need to be protected from family violence episodes. They believe the same intervention programs that are found to be useful for protecting abused children should be available to elders as well. Although the general population believes that family violence episodes represent a serious social problem that requires intervention, there is no evidence to suggest that their preferred response to such episodes is a punitive one. Clearly the preference is for treatment and counseling over arrest, charging, and jail time.

Perceptions of Woman Abuse in the United States

Researchers within the United States pioneered the systematic study of the prevalence and incidence of family violence. Beginning in 1975, Murray Straus and his colleagues used representative samples of adults in the general population to estimate the number of persons who abuse and who are abused by family members. The Straus teams studied the frequency or the "chronicity" of FAV episodes. Ironically, however, there has been no comprehensive survey of the country's general population to assess perceptions of how the state or private physicians or therapists should respond to FAV. No public opinion surveys are designed specifically to measure perceptions of how social institutions should work to prevent or treat family violence episodes throughout the United States.

We can, however, turn to other empirical projects that include clusters of survey questions that directly or indirectly measure what the general population believes regarding appropriate interventions for family violence episodes. Thus, we examine the Violence Against Women and Men in the United States (VAWM) survey, which is a nationwide study that polled a representative sample of 8,000 women and 8,000 men and asked them to disclose their family violence victimization experiences. Researchers also asked five questions to measure perceptions regarding the problem of woman abuse and intimate partner violence in American society (Tjaden and Thoennes 2000a). They posed the following questions to all their respondents:

- Overall, would you say that personal safety for women in this country has improved since you were a child, gotten worse, or stayed about the same?
- Do you think the following things are more of a problem for women today, less of a problem, or about the same?
  - violent crime
  - domestic violence
  - sexual harassment
  - sexual assault

While the researchers did not ask respondents to indicate what social service agencies or criminal justice agencies should do in response to woman abuse, they did ask men and women to disclose their perceptions of the seriousness of a particular form of family violence.

Sixty-five percent of the men who participated in the study and 56 percent of the women surveyed believe personal safety for women has gotten worse in recent years. More women (67 percent) than men (60 percent) think domestic violence is more of a problem today. Half of the women and 41 percent of the men think sexual harassment has gotten worse. Researchers found a substantial gender difference in perceptions of sexual assault. The majority of the men (54 percent) and the overwhelming majority of the women (76 percent) think that sexual assault is more of a problem today in the United States than it was in the past.

Table 8.1. Perceptions Regarding Woman Abuse from a National Survey

Item	Percent of Women	Percent of Men
Personal Safety for Women Has Gotten Worse*	56.3	65.4
Violent Crime for Women Is More of a Problem	87.8	86.5
Domestic Violence Is More of a Problem*	67.2	60.4
Sexual Harassment Is More of a Problem*	49.8	40.9
Sexual Assault Is More of a Problem*	76.1	54.1

Note: Items are from the Tjaden and Thoennes (2000a) study.
* Gender differences are statistically significant at the .05 level.

Table 8.1 summarizes the findings. Although there is no statistically significant gender difference in perceptions of violent crime in society, on all of the other perception questions women are more likely than men to think abuse against women has increased in severity over the recent years or decades. We cannot infer what accounts for these perceptions, but we can infer that most adults in the general population probably think additional social prevention or intervention measures are necessary to reduce the multidimensional problems of woman abuse, child abuse, and elder abuse.

A Vignette Study of Appropriate Social Responses to Family Abuse and Violence Episodes

For our analysis of family abuse and violence episodes, we surveyed married or cohabiting adults to measure perceptions of how the government or the state should respond to known episodes of intragenerational family violence. We used a vignette approach to ask 300 men and women, during the summer of 2003, what should happen to perpetrators whose FAV episode elicits police attention. After presenting the vignettes, we asked two questions regarding woman abuse that are similar to those used by Tjaden and

Table 8.2. Perceptions of Woman Abuse and Concerns for Personal Safety and Safety of Others

Item	Percent of Women	Percent of Men
Violent Crime Is More of a Problem*	76.1	48.0
Domestic Violence Is More of a Problem*	68.0	57.0
Somewhat or Very Concerned for Personal Safety*	61.1	45.5
Somewhat or Very Concerned for Safety of Family Members*	76.0	70.0
Somewhat or Very Concerned for Safety of Girls*	78.6	80.2
Somewhat or Very Concerned for Safety of Boys	76.5	74.5

* Gender differences are statistically significant at the .05 level.

Thoennes (2000a). We also asked a series of four questions, adapted from a study on concern for interpersonal violence or safety (Warr and Ellison 2000), to measure how concerned men and women are for themselves, for their family members, and for the boys and girls in contemporary society. Table 8.2 summarizes our findings of responses to these general questions about woman abuse and concern for interpersonal violence.

Our survey generated a nearly identical finding to the Tjaden and Thoennes (2000a) survey: Sixty-eight percent of the women, all of whom are currently in cohabiting relationships or married, believe domestic violence is more of a problem today than it was in the past. Both men and women are much more concerned for the safety of their family members than they are for their own personal safety. Men, compared to women, are more concerned for the safety of girls in their families or in their neighborhoods, but there is no statistical difference between the genders in how concerned married or cohabiting adults are for the safety of boys.

Men also perceive that domestic violence is more of a problem today than it was in the past. More than 70 percent of men and women said they are relatively concerned about the interpersonal violence that can affect their family members or girls and boys in their communities.

What should the state do in response to FAV episodes? Perhaps the state should respond to female and male perpetrators differently. Or perhaps the state should consider the composition of the family affected by violence or abuse. These issues—notably missing from the Canadian study—are important to gauge perceptions of the state's responsibility to diminish the consequences of family violence episodes.

Measuring Appropriate Family Violence Responses

We used a vignette approach, which is sometimes referred to in the published social science literature as a "factorial object survey design" (Rossi and Berk 1997; Rossi and Nock 1983), to measure the recommendations made by married or cohabiting men or women for how the government or the state should respond to FAV episodes. Sets of five randomly selected vignettes, chosen from a potential pool of forty-eight vignettes, were read to the participants. All the vignettes described physical assaults following a fight or argument between adult partners. The episodes of intragenerational family violence described visible injuries that resulted. The primary victims and abusers described in the vignettes vary along the dimensions of social status and family embeddedness, if they are married or cohabiting, and if they have young children at home. The vignettes implicitly described whether or not there are secondary social actors (the children) internal to the family violence episode.

The research participants recommended appropriate responses for the state to take when an FAV episode becomes known to the local police. They recommended a "criminal justice," a "therapeutic," or a "hands-off" response.

The vignettes describing FAV episodes were part of a computer-assisted, random-digit-dialing telephone survey administered by the Social Research Institute at Purdue University. Interviewers screened potential respondents to make sure they were currently married or living with an intimate partner. The vignette design is ideal for measuring perceptions of appropriate social responses to all types of complex events, including family violence episodes. Miller and Bukva measured normative definitions of dating violence among university students with a vignette study. Stalans (1996) measured judgments regarding appropriate sanctions for intimate partner violence with a vignette study, and Webster (1991) used a similar design to measure definitions of child abuse, partner abuse, and elder abuse in a community survey. Sniderman and Grob (1996) claim this research design has external validity (associated with probability sampling strategies) and internal validity (associated with the fully randomized experiment).

In our study we used the vignette design to measure the recommendations made by social actors external to family violence episodes. We focus on two key research questions: (1) Other things being equal, what accounts for punitive or therapeutic recommendations for family violence episodes? (2) What accounts for the quantity or the severity of punishment or therapy deemed appropriate for first-time or repeat offenders?

The Vignettes

Forty-eight vignettes were constructed to rotate, in a fully crossed (2 × 2 × 2 × 3 × 2) factorial design, the perpetrator's sex, marital status, if she or he has children, the social status of the neighborhood in which the FAV episode occurred, and if the police had knowledge of any prior FAV committed by the perpetrator. We show two examples in box 8.1 with bolded text to represent the vignette dimensions (for example, the abuser's sex) and their values (for example, "Tom" or "Linda"). All the vignettes were created to describe violence that results from an argument and that causes physical injury. No vignettes described weapons, hospitalization, or medical treatment.

In vignette A, the perpetrator is a man, and he is identified as a suspect with no prior police record of FAV. The couple has a relatively high level of family embeddedness because they are married and they have two young children. The children, because they likely witnessed or heard the violence that occurred within their home, may be considered secondary victims of FAV episodes. The family lives in what is described as a middle-class

Box 8.1.　Examples of Vignettes

Vignette A
Tom and his **wife** had a fight at the end of a day. During the fight, Tom pushed his wife to the floor. She bruised her arm and needed to stay home from work for two days. Tom and his wife have been married for about five years. They have **two children**, under age 6. They live in a comfortable home, in a **middle-class neighborhood**. Tom has **never done anything like this before**. The neighbors called the police.

Vignette B
During a fight, **Linda** hit her **boyfriend** in the face. His face was bruised and he missed two days of work as a result. Linda and her boyfriend have lived together **for about one year**. They live in a one-bedroom apartment, in a **working-class neighborhood**. Linda **has hit her boyfriend in the past** when they fought. The neighbors called the police.

neighborhood. In vignette B, the major dimensions of information are different: The perpetrator is a woman and she has a prior record. The couple has a low level of family embeddedness, there are no secondary victims, and they live in a working-class neighborhood.

The primary victim and the primary perpetrator, representing social actors internal to the family violence episode, are presented as heterosexual adults in all of the vignettes that we used in this study. Male or female abusers were assigned randomly to each vignette. The three values assigned to designate the social status of the neighborhood are working-class neighborhood, middle-class neighborhood, or upper-class neighborhood. For half the vignettes the abuser is described as a first-time offender and for the other half, she or he is described as a repeat offender.

After the interviewer read a randomly selected vignette from the total set of forty-eight vignettes, the research participant was asked: "Would you recommend jail, counseling, or nothing should happen?" If jail was the response, the interviewer asked: "How much time should be spent in jail?" Responses, coded on a five-point scale, ranged from one day in jail to more than six months in jail. If counseling was the response, the interviewer asked: "How many counseling sessions should be required?" Responses, coded on a four-point scale, ranged from one session to more than one year of counseling.

Participant Questionnaire

The second part of the research instrument was a traditional sample survey questionnaire. The research participant's marital status and family composition, race or ethnicity, age, educational level, and employment status were measured. We used a computer-assisted telephone interview (CATI) method to select potential respondents and to conduct the surveys and record the responses. Potential and eligible participants were asked: "We are conducting a national survey of attitudes about social problems in the United States. Do you have time now to answer some questions?"

Each social actor's answers to survey questions were appended to their vignette ratings. The resulting data file contains 1,500 cases, representing vignette judgments or ratings made by the 300 married or cohabiting adults. Each data case we prepared for analysis contains numerical codes for (a) the five dimensions of information rotated in the vignettes, (b) responses to survey questions, and (c) the five sets of vignette ratings that measure the type of response and the amount of jail time or counseling sessions that were recommended.

There are two types of dependent variables that we examine to assess general population perceptions for how the government should respond to intragenerational FAV episodes. The first represents the type of response the state should impose on the abuser: "jail," "counseling," or "nothing should happen." The second measures the level or amount of either the criminal justice (jail) or the therapeutic (counseling) response that the research participants recommended.

Table 8.3 shows the vignette ratings that represent how general population adults, in cohabiting or marital relationships, think the government should respond to all the FAV episodes we presented.

Only 21.5 percent of the 1,500 vignette ratings are recommendations for jail time. The majority of responses, 66.1 percent, are recommendations for counseling sessions, for intragenerational FAV episodes that caused physically visible injuries. In a small per-

Table 8.3. Vignette Ratings by Respondent Characteristics: What Should Happen to Perpetrators?

	"Jail Time"	"Counseling Sessions"	"Nothing Should Happen"
N of Responses	317	972	183
Percentage of Responses	21.5	66.1	12.4

centage of the cases (12.4 percent) the recommendation was "nothing should happen" to the abuser. These data clearly show that married or intimate partners believe the government ought to take some action in response to FAV episodes. However, a therapeutic, rather than a punitive, response appears to be the preferred response for most of the intragenerational FAV episodes the vignettes describe.

We find some differences in the vignette judgments based on the participant's sex and level of family embeddedness. There is a significant gender difference among participants. Women are more likely than men to recommend counseling sessions, and men are more likely than women to recommend either jail time or "nothing should happen" ($\chi^2 = 29.465$, df = 2, p < .001). We also find that married participants, compared to cohabiting participants, are significantly more likely to recommend jail time over counseling sessions ($\chi^2 = 12.797$, df = 2, p < .002). In addition, men and women who have children living with them at home, compared to those with no children in the household, are significantly more likely to respond punitively, with a recommendation for jail time ($\chi^2 = 25.368$, df = 2, p < .001).

When we examine differences in the general population's perceptions as a result of the vignette dimensions that we varied in this study, we find that vignettes describing female perpetrators, compared to those describing male perpetrators, are more likely to result in a "counseling" or "nothing should happen" recommendation. Jail recommendations tend to be reserved for male perpetrators ($\chi^2 = 60.244$, df =2, p < .001).

There are no significant differences in recommendations for perpetrators who are described as married (vs. cohabiting), or for perpetrators who are described as having young children or secondary victims in the home. The preferred government response is for counseling sessions. The vignette characteristic that most strongly affects perceptions or judgments is prior record. Vignettes that describe perpetrators with prior records of FAV are much more likely to result in recommendations for jail sanctions than vignettes that describe perpetrators with no prior record that is known to the police (χ^2 = 140.916, df = 2, p < .001). In summary, the participant's gender and level of family embeddedness influence recommendations for what the government should do regarding episodes of intragenerational FAV. In addition, a jail recommendation is more likely if the perpetrator is a man and has a prior record.

Amounts of Counseling or Jail Time Recommended

We also specified regression models to explain variation in the number of counseling sessions or the duration of a jail sentence that research participants recommend for FAV episodes. The regression models are shown in table 8.4.

When considering the vignette dimensions, we find research participants recommend a greater number of sessions for male perpetrators and for perpetrators who have children in their homes. If there are secondary victims of FAV episodes, married or cohabiting adults think that perpetrators should experience relatively long-term therapeutic intervention. We find that the respondents recommend longer jail terms for repeat offenders.

Although the research participants' age, sex, and race explain the number of counseling sessions recommended, they do not affect the amount of recommended jail time. Men, older participants, and working participants think fewer counseling sessions are necessary in response to FAV episodes. African American men and women, compared to Hispanic or white participants, recommend more counseling sessions. Only one characteristic—a higher level of education—is associated with a recommendation for less jail time for FAV episodes. It is clear that married or cohabiting adults in the United States, similar to the Canadian general population, call for therapeutic intervention, not necessarily jail time, when FAV episodes are brought to the attention of the police. Recommendations for a jail

Table 8.4. Amount of Counseling or Jail Time: OLS Models

Independent Variables	Amount of Counseling Beta (t)	Amount of Jail Time Beta (t)
Vignette Characteristics		
Perpetrator Is Male	.090	.015
	(2.630**)	(.264)
Perpetrator Is Married	.026	−.092
	(.757)	(−1.602)
Perpetrator Has Children	.071	−.066
	(2.076*)	(−1.150)
Perpetrator's Social Status	.016	−.057
	(.463)	(−.974)
Perpetrator's Prior Record	.179	.202
	(5.176)	(3.343***)
Research Participant Characteristics		
Male	-.134	.077
	(−3.133**)	(1.075)
Age	-.113	.010
	(−2.615**)	(.118)
African American	.096	.002
	(2.447*)	(.033)
Marital Embeddedness	.090	.080
	(1.906)	(1.020)
Education	.052	−.152
	(1.417)	(−2.381*)
Works	-.102	-.024
	(−2.840**)	(-.384)
Intercept	2.407	2.087
	(10.830***)	(3.570***)
N	767 263	
Adj. R2	.129	.197
F	7.700***	4.775***

Note: Numbers in parentheses are t values. * p < .05 ** p < .01 *** p < .001

sanction tend to be reserved for male offenders with prior histories of family violence. Social actors within ongoing intimate relationships tend to recommend a hands-off approach only if the perpetrator is a woman and has no prior history of family violence. More highly educated adults, African Americans, and employed persons tend to avoid recommending jail for FAV perpetrators.

Based on our vignette study, we conclude that men and women alike appear to be somewhat tolerant of the occasional act of physical aggression by a woman, and they appear to attribute more blame to men who aggress against women in intragenerational episodes of FAV. Social actors in the general population who are currently in married or cohabiting relationships seem to perceive what some researchers claim: The most egregious forms of family violence episodes injure women and children. Because not all FAV episodes are alike, general population adults tend to think the state should consider the context in which the act is perpetrated, the perpetrator's history of bad acts, and the motivation for the violence directed against a family member in order to determine the most appropriate response to a family violence and abuse episode.

We acknowledge that there are two important limitations to our study. One is its snapshot approach to estimating what adults think should happen to perpetrators. The second is a focus on FAV episodes that are perpetrated primarily against adult family members. One opinion research study, implemented by Johnson and Sigler, studied a single community for more than a decade, from 1986 to 1997, to observe changing opinions regarding what the state should do in response to family violence episodes that affect children and adults. That study answers some questions left unanswered by our vignette survey.

A Community Study of Changing Perceptions

Johnson and Sigler (1996 and 2000) distributed one of four research instruments, which are all self-administered survey questionnaires, to a sample of adults representing the community of Tuscaloosa, Alabama. They used the different survey instruments to measure perceptions of what constitutes child abuse and spouse abuse, to measure perceptions of appropriate state responses to FAV episodes, and to assess recommendations for what the state should do. They conducted their surveys at three points in time, first in 1986–1987, then in 1991–1992, and finally in 1996–1997. Their research team hand-delivered and retrieved the self-administered questionnaires to promote a high response rate. While their study is limited to one community and does not measure the most current opinions, it was a highly unusual and ongoing research program that examined changing definitions of FAV episodes and changes in perceptions of appropriate responses to the social problem.

In their first study, in 1986–1987, they found that respondents broadly define woman abuse and child abuse to include acts of hitting, emotional abuse, and sexual abuse, as well as the failure to care for and nurture dependent children. They report that "the use of physical force [is] unacceptable in almost any context with the exception of disciplinary procedures for children . . . [and] when occasional hitting becomes frequent hitting . . . the perception of behavior moves from child discipline to child physical abuse" (1995:485). We can generalize these findings to suggest that adults in the Tuscaloosa general population gauge the social actor's motivation to identify what constitutes FAV episodes.

Their second phase of data collection, in 1991–1992, resulted in perplexing findings. While the general population in Tuscaloosa showed less tolerance for all violent acts, including FAV episodes, they also indicated less willingness to call the police, compared to the willingness they expressed in 1986–1987 (Johnson and Sigler 1995). We contend that Johnson and Sigler uncovered changing definitions of what constitutes FAV episodes and changing perceptions about what the government should do in response to ongoing social problems.

In their more recent survey, conducted in 1996–1997, they found a strong pattern of change in definitions of spouse abuse. Whereas the 1986–1987 data showed that 44.3 percent of respondents believed that "hitting occasionally with open hand" was always wrong, the 1996–1997 data showed that 84.0 percent perceived that the behavior is always wrong. Other behaviors such as "hitting occasionally with belt or stick," "cursing her," or "never allowing her to have money" showed a similar pattern. Over time the community tended to define more specific acts of spouse abuse as always wrong. In addition, Johnson and Sigler measured perceptions of appropriate levels of punishment. They conclude "there appears to be general public support for a more punitive approach to defining and criminalizing acts of wife abuse. The public's perception . . . is becoming increasingly harsher over time"

(2000:177). Their studies support our claim that the general population's definition of what constitutes FAV episodes and perceptions of appropriate responses to the problem change over time. Changing definitions most likely reflect perceptions of the victim's vulnerability and the perpetrator's motivations for engaging in family violence episodes. If Johnson and Sigler had extended their research program into the new century, it is highly likely they would have found a shift from a punitive to a more therapeutic response to family violence perpetrators, which corresponds to shifting practices in American civil and criminal courts (Costello 2004; Hartley 2003; Madden and Wayne 2003).

The Centrality of the Courts for Responding to Family Violence Episodes

Prevention, and related public health and education efforts, are indisputably the most important tools a society has to address potential and existing FAV problems. However, because FAV episodes represent a very persistent social problem, the federal and local governments' action plans include programs and agencies that are designed and funded to respond to events that have already occurred—with the intention of preventing reoccurring violence and abuse.

Over the past three decades, the governments' response to FAV has been to take a somewhat therapeutic and remedial stance while simultaneously taking action to identify and punish perpetrators. In general the responses by states have corresponded to the general population's perceptions of what should be done.

The mandatory reporting of child abuse and neglect cases has at least two purposes: To identify and treat victims, and to identify and punish offenders or caretakers who fail to provide what a child needs to survive and thrive. Adult protective services, in most states, can petition the courts to remove abused or neglected elders from their homes. While the purpose is to provide appropriate guardians for vulnerable social actors, it is also to punish those responsible for elder abuse or neglect. Most police departments have developed preferred or mandatory arrest policies, and many prosecutors' offices claim to use no-drop policies for intimate partner violence cases, although the use of mandatory or preferred arrest and no-drop prosecution policies are extremely problematic (Bracher 1996; Ford 2003; Goodman, Dutton, and Bennett 2000; Henning and Feder 2004; Hirschel and Hutchison 2003; Hoctor 1997; Koss 2000; Mignon and Holmes 1995; Mills 1999; Sinden and Stephens 1999; Wanless 1996). The dual purpose is to protect victims and punish perpetrators, but the arrest and prosecution policies have had unintended and negative consequences. Unjustified, dual arrests, even by experienced officers, have resulted (Finn et al. 2004; Hirschel and Buzawa 2002). An increased probability of recidivism among those arrested for intimate partner violence as compared to those not arrested following police intervention is found in some of the most carefully designed empirical studies (Brinig 2002; Mills 1999). Victims can feel re-victimized by the courts when compelled or coerced to testify against their partners (Coker 1999; Ford 2003; Hanna 1996).

The dilemma faced by the criminal courts working to respond effectively to FAV is deeply rooted in the U.S. legal system. Individual social actors perpetrate bad acts and individual victims are harmed, but the arrest, the conviction, and the punishment that is meted out for a criminal conviction is accomplished in the name of the state or the collectivity. The purpose of criminal justice intervention transcends the needs or wishes of individuals. The purpose of criminal law is also to communicate legal expectations or legally prescribed or proscribed behaviors that apply to all persons in society (Salazar et al. 2003).

A contemporary trend in American justice is called therapeutic jurisprudence, which are legal processes that integrate healing, remedial therapy, and rehabilitation with formal means of social control (Madden and Wayne 2003; Nolan 2003; Stephan 2002). The therapeutic jurisprudence movement is being applied to child abuse cases (Brooks 1999) and intimate partner violence cases (Hora and Schma 1998; Simon 1995). It is most apparent in the creation of specialized domestic violence or family violence courts that are designed to help perpetrators solve problems and become productive members of families and the larger society (Ford et al. 1995; Karan, Keilitz, and Denaro 1999; Nolan 2003; Scott 2004; Tsai 2000).

The courts are spaces and places where FAV cases are alleged, disputed, and sometimes resolved. Communities, with sponsorship from local, state, and federal government funds, and assistance from charitable organizations and private foundations, have implemented diverse programs and policies that tend to funnel cases into the state courts. Consider the following all-too-typical cases:

- A neglected child is temporarily placed in foster care while her mother participates in a program that teaches her how to nurture and care for her children. When is the mother prepared to resume caring for her child?
- A woman approaches a domestic violence shelter with her children and tells the intake worker she needs a protection order but she does not know what to do. How can the shelter's legal advocate help her obtain the court order?
- A man is arrested on domestic battery charges. The police were called to his home by a neighbor who heard him throwing objects at and hitting his wife. Should he be arrested and prosecuted for a misdemeanor domestic violence offense?
- A woman was brought to a safe shelter by the police who witnessed mutual aggression when they arrived in response to a call for a domestic disturbance. She agreed to participate in an anger management program to avoid losing custody of her children. To avoid prosecution, to whom does she show proof that she successfully completed the program?
- A man, who has access to his mother's bank accounts, transfers all of her savings to his own account to buy a boat. His mother, as a consequence, cannot afford her monthly medical prescriptions. How can her caseworker recover her lost funds?

These examples, and countless others, represent cases comprising large portions of civil and criminal court dockets. Cases may be opened by various agencies or social actors external to the FAV episode—by a Child Protective Services Agency, by a police department, by a neighbor, or by an elder's physician—but all cases will be closed by the courts.

Courts in the United States are places where social actors adjudicate and settle disputes and other matters. They are social organizations that are critically important for addressing FAV problems. In response to changing social definitions of domestic violence, two distinctive models of jurisprudence—therapeutic and punitive—are discussed in the sociolegal research literature to describe the courts' responses to family abuse and violence episodes. The two models are ideal types, representing a constellation of legal values and structured normative beliefs that direct the agendas and activities of the courts and legal actors. As one model operates at the foreground of the sociolegal landscape, as it dominates legal discourse and practices, the other works in the background, supporting practices that complement the dominant model of jurisprudence. Shifts in sociopolitical attitudes; and changing public opinion about crime or specific forms of crime, such as FAV, alter the foreground and background, but not the components of the sociolegal landscape that supports a culture of social control (Garland 2001; Nolan 2001).

Punitive and therapeutic jurisprudence models symbolize and communicate different social control purposes, but they do not represent mutually exclusive or even competing practices. They are complements that expand the authority of legal institutions and organizations, making them powerful agents of formal or government social control. A punishment theme to characterize appropriate response to crime, such as deterrence or just deserts (i.e., deserved punishment), in principle calls for harsher sanctions than a therapeutic theme, such as rehabilitation. In practice, yearlong prison terms for two offenders, each convicted of a felony, fits the punitive and therapeutic jurisprudence models equally well: Two offenders, one sentenced for the purpose of punishment and one for the purpose of treatment, may indeed have qualitatively different experiences within prison programs. Nonetheless they experience no objective difference in the amount of time spent in state prison. Likewise, a court program that monitors therapy in the name of rehabilitation is no less social control than is a program monitoring probation in the name of punishment in response to FAV episodes.

Mutable justificatory themes of social control are more than a matter of changing tastes. Changeable themes expand the boundaries of social control practices. Nolan's analysis of problem-solving courts provides a definitive and contemporary illustration. In response to a persistent social problem (drug offenses), social control practices that once focused on delivering harsh punishments shifted, during the 1990s, to focus on graduating participants from court-administered treatment programs. Though a justificatory theme for directing social control activities—mandating court appearances, random drug and alcohol testing, and monitored social program participation—changed from punishment to treatment, an offender or a perpetrator remains controlled by government authorities for a specified period of time. Because treating an illness or condition, including an addiction, results in social approval, even protracted periods of social control escape critique: "Once justice can be plausibly spoken of as 'just treatment,' any objections based on 'just desert' become meaningless" (Nolan 2001:208).

To examine comprehensively how the state courts work in response to FAV problems, it is important to consider the relationship between punitive and therapeutic jurisprudence models and practices. Analytic distinctions between the two models of justice make it possible to examine, within a more general framework of social control, how both models work together to direct the behaviors of social actors, including those charged with the responsibility to respond to violence and to expand the boundaries of social control institutions.

Punitive Jurisprudence

By punitive jurisprudence we mean that legal institutions, organizations, and activities communicate the centrality of identifying and punishing wrongdoers for the primary purpose of controlling and preventing harm. The common-law theme of determining a defendant's guilt is paramount. Applied to FAV, a punitive jurisprudence model promotes legislation defining criminal behaviors and criminal sanctions. It encourages police departments and courts to develop and implement policies that capture and punish wrongdoers efficiently. It supports mandatory rather than discretionary behaviors among social workers, law enforcers, officers of the court, and corrections personnel. Thus it supports mandatory reporting, mandatory arrest, and the mandatory prosecution of family abuse and violence cases. Punitive jurisprudence communicates criminal law threats and practices that can remove and exclude convicted offenders from their homes and their communities for the purpose of incapacitating some and warning others.

Therapeutic Jurisprudence

By therapeutic jurisprudence we mean that legal institutions, organizations, and activities are focused on treating and healing practices that can reform or rehabilitate social deviants while helping victims. Intensive counseling or probation practices that center on helping the perpetrator to develop work or education skills while simultaneously developing family responsibilities, coupled with victim restitution, are exemplar. An example of a traditional sociolegal intervention in the name of therapeutic jurisprudence would be a mental health program that responds to certain types of deviant behavior. Whereas the individual defendant or perpetrator is ill and needs help or treatment, steps are taken to make sure the individual defendant or victim of crime is not re-victimized or harmed by a legal or court response.

Applied to FAV episodes, a therapeutic jurisprudence model supports legislation that provides funds for victim and perpetrator therapy programs. It encourages social service, public health, and criminal justice agencies to develop programs to provide resources such as training and counseling opportunities for perpetrators, victims, and their families. A therapeutic model communicates a stronger preventive and educational focus. By intersecting with health, mental health, social service, and legal authorities, therapeutic jurisprudence practices are comprehensive. They are also inclusive, designed to help all family members, and to keep the perpetrator, that is, the social deviant, within the family and within the community.

The Dominance of Punitive Jurisprudence

The sociolegal response to FAV throughout the 1980s and well into the 1990s in the United States can be characterized by punitive jurisprudence models that focus on perpetrators, stressing offender

arrest and punishment or incarceration. The widespread acceptance of arrest for FAV cases generated dramatic increases in the
number of cases referred for criminal prosecution (Garner, Fagan,
and Maxwell 1995; Hirschel and Buzawa 2002; Maxwell, Garner,
and Fagan 2001; Sherman et al. 1991; Sherman and Smith 1992).

No-drop prosecution policies, corresponding to mandatory arrest policies, take the discretion to prosecute an offender away
from the victim-witness (Hanna 1996). Approximately 66 percent
of the prosecutors' offices in urban jurisdictions currently claim to
maintain some form of no-drop policy for domestic violence cases
(Epstein 1999).

Proponents articulate three related justifications. First, empirical studies find that case attrition diminishes with the implementation of no-drop regulations. Second, legal practitioners contend
that victim-witnesses who are dependent financially or emotionally on their abusers are not in a position to make so-called reasonable choices. Shifting the witness burden from the victim to the
arresting police officer is the third justification. The police officer
who is empowered to be the complaining witness can give strong
testimony against an offender, precluding the need for a victim to
testify against his or her partner, while increasing the likelihood of
a criminal conviction. Such practices, however, cannot readily be
used in child abuse or elder abuse cases.

The state courts both contribute and respond to changing definitions of social problems, including FAV. Both punitive and therapeutic models of jurisprudence aim to correct the individual—whether
the individual is defined by the state to be deviant, criminal, or ill
and in need of punishment or therapy and rehabilitation. Researchers find that a therapeutic jurisprudence model, which incorporates practices based on healing and treating, appears to increase
the work of the state courts, or expand the state's level of social control activity, in response to FAV episodes (Nolan 2003).

The sociolegal movement toward therapeutic jurisprudence in
response to other social problems, which is documented by Nolan,
applies to FAV episodes as well. Punitive jurisprudence, the once-
preferred model for family violence cases, no longer dominates the
sociolegal landscape. A shift toward therapeutic justice, indicated
by the creation of dedicated family and domestic violence courts,

expands social control practices. More perpetrators, more victims, and more family members are regulated by court programs. It is possible indeed that the dominance of therapeutic jurisprudence in response to FAV will expand the boundaries of social control institutions without diminishing the problems. It does, however, represent what the general population thinks are the best means for responding to FAV episodes.

Can the United States Afford to Experiment? A Radical Proposal for Change: Intimate Abuse Circles

Since the 1960s communities throughout the United States have relied on formal institutional responses to FAV episodes. Some of the responses are determined by law and others are created within local communities. In all jurisdictions, physicians and classroom teachers must report suspected cases of child abuse. In forty-five states and the District of Columbia, physicians must report to the police any injuries they suspect have resulted from intimate partner or marital violence. Police have experimented with or tried mandatory or preferred arrest policies in intimate partner violence cases, and adult protection services have depended upon the courts to address the consequences of elder abuse. As jurisprudence models shift from a punitive to a therapeutic focus, there is no measurable indicator to suggest any decrease in the FAV cases brought into the courts throughout the United States. To the contrary, the number of FAV court cases continues to increase across all states (Jones and Keilitz 2002).

Does it seem reasonable to look outside the formal, institutional response to FAV to propose radically different ideas for how to respond to a persistent social problem? Based on what we know about perceptions within the general population, do we dare to step outside the justice system and other social institutions we have relied on thus far?

Linda Mills, a well-known scholar, social worker, and attorney, promoted her recent book *Insult to Injury* (2003) on television shows and in the print media for the purpose of communicating an innovative and perhaps even revolutionary change to how communities could respond to FAV episodes. According to her model, communities do not need to depend on police, prosecuting attorneys, or courts to respond effectively to primary and secondary victims and perpetrators. She proposes, instead, the use of an Intimate Abuse Circle (IAC), which is made up of mental health professionals, coworkers, family members, friends, and neighbors. The Intimate Abuse Circle process is proposed in lieu of a coordinated, comprehensive, criminal justice/social service response to FAV.

Relying on Intimate Abuse Circles to help families understand violence dynamics and to help them heal is a radical departure from the heavy reliance upon the law and the courts to define and respond to acts and patterns of FAV. It is a radical departure from relying upon a model of intervention that begins with a social actor reporting or discovering a case of abuse or violence. Such cases culminate with a treatment or punishment plan for perpetrators and victims, which the courts tend to legitimize. IACs take the legally defined social problem of FAV out of the public sector of society and into the private sector for treatment.

Mills's alternative proposal to meet the needs of the social actors internal to the family violence episode depend on actors external to the episode, including coworkers and neighbors. And it requires radical redefinition of the problem. The Intimate Abuse Circle, according to Mills's model, can empower and prevent FAV. The development and use of an IAC could help violent offenders and their primary and secondary victims, their adult intimate partners and their children, "have . . . the opportunity to gain insight into the violence that occurred" (2003:103).

Mills illustrates how the IAC process could work by describing a particular case with which she is familiar. In Brooklyn, unemployed Bob hit his cohabiting partner, Galla, who works as an exotic dancer, and choked her with a rope. That night, he put a gun under the pillow. The next morning he used the gun to sodomize Galla, the primary victim of FAV. Galla, while being attacked, screamed and awoke her son. Until that point, the young boy was a secondary victim of an FAV episode. When he heard the fight between Galla and Bob, he entered their bedroom. Bob threw the gun at the child, transforming the child into a primary victim. Bob was arrested after a neighbor called the police, and he was convicted of assault, sodomy, and child endangerment.

Mills writes that Bob's anger toward Galla increased dramatically because he was jailed. She argues that if, *instead of arrest, adjudication, and incarceration*, the IAC process had been initiated, "Galla and Bob, and perhaps even Galla's son, could have had the opportunity to gain insight into the violence that occurred that night and could have worked through issues of anger, responsibility, and blame more productively" (2003:103). This approach, the use of IACs, in lieu of a court-based response to domestic battery, sodomy, and child endangerment, is what can empower victims, according to Mills's model. We find this untenable.

Mills's conceptualization of a radically different method for responding to family violence needs to be examined carefully. She contends that traditional feminists do not understand that women are not necessarily the real victims. The "real" victims can be the perpetrators who had horrible childhoods: "if a grown man's violence is an expression of the helplessness he felt in childhood, it is as defensive an expression of violence as women's defensive aggression toward men" (2003:100). While childhood experiences may partly account for adult behaviors, we think an adult who commits acts of criminal violence against family members is a perpetrator and not a victim.

To begin the IAC process, an Intimate Abuse Assessment Team must be established. It consists initially of mental health professionals, but eventually the team will include neighbors, coworkers, family members, and friends. The primary role of the assessment team is to "determine the wishes of the party who filed the initial complaint" (2003:104). Its secondary responsibility is "to determine whether the violence is lethal and/or escalating" (2003:106). While we applaud thinking innovatively about responses to FAV episodes, we contend the Intimate Abuse Assessment Team can serve no purpose if the violence escalates and the victim is seriously injured or even killed. Sadly we know that thousands of women, men, and children die each year in the United States as a consequence of family abuse and violence episodes.

We know that prior acts of violence predict future acts of violence or abuse of children, adult partners, and elders. The abuse of alcohol or drugs, by the victim or the offender, unemployment, social isolation, and marital status are all possible contextual factors that predict escalating violence. Guns provide the mechanics for lethal acts of family violence. All told, it is our assessment that Linda Mills's IAC model is an interesting, provocative, and radical departure from extant practices and policies. While it may give us some important ideas to think about, it should not be used as a guide to develop alternatives to existing legal and social service responses to FAV episodes. Instead, a careful and critical analysis of all of the dimensions of FAV episodes can show communities, social change advocates, and social scientists what we need to do next in the continuous and changing struggle to respond to FAV episodes comprehensively and competently. We need to examine how beneficial or how harmful it would be to go outside the public institutional places we currently make available to respond to FAV episodes before we propose radical change. Indeed this is the message that the general population communicates when they describe to survey researchers how the government should respond to family abuse and violence episodes.

Discussion Questions

1. Why do perceptions of FAV vary across regions of the United States? Over time? Across urban and rural areas?
2. Should the U.S. government sponsor the collection of data on the family abuse and violence problem? Or should the government sponsor data collection on child abuse, intimate partner abuse, and elder abuse as distinctive social problems?

Research Project

Design a study to measure the extent to which different states (or local communities within a particular state) have adopted a therapeutic jurisprudence approach for responding to family abuse and violence problems. Compare the therapeutic jurisprudence response to FAV problems to the therapeutic jurisprudence response to drug and alcohol problems.

Notes

1. We must depend on a Canadian study because no comparable study is available for the U.S. general population.

2. These findings correspond closely to the American Medical Association's stance on family violence. Refer to the discussion in chapter 6.

V

*INTRA*GENERATIONAL FORMS OF FAMILY ABUSE AND VIOLENCE

9

Dating and Intimate Partner Abuse and Violence

The Family Abuse and Violence (FAV) Episode perspective is a conceptual framework integrating social structural characteristics with social psychological components in order to explain violence and abuse. By using multiple, distinctive dimensions of information to examine problems, the FAV framework can advance some of the persistent debates within the field of family violence. In this chapter, for example, we focus on intragenerational forms of violence and abuse, and we must address the intergenerational transmission of violence debate. Why? Because for decades, explanations of partner abuse have generally included a simplistic, determinist "violence begets violence" thesis even though most victims of child abuse or neglect do not, as adults, experience partner abuse, and most victims and perpetrators of intimate partner violence did not experience childhood violence, neglect, or abuse (Stith et al. 2000; Widom 1989).

Though the violence begets violence thesis lacks merit, it is indeed the case that children who witness adult violence and some children who are abused by their caretakers face an increased risk of experiencing dating violence and partner violence. Intuitively the violence begets violence thesis explains a social problem to the general population. Social scientists, practitioners, policymakers, and lawmakers, however, cannot rely on what are intuitively appealing but incomplete explanations. They must carefully specify the connections between childhood, adolescent, and adult relationships and how these connections can partly explain FAV episodes.

One dimension of the FAV framework—connections among social actors and groups of social actors—is particularly helpful for studying the problem of intragenerational violence and abuse. Connections among social actors and groups or organizations provide the bridges across social places and social spaces that actors enter and exit, taking with them an accumulation of experiences and observations that may result in intimate relationships characterized by abuse and violence.

By focusing on connections among social actors and groups or organizations that are external to FAV episodes, an analysis can examine how social actors engage in a continuous and cumulative process of learning cultural scripts, social norms, values, and meanings that affect gender identities and gender roles. The gender roles and identities that girls and boys take from their families of origin and into their school settings may be challenged or reinforced by social actors outside the home. Some actors in the school setting are authority figures, such as teachers or school administrators. They are like parents whose lessons can be internalized, modeled, or rejected. Other school actors are peers, including close friends as well as classmates or schoolmates, who may be observed—even idealized—but not known or understood.

Childhood and adolescent peers and peer groups are important resources for shaping or challenging identities and social roles that affect adult social relationships. Gary Alan Fine contends, "Adolescence is surely the most sociologically compelling moment of the life course. During these years the nexus of community, institution, and self becomes simultaneously powerful and precarious" (2004:1). His observational study of high school students is premised on the idea that self-images are linked to three sources: impulse, connections to core social institutions, and connections to peer groups.

We use Fine's thesis and argue that adolescents and teens come into school spaces with a guidebook, which consists of the norms, values, and gender scripts they learn from parents, caretakers, and other family members. In school, maps and directions are added to the guidebook, which help the social actor navigate among places and spaces she or he chooses to explore. The guidebook is not deterministic. While it contains family lessons, it also contains conflicting lessons learned from other social places. It may suggest to an adolescent that physical violence is the appropriate response to frustration or jealousy. Or it may suggest that aggression and violence result in harm and injury that need to be avoided. The guidebook shows the adolescent more than one path to take as he or she makes transitions from childhood to young adulthood. One important task the guidebook addresses is the development of intimate partnerships that can culminate in marriage or some other ritual or ceremony that initiates the formation of one's own family.[1]

We contend that a sufficient explanation of intimate partner violence, or an intragenerational form of an FAV episode, must account for how some adolescents and young adults accumulate experiences, gender scripts, and normative expectations that include violence and abuse in their early romantic relationships.

We define intragenerational family violence episodes as those characterized by perpetrators and victims of the same generation that can be a result of opportunity structures, motivations, levels of vulnerability, and levels of the social actors' subjective and objective power within interpersonal relationships. *Intra*generational violence takes place in private social spaces that can shield perpetrators from social actors external to the episode. The violence or abuse can alternatively occur in more public spaces and places, which can facilitate a response from other social actors and organizations.

Our analyses of dating violence and abuse studies are based on the important premise that in the United States, the normative expectation is for adolescent girls and boys to begin a process of rehearsing intimate partner relationships. Further, we argue that if intergenerational forms of family violence partly explain intragenerational forms, the researcher must specify the social processes that affect social actors at various developmental stages. Said differently, we think it is as important to look at how interpersonal violence is learned in places and spaces outside the family as it is to look at how violence is learned within the family.

Schools and Families: Places for Social Learning

The typical middle school in the United States sponsors dances and other gatherings that help adolescents initiate and imitate social interaction between candidates for intimate partners, a type of social interaction that is repeated throughout most of life's stages. Adolescent social actors go to the middle school dance and preview models for how to be a boyfriend or a husband, or a girlfriend or a wife, through learning how to "go with" someone, which begins the dating process.

If adolescent boys or girls live in two-parent or caretaker households, they are likely to observe and learn to replicate some of the behaviors that men and women engage in with their partners. Boys may observe the ways adult men and women show affection for each other and they may observe how men and women in their homes argue and fight. Without paying deliberate attention to behavioral patterns, boys and girls may internalize the moves for a subtle dance of control: If she moves toward a job that he does not want her to pursue, he embraces a job for himself that will require relocation, making her job prospects dim. If he brushes against her preference for a family meal each evening, she draws him closer with the promise of a glass of wine and some quiet time before dinner. The dance of control, of course, can be crude and ugly. She cries and raises her voice when he comes home later than planned. He insists that she not work outside the home. He impulsively strikes her emotionally or physically when dinner is not served on time. She belittles him in front of neighbors and friends.

Without recognizing what they are learning, boys and girls observe and internalize mechanics for feeling and expressing emotions, such as jealousy, disappointment, or sadness. They can perceive that an adult may believe an aspirin or a drink or a gift or even a therapist can help fix things that go wrong in an intimate relationship.

Girls and boys see up close what occurs within their own families and households, and they hear about what supposedly happens in their friends' households. With friends, siblings, other family members, or even alone, they consume movies, computer games, and television shows, cultural products that depict endlessly varied intimate relationships—limited only by the collective imaginations of those in the media. How adolescents internalize normative standards and idealized models for dating and mating is a wonderfully rich research subject. Unfortunately, the process of learning to date and mate also includes many harmful and hurtful lessons, and we address some of these in order to comprehensively understand the social problem of intragenerational family violence episodes.

Dating Violence

In 2003 a state supreme court ruled that boyfriend/girlfriend relationships are not covered by domestic violence protection orders (Wolfe 2003). Intimate partners must at least cohabit to be protected by state laws intended to guard citizens from domestic violence. While state and federal governments have enacted laws and created programs designed to respond to FAV, there is no corresponding law across the states to protect younger intimates who reside in separate households. Yet, there are well-designed and well-executed empirical studies that document an intimate partner violence problem within this demographic.

The Massachusetts Youth Risk Behavior Survey asked 4,163 teenagers, in grades nine through twelve, if they had "ever been hurt physically or sexually by a date or someone they were going out with." Approximately 20 percent of the girls disclosed that their dating partners had either physically or sexually abused them. Six percent of the teen girls said they had experienced both physical and sexual abuse by their dating partners (Buel 2002). As a consequence, researchers argued, the girls faced an increased risk of drug abuse, unhealthy weight control behavior, sexually risky behavior, and suicidal tendencies (Silverman et al. 2001).

The second wave of what is known as the Add Health Project[2] (the National Longitudinal Study of Adolescent Health) generated the largest and most representative national survey of abuse occurring within dating relationships (Cleveland, Herrera, and Stuewig 2003). Among the nearly 7,000 adolescents and teens enrolled in junior or senior high school who disclosed opposite-sex dating relationships, one-third reported some form of dating abuse, which was relatively broadly defined, and 12 percent reported physical violence by their dating partners (Hagan and Foster 2001; Halpern et al. 2001). Older respondents with more dating experiences had an increased risk of victimization, yet no age group escaped the negative consequences associated with dating violence, such as suicidal thoughts, lower emotional well-being, and depression (Ackard and Neumark-Sztainer 2002; Roberts and Klein 2003; Roberts, Klein, and Fisher 2003).

While the social science community documented the problem, the American Psychological Association (APA) took action to communicate the importance of the dating violence problem in the United States. The APA hosts a website called Teen Choices in consultation with representatives from the American Dietetic Association, American Medical Association, National Association of Social Workers, and the American Bar Association's Center on Children and the Law and Commission on Domestic Violence. Its first message is

> Believe It—It's Happening! Nearly one in 10 high school students will experience physical violence from someone they're going with. Even more teens will experience verbal or emotional abuse during the relationship.

The APA web page goes on to report

- Dating violence generally leads to marital violence.
- More than 90 percent of the injuries in dating violence happen to the woman in the relationship.
- Thirty-one percent of teen girls who report being forced to have sex identify their boyfriends as the perpetrators (APA 2004).

Empirical studies measuring the multiple influences of families and peers report that experiencing child abuse may or may not be a good predictor of students' dating-violence experiences. When comparing a Child Protective Services (CPS) sample to a high school sample of mid-adolescents, researchers found that CPS girls who label themselves as having experienced child abuse are more likely than girls in the general population to report they have experienced dating violence (Wekerle et al. 2001). Though intergenerational child abuse is found to be correlated with dating violence, most analysts recognize that the majority of perpetrators of adolescent or young adult violence did *not* experience intergenerational child abuse (Simons, Lin, and Gordon 1998; Smith and Williams 1992). It is possible, however, that the emotional and physical aggression inflicted by siblings or peers (intragenerational aggression) increases the likelihood of experiencing dating violence (Carr and VanDeusen 2002; Noland et al. 2004; Simonelli et al. 2002). It is, therefore, likely that an *intra*generational transmission of violence is at work among adolescents.

Adolescence includes the normative task of developing romantic relationships. Preteens—who are frequently identified as "tweens" to indicate the stage between childhood and the teenage years—and young teens lack the requisite social and emotional skill to maintain ongoing intimate relationships. Instead they experience "going-with" relationships that tend to be short-term. "Going with" someone is characterized by expectations for, but not the realization of, emotional intimacy (Merton 1996). Tweens and teens in "going-with" relationships tend to avoid disclosing their thoughts and feelings to their idealized boyfriend or girlfriend. The purpose for keeping feelings from the admired other is to present the self in ways that are designed to please or appeal to the other. Only with experience do tweens and teens develop the skill to initiate and sustain emotional intimacy in romantic relationships. The learning process itself can cause conflicts with friends or within friendship networks (Gembeck 1999), which sets the stage for the social isolation that dating violence victims tend to experience.

To whom does a girl turn, once she has started "going with" a boy or once she has a boyfriend who abuses her, if she is not confident that her friends will be supportive or that her parent or caretaker will understand? If she is concerned over the possibility of retaliatory violence, she will most likely avoid disclosing the violence or the abuse to friends, school personnel, or her family. Most victims tell no one (Bergman 1992), but researchers observe some variation by race and ethnicity. In one study of African American middle school students, researchers found that girls, who were far more likely than boys to experience dating violence, tended to turn to their friends for help; if boys perceived they were victims, they were more likely to turn to friends or to parents (Black and Weisz 2003).

Dating violence victims who approach the medical or legal arena for resolution or protection typically find little to no assistance in navigating what is for most teens and young adults a complex and confusing system (Goodmark and Klein 2004). A study of tenth-grade girls in New York State concludes that the Internet, rather than school officials or the doctor's office, can be the resource of choice for girls experiencing dating violence (Borzekowski and Rickert 2001).

Serious dating is the formation of intimate and exclusive relationships that launch the process of courtship, which is intended to culminate in marriage or cohabitation. According to most social scientists, this begins in high school. Thus, until this decade, most dating-violence research focused on high school or college-age social actors. It is not unusual, however, to see social events in middle school that mimic high school rituals and events and invite boys and girls to begin going with each other. It is here, in middle school, where friends and peers have a strong influence over the girls and boys who are or will become victims or perpetrators of dating violence (Arriaga and Foshee 2004; Bailey and Whittle 2004). A literature review of the published empirical studies identified the assumption that violence begins in high school as a clear limitation of many dating-violence studies (Lewis and Fremouw 2001).

Middle school, high school, and college students "try out" and "try on" many social statuses or social roles, only to discard most of them, but they retain a selection of their more successful social roles into young adulthood. A middle school girl wants the dress or the outfit for the school dance that will elicit approval from her girlfriends while it signals her attractiveness to the boys. A high school student joins a math club, not only to make friends with others with similar interests, but also to scrutinize potential occupational aspirations. College students select majors, join campus organizations, volunteer in their local community, engage in risk-taking behaviors, and pursue avenues for autonomy and independence. Beginning in middle school for some, and for others not beginning until college, most students pursue romance, companionship, sexual fulfillment, and potential life partners.

If interpersonal aggression and violence are socially learned behaviors, as Bandura and his colleagues (Bandura 1973) convincingly demonstrate, it is necessary to understand the implications of dating violence for the abuse and violence that occur within adult intimate relationships. It is imperative to understand how violence and aggression within all types of intimate or dating relationships are learned through observing friends and peer networks.

Dating violence includes acts of physical, emotional, and sexual aggression that can occur when adolescents begin going with each other. Friends, peer networks, and family members, who interact at home, in school, and within other social arenas, are sources for learning aggressive and violent behaviors. They also can be important resources for protecting social actors against the harm and injury associated with dating violence.

Known Estimates and Correlates of Dating Violence

In 1981, James Makepeace reported empirical findings from a seven-college survey of dating violence. Until he published his study, researchers depended on generalizations from child abuse or marital violence surveys to estimate the prevalence of dating violence and its correlates. Since the mid-1980s, however, nearly two hundred empirical studies of dating violence have appeared in the social science literature. Most depend on voluntary or convenience samples of high school or college students who self-report victimization or perpetration experiences. Clusters of studies are based on statewide or nationwide public health initiatives, such as the Add Health Survey, that represent adolescents or young adults within a general population. A very small number of studies include middle school students. Qualitative studies are outnumbered by quantitative studies, but they provide rich descriptions of relevant issues, such as the process that dating-violence victims engage in to sever intimate relationships to re-establish a sense of self and a network of supportive friends.

Is dating violence a major social problem or an infrequently occurring deviant behavior? Critiquing the prevalence data is problematic for several reasons. The numerous definitions of the problem and variations in sampling design and methods of data collection are likely to account for most of the variation in prevalence estimates. Nonetheless we can summarize the principal findings. A Minnesota survey estimates that 9 percent of girls and 6 percent of boys report date violence or rape (Ackard and Neumark-Sztainer 2002). A Massachusetts public health survey estimates that approximately 20 percent of high school–aged girls were either physically or sexually abused by dating partners (Silverman et al. 2001). The Add Health Survey of U.S. adolescents reports that 22.1 percent of girls and 21 percent of boys report being insulted in public, sworn at, threatened with violence, having something thrown at them, or being pushed or shoved by a dating partner (Roberts and Klein 2003). Prevalence estimates, therefore, range from 9 to 22 percent of teens who experience some form of verbal, physical, or sexual abuse within dating or dating-type relationships.

Except for the Add Health Survey, most dating-violence studies find that girls or young women are far more likely to be the victims of dating violence. Girls also are more likely to experience physical injuries as a consequence of dating violence. Whereas boys may be as likely as girls to be the victims of public insults, girls are many times more likely to experience sexual assault, rape, or physical assault (Buel 2002; Lewis and Fremouw 2001; Silverman et al. 2001). Fineran and Bennett (1999) find that 70 percent of high school victims of sexual assault or severe physical assault by their partners are girls.

Miller and White's (2003) study of African American dating-violence victims offers an important caution when interpreting findings that examine race and ethnicity differences. Their empirical observations focused on adolescents residing in a distressed neighborhood, and they argue race *cannot* be viewed as a personal characteristic that explains victimization experiences; poverty concentration within urban areas is a far more valid predictor of violence victimization than an individual's race. Sanderson et al. (2004) make a similar and important point regarding ethnicity.

They demonstrate that an acculturation process, not an individual's ethnicity, is a likely explanation of any variation in dating violence that may be empirically observed or counted. They studied ethnic identity as well as acculturation in a sample of Hispanic ninth graders from the Texas Lower Rio Grande Valley. They found female high school students whose parents were born outside the United States enjoyed a *reduced* risk of dating-violence victimization. Sanderson et al. conclude that greater acculturation, becoming "more American," is correlated with a higher prevalence of dating-violence victimization.

Drug use or alcohol abuse and other risk-taking behaviors, especially driving under the influence of alcohol or not engaging in safe-sex practices, are consistently found to be strong correlates of dating violence. These often-documented correlations are explained with a social control perspective that posits adolescents with weaker social ties are more likely to engage in risky behaviors (Gover 2004; Wingood et al. 2001). Contrary to intuition, which posits a relationship between urban living and urban violence, the Teen Assessment Project, which compared rural to suburban high school students, finds that students in rural school districts are more likely than urban students to perpetrate acts of dating violence (Spencer and Bryant 2000). These studies highlight the need to study the mechanics and the opportunity structures for FAV episodes.

While many studies have identified potential antecedents and correlates of dating violence, studies that attempt to explain the abuse or violence within ongoing and committed relationships are less common. One study, based on a mixed-method approach, explains that dimensions of a victim's social network, especially being able to count on a supportive response, can encourage young women to disclose problems and seek appropriate remedies (Mahlstedt and Keeny 1993). A study of college students found that satisfaction with relationship power, rather than the relative power that each partner actually experiences, explains the controlling violence that men perpetrate against women (Ronfeldt, Kimerling, and Arias 1998). The FAV Episode framework brings together these two important dimensions—subjectively experienced power and connections among social actors—in its explanation of *intra*generational abuse and violence.

We recognize many issues surrounding dating violence still need careful study and analysis. However, researchers have convincingly demonstrated several points:

1. Adolescents and young adults in predating and dating relationships experience abuse and violence, including emotional and psychological abuse, physical assaults, and sexual assaults.
2. Girls and young women tend to be the victims of the more serious forms of physical violence and sexual violence. Boys and young men are as likely as girls and young women to experience verbal and emotional or psychological abuse within dating relationships.
3. Substance abuse and other risky behaviors increase the likelihood of perpetrating dating violence.
4. Perceptions of power within the relationship can affect the risk of perpetrating or experiencing dating violence.
5. Social structural and cultural factors, such as the concentration of poverty in urban neighborhoods and the acculturation of ethnic group members, are better predictors of dating violence than are personal characteristics.
6. Social learning processes that begin when adolescents form going-with and dating relationships, along with family experiences, explain dating violence.

We are less certain about the root causes of dating violence, but we do contend that both *inter-* and *intra*generational explanations are tenable. While they warrant further investigation, we posit that cultural factors, social learning, social control, and gendered expectations within intimate relationships provide reasonable but incomplete explanations for dating violence. Table 9.1 summarizes a social learning model of dating violence that represents an integration of the existing studies, the learning process, and dimensions of the FAV Episode framework.

The table highlights the social places and spaces where dating violence can be learned through the processes of witnessing and modeling other social actors' behaviors. School and family are the most influential places for adolescents to learn from authority fig-

Table 9.1.   A Dating Violence Model: A Social Learning Component of the FAV Episode

Learning Places and Spaces	Teachers and Models	What Can Be Learned
Family	Authority	Gender: roles, scripts, and expectations
School	Authority, Peer	Hurting: learn to hurt and learn to be hurt
Other Places	Peer	Behaviors: physical and psychological aggression Emotions: jealousy, sadness, disappointment, satisfaction Power and Control

ures (such as parents or teachers) and to learn from their peers and peer networks. They are, of course, not the only places where social actors can observe and internalize the behavioral and emotional components of dating violence. Places of worship, work places, and recreational spaces and places can provide models of intimacy and caring as well as models of control and aggression. Social actors who approach dating and intimacy are continuously learning gender scripts, which include how to express the self, gender roles, and gendered expectations for behaviors, emotions, and attitudes.

Learned emotions, such as jealousy, sadness, loneliness, or insecurity, are the motivations for FAV episodes that can encourage abuse within dating relationships. Adolescent social actors can learn how to hurt the other or how to be hurt. While physically or psychologically aggressive behaviors are more apparent for the adolescent learner to observe, the more subtle control and power that a dating or intimate partner exercises over the other are potentially just as important. Learned behaviors can initiate and sustain abuse and violence among vulnerable middle school, high school, and young adult daters.

Adult Intimate Partner Violence

The social problem of marital or intimate partner violence has been the focus of intensive research in the United States since the 1970s. How much intimate partner violence affects women and men in the United States? Richard Gelles, unmistakably one of the nation's pioneers and leaders in the field, recognizes "there are yet no national surveys of reported spouse abuse that collect state data in the same manner that child maltreatment report data have been analyzed and collected; thus, most of the data on the extent of violence toward women and between partners come from self-report surveys" (2003:844). To estimate and explain the social problem of intimate partner violence in the United States, researchers need to consider data generated by three very different types of self-report social surveys.

The key self-report national surveys are

- The National Family Violence Surveys initiated by Murray Straus and his colleagues, which use the Conflict Tactics Scale.
- The U.S. Department of Justice's annual National Crime Victimization Survey.
- The National Violence Against Women Survey.[3]

The surveys, in principle, measure similar constructs and thus ought to generate similar prevalence estimates. Empirically, however, they generate substantial differences.

These self-report surveys all intend to represent the non-institutionalized, adult population of the United States. They depend on very large and therefore adequate sample sizes to guarantee the general population sampling design will capture a sufficient number of victims and perpetrators. Though FAV is a persistent and serious social problem, the number of victims or perpetrators, relative to the number of adults who get married or decide to live together each year, is very small. Consider, for example, a representative sample of 500 couples who intend to purchase new homes within the upcoming year. The sample size would be adequate for estimating the brands of new appliance purchases on the assumption that most if not all of the couples are likely to acquire new items for their homes. The same sample would not, however, be adequate to study couples that experience intimate partner violence or domestic violence. It is possible that the representative sample of couples would not include any social actors who perpetrated or were victimized by intimate partner violence.

The three self-report surveys that we focus on have different purposes. Thus they use different sampling designs, but large sample sizes, to represent men and women in the United States. They ask participants different questions, and the questions that are asked are contextualized differently within the larger research instrument. Before analyzing what the self-report surveys uncover regarding intragenerational forms of FAV, it is important to examine the purpose and context of each survey.

The national self-report surveys conducted by Murray Straus and his colleagues, called the National Family Violence Surveys (NFVS), are designed to measure family conflict and violence. Gelles, as Straus does, defines violence as "an act carried out with the intention or perceived intention of physically hurting another person. The 'hurt' can range from the slight pain caused by a slap or a spanking to harm that results in severe injury or even death" (Gelles 1992). The surveys designed to measure family violence distinguish kin relationships (pairs of social actors related by birth or marriage), intimate relationships (such as dating partners), and domestic relationships (people who live within the same household). Kin, intimate, and domestic relationships are the subjects of the National Family Violence Surveys.

For the initial NFVS, 2,143 households were surveyed. One adult from each household was interviewed. For the resurvey in 1985, 6,002 households were surveyed. The instrument used to measure family violence, called the Conflict Tactics Scale (CTS or its revised version, CTS 2), is discussed in detail in chapter 2. The revised version of the scale includes thirty-nine distinctive events that the respondent could have perpetrated or experienced. The CTS 2 items measure assaults, injuries, acts of psychological aggression, and acts of sexual coercion. Researchers can combine items into scales that vary along the dimension of severity. The CTS-based National Family Violence Survey takes a snapshot of all of the violence that was committed or experienced by couples within a one-year time frame.

The NCVS has been conducted[4] for the U.S. Bureau of Justice Statistics since 1973. Its original purpose was to fill in the gaps left by the Uniform Crime Reporting (UCR) system to allow the Federal Bureau of Investigation to compile personal-violent and property crime rates across jurisdictions and over time. Researchers found that the UCR[5] data underestimate the number of criminal events that occur throughout the United States because most victims do not report events to the police, which is the local organization that submits crime data to the UCR. Moreover, the UCR data are, by design, focused on crimes and perpetrators. They are not intended to generate information on how victims are injured by or recover from criminal events.

NCVS data are collected from 45,000 U.S. households[6] every six months. A sampled household is asked to complete an initial interview and remains in the sampling frame for three years. Respondents are asked through a series of screening questions to disclose criminal victimization experiences that occurred within the past six months. For each criminal event disclosed, the interviewer completes an incident report, which includes detailed information about the crime, the offender, the victim-offender relationship, consequences for the victim, and whether or not the crime was reported to police. Each incident report can take more than ten minutes to complete.

Classification of the criminal event, based on the information in the incident reports, is completed after the interview by NCVS staff. The staff classifies an incident as intimate partner violence if a violent crime (rape or sexual assault, robbery, simple assault, or aggravated assault) was committed by a current or ex-spouse or boyfriend or girlfriend. The NCVS, compared to the other two types of self-report surveys, in principle measures the most serious or injurious events. Thus, when comparing across surveys, the researcher expects to find that NCVS data will produce the lowest estimates of intimate partner violence that occur in the United States. The NCVS measures what the government defines as criminal events, and not what the victim defines as a victimization experience.

The third self-report survey, the National Violence Against Women Survey (NVAW), was conducted to obtain baseline measures of personal safety and the violence that affects women in the United States. The survey, sponsored by the Centers for Disease Control and the Department of Justice, was a result of the federal Violence Against Women Act passed in 1994. The NVAW survey (also known as the VAWM survey) is somewhat like the National Crime Victimization Survey in its approach to measuring detailed victimization experiences. Respondents answered a series of screening questions to determine if they had experienced any physical assault, rape or sexual assault, or stalking event within the past year. If any victimization was experienced, the researcher asked detailed follow-up questions to measure the victim-offender relationship, the number of times the respondent was victimized, and the physical, emotional, and social consequences of the experience.

The NVAW survey is the only self-report survey that measures stalking. Compared to the NFVS, the NVAW survey data should (and do) produce lower estimates of the prevalence and incidence of intimate partner violence—intragenerational FAV episodes. The lower estimates are expected because of the contextual and methodological differences in the surveys. They ask different questions, under different circumstances, and for different purposes. The NVAW survey should, on the other hand, be expected to produce *higher* estimates than those resulting from crime victimization surveys. The NCVS measures criminal events, not events defined by victims to be abusive. Together the three types of national surveys can be examined to estimate with relative accuracy how much violence affects women and men within their intimate or married partnerships.

Table 9.2, adapted from a National Institute of Justice Brief on Violence Against Women (Ford et al. 2002), summarizes the differences in the three surveys that influence variations in the estimates of intimate partner violence.

The data shown in table 9.2, pertaining to women only,[7] highlight some findings that result from the three surveys. These data are annual prevalence estimates of the number of women, age 18 and over, who disclosed that their partners, albeit defined differently by the different surveys, perpetrated intimate partner violence

Table 9.2. Differences in National Self-Report Surveys of Intimate Partner Violence

Survey Characteristic	NFVS	NCVS	NVAW
Sample	8,145 total 1975 and 1985	45,000 twice a year, 3 years	8,000 women 8,000 men 1995–1996
Relationship	Current Partner	Friends or Family Members	Current or Ex-Partner or Spouse
Stalking Measured?	No	No	Yes
Survey Context	Family Conflict	Victimization Survey	Personal Safety
Relative Estimates[a]	Highest	Lowest	Higher than NCVS, Lower than NFVS

[a] The relative estimates are based on our own analysis and not the Ford et al. (2002) report.

Table 9.3. Prevalence of FAV Episodes Perpetrated against Women per 1,000
Adult Women in the United States

SURVEY	Minor Violence[a]	Severe Violence[b]	Physical Violence	Physical Violence, Stalking, or Rape
1975 NFVS	100	38	—	—
1985 NFVS	80	34	—	—
1998 NCVS	—	—	13	18
1996 NVAW	—	—	7.7	—

Source: Gelles et al. 2003.
[a]Threw object, pushed, or slapped.
[b]Kicked/bit/hit or tried to hit w/object, beat up, threatened, or used weapon.

against them within twelve months of the interview or survey. Because a large number of the victims are likely to have experienced more than a single event or episode of intimate partner violence, the prevalence estimates derived from the self-report studies are considerably lower than what the estimates of incidents would be.

When comparing across time and across national surveys we can conclude that at least 8 women per 1,000 within the general population are victimized by events that the state would consider criminal. At least 13 women per 1,000 experience physical assaults; and approximately 18 per 1,000 women experience rape, physical assault, or stalking by their marital or cohabiting partners. In 1975, 100 women per 1,000 women in the general population experienced a "minor" form of assault or physical violence. By 1985 the number dropped to 80 out of 1,000 women. In 1975, 38 women per 1,000 women in the general population had experienced "severe violence." That prevalence level dropped only slightly to 34 women per 1,000 women in 1985.

The differences shown in table 9.3 suggest the prevalence of intimate partner violence has decreased in recent decades. The differences may be largely attributable to the methodological differences in the surveys. They may also be a consequence of a number of social factors, including the aging of the general population, the success of the battered women's movement, the changing socioeconomic circumstances of the United States, and the implementation of federal and state laws that criminalize FAV episodes. One troubling finding is the stability of "severe violence" against women by their intimate partners across time. "Severe violence" apparently did not decrease as much as "minor violence."

Recurring Violence

Rand and Saltzman designed a study aggregating eight years of National Crime Victimization Survey data (1992–1999) to examine how recurring and criminal intimate partner violence compares to single events. The events include aggravated and simple assaults, robbery, rape, and sexual assault. Rand and Saltzman report that on average, 639,000 intimate partner criminal events occur each year in the United States. They also find that 87 percent of recurring victims are women (Rand and Saltzman 2003).

Among the victims who experienced any form of intimate partner violence, 72 percent reported a single event within the six-month time frame measured by the victimization surveys. Nineteen percent reported between two and five events, 7 percent reported between six and twenty events and 2 percent of the crime victims reported more than twenty criminal intimate partner violence events within the recent six months. Sixty-eight percent of the events are assaults, but 16 percent are aggravated assaults, 7 percent are robberies, and 9 percent are rapes or sexual assaults by intimate partners.

It is the rape victims of intimate partner violence who are most likely to experience recurring events. Approximately 40 percent of the rape victims were raped more than once by their intimate partners within a six-month period of time. Rand and Saltzman found that victims of recurring intimate partner violence were significantly less likely to report the events to the police compared to the victims who experienced a single criminal event. There is, however, no difference in the percentage of victims who sustained physical injuries. Approximately half of all of the victims were injured physically.

Generally, when researchers are conducting NCVS interviews, they prepare a separate incident report for each distinctive criminal event a victim discloses. However, when someone discloses multiple victimizations that are similar or the same type of offense, the interviewer uses a "series protocol" to record the victimization experiences, because their recurring nature makes accurate recall of the details of the separate crimes difficult. Looking specifically at the 11 percent of intimate partner violence series victimizations found in the 1992–1999 victimization surveys, Rand and Saltzman found that in 99 percent of the cases, the victim reports the *same* offender committed the crimes, and in 51 percent of the cases, the criminal events occurred in the *same* place. The Rand and Saltzman study identifies two distinctive patterns:

1. A small number of women in the United States are the victims of recurring violence that is more likely to be a form of rape or sexual assault than simple assault.
2. Some victims are hurt repeatedly by the same perpetrators and they are usually victimized in the same social places.

An Empirical Typology Based on NVAW Survey

Family violence researchers argue that typologies of FAV episodes are useful for distinguishing among the different victimization experiences that tend to affect men and women. The National Violence Against Women Survey (NVAW) finds that women are three times more likely than men to be the victims of physical violence within their intimate relationships, but they are twenty-five times more likely to be the victims of rape or sexual assault by their partners. In the following section we take a detailed look at the National Violence Against Women Survey for the purpose of complementing the Rand and Saltzman study. Instead of observing differences between victims who experience single or repeated events, we focus on developing a typology to distinguish FAV victims who experience one type of event from those who experience two or three types of FAV episodes. The NVAW survey is the most appropriate for our purposes because it measures the prevalence of marital or partner rape. It also measures stalking, which is a type of FAV episode that is not measured by any of the other national self-report surveys.

A Profile of Respondents

The youngest women who participated in the NVAW survey are 18, and the average age is 44 years old. Nearly 10 percent of the women are African American and nearly 8 percent are Hispanic. Fifty-seven percent are married and 12 percent are divorced; 1 percent report ongoing or prior cohabiting, lesbian relationships. Typically, the women live in households with one child under age 18.

Most women (55.7 percent of the sample) have completed at least some post–high school years of formal education. Forty-six percent are employed full time and 12.5 percent are employed part time. Only 3.5 percent of the women indicated they were unemployed at the time they were interviewed.[8]

A number of women report some form of excessive or abusive control by their partners. Jealousy, shouting and swearing, and a partner insisting on knowing the woman's whereabouts at all times are among the most common forms of controlling behaviors or motivations for FAV episodes. In addition, nearly 4 percent of the women reported that their partners had threatened to kill or harm them.

The survey asked about childhood physical violence, including pushing, shoving, and slapping, that was perpetrated by parents or caretakers.[9] Nearly 40 percent of the women disclosed they had experienced some form of physical aggression (not necessarily abuse or violence) during childhood.

Types of Family Abuse and Violence Episodes

Table 9.4 shows the types of FAV episodes women report. Stalking, physical assault, and rape are the three unidimensional types that we examine. We then construct the typology by looking at the co-occurring types of violence that the women disclosed.

We find 18.9 percent of the women in the general population indicated they have experienced acts of physical assault that were perpetrated by their partners. This prevalence estimate corresponds to findings from studies that are based on general popula-

Table 9.4.   Four Types of Violence Reported by Women in the General Population

Type of Violence Reported	Number of Women Who Reported Physical Violence or Abuse	Percent of Women Who Reported Violence or Abuse
1. Physical Assault (1–12 Different Forms of Physical Violence) by Partner or Ex-Partner	1,512	18.90% of 8,000 Women
2. Physically Assaulted and Raped by Partner or Ex-Partner	468	31.0% of 1,512 Assaulted Women or 5.9% of 8,000 Women
3. Physically Assaulted and Stalked by Partner or Ex-Partner	351	23.2% of 1,512 Assaulted Women or 4.4% of 8,000 Women
4. Physically Assaulted, Raped, and Stalked by Partner or Ex-Partner	171	11.3% of 1,512 Assaulted Women or 2.1% of 8,000 Women

Note: Most women who disclose FAV episodes report that they experienced more than one type. A total of 864 women disclosed physical assaults and no other type. A total of 495 women disclosed rape by their current or ex-partner and no other type of violence. A total of 220 women disclosed stalking by a current or ex-partner and no other type of FAV episode.

tion samples (Abbott et al. 1995; Alpert et al. 2002; Brownridge and Halli 1999; Plichta and Falik 2001).

Among the women who experienced assaults, 31 percent also were raped by a current or ex-partner or spouse. The women represent 5.9 percent of the 8,000 women who participated in the NVAW survey. There is a statistically significant empirical association between experiencing physical assault and rape ($\chi^2 = 527.76$, df = 1, p < .001). These data show that if a woman is assaulted, she faces an increased risk of also being raped by a partner or spouse.[10] The prevalence estimates are comparable to the estimates of completed rape that were reported by the National Women's Study

(NWS). Data from NWS, based on a probability sample of 4,008 women over age 18, do not include "attempted rape" (Kilpatrick et al. 1988; Kilpatrick et al. 1992). Thus, these NVAW-based estimates should be interpreted as conservative estimates.

The data from the NVAW survey also show a strong association between physical assault and stalking (χ^2= 566.92, df = 1, p < .001). Among the women who experienced assaults by their partners or spouses, 23.2 percent also disclosed that they had been stalked.[11] There is a small but known percentage of women in the general population (2.1 percent) who have experienced all the forms of FAV that were measured by the survey, that is, physical assaults, stalking, and rape.

The distribution of the distinctive types of FAV reported by the women who participated in the survey show a strong "reverse J curve" distribution, which corresponds very closely to epidemiological studies of the severity of aggressive intimate partner behavior. As Gordon reports: "(a) a relatively high proportion of individuals in the general population engage in infrequent acts of physical aggression of relatively minor severity; and (b) a relatively small proportion of the population is responsible for serious and frequent aggressive behavior" (2000:752).

Data from NVAW respondents suggest

1. A high proportion of women in the general population, approximately 80 percent, do not report any type of family abuse or violence episode.
2. However, nearly 20 percent have experienced physical assaults during a marriage or cohabiting relationship.
3. Women in the general population who experience a physical assault by their husbands or partners face a known increased risk of being raped, stalked, or being raped and stalked by their current or ex-partners or spouses.

Explaining Types or Levels of FAV Episodes

The FAV Episode perspective indicates that intragenerational and intergenerational processes explain the types of violence women

Table 9.5. Levels of Family Abuse and Violence Reported by Women: Explained by Childhood Violence, Threats, and Abusive Control

Independent Variable	b (s.e.) β
Childhood Violence Experienced (7 item scale, α = .83)	.065 (.004) .142***
Partner Threatened to Kill or Harm (Yes/No)	.367 (.034) .100***
Partner Control Scale (13-Item Scale, α = .92)	.121 (.002) .528***
Intercept	−.022 (.008)
Adj. R²	.367***
(F Value)	(1515.233)
M (s.d.)	.368 (.907)
N	7,841

Note: Level of FAV is measured on a five-point scale; 0 = no violence reported, 1 = physical assault, 2 = physical assault and rape, 3 = physical assault, stalking, 4 = physical assault, stalking, and rape. Childhood violence is a scale of seven items. The partner control scale is a sum of 13 items. Both scales have high reliability coefficients.
*** p < .001

experience. To examine this pattern empirically, we constructed a five-point measure of the types of FAV women reported to NVAW researchers. The measure ranges from zero (indicating no FAV) to four (indicating a woman was the victim of assault and rape and stalking by her partner). We regressed the measure of FAV levels on three indicators: the woman's reports of childhood aggression, if the woman's partner threatened to hurt or kill her, and the level of control the woman's partner exercises over her within their relationship. Table 9.5 summarizes the regression analysis.

The data shown in table 9.5 indicate that among the women who reported FAV, those women who experienced more childhood aggression are more likely to have experienced more than one form of FAV. If a woman was threatened by her partner, she is more likely to experience multiple forms, that is, higher levels of FAV. Arguably the strongest predictor is the partner control scale. The more controlling the woman's partner is, which is a key motivation for FAV, the more likely she is to be the victim of stalking, and physical assault and rape by her intimate partner or her ex-intimate partner. This regression analysis neither refutes nor supports the "violence begets violence" thesis. What it shows clearly is the importance of examining simultaneously how *inter-* and *intragen*erational abuse or aggression can explain the FAV episodes that victimize women in the United States.

Although we do not show the findings in table form, we controlled for the women's personal characteristics of race and age and found they are not significantly associated with the levels of FAV. A woman's educational level does appear to protect her against experiencing multiple forms of FAV, but employment status does not.

The women who experience the highest levels of FAV—assault and rape, assault and stalking, or assault, stalking, and rape—and the women who experience recurring, criminal abuse and violence ought to be able to count on formal social and legal responses to family abuse and violence episodes. Criminal justice and social services are necessary to protect families and punish perpetrators. Moreover, victims of recurring or multiple forms of FAV ought to be able to depend on comprehensive community responses to meet their needs as primary victims and to meet the needs of other family members who are secondary victims of FAV episodes. Women who experience recurring violence or multiple forms of violence face the highest risks of injury, of losing their jobs and their children as a consequence of family abuse and violence, and they face the highest risk of experiencing an escalation in violence that can indeed be lethal.

Discussion Questions

1. What do you think high schools should do to prevent physical and sexual dating violence and abuse? Why should prevention programs be targeted at girls and boys together? Or why should the programs be designed for boys and girls separately? What community response would you predict for a public high school program that aims to prevent dating violence among same-sex couples?

2. How is the risk of perpetrating acts of intimate partner violence as an adult increased by witnessing violence as a child? How are inter- and intragenerational forms of family abuse and violence linked? Are they linked differently across the genders?

Research Projects

1. Document the history of stalking and anti-stalking laws in one particular state or across the states. Use newspaper accounts, state statutes, and legal cases.
2. Compose a cluster of questions that could be used in face-to-face interviews with intimate partner violence victims to ask if they have experienced marital or partner rape or attempted rape. Prepare a single set of questions that could be used for both male and female victims. Or, prepare one set of questions for men and another set for women.

Notes

1. Traditional sociologists call this a "nuclear family," a "family of origin," or a "family of procreation."
2. The Add Health survey is based on a nationally representative sample of adolescents in grades seven through twelve. The study was designed to measure risk behaviors and how they are associated with adolescent health issues. The first wave of the survey consisted of interviews conducted in school. The follow-up interviews were conducted in the students' homes one, two, or six years later. The third wave of the survey studies the transition between adolescence and young adulthood. Add Health is not designed to measure dating violence. It does, however, include survey questions about any violence or abuse that occurs within dating, romantic, or sexual relationships.
3. The CTS 2 items and the items from the NVAW—also known as the VAWM (Violence and Threats of Violence Against Women and Men in the United States)—that measure assaults, rapes, and stalking episodes are discussed in chapter 8.
4. The U.S. Bureau of the Census conducts the survey for the U.S. Bureau of Justice Statistics and the Department of Justice.

5. The National Incident Reporting System is planned to replace the Uniform Crime Reporting System in the near future. A number of states currently collect NIRS data. The data reflect more types of criminal events, including domestic violence, and a more refined picture of what occurs when crimes are committed.

6. The household's address is the sampled unit. If a family moves out of a home, the address stays in the sample for three years. The family that moved is not followed by researchers.

7. Gender differences are presented in chapter 8.

8. Students and retired women comprise 22.5 percent of the sample and homemakers comprise 15.4 percent of the sample.

9. Respondents were not told any age or cutoff point for responding to events that occurred during childhood. Childhood is self-defined by each respondent.

10. Among the women who report being raped (or experiencing an attempted rape) by their partners or spouses, 107 did *not* report any form of physical assault. In a small percentage of cases, women experience marital rape as the single type of FAV.

11. Among the woman stalked (N = 651), 300 did not report that they had been assaulted or raped by their partners or ex-partners.

10

Consequences of Intragenerational Family Abuse and Violence

It is difficult if not impossible to summarize the personal, interpersonal, and social costs of family abuse and violence episodes. While the Centers for Disease Control and Prevention (CDC) measures the financial costs associated with health and mental health care following episodes of FAV, the CDC also recognizes that deaths and millions of injuries that do not require medical intervention are not counted.

Government data, agency data, and national survey data paste a collage portraying family abuse and violence (FAV) episodes. Children, adult intimate partners, and elders experience abuse and violence that varies in its severity, chronicity, and physical and emotional harm and injury. The data, however, regardless of their reliability and validity, cannot speak. They cannot adequately communicate the victim's account, or the subjective experience of what it feels like to be a social actor within an episode of family violence. To understand the subjective experiences and the consequences of FAV episodes, scholars need to study social actors' narratives, in addition to the experts' data and claims. To begin this analysis of the consequences of FAV, we attempt to listen to what the victims tell us.

Narratives of Family Violence Episodes

Consider Fisher's position, that social actors "experience and comprehend life as a series of ongoing narratives" (Fisher 1987). Narratives generally listen to the social actors who are internal to the FAV episode. They can tell us how violence and abuse is subjectively understood and how social actors external to the FAV episode affect it. Perceptions of the social context in which abuse occurs can be understood by listening to narratives.

Children's Voices

Narrative research on children's experiences is highly unusual, in part because researchers face heightened scrutiny by their institutional review boards when persons younger than age 18 are their research subjects. Berman's extraordinary study compares children who witnessed and survived war to children in the United States or Canada who witnessed and survived FAV episodes that targeted their mothers. The U.S. and Canadian children who participated in the study (N = 16) ranged in age from 10 to 17. At the time they were interviewed, they were living with their mothers but no longer with their mother's abuser. A 15-year-old girl, Donna, describes the extreme fear she experienced that seemed to paralyze her and her siblings. The control that family abuse and violence episodes had over her young life makes her story sound as if it comes from a prison instead of a home.

> You would only go in your bedroom to sleep, you don't go to play or nothing. You stay in the basement until it's time for bed, on the weekends you stay down there. We had toys down there, but you couldn't play with the toys because that would make a mess. I would have to clean the basement and make sure the toilets were clean. He would swear at us and poke us a lot. It would leave bruises. Or he'd slap us across the head and say, "You're stupid." We never showed mom the bruises because we were scared. We weren't allowed around our mom because he was possessive. (Berman 2000)

Some children appear to construct accounts, but not excuses, for the abuse that their mothers experienced. They want to make sense out of recurring and nightmarish events by reaching for some type of causal explanation for family violence. A 15-year-old, Mardelle, recalls,

> He was abusive to my mom, not really to me. . . . I think that was abuse, to see my mom go through it. He wasn't really mean to me, he just never talked to me. . . . He acted like he loved her a lot. But his problem was alcohol or something. If he drank he would get really possessive and take his anger out on her. Like one time he sliced my mom's stomach with a knife when she was pregnant. Just like a little slice, not real big or nothing. He took an anger control class and was doing good until he got angry at the teacher. (Berman 2000:117–118)

The children's narratives highlight the importance of examining how FAV episodes can affect primary and secondary victims. They tell social actors who are external to the FAV episode to remember the children when they respond to the adults who disclose abuse. When FAV episodes are not prevented, they can cause harm and injury to adults and children who require understanding and healing.

Women's Voices

We switch focus to the studies designed to describe how adult women, who were victimized by intimate partner violence, disclose to interviewers what they experienced. Julia Wood interviewed twenty women who had experienced both emotional and physical abuse within their young-adult dating relationships. The women described how gender norms made them vulnerable to abuse. Janelle, for example, disclosed that her boyfriend spoke critically of her appearance. As a consequence she thought "I had to look a certain way for him and definitely in terms of . . . well, I'm supposed to please him." Desire acknowledged, "I wanted to be like he wanted me to be, so I kept trying to figure out what he liked" (Wood 2001:250).

Some women believed the violence and abuse they experienced was not as bad as what others experienced. Mary told about her friend who had been beaten

> so bad that she's been in the hospital. And I mean, maybe I looked at it as I looked at her, and I saw how Luke beat her and she still stayed with him, that I considered myself lucky. That, you know, I just had, like, bruises and I didn't have a broken jaw or a broken nose or anything like that. (Wood 2001:250)

Other women who experience violence and abuse hold on to the notion that their partners' authentic selves are good and kind. It was some aberrant circumstance that caused the partner to hit or to verbally abuse them. Wood hears five different women's attempts to justify supposedly aberrant behavior. Beverly said,

> That wasn't the real Charles. . . . This wasn't the Charles I first met, the guy I fell in love with. It was just that he wasn't himself, you know. But nobody is nice all the time. So I figured he'd just been not himself or something, that he had been in a bad mood, but it was over and we were okay. I didn't want to make too big a deal over it or anything.

Janelle explained that "I know he's a better person than that . . . maybe that wasn't him that night. . . . Well, he was a good person. He had a bad day." Desire thought she understood the good side and the bad side of her partner:

> He just got into these mean moods, but most of the time he was his regular self. And so I tried to remind myself that this wasn't how he really was. I mean, everybody's got a bad side or has bad moods, so I understood that.

Mehnessah believed substance abuse accounts for her partner's violence. She said,

> He was only ugly or mean if he'd been drinking or doing drugs. The rest of the time he was his true self . . . real Greg—the nice one who cared about me and was warm and thoughtful and nice to me—that was the real Greg. . . . Sometimes the real Greg was hid-

den beneath all of the bad stuff, but that's who he really was. . . .
His anger would just get away from him sometimes, that's all. It
wasn't like that was who he was or anything.

Bailey was convinced that only when her partner lost control
over his emotions and behaviors did he become abusive: "I hated
those things he did, but I loved him. . . . He just couldn't control
himself. . . . I knew he would never purposely hurt me, but in that
instant he was somewhere else" (Wood 2001:252–253).

Stevens and Richards (1998) wrote up a clinical case study that
centers on an HIV-infected and battered woman who experienced
many years of intimate partner violence. Koral, one of their subjects, describes the range of injuries she experienced: "He . . . broke
my jaw. He had broke[n] my ribs. He had set me on fire. He had
stabbed me. You name it, he did it. Short of killing me."
She also disclosed her account of what motivated the abuse:

[I thought] things will go back to the way they used to be. . . . That
never happened. It's a shame because he was a good man. In the
beginning he was good. He didn't do drugs and he wasn't beating me. It was just when we moved to Florida that he started all
that. He wasn't strong enough to say no. And I tried, and I tried,
and I tried and it just. . . . Nothing I did was any good or it wasn't
enough.

After Eddie, her partner, beat her in front of a social actor who
was external to the FAV episode, Koral left him. She explains,

That night it happened in front of his boss. They had been doing
drugs at our house. They were smoking crack. And when it was
gone, Eddie went crazy, like he always did. . . . He'd be looking
on the floor for anything white. And he jumped on me in front of
his boss. And he choked me to the point where I went out. It was
one of his favorite things to do. And the next morning I just said
to myself, if I stay one of us is going to end up dead. And it's just
not worth it.

When reflecting on her experiences, she realized, "I do a lot of
thinking these days. I think about if I could do my life all over
again, would I have made the mistake of marrying him. And, you

know, I probably would, because in the beginning, he was good" (Stevens and Richards 1998:12–13, 15).

Riger and her colleagues, who interviewed fifteen abused women, consider the connections and relationships among social actors who are internal and external to the FAV episode. One of the women reported,

> When I left the shelter, I moved [in] with my sister. And so my boyfriend I was telling you about, he cannot come around my family because he . . . [has] beaten [me] up so much, you know. So he was coming here to see me . . . busted all the windows, you know, and the police had to come. So that's why I said, well then they don't need me being here, and he's causing all this confusion at my sister's house. He came back, and my aunt lives next door to me in another apartment. He came back with a shotgun, a shotgun. . . . He broke my front door. . . . I don't know how he broke my aunt's door from the side. (Riger, Raja, and Camacho 2002)

Poverty and intimate partner abuse tend to co-occur in the United States (and in other countries). In many women's lives, it is the experience of reoccurring violence and abuse that causes them to drift into extreme poverty. Sharon Hays estimates approximately 60 percent of welfare mothers have experienced FAV episodes. She argues, "Domestic violence—the single most dramatic indicator of gender conflict—is also the single most prevalent cultural pattern in the lives of welfare mothers. Welfare mothers are more likely to share this experience in common than any other life condition" (Hays 2003:212). Many of the extremely impoverished women she interviewed talked about the violence they had experienced. One of the women, Joy, explains why she left her abusive husband:

> If I hadn't left him . . . I'd probably still be being beaten and molested (or whatever it's called when it's your husband that does it). Yea, he slapped me a few times and a couple of times he beat me bad. He actually, well, he decided to force himself on me. He raped me. And I wanted to prosecute him, but see, here in [this] state the law says "You're mad at him, you say no, and it doesn't matter. . . . You turned him on, you're to blame, so that's that." I said no, but that's not enough. (Hays 2003:196)

Men's Voices

Narrative analyses of men who are victimized by FAV episodes are unusual. Male victims, compared to women, are less willing to disclose their experiences, and they are even less willing to talk about their feelings or emotions in response to their victimization. Migliaccio (2002) interviewed twelve men who were participating in men's groups that addressed divorce and child custody issues. All of the men were physically assaulted by their adult, female partners in FAV episodes that could not be attributed to defensive violence by the women. Karl recalled,

> One night . . . she got really out of control. I had accidentally left the toilet seat up. . . . Well . . . she fell into the toilet. She started yelling and screaming and stomping around the apartment. Then she came into the bedroom. I was pretending to be asleep, but I could see her shadow. She had something in her hands, raised above her head. I figured it was a wooden spoon . . . or something like that because she had hit me with those before. So I waited until she came around to my side of the bed, then rolled over. . . . When I turned back over, I saw that she had stuck two of the biggest steak knives into the bed up to the handles exactly where I had been laying. I grabbed my pants, ran out of the apartment, and jumped into the car. (Migliaccio 2002:36)

Another participant, Tim, talked about verbal abuse that was followed by a physical assault.

> I was just sitting there, conducting myself in a cold, lifeless manner, the same way I always conducted myself in conversations when she was getting angry, which, I am sure, would make her even angrier. And I finally said something that just set her off. She jumped on top of the bed . . . pinning me down and started whaling away on me. (Migliaccio 2002:37)

The men's narratives attribute their partners entering an out-of-control state as a plausible explanation for why women initiated violent acts against them. They do not connect losing control to drug or alcohol abuse as the women tend to. While the women seem to present a Dr. Jekyll and Mr. Hyde explanation for recurring violence, the men appear to be somewhat puzzled by the outbursts of physical aggression that were perpetrated by their intimate partners.

Narrative accounts, from the victims' perspectives, sensitize researchers to the experiences that women, children, and men have as a consequence of FAV episodes. While there is no substitute for listening to those affected by family violence, researchers also need to look beyond the victim's story and see clearly that many FAV episodes are criminal events that deserve punishment imposed by the state. To do otherwise is to blame or "frame the victim" (Berns 2004). During phases of the battered women's movement, social change advocates struggled to empower women and to make policymakers and social service agencies aware of the victim-blaming perspectives that diminished the importance of surviving domestic violence.

Many contemporary researchers focus almost exclusively on the victims-survivors of FAV episodes (Carlson et al. 2002; Choice, Lamke, and Pittman 1995; Coker 1999; Ferraro and Johnson 1983; Mills 1998). Like Berns (2004) we contend it is important to take the perspective of the victim to understand experiences and consequences of family abuse and violence; and it is equally important to focus on the perpetrators of criminal violence and abuse as well as on the structural and cultural factors that engender FAV episodes.

Miller's (2002) study of a group of sixteen men who were attending a court-ordered twelve-week counseling program as a consequence of misdemeanor domestic violence convictions illustrates some of the motivations and justifications for FAV episodes that batterers communicate. Don, recently released from state prison, was, at the time he participated in the counseling program, living with a new girlfriend. He referred to his ex-wife as "The woman who cost me six years in prison." Don agreed "voluntarily" to participate in the counseling program to avoid a jail term after he was arrested for hitting his new girlfriend. He explains,

> The only thing that happened was that one night, at 2 a.m., me and my girlfriend had been drinking enough rocket fuel to light

up Chicago when I hit her. It's drinking that gets me in trouble with her—that the police had come over for. (Miller 2002:10)

Don also talked about his need to control the decisions his new girlfriend was trying to make about their new apartment. In a discussion about relationship issues that are negotiable versus those that are not, he told the group:

The color of the living room walls is *not* something to negotiate. I pay the rent. And we also fight over appliances. She wants a glass-top stove and I won't buy it because she throws temper tantrums . . . and would break the $700 glass-top one. But, it's her stove and it's *my* refrigerator. It's not "ours." (Miller 2002:35)

Kyle, who lost his job as a firefighter following a criminal conviction for domestic violence, claimed, "I have no anger issues." When asked about his activities over the past week, he referred to problems he had with his stepson.

I could strangle him. He's 14 years old. The boy is a freak and stole ice cream sandwiches [from my freezer]. When he was caught he smashed his window. It was just a small cut on the back of his hand. I know because I was a firefighter when a cut needs stitches. It wasn't that serious. His therapist says I should have brought him to the hospital. But it was on a Friday night. Do you know how long it would take on a Friday night? A little scar. Big deal. He's not a *girl*. I just don't want Child Services coming back into my life. The kid is OK. He gets food, he lives in my house. I'm not abusing him. OK? What's the problem? The child is a total mess. He is *really* a mess. He's *actually* sick. He takes medicine for it. (Miller 2002:36)

Will, like most of the other men in the group, disclosed how hard he works to support his wife and how dependent she is on him. When asked what he did over the weekend, he reported,

I fixed the freakin' brakes on the wife's car, but not soon enough for her yacking and complaining to stop. I work seventy hours a week [at a local store] to advance to the next level. I even go without sleep. I drive my wife one-and-a-half hours each way to visit our children [who are in a foster care home]. . . . My wife got her first paycheck this week. I'm proud of her. But that's the problem with her. She has no goals. 'Til now all she did was stay home. (Miller 2002:12)

The men tend to blame their victims for their own problems. Their problems are then used to account for their FAV episodes. The devil made them do it, whether the devil takes the form of alcohol, too much yakking, work stress, or stepchildren. What they unintentionally disclose are their motivations to control their partners.

Physical, Psychological, and Social Consequences of FAV Episodes

The research literature demonstrates that the immediate, short-term, and long-term consequences of FAV episodes vary dramatically, based on a number of personal, social psychological, and social-supportive factors. Female victims, as compared to male victims, are more likely to be physically injured as a consequence of FAV (Tjaden and Thoennes 2000). They also are more likely to suffer emotional distress, including depression and longer-term post-traumatic stress disorder (PTSD). Employed and well-educated women, because they are more likely than unemployed and less-educated women to have strong social support networks, are less likely to suffer depression or PTSD symptoms as a consequence of intimate partner violence. What will she experience as a consequence of FAV?

Low-income victims are especially vulnerable to physical and emotional distress (Leone et al. 2004). Arguably one consequence of FAV victimization is the increased risk of perpetrating intra- or intergenerational offenses. To illustrate: Sibling violence victims face an increased risk of perpetrating dating violence. Perpetrators of dating violence are at an increased risk for committing intimate partner violence in a subsequent intimate relationship (Anda et al. 2001; Bailey and Whittle 2004; Hoffman and Edwards 2004; Noland et al. 2004).

Estimating the long-term effects of FAV, especially for younger victims, is problematic for two important reasons. Many children and adolescents who experience or witness violence within their homes also are exposed to violence in other social settings. Disentangling the consequences of FAV from neighborhood or dating violence is not possible in many studies. In addition, children and adolescents are exposed to violence at various developmental phases, which can affect short-term as well as long-term consequences (Margolin and Gordis 2000).

It is necessary to accurately identify the consequences of FAV episodes to determine the appropriate treatment or social response. Does the victim suffer from depression? Post-traumatic stress disorder? Low self-esteem? A review of the published research literature on PTSD, using a systematic research synthesis method, found that women who experienced multiple forms of family violence and the women who turned to safe shelters in response to FAV episodes are more likely than other types of victims to manifest symptoms of PTSD (Jones, Hughes, and Unterstaller 2001). Intimate partner victims are likely to show other mental health problems, including substance abuse and depression. Clinicians and social service agencies, if unfamiliar with trauma symptoms, can (mis)treat a person for depression.

A Summary of the Known Consequences of Intimate Partner Violence

It is not possible to make valid statements about the consequences of intimate partner violence for each social actor who experiences one-time or chronic FAV episodes. A woman, one who is most likely surrounded by supportive friends, coworkers, and family members, may "walk it off," as if the event or episodes were more like a leg cramp than a torn ligament. A man, one who is most likely too embarrassed to disclose his experiences to friends or coworkers, may "suffer in silence" and experience high blood pressure, insomnia, and anxiety attacks as a result. Another man may quickly separate from his abusive partner. Each unique social actor experiences the consequences of FAV in unique ways. Though every researcher needs to pause to recognize the exceptional experiences of the unique person, they also must aggregate or summarize what the empirical data suggest. To summarize the overall consequences of intragenerational forms of family violence episodes, we look at (a) the economic costs, (b) the health and mental health consequences, (c) the gender differences in injuries and social costs, and (d) the risk factors for rape and physical assault–related injuries.

In a government sponsored study, Miller and his colleagues set the total financial cost associated with intimate partner violence victimization at $67 billion annually in the United States (Miller, Cohen, and Wiersema 1996). Most of the tangible costs are due to medical expenses, mental health expenses, and lost wages and worker productivity. They also estimate that violence against children, with approximately 40 percent of cases representing FAV episodes, cost $164 billion.

Health and public health researchers study the health and mental health consequences of FAV. In a comprehensive review of the literature, Walker and his colleagues report that family abuse and violence victims, compared to similar social actors within the general population, are more likely to experience acute physical injuries, such as broken bones, or chronic physical injuries, such as back problems. Existing health problems, such as skin disorders or irritable bowel syndrome, are likely to be exacerbated by FAV. Stress, PTSD, depression, and anxiety are more likely to be reported by general population samples of victims of family abuse and violence. The likelihood of mental health and stress disorders is highest when sheltered victims are compared to general population victims or to general population adults who do not experience FAV. Substance abuse, in the form of alcohol abuse, illicit drug use, or dependence on prescription medication, is correlated with family abuse and violence victimization (Walker et al. 2004). What remains uncertain is the direction of the empirical relationship. Does FAV cause victims to treat their physical and emotional pain with alcohol or drugs, or does the abuse of alcohol or drugs increase the likelihood of FAV victimization?

Violence Against Women and Men
in the U.S.: Survey Data

We analyzed the Violence Against Women and Men (VAWM)[1] survey data to examine the consequences of intimate partner violence that were disclosed by 8,000 women and 8,000 men (Tjaden and Thoennes 2000). A total of 682 out of the 16,000 general population respondents reported physical injuries as a consequence of FAV. Women, compared to men, are significantly more likely to be injured as a consequence of family abuse and violence episodes ($\chi^2 = 42.418$, df = 17, p < .05). The injuries range from head injuries or broken bones to bruises, sprains, and scratches. There is no statistical gender difference among those injured who seek medical help. Men are no less or more likely than women to go to the doctor's office or to the hospital. There is, however, a significant difference across the genders in seeking mental healthcare or counseling in response to FAV episodes ($\chi^2 = 9.496$, df = 2, p < .05). Women perceive a greater need than men to get advice and help in response to a victimization experience. Among those who sought mental health help (N = 344), 70 percent are women and 30 percent are men.

The social costs associated with FAV include lost time to care for children and lost time to donate volunteer hours in the community. These are social costs that women experience, and that men rarely experience, partly because these activities are "women's work." Missing days from paid employment, on the other hand, is a cost that both men and women can experience. A total of 302 respondents in the VAWM survey reported losing one or more days from work. Again we find that women, compared to men, are significantly more likely to experience a cost, including a financial cost, as a consequence of intimate partner violence ($\chi^2 = 10.898$, df = 2. p < .05). Nearly 80 percent of the victims who were injured seriously enough to miss work are women, and 20 percent of the victims are men.

Tjaden and Thoennes (2000) used logistic regression to estimate the probability of injury as a consequence of rape and as a consequence of assault. They found that victims who were raped by their partners were more likely to suffer injuries in addition to the rape itself than women who were raped by strangers or acquaintances. What predicts an increased risk of injury from an assault? For male victims, being assaulted by an intimate partner decreases the risk of injury. For women, being assaulted by an intimate partner increases the risk of physical injury.

Generalizations

The generalizations that researchers can make, based on reviews of empirical studies and analyses of general population and shelter population victims of intragenerational family violence episodes, are

1. The consequences of FAV may include acute or chronic physical injuries.
2. The consequences include stress, depression, anxiety disorders, and PTSD.
3. The consequences include economic or financial costs as well as social costs.
4. Consequences vary by gender. Women, compared to men, suffer more physical injuries, more severe injuries, more mental health problems, and women experience greater social and economic costs.

The most severe consequence of a family violence episode is homicide. While homicide trends in the United States continue to decrease, the Department of Justice notes one exception: "Except for white girlfriends, the homicide victimization rate for intimate partners in each racial group has fallen" (Fox and Zawitz 2004). Although rates of intimate partner violence homicides decrease, individual and unique social actors continue to be killed by their companions, partners, and spouses. To tell that story, we turn to an FAV episode that took place in a university town. It is an ordinary case of a husband who killed his wife: A well-educated, white, middle-class mother of two young children was killed by a controlling partner when she decided to leave him. The victim had never sought help for domestic violence.

The Professor's Wife:
A Victim of Separation Violence?

We examine a murder that occurred in a midwestern state to illustrate how a domestic violence event, an intragenerational form of FAV, has multiple consequences. The case is not unusual, but it does challenge prevailing stereotypes of FAV.[2] The perpetrator and his victim, though from somewhat different social backgrounds, enjoyed the privileges of raising a young family in a town where serious felony offenses are relatively rare. We tell the story with five years of newspaper coverage of the murder and legal proceedings, which included a trial, sentencing hearing, a resentencing hearing, and lawsuits initiated by the victim's family, the convicted offender, and the offender's friends.

A murder was committed by an assistant professor of computer science. Edgar Knapp, Jr., a well-educated, white professional, killed his wife and the mother of their two children. His wife, Brenda, was killed with her own gun, a .38 caliber revolver she had bought several years earlier when she worked as a police officer. Their neighbors expressed surprise: How could something like this happen in their quiet, middle-class neighborhood? They had failed to hear the sounds of violence.

On July 24, 1994, Edgar Knapp, Jr., (EK) called 911. Portions of the transcript of his call to the police dispatcher (D) appeared in the local newspaper:[3]

D: What is your emergency?

EK: (crying) I just shot my wife.

D: What? What happened?

EK: I just shot my wife (crying).

D: OK. . . . I need you to take a deep breath 'cause I need to know what's going on.

EK: I just shot my wife (crying).

D: You just shot your wife?

EK: Yes (crying).

D: OK.

EK: Hurry up.

D: OK, we've got officers, I'm getting the medics going, OK?

OK, stay . . . on the line with me. Hey, I need you, OK . . . to take a deep breath 'cause I need to be able to get information from you, OK?

EK: (crying) Yes.

D: OK. . . . Where, where is she at right now?

EK: In the bedroom.

D: She's in the bedroom. OK. Was this, was this an accident? How did it happen?

EK: No. It's not an accident.

D: It's . . . not an accident.

EK: She went after me. We had an argument here.

D: OK.

EK: A very bad argument, after me.

D: OK. Let me get that and then I need some more information. Unit 41, units en route. Subject advising this is not an accident. Not an accident. Female subject and he were arguing, then she went after him and he shot her. OK, where's the weapon at now?

EK: I don't know. It's wherever it fell. I have no idea. Probably in the bedroom.

D: OK. . . . She's in the bedroom, where . . . where is she injured? Where did you shoot her?

EK: I don't know . . . I struggled for the gun and it went off. . . . And I just shot and shot and shot (crying).

D: OK. . . . Where's the weapon at now? Do you know where in the house . . . it's at?

EK: I said it's probably in the bedroom. I don't know.

D: Units at the scene, subject is advising he's unsure where the weapon is. He believes it may be in the bedroom, but he is unsure where he dropped it.

When police arrived at the scene, they found a "10-inch-wide pool of blood next to [Brenda's] . . . head" and her right-hand thumb resting on the grip of the revolver that Knapp used to shoot her four times.[4] At his trial, Edgar Knapp, Jr., pleaded self-defense. His attorney argued that Knapp thought his life was endangered by his wife. Although he did not disclose the information to the police dispatcher, Knapp had apparently placed the murder weapon in a position that would help him portray a self-defensive act.

Knapp was convicted of murdering his wife and sentenced to serve forty years in prison, in a state that will reduce his sanction by 50 percent unless he loses good time credit. In practice, Edgar Knapp, Jr., at age 35 was ordered by the state to spend twenty years in a state prison. When he is 55 years old, he will likely find it impossible or at least difficult to achieve his career aspirations or meaningful relationships with his two children. But, he is likely to be alive.

The police who investigated Knapp's crime told the newspaper journalists they had received no prior calls about domestic violence in the Knapp home. This is in stark contrast to the most typical FAV case, in which social service agencies and police, in the same jurisdiction in which the murder of Brenda occurred, are very familiar with the chronic violence and abuse that victimizes women.

Caution: BIOHAZARD

A July 26, 1994, newspaper photograph shows Assistant Professor Edgar Knapp, Jr., wearing handcuffs and a T-shirt, with the slogan CAUTION: BIOHAZARD. The front-page headline reads, "I killed my wife!" Additional photos accompany the first reports of a domestic homicide. One is a portrait of the victim, with the caption "Brenda in an undated photo." One is a picture of a blood-splatter specialist who works for the state police. In the background is a two-story house, owned by Knapp and Brenda. Outside the house is a backyard toy.

Another picture shows two young children being taken from a neighbor's house by a Child Protective Services worker. Both clutch stuffed animals. The younger child, age 2, carries a teddy bear. The older child, age 4 at the time her mother was killed, is pictured standing behind her brother, holding a toy rabbit with both of her hands. Her face shows an unmistakable frown. Their next-door neighbor, who took the children in on Sunday night, according to the photo's caption, has her hand on the child's shoulder.[5]

"Not the kind of person who usually comes through the court system" is how one of the prosecuting attorneys described[6] Professor Knapp, a German resident, who was 35 when he killed his 37-year-old wife. He had completed his Ph.D. program in 1992 and was appointed assistant professor in a department ranked tenth in the nation. His parents came to the United States to attend their son's trial. They stayed through the trial, which led to a murder conviction, until the sentencing hearing a month later. At that time the professor's defense attorney argued that the sentencing judge, in a presumptive sentencing jurisdiction, should consider the mitigating circumstances surrounding the murder and impose the more lenient sanction specified by statute. The mitigating circumstances are that the professor is well-educated, has close family ties, and no criminal history prior to killing his wife. His defense attorney claimed, "He has done everything we want a good citizen to do."[7]

Perhaps the professor did what his defense attorney thinks "good citizens do." The judge apparently disagreed, and in 1994 he sentenced the convicted murderer to fifty years in state prison. In 1999 the term was reduced to forty years[8] after the state's appellate court ordered a reconsideration of sentences for murder that were handed out the year the professor killed his wife. Although he testified at his sentencing hearing that he loved his wife and his children, the professor hired an attorney to appeal his conviction and to petition the state in 1999 to move him to Germany to serve out his sentence, where he "can be close to his family and friends"[9] (not including his two children).

Brenda met her husband in Texas, where she was teaching junior high school. Before that job, Brenda taught science in a middle school in Florida, her home state. She completed her master's degree in education and had started work in a doctoral program in curriculum and instruction in January, six months before she was murdered.

Education was a career change for Brenda. During the mid-1970s she worked first as a police aide, eventually becoming a police officer in Florida. A police captain who worked with her described Brenda as a "happy-go-lucky, bouncy person."[10] When she changed career aspirations, she took with her the .38 caliber Smith and Wesson revolver that she purchased while working as a police officer.

Knapp shot his wife four times at close range. One of the wounds was superficial. Each of the other three was deadly. An investigator for the state police and a pathologist from a university medical center testified that one shot, to Brenda's right temple, was fired while she lay on her bedroom floor. The bullet passed through her brain, lodging in the skin under her left ear. It was an incapacitating wound that would have caused her death within one hour. Another bullet wound, a front-to-back wound, entered her left breast, while she lay on her bed, puncturing her lung, and exiting her back. The pathologist testified that the chest wound would have caused Brenda's death within an hour. Also while lying on her back, Brenda was shot in her upper abdomen. The bullet tore her liver and was lodged in her spine.

The pathologist testified the shot to her abdomen was a "contact wound," that is, the offender held the barrel of the gun directly against Brenda's body as he fired the shot; the pathologist testified the shot would have paralyzed her from the waist down. Although the forensic experts could not determine the sequence of the gunshot wounds, the blood-spatter expert testified the shot to her temple was fired as she lay on the floor, where the emergency technicians found her.[11]

Four gunshot wounds, three of them deadly, entered Brenda's body while she lay on her bed and on the bedroom floor. When the emergency technicians arrived at the scene, they found Brenda's thumb "resting on the grip of her own . . . revolver."[12] Her head rested in a ten-inch-wide pool of blood.

Professor Knapp argued that he killed Brenda in self-defense. He stated that Brenda was "under great stress" on account of her course work, her teaching, and research responsibilities. As a result, on the evening of her death, the professor and Brenda began arguing as they prepared for bed. According to his story, Brenda told him that she wanted a legal separation, which caused an escalation in their fight. He testified that he went into the bathroom to brush his teeth; when he returned he found Brenda pointing a gun at him and telling him to leave the house that night. "Her face was distorted. . . . I was terrified. I had never seen her like that. . . . I was absolutely convinced she was trying to kill me, and that's when I panicked."[13] He testified that he struggled with Brenda, trying to get the gun away from her and trying to point the gun away from both of them. If there was any struggle, it left no visible signs on the professor. He was not bruised, not scratched, and certainly not shot.

At his trial, the professor remembered shooting Brenda three times. He forgot about the contact wound, the shot fired from the gun pressed against her that split her liver and would have paralyzed her. However, he remembered the shot that hit Brenda in the head. According to the professor, that particular shot was fired when he got his finger on the trigger for the first time. The prosecuting attorney, John Meyers, remarked on the professor's testimony about the gunshots and summarized his position: "Generally, I thought the account he gave was good for us [for the state's case against the professor]."[14]

Brenda and Professor Knapp lived in a quiet middle-class neighborhood, on a secluded street. They were the parents of two children. Brenda left behind a mother, who is described as a quiet, 57-year-old white-haired woman who uses a wheelchair. She thanked Mr. Meyers for the conviction. Brenda's siblings were at the trial. One of her sisters was awarded custody of Brenda's children, and she and her husband planned to adopt them. The professor objected, declaring the same sister was the executor of Brenda's estate, and that because he—the convicted murderer—was the sole beneficiary specified in Brenda's will he should be named executor. The judge disagreed.

The professor's parents, Edgar Knapp, Sr., and Ilse Knapp, were in their late 50s and resided in Germany. Although they initially petitioned the court for custody of the children, they settled the custody dispute with Brenda's surviving relatives. The only other information the reader obtains about the Knapps is the ironic detail that Edgar Knapp, Sr., was orphaned at a young age, and thus has a special appreciation for the need of children to have a father in their lives.

The morning before she was murdered, Brenda had called a marriage and family therapist, Dr. Sprenkle, to tell him she wanted to terminate her marriage. According to the testimony he gave at Knapp's trial, Dr. Sprenkle had been seeing Brenda and her husband for marital counseling for approximately one month. In his last conversation with her, he advised Brenda to consult an attorney.[15] Like many other homicides, the murder of Brenda appears to be a separation homicide. It is possible that Edgar Knapp was motivated to kill his wife once he heard that she intended to terminate their marriage. According to a newspaper report, Knapp himself disclosed during his trial: "'She told me she wanted me out by Wednesday.' She told him he'd better shape up during the separation or she would seek a divorce, get custody of the children, and take a big chunk of his income. 'I told her that I was no dummy either,' he said."[16]

Newspaper stories give readers a glimpse into Brenda's life and her troubled marriage. Her mother testified that Knapp had had an extramarital affair during Brenda's second pregnancy. She also testified that "there was a lot of verbal abuse. . . . He was very dominating and she [Brenda] couldn't please him."[17] Brenda had confided in her older sister, who also testified at Knapp's trial, that she and Knapp had spoken on the phone the day before the murder. Brenda disclosed that she had told Knapp, "I want you out of here." Brenda's sister claimed that "this time, I could tell she meant it." Brenda had friends who testified Knapp was demeaning and failed to help care for their children.

Knapp's friends testified during his trial and at his sentencing. An especially sympathetic woman, Elizabeth Vogt, told the sentencing judge that Brenda's sister and brother-in-law "have cut the children off from their father," but explained that "Knapp has been understanding." A total of "ten friends and colleagues" loaned the professor $25,000 for his legal expenses. Six months later they sued him, claiming he was in "default on the loan." The newspaper reports that five of the professor's friends were found by police inside of the Knapp house, retrieving items to sell, including "kitchen appliances, bedding, pots and pans, books, and toys" estimated to be worth $1,365 before the court issued an order to freeze the family's assets.[18]

While the court granted custody to Brenda's sister, the judge also ruled that Knapp's parents could visit the children each summer and that Brenda's sister must make it possible for the convicted murderer to have contact with his children while imprisoned. If this case had been adjudicated in another state, Massachusetts, for example, the judge would have been prohibited from ordering the children to visit the person who was convicted of the murder of their mother. The attorney representing the children said, "We can't blame Edgar's parents for what Edgar did, and certainly the children should maintain a relationship with their grandparents," although the children's guardians have "some reservations about whether extensive contact with their father will be good for the children."[19]

In 1999 Knapp sued the state, claiming his Eighth Amendment right to be free from cruel and unusual punishment was violated. His prison cellmates tended to smoke, causing him to "suffer headaches, swollen sinuses, nausea, nosebleeds, and eye irritation that prevented him from wearing his contact lenses." He sought $5,000 in compensatory damages and $5,000 in punitive damages. The United States Court of Appeals for the Seventh Circuit, forgoing oral argument, affirmed the district court's decision to deny payment to Professor Knapp.

This murder is an FAV episode, but it also is a somewhat unusual event: It is a homicide committed by a professor against a graduate student and teaching and research assistant at the same university. The *Chronicle of Higher Education,* on August 9, 2001, published an article about a university graduate student who killed two graduate students. On March 27, 1997, it published an article about campus murders and mentioned a mother-child homicide that occurred on the same campus. On February 22, 2002, we sent a letter of inquiry to the *Chronicle*: "Would you please tell me how deaths in academe are covered by the *Chronicle*. . . . The murder of a graduate student . . . by her professor-husband (Edgar Knapp) . . . went totally uncovered. Is there any particular policy that precludes coverage of a murder OF a student BY a professor? Are spousal murders in academe covered?"

Edith Taylor, on February 25, 2002, responded,

The Chronicle does not have a formal policy about homicides in academe. We do list deaths of faculty and staff members in higher education, natural and otherwise, on a weekly basis—but we do not give the cause of death. . . . If people are murdered in their off-campus homes for domestic or personal reasons, it is usually for reasons not to do with higher education, per se, and we do not write news stories about them. . . . The only exception I can think of . . . is that of a Midwestern college president who murdered his wife at their summer home some years ago, and that story we covered because it had an immediate impact on his campus—i.e., he had to be replaced immediately.

Less than three months later, in an article published in the *Chronicle*, titled "Professor Charged with Murdering His Wife," the author, Piper Fogg (2002), wrote,

A Professor at East Georgia College was arrested this month and charged with murdering his wife, who was also a professor at the two-year college. Walter C. Mason, Jr., 48, an associate professor of physical education, was being held without bond in the death of Emily Pestana-Mason, 38 . . . an assistant professor of English [who] was found stabbed to death at the couple's home, in Swainsboro, Ga., on April 29. . . . The couple's two daughters, Naomi 4, and Becky 2, were home at the time.

The story continues to say that the mother, an apparent victim of a family homicide, taught creative writing courses. The students and faculty members were shocked by the murder. The president of the college said he "had spoken with both Mr. Mason and Ms. Pestana-Mason on a regular basis, and that everything seemed fine."

Why was the East Georgia College homicide newsworthy, according to the *Chronicle of Higher Education*, but the murder committed by Professor Knapp, Jr., was not? The professor was arrested, tried, and found guilty of murder. He killed the mother of two young children; she also was a graduate student with teaching and research responsibilities on campus. Did this FAV episode not shock the faculty sufficiently to warrant coverage? Was the primary victim of an FAV episode not newsworthy to the *Chronicle*? We have no way of knowing how much family violence known to colleges and universities goes unnoticed and undetected. Even when it comes to murder, the *Chronicle of Higher Education* does not find it newsworthy to report the FAV episodes that occur on our campuses. Tragically these events remind us that academic families, like all other upscale families, can be victims of FAV episodes, including the most severe, which result in death and orphaned children.

Applying the Family Abuse and Violence Episode Perspective

In this case of family violence, the perpetrator and the primary victim, who are the social actors internal to the FAV episode, vary in ethnicity, educational level, and earned income levels. The relatively advantaged social actor is in prison. The space and place where this family violence occurred explain in part its consequences. The professor and his wife lived in a private home, in a quiet neighborhood where the sounds of violence are not recognized.

In this case, young children are also primary victims. We also know that the victim's mother and her siblings are secondary victims. What the future holds for them is uncertain. The court requires Brenda's children to obtain counseling for as long as they need it. The court cannot help Brenda's extended family members.

The connections among social actors are important. Brenda had a large extended family, but all of her family members lived thousands of miles away from her. They could not help insulate her from the abuse and violence that killed her. The man who murdered her enjoyed a network of colleagues and friends who sufficiently sympathized with him to collect $25,000 to help defend him against a murder charge.

The perpetrator had opportunities to abuse his marital partner that were structured by their living arrangements. Like a classic textbook case of family homicide, Brenda became vulnerable to murder by announcing to her abuser she was about to terminate their marital relationship (Hardesty 2002; Kurz 1996). While the perpetrator argued that Brenda experienced "stress" from her studies and work, the newspaper accounts of the professor's motivations included the "stress" that untenured assistant professors experience.

The mechanics of the FAV episode are significant. Most importantly, a loaded gun was available and used by the professor to kill his wife. The same sequence of events could have occurred with a very different outcome if the gun had not been in the household. Given the same argument and the same threats taking place, it is possible that the professor would have struck or injured Brenda. Without a weapon, however, Edgar Knapp, Jr., might not have had the mechanics necessary to kill his wife. A family murder might have been prevented if the mechanics of the FAV episode had differed (Brantingham and Brantingham 2001).

The most important and relevant question regarding this case is why did he kill her? A post hoc explanation, but one based on the separation violence studies, is Knapp's motivation to control Brenda and prevent her from leaving him. An FAV episode framework provides no causal explanation, but it does address issues that suggest strategies to prevent family homicides: keep weapons out of the hands of abusers, empower potential victims with connections to social actors and social organizations that can provide survival resources, redefine threats to be deviant or criminal behaviors, and educate marriage therapists to recognize the signs of separation violence or the risks of escalating or lethal violence.

Based on court testimony, we know that Brenda was planning to leave her abusive husband. We may be tempted to ask, why didn't she leave earlier? Would he have killed her then? Or could she have survived? While it is imperative not to blame the victim for her murder, it is important to see if there are constraints against leaving that need to be addressed by FAV researchers.

Ola Barnett, whose studies of sheltered women are exemplary, addresses the question of why battered women do not leave in a systematic two-part review of the research that has been published since the early 1980s (Barnett 2000; Barnett 2001). Barnett's work, which can be incorporated into an FAV episodes framework, finds that women who make final decisions to leave their abusive partners have attempted to sever their relationships on an average of five prior occasions. Many women, perhaps like Brenda, must go through a process, characterized by several stages, to separate from their partners and let go of their hopes and aspirations to maintain a family for their children. Although Brenda worked, her earned income was not sufficient to support herself and two children, making her economically dependent on her abusive spouse (Barnett 2000:348).

Brenda had disclosed to her therapist that Edgar Knapp, Jr., was abusive and threatening. Her therapist advised her (by phone) to plan to terminate her marriage. What would her experiences have been if she had contacted the police to report Knapp's threats? What would have happened if she had filed an order for protection in civil court? By 1994 protection orders were available in all the states. In 65 percent of the cases, a court order can help a victim remain safe from subsequent violence (Keilitz et al. 1996). Barnett reports that the American Bar Association, in 1997, concluded that "so generally flawed was the legal profession's representation of victims that the Commission [on Domestic Violence] issued a series of recommendations concerning legal education" (Barnett 2000:356). Attorneys, in general, poorly represent FAV victims as they seek orders of protection and as they seek lawful divorces from violent and abusive partners.

Barnett's research shows that women like Brenda face many factors internal to their marital relationship that inhibit them from leaving an abusive partnership. In addition, factors external to their relationship prevent women from leaving. Patriarchal institutions, such as the family, and patriarchal and sexist social structures, such as gendered economic and political structures, disadvantage women and make leaving an abusive relationship problematic—not only for the primary victim but also for the secondary victims of family abuse and violence episodes. It is possible that Brenda wanted to leave her abusive husband but could not until she figured out an exit plan that would financially support her and her children. It is possible that whenever she left him, Knapp would have killed her. It is certain that he did kill her.

Discussion Questions

1. What are some of the consequences of intragenerational FAV that men, but not women, are likely to experience?

2. How do women tend to experience the consequences of intragenerational FAV in ways that vary by their social class, location, race or ethnicity, and age?
3. Why are women who have been raped by their partners more likely to suffer severe injuries than women raped by strangers and acquaintances? Why are men who are assaulted by their partners less likely to experience injuries compared to men who are assaulted by strangers or acquaintances?
4. What, if anything, could social actors external to the FAV episode have done to prevent Brenda's murder? How are Brenda's children, her parents, and her siblings the primary or the secondary victims of family abuse and violence?

Research Projects

1. Visit the U.S. Department of Justice, Office on Violence Against Women, at www.usdoj.gov/ovw/. Summarize the research programs that the office promotes. What types of additional research programs should the office develop to ameliorate the consequences of intragenerational forms of family abuse and violence?
2. Visit the U.S. Department of Justice, Office of Justice Programs, Bureau of Justice Statistics, at www.ojp.usdoj.gov/bjs/. Examine the statistics about crime and victims and the Incident Based Statistics. Summarize what the statistics indicate about family violence.

Notes

1. This national study is often called the Violence Against Women Survey because it was mandated by the Violence Against Women Act of 1994. Researchers sampled 8,000 women and 8,000 men in the general population. The original name of the survey was Violence Against Women and Men, and we use that name in this chapter because we analyze data comparing the consequences of FAV for men and women.

2. The stereotype of the FAV victim that we refer to is a poor, undereducated woman who is trapped by a bad relationship and by a bad (i.e.,

high crime rate) neighborhood in an urban ghetto. The stereotype of the FAV perpetrator is a poor, undereducated man who is likely to be a "drunken bum."

3. *Lafayette Journal and Courier*, November 4, 1994, Page B2.

4. *Lafayette Journal and Courier*, November 3, 1994, Page A10.

5. *Lafayette Journal and Courier*, July 26, 1994, Page A1.

6. *Lafayette Journal and Courier*, December 8, 1994, Page A1.

7. *Lafayette Journal and Courier*, December 8, 1994, Page A1.

8. *Lafayette Journal and Courier*, October 23, 1999, Page B1.

9. *Lafayette Journal and Courier*, October 23, 1999, Page B1.

10. *Lafayette Journal and Courier*, July 27, 1994, Page B1.

11. *Lafayette Journal and Courier*, November 2, 1994, Page A1 and Page A10.

12. *Lafayette Journal and Courier*, November 3, 1994, Page A10.

13. *Lafayette Journal and Courier*, November 8, 1994, Back Page of Section A.

14. *Lafayette Journal and Courier*, November 8, 1994, Back Page of Section A.

15. *Lafayette Journal and Courier*, November 3, Page A10.

16. *Lafayette Journal and Courier*, November 8, 1994, Page A1 and Back Page.

17. *Lafayette Journal and Courier*, November 5, 1994, Page A7.

18. *Lafayette Journal and Courier*, February 3, 1995, Page A8.

19. *Lafayette Journal and Courier*, September 13, 1995, Page A1.

VI

DEPENDENTS

11

Neglect: The Failure to Act on Behalf of Dependents

Neglect is the most pernicious, damaging, and persistent form of family abuse and violence, in part, because its victims, children and elders, are dependent on other family members for their basic care. Unlike physical, sexual, or emotional forms of family abuse and violence (FAV), wherein the actions are obvious and the consequences often immediate, the signature lack of action in neglect may be largely invisible, and its consequences may not be evident for months or even years. For elders, neglect has serious consequences for physical and mental health that often lead to increased dependency and vulnerability, economic exploitation, and physical and sexual violence. For children, neglect over an extended period of time may lead to a serious physical disability or other health issues, impeded mental or psychological development, an ignorance of social norms or values, a lack of interpersonal skills, and other negative effects, including death. The slow but persistent and incremental effects of parental failure to act often culminate in severe problems, especially for very young children (Hildyard and Wolfe 2002; Holton and Oshana 2004). These forms of intergenerational family abuse and violence are potentially more serious than those resulting from physical abuse. They can also be more difficult (or impossible) to treat or heal.

In spite of documented effects, there is a relative lack of research regarding the issue of child neglect. Less than 10 percent of published articles on child maltreatment focus on neglect (Behl et al. 2001; Garbarino and Collins 1999; Zuravin 1999). This "neglect of neglect" continues despite Child Protective Services (CPS) records that consistently indicate at least half of all children who are mistreated each year suffer from neglect, totaling more children than those who are physically, emotionally, and sexually abused combined.

Both elder and child neglect involve dependency on others. But the long-term effects for each are reversed: Children become less dependent as they age while elders become more dependent. Although they are both types of intergenerational family abuse and violence, we consider them separately in this chapter.

Child Neglect: Educational, Emotional, Medical, Physical, and Supervisory

Child neglect, as defined by federal agencies, is an act of omission, specifically the failure of a parent or other person legally responsible for a child's welfare to provide for the child's basic needs and proper level of care with respect to food, shelter, hygiene, medical attention, or supervision (National Center on Child Abuse and Neglect 1978). The problem of parental inability or unwillingness to provide appropriate care for children has always existed, with communities frequently attempting to force parents or caretakers to provide adequate, consistent care, but at other times undertaking care of neglected children directly.

With the 1974 Child Abuse Prevention and Treatment Act (CAPTA), and subsequent extensions of the federal law, there has been a massive expansion of social services and new agencies to deal with those parents and caretakers who fail to provide for the physical, emotional, or educational well-being of children. Parental participation in programs provided by these service agencies is bolstered by both enticing them and coercing them, if necessary, with promises of better lives or through legal action that could result in the loss of parental rights. Nonetheless it is often difficult to get neglectful parents or caretakers who need to learn how to care for their dependent children to attend classes or workshops. Some-

Box 11.1

November 15, 2005
Westchester Child Agency Is Called Poorly Managed
By Anahad O'Connor

A Westchester County grand jury investigating the scalding deaths of two boys in Yonkers released a report on Monday that harshly criticized the county's Department of Social Services.

. . . . The department has faced unusually intense and widespread criticism this year, particularly for its handling of the Yonkers case, in which Elijaha Santana, who was nearly 3, and his 20-month-old half brother, David Maldonado Jr., were burned to death after they were locked in a bathroom as scalding hot water poured from a tub.

As the boys struggled to escape from the bathroom, their parents were in a drug-induced sleep in a nearby room. An investigation by county legislators later revealed that a caseworker assigned to the family had repeatedly missed visits to the home and that the worker's supervisor may have failed to keep tabs on her.

. . . . [In another case] a social worker visited a home after getting a tip about a neglected infant. Despite learning that the parents were never home, that the family was about to be evicted and that the father would often fly into rages and throw objects at the baby, the report said the worker determined that the child was safe.

Within weeks of that visit, the mother left the unidentified baby with a neighbor but regained custody about seven months later. As the weeks passed, the report said, there were more reports about neglect and more signs that the father, who was not complying with a drug treatment program, was endangering the infant. The child was taken away this spring when the father threw the baby at a wall, fracturing its skull.

times this is because overworked caseworkers do not substantiate cases of neglect warranting intervention.

Box 11.1 is an excerpt from a newspaper story documenting how one particular local agency failed to respond appropriately to reports of child neglect. How many agencies across the United States, within recent months, have been cited for neglecting the neglected?

As with other types of child maltreatment, the difference between legally defining "neglect" and then applying that definition in practice—an operational definition—is important. Regardless of how the legal definitions are developed, in application they necessarily involve a standard of appropriate care against which the judgment is to be made. This standard is set not only by those who administer and provide services directly to individuals and families, but also by researchers seeking new insights into the causes and consequences of child neglect (Gough 1996). Controversy about how neglect should be examined centers around three issues:

1. how broadly or narrowly the standard of neglect should be defined;
2. whether emotional and psychological neglect is to be included;
3. if standards that are developed should apply to all families, regardless of the parents' or caretakers' ethnic, cultural, or social class backgrounds.

CPS and social services must develop operational definitions of neglect for practical reasons, as the following hypothetical situations indicate:

- Should a young child who is left at home alone after school while his parent works, a condition that exists for an estimated 3,325,000 children aged 6 to 12 years old,[1] be considered neglected?
- Should caretakers be considered neglectful if they fail to provide intellectual stimulation so the child can reach her full potential?
- Are unresponsive parents neglectful?
- Are parents or caretakers who regularly address their child with negative attributions neglectful?
- Are parents who place inappropriate expectations on their children neglectful?
- If a couple decides to have a home birth instead of going to a hospital, and complications develop that could have been prevented or treated at a birthing center, resulting in a severely disabled child who will require total care for life, should the parents be prosecuted on neglect charges?

- If a seriously ill child is not taken to a medical facility for care because of the parents' religious beliefs, should the state intervene?
- How should the state respond to parents who lack the basic knowledge and skills of child care, and consequently who *unintentionally* fail to protect and provide an appropriate home, thereby threatening the lives and futures of their children?

Consider two hypothetical cases of single mothers, each with two children, aged 6 and 8. One completed two years of college, and works full time as an administrative assistant in a small firm. She earns $31,000 per year before taxes. The other graduated from high school and has few marketable skills. She works as a part-time laundry assistant and earns $10,500 per year before taxes. Both women live in an urban area and neither receives financial support from the children's fathers beyond the occasional gifts they give them. Both women are concerned about the quality of life for their children.

One woman believes her children can be left alone after school until she returns from work, usually within three hours. When they play outside, they have a cell phone to use to contact their mother. When they are injured they rely on private medical care, thanks to medical insurance benefits. The other woman believes her children are best cared for by her, at home. She deliberately arranges her work hours to be home with her children after school. As a consequence, her income is less than adequate to cover housing, clothing, and food. In addition she has no medical insurance. When her 8-year-old was injured in a playground accident in the neighborhood, he was taken to a nearby hospital for medical care. The attending physician contacted CPS on the suspicion that the child was neglected. Are one or both of these women neglectful?

Child Protective Service workers and social service providers must make judgments about the harm or existing danger to a child. If harm or danger due to a lack of action is determined, these workers must decide who is responsible, using operational definitions of child neglect that are not based on precise, objective measures or standards. In most cases of neglect, the intensity, duration, and immediate consequences of omissions and the intentions of a parent—essential features of definitions of abuse—are neither measurable nor relevant. Neglect, like abuse, is defined operationally, first by the person reporting it and then by the investigator, whose judgments reflect administrative guidelines and inevitably are influenced by personal perspectives and attitudes.

As a result of these circumstances, there is tremendous inconsistency in the operational definitions and decisions about what constitutes child neglect among states and local communities. In 2002, for example, more than 90 percent of child maltreatment cases investigated by CPS agencies in New York and North Carolina were defined, classified, and reported to be cases of neglect, compared to 6.2 percent and 3.9 percent in Vermont and Pennsylvania, respectively (Administration for Children and Families 2004). Given the lack of clear demographic differences among these states, which might explain such differences or discrepancies, it is likely these rates reflect the influence of administrative decisions made and the operational definitions used by CPS investigators.

In contrast, the operational definitions of child neglect used by researchers are designed to provide data about causal factors, processes, and consequences. The data, in principle, can be generalized to larger populations and compared to other research findings. Unfortunately, much of the available research focuses on individuals, rather than giving consideration to family circumstances, and often ignores the difference between chronic and episodic child neglect (Nelson, Saunders, and Landsman 1993). Further, researchers may fail to consider the dynamics of family traditions, culture, and ethnicity, as well as the neighborhood or regional context, which are critical for understanding CPS decisions. As a result, service providers often view social science research as very limited in applicability to the decisions they must make about parents and the neglect of their children. A continuing issue is the interface between these two approaches: How can the information that is generated by researchers, who seek precision, comparability, and generalizations, be elaborated and applied to a problem in practice (Guterman 2002)? The challenges to answering this question are numerous and not easily resolved.

Research issues related to the quality of data, such as sampling, validity and reliability, prospective-retrospective approaches, and definitional precision, appear to be more significant for child neglect than for child abuse, in part because of the complexity of neglect. Some researchers have used the operational definitions of neglect found in case records that were applied by official agency personnel during or after investigations. However, many children experience multiple forms of maltreatment (Claussen and Crittenden 1991; McGee et al. 1995), and classifying children by only one type of maltreatment, usually for administrative and reporting purposes, does not allow the precision or clarity sought in research. In addition, because only reported cases are included in CPS records and much neglect is never reported to CPS agencies, the samples drawn and consequently the data that result may underestimate the prevalence and severity of all types of child neglect. In contrast, studies based on general population data (rather than CPS data) may include unreported and officially unidentified cases, but the lack of standardized measures of neglect make meaningful comparisons difficult.

Attempts to develop objective measures of neglect have been ongoing for many years, but the issue continues to challenge researchers. Zuravin, in a review of twenty-five studies of child neglect that were published from 1992 to 1996, evaluated both the sources of data and the operational definitions used, and found great variation in sampling and approaches to measurement. She concluded that to advance knowledge regarding causal factors and the unique consequences of child neglect, future research must use multiple sources of data, multidimensional classification schemes to encompass the various types of neglect, and build on existing measurement schemes that have established validity and reliability (1999).

The decisions of CPS agencies have been the primary source for defining child neglect in most studies, but some social science researchers have used their own measures of neglect, either alone or in combination with CPS evaluations. Others have relied on self-reported, retrospective information.

Despite the limitations of using various definitions and approaches to study the problem, there are strong and consistent findings about neglectful families and neglected children, their circumstances, and the consequences that result. Though states have somewhat different statutes, and those who investigate reports obviously use different operational definitions of neglect, CPS reports are an important source of data. When combined with the numerous studies that have been undertaken by governmental agencies, academics, and applied researchers, some conclusions are possible.

Incidence and Prevalence of Child Neglect

Incidence is a measure of the amount of neglect in a given time period, typically a year, and includes the number of incidents or reports regarding children who have been reported as victims of parental failure to provide adequate care. Incidence rates rarely distinguish between chronic or long-term child neglect, such as the failure to provide adequate food or shelter over several months or years, from single episodes of neglect, such as the lack of supervision of a 5-year-old who wanders away while the parent is asleep.

Lifetime prevalence refers to the number or the proportion of all children under the age of 18 who have ever been neglected. Some researchers suggest that prevalence refers to a measure of the chronic condition of neglect. While the number of children who are neglected is an appropriate focus, nearly all the available reports rely on either the number of children who have been neglected in a specific year, or a rate based on the number of children neglected per 1,000 children.

According to tabulations of cases investigated and verified by Child Protective Services, in 2002 in the United States more than 542,000 children, or about 60 percent of all maltreated children, were reported as victims of physical and medical child neglect. This reflects an increase from the approximately 482,000 verified cases reported in 1998 (Administration for Children and Families 2004).

In an effort to provide data about children who were recognized as neglected but not reported to CPS agencies, three National Incidence Studies (NIS 1, 2, and 3) were undertaken. They offer an alternative source of information about the incidence of neglect

(Sedlak and Broadhurst, 1996). Information was collected about cases that were identified by CPS or other agencies during the study period and met the criteria of age, residence, custody status, currency, and maltreatment that was nonaccidental and avoidable. For NIS 1 and 2, cases were screened to eliminate duplication and classified by level of severity, using both the harm standard—those who were seriously harmed as a result of neglect—and the more inclusive endangerment standard, in which both children seriously harmed, and those who had experienced neglect that put them in danger of being harmed, were counted.

Four types of neglect were defined by the NIS: "physical," "educational," "emotional," and "other." Physical neglect refers to parental or custodial refusal to seek health care or a delay in obtaining health care, abandonment, expulsion/refusal of custody, inadequate supervision, and other custody or physical neglect. Educational neglect is defined in terms of permitting chronic truancy, failure to enroll, and inattention to special educational need. Emotional neglect is the inadequate nurturance/affection, chronic/extreme spouse abuse, permitted drug/alcohol abuse, permitted other maladaptive behavior, refusal, delay, or failure to obtain psychological care, and other inattention to emotional needs. Other neglect is a category that includes involuntary neglect, chemically dependent newborns, or other aspects of maltreatment, such as overprotective restrictions that foster emotional overdependence or the chronic application of age-inappropriate expectations.

Based on these data, researchers estimate about 879,000 children were neglected in 1993, approximately 3 per 1,000 children. Nearly 339,000 of the victims experienced physical neglect, 212,800 were victims of emotional neglect, and 397,300 were neglected educationally. If the endangerment standard is used, the total number of children neglected reached nearly 2 million in 1993; this number is double that for 1988, and more than three times the 523,049 substantiated cases reported by CPS (U.S. Department of Health and Human Services 1997).

Only 28 percent of the children identified as abused or neglected by the harm standard, and only 33 percent of those falling under the endangerment standard in the NIS 3 study, were reported to CPS. And not all the reports of neglected children are investigated. As a result of such evidence, some have suggested that "the CPS system has reached its capacity to respond to the maltreated population" (Sedlak and Broadhurst 1996:16). Even the NIS figures represent a conservative estimate of child neglect because they do not include children who have been maltreated but unreported to either CPS or NIS by individuals in private therapy, families, or friends.

A third approach to measuring the incidence and prevalence of child neglect used the Parent-to-Child items of the Conflict Tactics Scale in the National Family Violence Surveys. Parents were asked to indicate if, in the past year or ever, they personally had acted certain ways. The parents were asked how many times "you (1) had to leave your child at home alone, even when you thought some adult should be with him/her; (2) were so caught up with your own problems that you were not able to show or tell your child that you loved him/her; (3) were not able to make sure your child got the food he/she needed; (4) were not able to make sure your child got to a doctor or hospital when he/she needed it; and (5) were too drunk or high (so) that you had a problem taking care of your child" (Straus et al. 1998:269).

A large number of parents, a rate of 195 per 1,000, said they had left their child alone during the last year, with an average of 6 times during the year; 213 per 1,000 indicated they had done so at some time. Combining all the types of neglect responses measured, 270 per 1,000 parents admitted to one or more types of omissions during the past year and 306 per 1,000 parents admitted that they had, at one point or another, ever engaged in one of these types of omissions. Clearly this suggests that what is legally defined as child neglect is relatively common but usually unreported and uninvestigated.

This measure, the rate of neglect, allows some comparisons, though not perfect ones. Based on the harm standard of neglect, the NIS 3 reports a rate of 13.1 per 1,000 children were neglected. Using the endangerment standard, the rate is 29.2 per 1,000 children. These figures are derived from reports of professionals who are involved with children in their communities, but the estimates, even for endangerment, are much smaller—about one-tenth of those provided by parents themselves. Similar results were found in a study of Memphis, Tennessee, residents who were asked to recall their childhood experiences, with about 5 percent reporting emotional neglect, and 18 percent indicating they had experienced physical neglect as children (Scher et al. 2004).

A comparison of victim characteristics provides some insight into the effects of differing definitions and identifications of child neglect. According to the 1995 CPS figures, children aged 0–3 were most likely to be neglected, followed by those aged 4–7, 8–11, and then 12 and older (U.S. Department of Health and Human Services 1997). The figures, derived from the NIS data, indicate the neglect rate is highest for those aged 6–8, while the rate for children under the age of 2 and those aged 3–5 is less than half that of older children (Sedlak and Broadhurst 1996).

While these data are not strictly comparable, they suggest that CPS involvement is more likely with very young children, probably due to the frequent and regular contact that parents have with health care professionals who are most likely to report medical child neglect. As children grow and develop, there is less contact with health professionals; and the neglect of older children, especially emotional neglect, is less obvious or socially visible. It is more likely to be overlooked, and consequently less likely to be reported to CPS by neighbors, friends, relatives, or other social actors. In addition, confusion about reporting and concerns about intervention among educational personnel and others in the community who interact with older children may reduce reports to CPS, despite awareness of possible child neglect.

There appears to be only slight differences in rates of neglect by the child's sex. CPS reports for 1995 indicate that boys were 51 percent of the total neglect cases, and about 53 percent of medical neglect cases (U.S. Department of Health and Human Services 1997). The NIS 3 data, using the harm standard, indicated no statistically significant differences in rates of neglect, but the endangerment standard indicated that boys, with a rate of 9.2 per 1,000, were slightly more likely to experience emotional neglect than girls (Sedlak and Broadhurst 1996).

Similarly, race appears to be unrelated to neglect, despite numerous studies that have identified different goals and child-rearing expectations across various racial and ethnic groups (Amato and Fowler 2002; Ferrari 2002; Korbin 2002; Rose and Meezan 1996) and the historic discriminatory applications of social welfare rules (Lawrence-Webb 1997). The three NIS reports do not indicate significant differences by race in the incidence of maltreatment, whether the harm or the endangerment standard is used. While there is a disproportionate representation of children of color in the child welfare population, the findings of the NIS reports suggest that differences, based on race, are due to the process of referral, investigation, and service allocation. The differences do not reflect race differences in rates of abuse and neglect. Undoubtedly the causes of neglect transcend racial, ethnic, and cultural factors.

The Context of Neglect

The long history of the neglect of children by their parents and the failure of many efforts to eliminate or minimize neglect has produced a litany of potential causal factors and persuasive arguments about its inevitability. These factors include personal attributes, such as ignorance, laziness, depression, mental illness, mental retardation, and temperament, as well as social conditions such as poverty, stress, large family size, dysfunctional families, or the lack of social support for parenting. However, none of these factors alone is adequate to explain child neglect, and no direct causal links between these personal attributes or conditions and neglect have been consistently identified. Instead, as Belsky (1993) suggested more than a decade ago, the social context is probably the most significant contributor to neglect.

Community responsibility for the poor, largely patterned after the English system of poor laws in the early years of the United States, gradually was replaced by Aid to Dependent Children in the 1930s, by Aid to Families with Dependent Children (AFDC) in the 1950s, and by entitlement programs and mandatory work programs for welfare recipients in the 1960s, which were intensified during the 1970s. While providing less than enough income to survive for most families, even these programs were so unpopular that child neglect—seen as an issue of the poor—was excluded from the legislation first introduced after child abuse was "rediscovered" in the early 1960s. Further, it appears unlikely the Child

Abuse Prevention and Treatment Act would have passed had neglect been included (Nelson 1984). The emphasis on the "classlessness" of abuse was essential for passage of that legislation.

In the 1980s, welfare cuts began in the face of rising numbers of claimants, and in 1996 the Personal Responsibility and Work Opportunity Act (PRWOA) was enacted, awarding block grants to the states that then set mandatory rules for work and a limit of five years on welfare. Arguments for this recent reform of welfare included the alleged effects of long-term dependency, especially the undermining of the work ethic and the encouragement of illegitimacy, family disruption, and irresponsible behavior among the urban poor, whose values purportedly deviated from core American values.

The effects of PRWOA are not yet fully understood and continue to be documented. Research on its impact on child maltreatment generally and the child neglect rate specifically is unclear, in part due to limited data regarding the direct linkages of poverty and child neglect. Some evidence from the National Longitudinal Survey of Youth, however, suggests that poverty has consequences for routine medical and dental care. For single parents who are employed, the risk of child neglect increases because employment is associated with poorer care giving for the child (Berger 2004). Most research on child neglect, for obvious ethical reasons, has been retrospective, and directed toward the identification of those characteristics or conditions that are shared by large numbers of families after they have been identified as neglectful. Poverty is the one factor that appears in nearly every study, along with the conditions associated with poverty: stress, underemployment or unemployment, low educational achievement, young and often unmarried parents, and poor mental and physical health (Drake and Pandey 1996; Giovannoni and Billingsley 1970; Kotch et al. 1995; Musick 1994; Wolock and Horowitz 1979; Zuravin and DiBlasio 1996). However, despite the fact that it has such importance, poverty is neither a sufficient nor a necessary cause of child neglect. As Crittenden (1999) notes, only some of the people who live in poverty neglect their children, and most of the children born to poor and often large families are not neglected.

Efforts to identify those distinctive circumstances or factors that distinguish neglectful poor families from non-neglectful ones have focused on parental conceptions of appropriate and inappropriate child care and family dynamics. A study of 400 parents in twenty neighborhoods that had different profiles of risk for child maltreatment found respondents gave similar definitions in response to the survey's open-ended question regarding what they would consider child abuse and neglect. Respondents identified inadequate food most often, followed by beating a child, lack of supervision, lack of cleanliness, and leaving the child alone. When respondents were given a list and then asked about the etiology of maltreatment, there was agreement among them about the causes of neglect. Drugs and alcohol were seen as major contributors, followed by stress, lack of family values, childhood abuse, psychological problems, poverty, unemployment, teen parents, and lack of knowledge (Korbin et al. 2000). Consistently studies report that families investigated for child neglect, compared to physically abusing families and non-maltreating families, are likely to be poorer, more reliant on public income, more likely to be headed by a single parent, and more likely to have medical, mental health, and substance abuse problems (Bath and Haapala 1993; Dubowitz et al. 1998; Zuravin and DiBlasio 1996). It is possible that most neglectful parents lack competence because of inadequate resources, poor preparation and support in their parental role, and impairment in coping due to overwhelming sources of stress, due to both familial and community factors.

Crittenden suggests that both poverty and chronic, long-term neglect may be effects of "learning to process information in distorted and limiting ways" (1999:66) and identifies three types of neglect related to invalid or inappropriate cognitive functioning. The "disorganized" type of neglect refers to multiproblem and crisis-prone families in which parents offer inconsistent parenting. "Emotional neglect" involves highly structured families in which parents focus on material or cognitive aspects but fail to express affection or adequately address the emotional needs of their children. "Depressed neglect" families are characterized by the mindless passivity or helplessness of the parents toward their children, in part because of a failure to perceive the child's needs or a failure to respond to them.

Though not using these classifications specifically, the research literature provides empirical evidence of these types of neglect.

Circumstances or general conditions that are often identified with child neglect include isolation, lack of social support, loneliness, depression, stress, and adolescent parenthood. Though operational definitions of these factors are not well-developed, making it difficult to compare the results of various studies, findings from studies using comparison groups suggest neglectful families, especially the depressed and the disorganized types, have multiple problems that are overwhelming. Chaffin and colleagues examined the onset of child abuse and neglect, noting that poverty, substance abuse, and mental health issues were significant factors in the development of neglectful behavior (1996). Based on intensive interviews with low-income African American mothers, Beeman (1997) reports those who had neglected were more dependent on others and their interactions were more likely to involve conflict and distrust, compared to those who did not neglect. Ethier et al. (1995) find that negligent mothers experienced more stress and depression than those in a comparison group.

One study of the importance of social isolation compared groups of mothers: 45 who had physically abused, 69 who had neglected, and 36 who had both abused and neglected their children. All were drawn from CPS records. A comparison group of 150 nonmaltreating mothers was recruited from schools in the same neighborhoods. The size, composition, and function of the mother's social networks were a focus of the study. Compared to mothers who did not abuse or neglect their children, neglectful-only mothers "had fewer members in their networks, had fewer total contacts, had less contact with the members they did have, [and] perceived their members to be less supportive . . . [they] received fewer instrumental and emotional resources from their network members" (Coohey 1996:249).

Despite consistency among studies of neglectful parents, questions of causality remain. Do loneliness, depression, stress, and isolation, all conditions that have been found to be associated with neglectful behavior, cause child neglect? Or is child neglect the result of other factors, such as parental alcohol and drug abuse, poverty, family disorganization, and inadequate early learning? These factors can lead to deficiencies in educational achievement, unemployment, and social and emotional deficits, which can in turn affect both perceptions and behavior, thereby creating neglectful behavior. Though there is no clear path of causality, the association of multiple factors with child neglect across generations within families suggests that there is a cycle of neglect that is continued in various ways. A lack of prenatal care creates conditions that can affect the child later, and early childhood experiences often produce the attitudes, values, and behaviors that perpetuate inadequate parenting (Zelenko et al. 2000). A child's early experiences are further complicated by problems associated with poverty, such as social isolation, poor schools and neighborhoods, inadequate housing and health care, which place greater responsibilities on parents to moderate the harsh effects of negative experiences. Increased levels of substance abuse by parents, during pregnancy and following birth, are related to increased rates and severity of child neglect (Chasnoff and Lowder 1999; Jaudes et al. 1995). The effects of a parent's incapacity to care for children include low birth weight, malnutrition, and related health concerns that may already be affected by income and other family factors (Berger 2004).

The consequences of neglect for children have been identified for many years, and the various types of neglect often produce different consequences. A failure to provide intellectual stimulation, which is often considered emotional and educational neglect, is related to a temperamental or "difficult child." The difficult child is more likely than other children to manifest difficulties in intellectual development and academic achievement (Kendall-Tackett and Eckenrode 1996) as well as social, affective, and psychological problems (Crouch and Milner 1993; Gaudin 1999). A lack of supervision may lead to injury and harm. Physical neglect, including the failure to have a child immunized and the failure to provide adequate nutrition, has obvious consequences for growth and development.

What types of intervention are needed to protect children from these multiple types of neglect? The evidence about neglectful families, based on decades of research, is that they are multiproblem families. They may face problems within the family regarding interaction, organization, management, communication, and nurturance. They face extrafamilial problems as well, such as poverty, a lack of work skills, inadequate medical care, deficient housing, and social isolation. In a Florida study, more than one-fourth of those families with substantiated reports of child neglect and provision of in-home services had a recurrent report within two years (Lipien and Forthofer 2004). These problems are magnified by major life events, such as the need to move, having a new baby, or being arrested (McDaniel and Slack 2005). Noting that "neglect results from a complex interplay of both risk and protective factors" (1999:229), and that both the internal operation of the family and its relationship to the community must be altered, DePanfilis suggests six components that are essential to an intervention and prevention program for neglectful families:

- Concrete services, such as housing assistance advocacy, transportation, medical care, child care, and similar actions
- Social services, such as individual mentoring, neighborhood center activities, cultural festivals, and similar programs
- Developmental interventions, such as individual assistance with parenting, educational programs, mentoring, and therapeutic day care as needed
- Cognitive-behavioral intervention, such as teaching social skills, home management, education in financial management, child-rearing, and communication skills
- Individual programs, such as alcohol or other drug counseling, mental health and stress management
- Family system programs, focused on family-centered issues, such as family functioning, nurturance, and family roles and responsibilities

Comprehensive programs are expensive, intensive, and require long-term involvement with neglectful families (Dore and Lee 1999). It appears doubtful that public support will emerge to support an investment in neglected children, though several analyses suggest that some programs, particularly a health care insurance program, would prove to be cost-effective. An analysis of costs associated with health coverage estimated that an additional $48 billion—from the current $125 billion to $173 billion—would be required to cover all U.S. citizens. Health care costs for uninsured persons currently include $34.6 billion provided from federal funds, and another $5 billion paid by other governments, hospitals, or health care providers (Hadley and

Holahan 2004). Numerous benefits could result from a comprehensive program, notably preventive care that would improve personal health and lower mortality—saving perhaps 18,000 children and adults every year.

As Zelizer (1985) observes, the social value of a child has evolved during the past century and continues to change in the United States. But how does one place a value on the life of one child, or one thousand children? What factors, conditions, or issues should be considered in making policy decisions about interventions in the lives of families? No clear answers have emerged in the past sixty years, to the detriment of the entire U.S. society, but especially to the children who are neglected by their parents, and then again by the public agencies that are created to help.

Elder Neglect

The "neglect of neglect" that characterizes the research literature on child neglect applies to elder neglect as well. Lawmakers and policymakers in the United States recognized elder neglect as a social problem as early as 1953. However, elder neglect remains an understudied problem in family abuse and violence. Most of the published papers on elder neglect are essays, not empirical studies conducted by social and health scientists. Until the most recent decade, the research that was published almost exclusively examined how or why employees, such as nursing assistants, abused or failed to care for their clients in long-term residential or nursing care facilities. It is only in the most contemporary research literature that we find elder neglect studied as a family abuse and violence problem that occurs within private residences. Nowadays it tends to be a social problem that is generally attributed to adult children who have willingly or reluctantly agreed to live with or care for an older family member.

Defining the Neglect of Dependent Elders

Elder neglect may be generally defined as the failure to provide for the goods or services that are necessary to avoid physical harm, mental anguish, or mental illness; or the failure of a caregiver to provide those goods or services. The National Center on Elder Abuse has identified three types of maltreatment that can be classified as neglect:

1. Neglect: The refusal or failure to fulfill any part of a person's obligations or duties to an elderly person.
2. Abandonment: The desertion of an elderly person by an individual who has physical custody of the elder or by a person who has assumed responsibility for providing care to the elder.
3. Self-neglect: Those behaviors of an elderly person that threaten the elder's health or safety. (National Center on Elder Abuse 1995)

Blameworthiness

Elder neglect ranges in severity from abandonment to the negligent failure to provide access to voting opportunities. State laws define what constitutes various forms of elder neglect and address the blameworthiness of the caretaker's omissions by distinguishing between intentional neglect and neglect that occurred in error or due to negligence (Brinig et al. 2004). The withholding of medication illustrates this distinction: A caregiver may, by mistake or negligence, fail to give an elder parent blood pressure medication because the caretaker was distracted by other responsibilities, or erroneously believed that the daily dose was not necessary. A more egregious omission is the deliberate withholding of the medication with the intention of increasing blood pressure and thereby increasing the elder's prospects of suffering a stroke.

Failure to provide services to guarantee an elder social actor's basic civil and human rights is also a form of neglect. Adults, unlike children, are entitled to vote. To deny a citizen's right intentionally is a violation of federal voting rights law, making a caretaker obligated to facilitate transportation to a voting place or to assist an adult in obtaining an absentee ballot. Elder adults, whether they are frail or strong, are entitled to receive mail and other forms of communication (phone calls, electronic mail, and so forth). To deny a dependent adult's opportunity for social contacts is a neglectful behavior that can be connected to other forms of elder abuse, such as financial exploitation (Choi, Kulick, and Mayer 1999; Choi and Mayer 2000). It can also lead to a degree of social isolation that can initiate a state of clinical depression or anxiety (Coyne, Reichman, and Berbig 1993; Guterman, Beavers et al. 1995; Dyer, Pavlik et al. 2000).

Elders, even if they become homebound, are entitled to believe and practice religiously prescribed and proscribed behaviors. To make available for an elder only food that is proscribed by his or her chosen religion (beef or pork, for example) is a neglectful behavior that can lead to malnutrition. Likewise, to fail to make religious practices available to an elder adult who desires to attend a place of worship, only because a caretaker does not want to provide the service, is a form of neglect (Heisler and Quinn 1995).

Failing to provide privacy for an elder family member is a neglectful form of abuse that generally does not apply to preadolescent children. Adults, socialized to seek privacy when bathing or defecating, experience abusive neglect if a bathroom door is removed or if a surveillance camera is used only to make the caretaker's daily chores easier to accomplish (Marshall et al. 2000).

Self-Neglect by Elders

Self-neglect is a type of FAV episode that applies by law exclusively to elders. It can be described as "the failure to engage in activities that a given culture deems necessary to maintain a socially accepted standard of personal and household hygiene, and to carry out activities needed to maintain health status" (Lauder et al. 2002:331). A study of all the states' statutes, which was sponsored by the Centers for Disease Control and Prevention, reports that only ten states define self-neglect with specific laws. Most of the states that define self-neglect (N = 21) subsume the definition within a broader definition of neglect (Brinig et al. 2004). State regulations, administrative laws, and court decisions also produce definitions of elder neglect that include self-neglect. Hoarding behavior, considered by many local communities to produce public health threats, is an example of elder self-neglect that is subsumed by regulatory law. The self-neglecting hoarder, that is, the elder who may live alone or with an adult child, fails to maintain a sufficiently clean residence. As a consequence the self-neglecting hoarder is at risk for falls and injury and disease and illness.

Like all other forms of FAV, self-neglect is socially defined and constructed. Contemporary values and norms guide standards for hygiene and health. In colonial America only the most obsessive person would attempt to bathe on a daily basis. To require an elder to bathe daily would certainly be abusive. In the contemporary United States, most would judge the older person who has not bathed within the past month to be unhygienic.

What is health? While one person may gauge her health status by an ability to run or jog or solve crossword puzzles, another may gauge it by longevity, even if the elder social actor is bedridden, suffering from memory impairment, and homebound. Defining health is only one dimension of the complex problem of determining self-neglect by an elder. Legal and medical determinations of competence, based on various measures of ability or mental health, are necessary to ascertain if an elder client has engaged in self-neglecting behavior by deciding not to seek medical intervention, not to take prescribed medications, or not to follow the financial or legal advice offered by an appointed guardian or other adviser (Bond et al. 1999; Quinn 2000).

Self-neglect represents a large percentage of the elder neglect cases to which agencies such as Adult Protective Services or a local Area Agency on Aging must respond. Because self-neglect is not adequately studied and because it gets included or overshadowed by other important debates, such as the right to die, researchers can make more valid claims about its correlates than its causes or consequences. Factors such as malnutrition, depression, memory impairment, substance abuse, poverty, social isolation, and illness, especially a chronic illness requiring numerous medications, are among the known correlates of self-neglect (Cooney and Mortimer 1995; Choi and Mayer 2000; Mays 2002; Kahn and Paris 2003). Although race or ethnicity is not correlated with elder neglect, living in rural areas increases the likelihood of women facing a deprivational form of elder neglect (Dimah and Dimah 2003).

Child neglect and elder neglect are similar problems because they are premised on the notion that adults within a family have a social, moral, and legal responsibility to nurture and care for persons who are dependent upon them. The failure to provide the services and materials necessary for dependents to survive or thrive constitutes a form of family abuse that highlights the issue of autonomy/dependence within familial relationships. Chronic neglect results in physical harm, emotional harm, and even death.

Privacy is an issue that separates elder neglect from child neglect. The crowded bedroom and the lack of privacy may be acceptable for children, but adults, in contemporary U.S. society, expect privacy to care for the self. The failure to provide privacy is a form of elder abuse only because it is culturally and normatively defined.

The neglect of a child and the neglect of a dependent elder are persistent problems that evolve as families and society change. What also persists is a strong need for U.S. policymakers and social scientists to consider a small number of very important questions: How important is the family care work that our dependents require to survive and thrive? Who provides the care work that our dependents need? How highly do we value our family dependents, who represent our future and our past?

Discussion Questions

1. How can the "neglect of neglect" of children and elders in the research literature be explained?
2. Identify the types of neglect that you think have the most serious consequences for both elders and dependent children.
3. Take and justify a position on one of the following claims: (a) child neglect is the most insidious form of intergenerational family abuse and violence in the United States; (b) elder abuse should not be tolerated within the United States because this country is wealthy enough to end all forms of elder abuse.

4. Prioritize, in order of their importance, the factors that cause the neglect of children and the neglect of elders: ignorance, psychological problems, poverty, drug or alcohol abuse, illness, social or physical isolation, and depression. What are the additional factors that should be considered?
5. If an elder and ill person deliberately refuses to eat or rejects medication because she or he wishes to die, should the state consider the refusals acts of self-neglect? Would family members be held responsible for an elder's death under such circumstances? Under what circumstances would the state be justified in removing the elder family member from her or his home and placing the elder in a hospital or residential facility?
6. Poverty is a known contributor to child neglect. How does poverty directly and indirectly increase the risk of child neglect? Why don't most families in poverty neglect their children?

Research Project

Identify the key causes of poverty in a local community. Design a comprehensive community program that would mitigate the effects of a particular cause of poverty within the community. If necessary limit the program to serve a particular neighborhood or geographic area within the city. Locate an office or a building to house the program. Draft newspaper advertisements to recruit volunteer staff for the program. Identify a private foundation that could fund the creation and maintenance of the program for one year. Outline specific program services.

Note

1. See, e.g., Vaddivere et al. 2003.

VII

ASSESSING THE SITUATION

12

Persistent Controversies and Emerging Issues

What if a researcher chose to search the Books in Print database, available at most university libraries and in many public libraries, to see how many books there are on family violence and related topics. What would the researcher find? Here are the results of a November 24, 2005, keyword search in Books in Print:

- 2,274 books on child abuse
- 501 books on domestic violence
- 119 books on woman abuse
- 63 books on elder abuse
- 10 books on intimate partner violence

Are societies and writers more concerned about child abuse than domestic violence or elder abuse? Why are there 501 books on domestic violence but only 10 on intimate partner violence? With more than 2,000 books on child abuse, is there any part of this problem that has not been studied?

The keywords or the *terms* themselves represent one of the long-standing controversies in the study of FAV episodes: What do we call the problem? What difference does a term make? To distinguish between abuse and neglect or abuse and violence is problematic. The problems, whatever we call them, tend to co-occur. Nonetheless, one term, based on the politics of lawmaking or the particular social science theory that guides a research design, gets preference over another and may erroneously communicate the dimensions or the persistence of the social problem.

A parent or spouse who hits a child or spouse with a chair has committed a violent act. For some researchers, that is the story. For others, it is only the beginning: The victim can be affected psychologically or emotionally by family abuse and violence episodes. A violent act can also be an abusive and controlling episode. Moreover, if others witness it, it can affect secondary victims.

Also problematic are the distinctions that researchers and social change advocates make among the terms "domestic violence," "spouse abuse," "woman abuse," "battered wife," "wife abuse," and "intimate partner violence." During the 1970s wife abuse and spouse abuse were for some writers nearly interchangeable terms, yet for others they were contentious terms. "Wife abuse" can imply that only women within marriages are the subjects or the potential victims of the social problem. Another term, "spouse abuse," implies that men and women, within their marriages, are potential victims.

Woman abuse, especially for feminist researchers, was a corrective term used to heighten awareness that women and girls within patriarchal societies are the subject of abuse and violence within their intimate relationships and also within public places and spaces. As woman abuse researchers study FAV episodes, including marital or partner rape, they tend to pay careful attention to a cluster of related problems, especially stalking and sexual assault and sexual harassment in school or at work.

"Partner abuse" was the term used by Claire Renzetti (1992) in her study of violence and abuse within lesbian relationships. Renzetti's exemplary scholarship, which is theoretically driven and empirically strong, takes a social problems approach to uncovering a form of intragenerational FAV that social actors in legal, medical, and social service work tend to ignore or avoid. The appendixes to her book, *Violent Betrayal*, include the research instruments she used to gather data from victims and from service providers.

We use the term "intimate partner violence" for a number of reasons. It can be used to study the FAV episodes that harm married or cohabiting heterosexual couples, dating partners, and same-sex couples. It is an inclusive term. The term also is conceptually rich because it generates distinctions between situational couple violence and intimate partner terrorism (Johnson and Ferraro 2000), which have different causes and imply different consequences for victims and for perpetrators.

The terms chosen certainly represent persistent debates in the field of FAV. In *Current Controversies on Family Violence*, the editors (Gelles and Loseke 1993) begin their book with essays on issues surrounding the terms researchers use and the related conceptualizations of FAV problems. In the second edition, published more than a decade later, the editors (Gelles et al. 2004) also include a number of essays on the controversial topic of using and defining various terms.

A second controversy that has persisted across the decades is the question of whether family abuse and violence or the separate and specific types of abuse and violence that affect children, adults, and dependent elders ought to be the focus of theory and research. Clearly we weigh in on the debate. Our position is that social scientists must study *families* and family-type relationships in the United States in order to understand the problems that children, adult partners, and parents experience. We do not think that a single theory is desirable or adequate for explaining all forms of FAV or that a single research project can adequately study the problem. Our position is that families or family-type relationships make the social spaces where abuse and violence can occur. U.S. families today have the responsibility to provide high-quality care to enrich the lives of family members who range from newborn infants to dying parents. Some of the forms of abuse and violence that take place within families also take place in other social spaces that families depend on to care for family members—in schools, in hospitals, or in some other institution or facility. Our position is that social scientists, policymakers, and lawmakers need to understand

- how U.S. families and expectations for them are different now
- why some families and family-type relationships experience family violence and abuse while others do not.

The facts and figures that purportedly describe and document the multiple forms of family abuse and violence in the United States represent the third major controversy that has persisted across the decades. Best (2001, 2005) amuses his readers as he illustrates how social movement activists, politicians, the media, and other well-intentioned social actors knowingly or naïvely misuse or misrepresent statistical data in the social construction of problems, including family abuse and violence. Richard Gelles posts, on the Minnesota Center Against Violence and Abuse web page, a series of "Domestic Violence Factoids." The factoids, all of which are excellent candidates for Best's next sequel to *Damned Lies and Statistics*, are myths or supposed statistics summarizing the problem of intimate partner violence. They include the following misrepresentations, which have been repeated in speeches and public addresses to the extent they are elements of the popular discourse on intimate partner violence:

- According to the FBI, a woman is beaten ever nine (or fifteen) seconds.
- There are four million women beaten and abused each year.
- Four thousand women each year are killed by their husbands, ex-husbands, or boyfriends.
- The March of Dimes reports battering during pregnancy is the leading cause of birth defects.
- Family violence has killed more women in the last five years than the total number of Americans who were killed in the Vietnam War.
- Women are as violent as men, and women initiate violence as often as men.
- Fifty percent of all homeless women and children are on the streets because of violence in the home.
- There are nearly three times as many animal shelters in the United States as there are shelters for battered women and their children.

Gelles provides sources for each factoid and corrections for all of them. While the factoids are myths, there are systematic attempts to collect reliable and valid data to summarize some but not all forms of inter- and intragenerational family abuse and violence in the United States. Until the federal government commits to gathering and compiling accurate data on all forms of FAV, the controversy of what to count and how to count episodes of FAV will continue. Thus policymakers, social program designers, and researchers will remain committed to or limited by the controversial and inaccurate statistics that summarize and explain a substantial social problem.

Child Abuse and Neglect Controversies

Some of the controversies regarding *inter*generational forms of FAV seem to have been put to rest. No longer are specialty journals in the social sciences devoted to mysteriously missing children or satanic or ritual forms of child abuse in the United States. Box 12.1, however, reminds us that allegations and zealous prosecution do indeed persist in isolated cases.

Also we now know the supposed problem of *repressed* memory in adolescence or adulthood, in response to childhood sexual abuse, is actually the problem of *constructed* memories, which are associated with particular intervention strategies. We know that social interventions in response to allegations of child sexual abuse can be witch hunts rather than effective strategies to keep children safe. The persistent controversies are less sensational than the ones from decades earlier, which were as likely to appear in an issue of the *National Enquirer* as in an academic journal. Now we tend to be most concerned with controversies addressing what happens to children in their families: How does emotional abuse or neglect affect a baby or an older child? What are the long-term consequences of fetal alcohol syndrome? Should drug-addicted parents or caretakers lose custody of their child or children?

Emotional Abuse and Neglect

Few would deny that psychological or emotional abuse is a common experience for children, but the problem continues to challenge

Box 12.1.   Ritual Child Abuse Accusations

March 18, 2002
Justice, Not So Swift
By Katha Pollit

On October 31 Governor Jane Swift of Massachusetts pardoned five women who had been convicted and executed in the Salem witch trials in 1692. On February 20 she rejected the recommendation of the state parole board, known for its sternness and strictness, and refused to commute the thirty-to-forty-year sentence of Gerald Amirault, who was convicted in the 1986 Fells Acre Day School sex abuse case and who has already served sixteen years in prison.

Since the 1980s, when a wave of now notorious prosecutions of alleged ritual child sex abuse swept the country, many of the techniques used to elicit children's stories of abuse have been discredited: leading and coercive questions, multiple interviews, promises of rewards, suggestive use of anatomical dolls. It's no longer iron-clad doctrine that certain behaviors, like bed-wetting, masturbation and sexualized play, reliably indicate sex abuse.

. . . . [In] the Amirault case . . . [the] result was that a respected working-class family who had run a popular daycare center in Malden for twenty years—a place where parents were constantly popping in and out of—were convicted of a total of twenty-six counts of child abuse involving nine children in trials that included accusations of extravagant and flamboyant behavior: children were being raped with butcher knives (which left no wounds), tied to trees on the front lawn while other teachers watched . . . thrown about by robots, tortured in a magic room by an evil clown. One child claimed sixteen children had been killed at the center. Obvious questions went unasked: How come no kids who went to Fells Acre in previous years had these alarming experiences? Why was an expert witness permitted to testify about a child-pornography ring when no pornographic photos of the Fells Acre kids were ever found?

Massachusetts—liberal, modern, technocratic Massachusetts—is the only state in which people convicted in the 1980s wave of ritual child abuse cases are still in prison. . . . Will it take another 300 years for the state to acknowledge that Salem was not its last miscarriage of justice?

Source: Katha Pollitt, *The Nation*, March 18, 2002. Reprinted by permission.

researchers and protective service workers. There is a long and well-documented history of research on the significance of *early child-rearing* behaviors on the short-term and the long-term emotional and social health of individuals. In addition, the factors that affect social attachments and the consequences of insecure attachment for both children and their parents or caretakers are well-documented. There is less definitive information about the emotional neglect and abuse that harms *older children.*

There appears to be less agreement over the types of actions or the omissions that constitute emotional or psychological maltreatment of older children. Consider the following forms of abuse:

- confining to a small space
- public humiliation
- the Cinderella syndrome
- scapegoating
- severe verbal abuse
- coercing a child or adolescent to commit delinquent or criminal acts
- threatening or refusing psychiatric treatment.

Abusive behaviors such as denigration or verbal attacks are often combined with child neglect. A research effort to develop definitions of psychological maltreatment by the American Professional Society on the Abuse of Children resulted in six abuse and neglect categories. After reviewing their applicability, the six types of maltreatment were revised by Glaser (2002) into five basic categories:

- emotional unavailability
- negative attributions or misattributions to the child
- developmentally inappropriate or inconsistent interactions with the child
- failure to recognize/acknowledge the child's individuality
- failing to promote the child's social adaptation.

These are not discrete categories, however, as many children experience more than one type of abuse. All of them can lead to some impairment of emotional and social development.

Emotional or psychological abuse includes actively violent parental practices that appear to occur most frequently in families in which one child is the scapegoat, there is a domineering father or a rigid or manipulative mother, or the parents are generally incompetent (Gagne and Bouchard 2004). Some laws and some researchers include witnessing intimate partner violence as a dimension of emotional abuse of children (Jellen et al. 2001).

Unfortunately, in older children both emotional neglect and abuse are often overlooked, and some children may deny they have been victims of maltreatment and therefore avoid engaging in the processes necessary to mitigate or negate the harm they suffered. As Hart and Brassard suggested two decades ago, parental behaviors that may be seen as emotional or psychological abuse or neglect by observers may not be interpreted as maltreatment by the child, but relatively few studies have attempted to address this issue.

Child care—or care work—by extended family members or by someone outside the family is an extremely important issue that must be addressed by social actors and organizations that are seriously interested in the problems of child abuse and neglect. Given the high rate of dual parent or single parent employment, too many parents and caretakers must depend on insufficient and inadequate care for their preschool and school-aged children. A 1997 study, conducted before the effects of revised welfare laws were documented, found that 81 percent of infants were in some form of regular nonmaternal child care during their first twelve months of life, with most starting prior to 4 months of age and enrolled for nearly thirty hours per week (NICHD 1997). The study noted the connection between stability of care and developmental outcomes.

An ambitious national study of child care examined media reports, legal records, and ethnographic data. The researchers explained variation in fatality rates and injuries sustained by preschoolers as a function of the type of day care facility. Is child care in someone's home safer or more dangerous for preschoolers compared to child care in licensed centers? The researchers conclude that child care centers provide "protection against fatalities, especially fatalities from violence" (Wrigley and Dreby 2005:753). Child death rates for preschoolers cared for in private homes are sixteen-times higher than for preschoolers in child care centers. Children also face an increased risk of injury or sexual abuse if they are cared for by non-family members in private homes. Clearly the lack of consistent, quality child care and the potential negative effects that may emerge in the future present a substantial challenge for U.S. society that must be addressed.

Prenatal Maltreatment

Fetal alcohol syndrome (FAS) appeared in the research literature as early as 1973, when several genetically related problems in newborns were found to be related to their mothers' consumption of alcohol during pregnancy. The problems included underdeveloped or malformed joints, genital or heart defects, cardiovascular abnormalities, low birth weight, mental retardation, and neurological defects. While other maternal behaviors or conditions, including drug use, smoking, and workplace environments, also were associated with birth abnormalities, attention was directed to drugs and alcohol because of their quick and measurable effects on the fetus.[1]

Several states passed laws for the mandatory screening of suspected drug or substance abuse in hospitals and the reporting of drug or alcohol abuse to Child Protection Services if the screens were positive. The Center for Reproductive Law reported that by the mid-1990s, 70 percent of the states "had prosecuted women for talking illicit drugs while they were pregnant" (Hines and Malley-Morrison 2005:300).

The response to a woman's drug and alcohol abuse, while pregnant, was and is not consistent across or within states. Only a small number of states include in their laws fetal abuse through drug exposure as an explicit type of child abuse. Moreover, some CPS agencies respond to referrals aggressively, while others do not (Ondersma et al. 2001). Expectations about subsequent abuse or neglect by those who are referred because of prenatal drug or alcohol use appear to influence the way CPS agencies respond (Smith and Testa 2002), though CPS responses also may differ as a function of the type of addiction or drug (Hohman et al. 2003).

Numerous problems appeared as quickly as the laws requiring drug screenings or CPS investigations of prenatal drug use. The inaccuracy of most drug screens is a key problem. False positive results as well as false negatives were common. In addition, discrimination in the application of screening was apparent from the beginning. African Americans, single mothers, those who had no prenatal care, or who were known to CPS were far more likely to be tested than others. Court rulings often were inconsistent even within a state and

Box 12.2.   Child Endangerment

April 26, 2004
Pregnant and Dangerous
By Katha Pollitt

The good news is that Utah has dropped murder charges against Melissa Rowland, who rejected her doctors' advice to undergo an immediate Caesarean
section and gave birth to a stillborn boy and a girl who tested positive for cocaine. . . . She has accepted a plea to two counts of child endangerment for using drugs during pregnancy. . . .
    Rowland is a deeply troubled woman: mentally ill, estranged from her fam-
ily, sometimes homeless; she was confined to a mental hospital at 12, bore
twins at 14, has tried to kill herself twice; four years ago her daughter was
placed in foster care after Rowland was convicted of child abuse. . . . Her
boyfriend, father of the second set of twins, abandoned her. . . . Lorna Vogt of
the Utah Progressive Network says Rowland told her that the reason she was
in Utah . . . was that she had been brought to Salt Lake City from Florida by an
adoption agency to deliver the babies and give them up. (Utah has lax adoption laws, and apparently this practice is not uncommon.)
    Rowland lacked everything a pregnant woman should have: support, secu-
rity, understanding, respect.
    . . . . what is becoming an American tradition [is] arresting poor women for
illegal drug use during pregnancy. For the past eight years, South Carolina has
been charging women, mostly poor and black, with child abuse if they deliver
babies who test positive for illegal drugs; the Supreme Court recently refused
to hear the appeal of Regina McKnight, who is serving twelve years in maxi-
mum security for "homicide by child abuse" after delivering a stillborn baby
who tested positive for cocaine.
    Melissa Rowland's case is one that never should have happened. . . . the
State of Utah should be asking itself how it can improve services for poor, pregnant, mentally ill substance abusers—and maybe take a look at its adoption
agency practices, too.

Source: Katha Pollitt, The Nation, April 26, 2004. Reprinted by permission.

depended on a judge to define a mother's criminal liability. Finally,
the inaccessibility or severe shortage of treatment facilities and other
services for addicted women meant that many, if not most, addicted
mothers continued to use alcohol and drugs, and many consequently faced criminal proceedings when their children were born
(Zivi 2000). Box 12.2 describes the dilemma that a pregnant, cocaine
abusing, mentally ill woman faced.

With the obvious lack of consensus regarding what is in the best interest of the child, no clear solution has emerged for the problem of drug or alcohol abusing mothers or pregnant women. While some research indicates that the early effects of FAS and other substances are severe, other research suggests the consequences of fetal alcohol and drug use are mitigated or disappear with later care (Wattendorf and Muenke 2005). Clearly continued research is needed to clarify the long-term effects of alcohol, illicit and legal drugs, and other ingested substances.

Perhaps more importantly, empirical research is necessary to determine the effects of toxic environments on fetuses, babies, and children. The effects of procreating adults' work settings, air and water pollution, the proximity of toxic waste sites, and other environmental hazards on the developing fetus or the school-aged child or adolescent need to be established empirically.

It is an easy and reasonable claim: Research is necessary to give us an adequate understanding of child abuse in the United States. Yet some suspected types of child abuse remain controversial precisely because we cannot depend on researchers to figure out if a child has a medical or genetic problem or is the victim of maltreatment or neglect. Consider the layers of tragedies documented in box 12.3. Parents who have already experienced the death of one of their children have also lost custody of their surviving children. Perhaps this is because researchers cannot yet figure out what constitutes a neurological condition and what constitutes a controversial mental illness (Munchausen by proxy syndrome). Clearly the parents should not be told "wait until the research is conducted."

Intimate Partner Violence
Controversies and Emerging Problems

Some controversies are likely to persist for decades in discussions of intimate partner family abuse and violence: Is there gender parity in domestic or partner violence? Do criminal justice interventions help or hurt? Other issues have recently emerged: How should the state respond to mothers whose children are exposed to violence within the family? In this section we look at examples of

Box 12.3. Munchausen by Proxy?

April 19, 2005
Expert Declares Accused Parents 'Normal':
  Munchausen by Proxy at Core of Butler Trial
By Karen Kane

A nationally known expert in the study of Munchausen syndrome by proxy testified yesterday that a Butler County couple who lost custody of their children last fall are "normal parents" who were swept up in the medical community's confusion over a neurological disease that is difficult to diagnose.

Dr. Loren Pankratz, a medical pathologist and clinical professor . . . told Butler County juvenile court he flew to Pittsburgh at his own expense and is forgoing his usual $15,000 witness fee because he is convinced that Mannie and Ron . . . are innocent of accusations that they concocted a set of medical ailments for two of their three children.

Pankratz testified he has been studying the range of "patients who deceive in the medical setting" for 30 years.

The children . . . were taken away from their home in September by Butler County Children and Youth Services [who] said that Mannie and Ron manipulated doctors into giving [the children] narcotic drugs and feeding tubes.

The parents contend [that their children] have mitochondrial disease, in which the mitochondria—the part of the cell responsible for energy production—fails to work properly.

. . . . [T]estimony presented during 10 court days from medical and school professionals [gave] contrasting pictures of children who were failing to thrive under the parents' care and who now are doing well in foster care.

Pankratz said he has found the "separation test" to be unreliable proof of Munchausen's because children's conditions can improve for a variety of reasons, including changes in medical treatment.

He said that if he were [Mannie and Ron] he would be predisposed to believing the children had mitochondrial disease because of medical symptoms that were objectively noted by doctors as well as medical indications that a sibling had died just shy of his third birthday . . . from complications of the disease, which often runs in families.

Pankratz said the couple are "worthy parents" who "were caught up in the doctors' differences of opinions as to how the children should be managed medically."

both persistent and emerging controversies that policymakers address when responding to *intra*generational forms of FAV episodes.

We find that studies of adolescent dating partner abuse tend to report that girls hit or initiate aggressive behaviors as frequently as boys (Cleveland, Herrera, and Stuewig 2003). A meta-analysis of the published empirical research on heterosexual couples shows that women, especially when they are younger, are no less likely than men to engage in physical aggression. Men, however, are much less likely than women to experience injuries as a consequence (Archer 2000).

A number of factors explain the gender parity controversy, such as the sampling strategy and data-collection instrument used. The gender parity question is an important one when emotional and psychological abuse and non–life-threatening events are the focus of inquiry. Verbally, emotionally, and psychologically abused men can indeed be harmed and seriously affected by their intimate partners. Men within their families need to be studied carefully to see how, as primary victims of FAV episodes, they may, in response, become primary perpetrators and cause psychological or physical injuries to other immediate family members or to extended family members, coworkers, and friends who are external to the FAV episode.

There is no gender parity question when the focus changes from all forms of FAV episodes to those that cause serious injuries or death. Women, not men, are the victims in most cases. There are, of course, notable exceptions to the empirical pattern. Remember Billy? We described his homicide in chapter 1. *He* and his extended family are tragic victims of family abuse and violence.

Intimate partner homicides and attempted homicides[2] have decreased dramatically since the mid-1970s. Fox and Zawitz (2004) find that the decline is especially sharp for male victims. For each race by gender group, some decrease is noted, with one exception: white girlfriends. White women not married to their abusers represent the single group in the United States that has not experienced a decline in FAV homicides. In addition, it is important to note that not all groups of married persons are equally protected against the risk of domestic homicides. Zahn finds that the decline in homicide among married couples is "greater for men and for blacks and less pronounced for white women" (Zahn 2003).

What are the predictors of FAV that result in death? The mechanics of the FAV episode are important. If the perpetrator, a social actor internal to the episode, possesses a gun or has access to other weapons, and if he uses alcohol daily or excessively, he increases the risk of his partner's death as a consequence of his FAV. Women may experience life-threatening or life-ending forms of FAV when they decide to leave their abusers, especially if their abusers are pathologically jealous (Block 2003). Women who are stalked by their abusive partners, and who experience forced sex or abuse during pregnancy, also experience an increased risk of homicide victimization (Campbell et al. 2003).

There are three extremely important controversies for lawmakers, policymakers, and service providers to consider when developing programs, interventions, or ideas to reduce the risk of FAV homicides:

1. How useful are danger assessment tools?
2. Does the use of community resources increase or decrease a woman's risk of homicide?
3. Can police or prosecutorial behaviors trigger homicide?

Campbell developed a "Danger Assessment" tool in 1985 and refined it based on reliability and validity studies. It is available online, via a Johns Hopkins University web page, along with instructions for how to use it properly.[3] When used by social organizations, such as a domestic violence treatment program or a police department, the tool can assess how grave the risk is for an abused woman to be killed by an abusive partner. Campbell's multi-city homicide study found that 83 percent of the women who were killed had scores of "4 or higher [on the Danger Assessment tool], but so did almost 40 percent of the women who were *not* killed" (Campbell et al. 2003). Thus, the dilemma: A number of women who died as a consequence of FAV faced a risk that they or social organizations external to the FAV episode failed to recognize. Yet a number of women whose recent experiences would put them at risk of death were not killed.

Which is more problematic for the policymaker or the police department? Failing to correctly identify the woman who *will die* as a consequence of FAV? Or incorrectly estimating that a perpetrator *will kill*—and therefore incapacitating him—when he would not have killed? The dilemma, balancing the consequences of false negative and false positive errors, has life and death consequences.

Well-intentioned men and women routinely encourage adult FAV victims whom they know to seek help from local social service or criminal justice agencies, premised on the notion that protection orders, arrests, prosecution, or safe shelter services can only help victims. Homicide studies challenge many commonsense recommendations and therefore elicit controversy. Campbell's twelve-city control-group study of female, adult FAV victims found that only 4 percent "of the victims of actual and attempted femicide actually" contacted domestic violence shelters (Campbell et al. 2003). In chapter 10, when describing the murder of Brenda by her husband, we noted that she had never contacted a domestic violence intervention program.

Nearly half of the homicide victims in Campbell's studies had been seen by physicians for FAV injuries during the year of their deaths. The implications of her research, and the homicide studies conducted by others, are that health care providers need to recognize the signs of FAV and talk with their patients to assist the women in making decisions that can save their lives.

Most women killed by their husbands or intimate partners did not turn to domestic violence shelters. Why didn't they? Some were ashamed, others were afraid. Some may have been concerned about their social position or social status or about what would happen to their abusers. A number of homicide victims probably had experienced only one or no prior violent assaults.

Dugan et al. report that FAV victims may be helped or actually harmed by intervention programs. They report that "unmarried black women [who are FAV victims] may be especially vulnerable to homicide if they elect to use domestic violence resources" (Dugan, Nagin, and Rosenfeld 2003). For all victims a "retaliation effect or backlash may also be triggered by an intervention—such as a restraining order, arrest, or shelter protection—that angers or threatens the abuser without effectively reducing contact with the victim" (2003:23). These researchers point out that the following types of interventions for FAV can be equally helpful or harmful for victims of all race and ethnic groups: Mandatory arrest for protection order violations, state laws that provide no-contact orders for those who do not cohabit, and mandatory arrest for domestic assault.

Children Who Witness Intimate Partner Abuse and Violence

The FAV Episode perspective is useful for recognizing the *intra*- and *inter*generational behaviors that can injure and harm primary and secondary victims. It also addresses a controversial issue that has emerged in FAV policy and law: Should children in a violent or abusive home be removed from their mother's custody? Some argue that children who witness what is commonly called domestic violence should be removed from the home. Some argue that mothers should be held accountable for failing to protect their children from the emotional abuse that can result from witnessing violence. What should the state do when a pregnant woman is assaulted by an abusive partner? Are mothers or pregnant women who are victimized by FAV unfit mothers? Some legal analysts conclude that removing a child from a mother's custody because she is a victim of FAV results in the re-victimization of the primary victim and possibly the re-victimization of the children—the secondary victims of FAV. Others take a stronger position and claim systemic misogyny accounts for legal proceedings that fail to respond to the gendered nature of FAV and the state's response to the problem (Lemon 2001, 2006).

Elder Abuse and Neglect Controversies and Emerging Issues

Consider the family events, ceremonies, and rituals that our local newspapers report on every week: births, deaths, and weddings. When our local newspaper reported on a wedding in 1965, it most likely described a bride and a groom with one set of parents each. Today, newspaper readers need to pay attention to the details to figure out how many marriages were blended by the time a couple of 25-year-olds got married. The consequences of increasingly complex families and increased longevity are causes for celebration. They are also causes for concern. We end this chapter with a discussion of some of the problems that unfortunately represent emerging issues regarding elder abuse and neglect.

Researchers and practitioners interested in *intra*generational forms of FAV can no longer make the mistake of thinking that intimate partner violence is a social problem that affects younger adults, ending with later-life stage transitions, such as retirement for men or women or menopause for women. An emerging issue that social organizations external to FAV episodes must address is the problem of physical and sexual violence that older women and some men experience. Safe shelters are not the preferred living option for any FAV victim. Nonetheless they tend to be funded and organized to provide the services that mothers and their dependent children need to survive. Few communities have planned and initiated the comprehensive programs that older victims need.

Many elder parents, some who retire and relocate to housing developments designed for an active lifestyle, find themselves unable to remain independent once chronic illness or disability or financial limitations dominate their everyday activities. New forms of abuse, or those made easier or more possible with home computers, put elders at risk for mortgage and other forms of financial fraud and identity thefts, sometimes by immediate or extended family members.

For decades researchers have debated the question: Why do some family caregivers abuse elders? Early research presented the case for stress as a cause of social deviance. More recent studies tend to take a stress versus crime position. Either the caretaker is under extreme stress, with little social support or relief from the need to provide constant care; or the abuser is criminal and deserves punishment, even if she or he is the victim's child (Forbat 2002; Payne 2002). It is imperative to avoid victim blaming when addressing any form of FAV. It is also important to recognize that the consequences of a punitive response to elder abusers can be life threatening *for the victim*. In the United States we have a foster care system for children, but we do not have a foster care system for elder and dependent parents. If a perpetrator loses employment and income as a consequence of a conviction of elder abuse, the perpetrator may no longer be able to care for her or his dependent. This is an emerging and urgent issue that is sometimes discussed with the theme of family preservation that used to be reserved for the child-parent relationship.

Complex and changing families face emerging issues that can result in emotional neglect and abuse of elders. Debates in the near future will address the financial responsibilities that families have to care for their dependent and elder parents. They will approach the right to die question, and they will recognize the rights of grandparents. Right now, policymakers, lawmakers, and local communities need to recognize the importance of quality care work and provide care workers for family dependents: children and elders. Child care and elder care work can be provided by family members and by non–family members. Quality care work needs to be valued by families, by communities, and by the larger society. Care workers need to be well-educated, dedicated to their work, and they certainly need to be well-paid. Our state and federal governments urgently need to address the important question of supporting care work in their attempts to reduce the problems of family abuse and violence.

Discussion Questions

1. What are the most recent or emerging issues or controversies in the field of intragenerational family abuse and violence?
2. What are the most recent or emerging issues or controversies in the field of intergenerational family abuse and violence?
3. What would social actors, social organizations, social institutions, and the state need to do to improve the quality of care work for children and dependent elders within the United States?

Research Projects

1. Select a specific type of intergenerational FAV and a specific type of intragenerational FAV. Search the research literature

for professional journal articles on those two types of FAV that have been published over the most recent decade. Retrieve only the abstracts for the articles. Classify the articles according to academic field, theory or perspective, and data collection and analysis methods. What patterns characterize the empirical research that you investigated?

2. How do prosecutorial practices vary across the states for interviewing child witness/victims of family abuse and violence?

3. Through online law and legal research search engines, identify several child custody cases in at least two states. How do the states interpret "the best interest of the child?" Do the states place a child who witnesses family violence or intimate partner violence in foster care? Do the states remove children from the custody of their parents if the parents are arrested on illicit drug use or distribution charges?

4. Identify the laws across the states that regulate home schooling.

5. Conduct a search of all the news coverage of the Andrea Yates case. Analyze the case with the ten dimensions of the Family Abuse and Violence Episodes perspective.

Notes

1. The moral panic over a pregnant mother drinking a glass of wine in a restaurant reminds us that policymakers' supposed responses to issues, such as FAV, are actually responses to socially constructed problems that grab their attention and sympathy.

2. Researchers have a distinct advantage when studying homicides. Few homicides go undetected. States and cities compile homicide data sets, the FBI compiles data collected from police departments, which contain much more information than the data reported on other forms of crime; and a number of exceptional FAV researchers, such as Jacquelyn Campbell, have designed multi-city studies to develop "Danger Assessment" tools.

3. www.son.jhmi.edu/research/CNR/homicide/DANGER.htm

13

What Do We Know?
What Should We Do?

We conclude our study of family abuse and violence with a summary of what we know and an informed assessment of what we need to do to prevent or respond to episodes of child abuse, intimate partner violence, and elder neglect. We know with certainty that family abuse and violence (FAV) episodes constitute a persistent, widespread social problem within the United States. In this analysis we do not attempt to compare the FAV problem in the United States to that of other cultures or societies. We recognize that most cultures and societies have FAV problems, some more severe and some less severe than in the United States.

What is counted and measured by all the public and private agencies working to prevent or respond to FAV episodes varies as a function of a society's laws and as a function of a society's customs.[1] Social movements, professional associations, and the media have the greatest influence on lawmakers, who generate regulations for what family members are supposed to do, what they are forbidden to do, and what they need to do to avoid exposing others to potential harms. Lawmakers charge social agencies and social organizations, most of which operate within local communities, with the responsibility of determining FAV episodes, the blameworthiness of perpetrators, and the appropriate sanctions or treatments. Family and criminal laws throughout the United States reflect how U.S. society values family, men and women, and children. Federal and state laws, along with other social forces, reflect and affect the values that this society associates with education and work, including care work, as well as the degree to which this society values privacy and autonomy. The cultural context in which FAV occurs is identified and either sanctioned or condemned by law.

What explains and what counts as an episode of elder neglect or child abuse or intimate partner violence varies from place to place and across time. Thirty years earlier, if we had been doing this research, we would have been most attentive to the elder abuse and neglect that occurs within nursing homes and other types of residential facilities for dependent and older family members. We would have examined carefully foster homes and boarding schools, usually associated with religious organizations, which replaced orphanages from an earlier time. We would have looked at what the social science research community knew about the abuse of women who refused to conform and were therefore placed in psychiatric wards in private and public hospitals and state psychiatric hospitals. We know that in contemporary society, much of the neglect, abuse, and violence episodes that social actors perpetrate or experience, which once occurred in nursing homes, hospitals, and schools, now occur within families.

Contemporary families need to be studied carefully to understand family abuse. Consider some of the ways in which families have changed in recent decades. More young adults, especially in the early phases of their marital or cohabiting relationships, live thousands of miles away from their parents. Yet more elder parents reside with or close to their adult children. Even if the generations live far apart they can remain virtually in touch, via telephone and e-mail; and they can visit each other often via affordable travel.

More women and men postpone marriage and family formation for the purpose of establishing their careers. Fewer teens are having babies but more single mothers, more single fathers, and more same-sex or heterosexual couples form families with the assistance of surrogates or by adopting children from their home state or from a country on the other side of the globe.

Fathers today are expected to engage actively in parenting work, a form of unpaid care work. The well-educated and high-income-earning father provides care work for his children, as does the impoverished and unemployed father who may be a single parent (Roy 2004). And more mothers work full-time or more, some because they choose to, others because they must. Unhappy families and troubled families find the dissolution of the marital or cohabiting relationship more socially acceptable and more legally available than it was decades earlier.[2] The women and men who leave especially abusive and controlling relationships face an increased risk of family violence or stalking. Separation violence is real and it can be deadly.

Family members' expectations of each other affect relationships in both positive and negative ways. The work of developing and maintaining intimacy and dealing with emotions is, in many families, expected for men and women, young children and teens. Preschoolers are taught to communicate how they feel and how to recognize and acknowledge the other's feelings. In principle, the family with strong emotional skills can avoid many of the stresses and frustrations associated with abusive or aggressive behaviors.

U.S. families only need to watch an hour of commercial television programming to see the components of the American dream: a fine home, plenty of good food and drink, resort or cruise-ship vacations, legal pharmaceuticals for every possible ailment or intimate desire, a new car, plenty of toys, and credit cards. The desire to have it all can introduce economic or psychological stress into family relationships, as can the perception of not having enough. Family stresses can lead to circumstances that increase the likelihood of family abuse and violence episodes. Worse yet, the objective economic hardships that rural, suburban, or urban families can experience within the United States can bring problems into the family's space.[3] The more stressed a family member is, the more likely she or he is to become socially isolated and therefore more vulnerable to abuse or violence within the family.

U.S. social scientists need to continue their work on understanding families in order for policymakers to work toward ameliorating the family abuse and violence problems. The family may indeed be a patriarchal social institution that perpetuates the domination and control of women and children by men. It is, however, anything but a monolithic social institution. Lesbians and gays form families, and innumerable heterosexual couples engage in behaviors and events in deliberate attempts to achieve gender equality. Social scientists who want to understand FAV episodes must discard the ideological blindfolds that prevent them from seeing the consequences of such social forces as patriarchy, religion, and family systems theories. Likewise they must see more than only what their preferred vantage point shows them.

While social scientists continuously ask how successful social actors are in pursuit of education and employment, few researchers dare ask the question: How successful or effective is your *family*? Your parenting? Your care work? How would the social scientist measure the outcome or the effectiveness of family work? Does successful parenting mean that the products—the new adults—are happy? Economically successful? Independent? Creative? Good citizens? We know a problematic family or a troubled family member when one comes to the attention of a police officer, a doctor, a teacher, or a social worker. We do not study what accounts for the lack or the *absence* of problems within or across family type relationships.[4] We need to establish what makes some families likely victims of family violence (or vulnerable to abuse) and what makes others unlikely victims.

For decades social scientists have reported strong empirical correlations between a long list of factors and various forms of family abuse and violence. For at least a decade, groups of researchers have called for the systematic collection of uniform data on family violence and abuse. As a society do we need to know what *causes* FAV or do we need to know what the risk factors are in order to prevent abuse or violence? Perhaps the social science community ought to establish causal explanations for FAV. Perhaps the public and private agencies that work to prevent or respond to FAV do not need causal explanations. What they need are the known correlates of FAV, to determine who or which family is at risk in order to prevent abuse or reoccurring episodes.

This duality may keep academics and social service providers focused on different issues, but it does not mean academics and service providers can afford to ignore each other. Consider, for example, the HIV/AIDS problem. Physicians do not need to develop or test causal theories of the virus to treat HIV-exposed or AIDS patients effectively. We do not hold practicing physicians responsible for discovering or even knowing the origins of HIV. We do, however, hold them responsible for knowing the risk of acquiring what can be a deadly virus and for knowing the risk of death if HIV/AIDS goes untreated. We also need to remember that without causal explanations for the HIV virus, the world's AIDS problem cannot and will not be cured. Likewise, judges and social service agencies do not need to test causal theories of family abuse and violence. They are responsible for knowing the risks of reoccurring family abuse and violence. They are responsible for treating individual cases that come to their attention for the purpose of preventing more harm. It is the social science community that is responsible for understanding the causes and consequences of FAV episodes. It takes an academic and practitioner partnership to understand and treat the problem most effectively.

Family and family-type relationships cross generational boundaries. We know that FAV researchers need to account for *inter*- and *intra*generational problems. Within a generation, partners, including dating, cohabiting, and marital partners, can be abusive or physically or sexually violent. Abusive adult partners expose children and other family members to violence and abuse. What children witness or experience in their homes, they can learn to repeat, either in its original form or in a modified form, and they can act out what they learned in other social settings.

Across the generations, problems of neglect can arise. Parents or guardians can neglect children by failing to provide education, medical attention, nutrition, and safe housing. A negligent caretaker is one who fails to take the steps necessary to prevent harm. A neglectful care worker, within the family, is one who fails to provide what a dependent family member needs to survive and to thrive. The caretaker or the family care workers are responsible for dependent children and for dependent elders.

Elder family members, on account of their dependent status, which can result from financial, medical, or emotional circumstances, can be neglected and abused in unique ways. Elders can be denied privacy or their voting rights. They can be denied the right to practice their chosen religion or their right to visit their grandchildren. Some manifestations of elder abuse and elder neglect, including self-neglect, are a function of increased longevity, changing family expectations, and changing laws and rights. We know that a systematic study of neglect must distinguish the forms of neglect that children or elders can experience, but we also know that a dependent status makes elders and children at risk for abuse and neglect.

A debate in the research literature challenges assumptions about the cause of child and elder abuse and neglect: Does the caretaker act abusively, or fail to act appropriately, due to stress? Or is the neglectful or abusive family care worker deviant? Paid care work is an "occupation in which workers are supposed to provide a face-to-face service that develops the human capabilities of the recipient." Care work returns at least a 5–6 percent wage penalty. A wage penalty means that those in an occupation "receive, on average, lower hourly pay than we would predict them to have based on the other characteristics of the jobs, their skill demands, and the qualifications of those holding the jobs" (England et al. 2002:455). The care work occupation with the largest wage penalty is that of child care, an occupation dominated by women. A woman who takes a child care job, rather than another job for which she is qualified or trained, can expect a 41 percent wage penalty (England et al. 2002:467). If the market devalues child care work, which in principle is fulfilling work, can we assume that it devalues elder care work as well? Can we expect *unpaid* care work, within the family, to be highly valued? Is it something that most men and women aspire to do well?

A ten-dimensional perspective that accounts for intra- and intergenerational problems framed our analysis of family abuse and violence episodes. The perspective considers the subjective and objective power and vulnerability of social actors internal to the episode. It incorporates the motivation to commit acts of violence or abuse and establishes a connection between what goes on within the family in response to social organizations and actors external to the family. We show how opportunity structures for abusive episodes are a function of the social spaces and places in which social actors live, work, and engage in activities within their communities. Opportunity structures for abuse can be connected to physical isolation, which we tend to associate with rural family abuse or violence. Or they can emerge as a function of social isolation, which is imposed by the self or by the other in a marital or family-type relationship. We also examine the mechanics of an episode, including the weapons that can be used to injure, and the behavioral sequences that can culminate in deviant or criminal behavior. The FAV perspective provides a framework for (a) integrating extant theories and studies of child abuse, intimate partner violence, and elder abuse and neglect; (b) guiding an interpretation of empirical data; and for (c) informing research designs to comprehensively study the multidimensional problem of abuse and violence within the family. The framework helps social science researchers make sense of the literature and encourages empirical study to further a comprehensive understanding of the abuse and violence that occur within families.

Throughout this book we have examined FAV episodes as a social problem. Changing definitions and changing public responses to child abuse, partner abuse, and elder abuse characterize the recent history of the problem. All told we know that family abuse and violence, once considered private troubles, became a social problem, a problem with responses that have transformed in the recent decades from medical to legal, and then to a social service or therapeutic type of social response. As the social problem became institutionalized, organizations in the public and private sectors responded. Foundations and the state sponsored programs. Federal and state laws were promulgated. A decade ago social change advocates were quick to point out that shelters for animals outnumbered safe shelters for victims of family violence. Today, as a consequence of the institutionalization of the family violence problem, we face a different problem, and we face a new question: How should we examine the state-community partnerships that work to ameliorate the social problem?

As long as intimate partner violence, child abuse, and elder abuse remained private problems, women, men, and children could not count on the criminal or civil courts, or the state and federal governments, to communicate unambiguously the wrongfulness of family abuse and violence. As long as family abuse remained a private problem, its burden remained exclusively with the family. But for thousands of persons, these problems were never resolved.

However, state intervention alone is insufficient to address social problems. Some women, concerned about the consequences of police intervention, remain reluctant to turn to the state to stop the violence.[5] Some well-intentioned neighbors, physicians, or teachers are reluctant to report suspected cases of neglect or abuse, convinced (perhaps correctly) that a child or an elder is better off in a troubled family than in foster care or an institution where abuse is even more likely to occur. Community organizations are necessary to prevent abuse and violence, to protect potential victims, to sanction perpetrators, and to help families recover. Moreover, such public and private organizations, as some analysts have demonstrated, are "here to stay" (Kelly 2004).

Table 13.1, adapted from Kelly (2004), shows some of the state, community, and family groups that are autonomous social organizations working with the FAV problem. A judge, for example, in response to a child neglect case may order a parent to participate in a program run by a mental health care organization that teaches

Table 13.1. Groups that Work on FAV Problems or that Prevent FAV Problems

State Groups	Community Groups	Family Groups
Legislative Bodies	Social Movement Organizations	Nuclear Family
Local Governments	Special Interest Groups	Extended Family
Courts	Corporations / Employers	Intimate Relationships
Criminal Justice Agencies	Schools and Universities	Close Friendships
Police Departments	Neighborhood Associations	
Social Welfare Agencies	Religious Organizations Philanthropic Organizations Health and Mental Health Care Organizations Media	

Source: Kelly 2004: 37.

stress management skills. To gauge how well a parent puts into practice what she or he learned, an extended family member, such as a child's grandparent, may be called on to tell the court about the parent-child interactions he or she observed. A criminal court judge, when sentencing a convicted domestic violence offender, may impose a sanction that includes the completion of an anger management class and active participation in 12-step meetings. Friends and an Alcoholics Anonymous or Narcotics Anonymous sponsor may be called upon by the state (the court) to disclose their perceptions of the offender's progress. When the state crosses boundaries, into a community organization and into a family group, it brings together a network of social actors who have an interest in a family's well-being and in a community's well-being.

How do we examine the state-community partnerships? What are the questions social scientists need to ask to determine if these partnerships are preferable? Nancy Jurik uses the phrase "new privatization" to refer to the "discursive and programmatic restructuring of public sector organizations . . . to become more like businesses" (Jurik 2004:4–5). New privatization means that a community domestic violence prevention program, likely funded with a mix of federal and state monies and local business contributions, must show how effective and efficient it is in order to stay in business. New privatization means that a community mental health center must develop and use performance measures to show how well it is preventing elders from returning to self-neglecting patterns. New privatization means a public agency may spend too much of its limited resources on strategic planning and developing metrics to measure success—and too little of its resources on providing the services that social actors need.

We think social scientists ought to be critical of new privatization and how it affects the community-state partnerships that have emerged (and are here to stay) in response to family abuse and violence episodes within the United States. Critical means that we need to ask effective questions about extant problems and programs. Critical means that we need to challenge whether the metrics and measures imposed by the culture of new privatization are reasonable for judging FAV services and programs. It does not mean that we need to consider returning a public problem to the private domain. To contribute to the well-being of the collectivity, families, community organizations, and the state need to work diligently to diminish the widespread social problem of family abuse and violence. Practitioners in local communities need to respond to the needs of victims and to the wrongful deeds of perpetrators. And social scientists need to work diligently to understand families, to understand the value of family care work, and to understand why some families are abusive while most are not.

We end with a plea: Academics and practitioners need to talk to each other and they need to work together to address effectively the widespread social problem of family abuse and violence. Too few academics are willing to work with local social service agencies, criminal justice agencies, or courts. And too few local agencies or organizations are willing to ask the academic to work with them. Academic researchers, on one side of the river, work to understand and explain social problems. Practitioners, on the other side of the river, work with people who experience the problems. Both make the claim that those on the other side do not understand.

Imagine the academic who meets her graduate seminar and tells students not to trust their personal experiences to inform them about the social problems they study. A judge, who gave a presentation to the seminar, meets the professor for lunch and claims it is different in the real world—in the community—where he works. Personal experiences are what really count. He is smart, clever, and an exceptionally courageous judge. He wants to do good things for his community. He wants to keep his community safe by helping the offenders he sentences, including those who have serious family problems, avoid subsequent crime or drug and alcohol abuse. Because he sees the big picture he understands that many experts, including social scientists, can inform his work in problem solving courts and make it effective (Berman and Feinblatt 2005). Should the academic accept the judge's invitation to study his court programs? She cannot take her academic perspective alone into the community and hope to help. She must listen carefully to understand what really does occur in her community. She must learn from the judge if she wants to contribute to what he is working to accomplish. Likewise he must trust her to deliver relevant theory and research. Together academics, practitioners, and community leaders can make a difference. We conclude by stating that it is necessary to form academic-community partnerships and collaborations to diminish the social problem of family abuse and violence within the United States. Local courts, social service agencies, and criminal justice agencies need to invite the academics to the table. And the academics must be willing to learn. The family abuse problem happens in private spaces, and only local communities have the resources to help and heal.

Notes

1. Many cultures and groups within U.S. society, defined by their religion, ethnicity, race, or nationality, define family relationships and families in ways that we do not address here. Thus, within these cultures or groups, events or episodes are differently defined to be abusive or violent or neglectful.

2. This does not account for the strong discouragement of divorce associated with some religions and ethnic groups within the United States.

3. It is important to remember that family violence experiences can *cause* poverty. A woman who leaves a violent intimate relationship may drift into poverty, especially if she has young children to care for and few work opportunities. Homeless teens include children who ran away from home to escape physical and sexual abuse within their families.

4. A problem-free family and successful parenting may be conflicting constructs. What if successful parenting means, among other things, the production of an adult who is independent and successful at a chosen profession or occupation? Many creative geniuses come from troubled and abusive homes. For example, Kathryn Harrison is a successful novelist who, in her memoir entitled *The Kiss*, vividly describes her childhood in a white, middle-class home—and a horribly abusive father.

5. Women of color, concerned that a criminal justice response will be a racist response to social problem, may be reluctant to initiate state intervention. Likewise, new immigrants may fear reprisal.

Appendix: Resources

A. Interdisciplinary Specialty Journals

Many professional journals, some interdisciplinary and some associated with academic disciplines or professional associations, occasionally publish research articles on family abuse and violence problems. Journals on social work, sociology, political science, criminology, criminal justice, public health, psychology, public policy, and law can be searched for relevant articles on child abuse and neglect, domestic and intimate partner violence, and elder abuse and neglect.

Child Abuse and Neglect
Child Maltreatment
Children and Youth Services Review
Journal of Elder Abuse and Neglect
Journal of Family Violence
Journal of Interpersonal Violence
Trauma, Violence, and Abuse
Violence Against Women
Violence and Abuse Abstracts
Violence and Victims

B. Higher Education / Graduate Programs

A number of graduate programs (in Sociology, Social Work, Psychology, and Public Administration) have masters' certificate programs in family violence fields. For example, the University of Central Florida has an Applied Sociology Program in Domestic Violence.

Family Research Laboratory
University of New Hampshire
www.unh.edu/frl/

Graduate School of Public Affairs
The Program on Domestic Violence
University of Colorado
carbon.cudenver.edu/public/gspa/programs/c054.html

Institute for Family Violence Studies
School of Social Work
Florida State University
familyvio.ssw.fsu.edu/

C. U.S. Government Websites

This is not an exhaustive list nor does it include the many excellent state web pages.

Violence Against Women and Family Violence
National Institute of Justice
www.ojp.usdoj.gov/nij/vawprog/

U.S. Department of Health and Human Services
Administration for Children and Families
nccanch.acf.hhs.gov/

Centers for Disease Control and Prevention
www.cdc.gov/

MedlinePlus, a Service of the U.S. Library of Medicine and the National Institutes of Health
www.nlm.nih.gov/medlineplus/

D. Professional Associations, Organizations, and National Centers

American Bar Association[1]
www.abanet.org/home.cfm

American Medical Association[2]
www.ama-assn.org/

American Psychological Association
www.apa.org/

The Family Violence and Sexual Assault Institute
www.fvsai.org/

Family Violence Prevention Fund
endabuse.org/

National Center for State Courts
www.ncsconline.org/

National Center on Elder Abuse
www.elderabusecenter.org/

National Coalition Against Domestic Violence
www.ncadv.org/

National Council of Juvenile and Family Court Judges
www.ncjfcj.org/

National Council on Child Abuse and Family Violence
www.nccafv.org/

Notes

1. This exceptionally rich source has a section called "Resources for the Public" that includes materials on children and the law, family law, domestic violence, and senior citizens.

2. The "For Patients" section and a searchable database contain articles on family abuse and violence.

Glossary

co-occurring family abuse or violence Multiple types or events of abuse or violence that are perpetrated by a single social actor or experienced by a single victim, such as neglect and abuse; or assault, stalking, and rape.

cultural factors Shared beliefs, values, norms, moral codes, and customs that guide social interaction.

elder abuse The abuse of an elder generally means the abuse of a dependent by a younger family member or caregiver. The victim may be physically, mentally, or emotionally abused or neglected. It includes self-neglect that is not prevented by family or family-type members.

episode An isolated event or reoccurring events in which a violent or abusive act or acts occur over a period of time and within a specific context.

external actors Social actors outside the family or episodes occurring within the family or family-type relationship who have direct or indirect access to resources that can alter the social space in which family abuse and violence occurs. Examples include neighbors, police, social service workers, teachers, and coworkers.

facilitating objects Items such as weapons or household or workplace objects that can be used to intimidate, threaten, or injure someone in an episode of family abuse and violence. Examples include guns, knives, sticks, telephones, or other objects that can injure the victim physically.

family embeddedness   The level of connectedness to one's family or family-type relationship, such that an unmarried couple is less embedded than a married couple, and a married couple with children is more embedded than a married couple with no children. Laws and customs define levels of family embeddedness.

intergenerational abuse or violence   Abuse or violence that occurs across family or family-type members of different generations, such as abuse or violence by mother-to-child or caretaker-to-child.

intergenerational episode   A violent or abusive event or reoccurring events that are committed by a social actor of one generation against a social actor of a different generation.

intimate partner   Social actor with whom another social actor has a romantic, sexual, or marital relationship.

intimate partner abuse   Physical, emotional, or sexual abuse by a husband or wife, or by a boyfriend or girlfriend. Includes heterosexual and same-sex partners. Includes dating, cohabiting, and married, separated, or divorced partners.

intimate partner violence   A violent act, such as hitting or kicking, or forcing sexual activity, that is perpetrated by an intimate partner.

intragenerational abuse   Abuse or violence that is perpetrated by a family or family-type member against another member of the same generation, such as husband-to-wife abuse or partner-to-partner abuse or sibling abuse.

intragenerational episode   A violent or abusive event or reoccurring events that are committed by a social actor against another actor of the same generation.

mechanics   A series or chain of events or activities that occur with or without facilitating objects. Includes weapons and the use of weapons.

objective resources   Monetary, economic, or material resources that can be used to obtain or sustain a relative position of social power over another or others within a social relationship or a social group.

primary perpetrator The individual social actor who uses or directs violence or abuse against a primary victim. Includes neglect.

primary victim The individual social actor at whom an act of violence or abuse is directed. Includes neglect.

secondary victim Social actor who is indirectly affected by or harmed by neglect, abuse, or violence.

social actor An individual who interacts with others and directly or indirectly affects their perceptions, emotions, and behaviors.

social climate The social and historical context in which social actors, through interaction structured by institutions and organizations, generate definitions of appropriate or deviant behaviors and thus definitions of abusive or violent behaviors.

social problems perspective Influenced by C. Wright Mills, a social problems perspective connects private troubles with public issues. Historical contextualization is necessary to make the connections. A woman, for example, is the victim of partner violence. A social problems perspective explains her situation and how it is connected to the widespread problem of women abuse in the United States. To make sense of the woman abuse problem it is necessary to understand the gendered history of the United States that contemporarily results in inequitable distribution of resources across gender groups that vary by social class, age, race, and ethnicity.

social structure Patterned, recurring, and enduring social relationships among a set of social actors, be they persons, occupants of positions, enactors of roles, or organizations.

social time The temporal ordering of social interaction, such as time for work and family or time for leisure. It is perceived and constructed by social actors yet constrained by social relations and social institutional forces. For example, the most privileged workers choose when and when not to work, yet all workers arrange for family time and leisure time.

space and place Specific social arena, bounded by location and time, in which social interaction and physical experiences, including abuse and violence, occur. Examples include the work place, a car trip, or a school day.

subjective resources Nonmaterial resources, such as prestige or influence within a social group that can be used by social actors to obtain or sustain a relative position of social power over another or others within a social relationship or within a social group.

References

Abbott, J., Johnson, R., Koziolmclain, J., and Lowenstein, S. R. 1995. "Domestic Violence against Women: Incidence and Prevalence in an Emergency Department Population." *JAMA: Journal of the American Medical Association* 273: 1763–1767.

Ackard, D. M., and Neumark-Sztainer, D. 2002. "Date Violence and Date Rape among Adolescents: Associations with Disordered Eating Behaviors and Psychological Health." *Child Abuse and Neglect* 26: 455–473.

Ackerman, P. T., Newton, J. E. O., McPherson, W. B., Jones, J. G., and Dykman, R. A. 1998. "Prevalence of Post-Traumatic Stress Disorder and Other Psychiatric Diagnoses in Three Groups of Abused Children (Sexual, Physical, and Both)." *Child Abuse and Neglect* 22: 759–774.

Adams, J. F. 2001. "Impact of Parent Training on Family Functioning." *Child and Family Therapy* 23: 29–43.

Administration for Children and Families. 2004. "Summary: Child Maltreatment, 2002." Washington, DC: U.S. Department of Health and Human Services. www.acf.hhs. gov/programs/cb/Publications

Adoption and Safe Families Act. 1997. Washington, DC: U.S. Government Printing Office.

Adoption Assistance and Child Welfare Act. 1980. Public Law 96-272. Washington, DC: U.S. Government Printing Office.

Alaggia, R. 2004. "Many Ways of Telling: Expanding Conceptualizations of Child Sexual Abuse." *Child Abuse and Neglect* 28: 1213–1227.

Aldridge, N. C. 1998. "Strengths and Limitations of Forensic Child Sexual Abuse Interviews with Anatomical Dolls: An Empirical Review." *Journal of Psychopathology and Behavioral Assessment* 20: 1–41.

Alexander, P. C., Moore, S., and Alexander, E. R., III. 1991. "What Is Transmitted in the Intergenerational Transmission of Violence?" *Journal of Marriage and the Family* 53: 657–668.

Alpert, E. J., Shannon, D., Velonis, A., Georges, M., and Rich, R. A. 2002. "Family Violence and Public Health Education: A Call for Action." *Violence against Women* 8: 746–778.

Amato, P. R., and Fowler, F. 2002. "Parenting Practices, Child Adjustment and Family Diversity." *Journal of Marriage and Family* 64: 703–716.

American Bar Association. 2002. Recommendation: Commission on Legal Problems of the Elderly. Report to the House of Delegates. Chicago: American Bar Association: 14.

———. 2003. Report to the House of Delegates. Commission on Domestic Violence. Section of Family Law. Young Lawyers Division. National Association of Women Lawyers. Health Law Section. Section of Taxation. Steering committee on Unmet Legal Needs of Children. Chicago: American Bar Association.

———. 2004. "What Is a Unified Family Court?" Chicago: American Bar Association.

American Humane Association. 1967. Child Protective Services: A National Survey. Denver: American Humane Association.

American Medical Association. 1992. "Diagnostic and Treatment Guidelines on Elder Abuse." Chicago: American Medical Association.

American Psychiatric Association. 1994. *Diagnostic and Statistical Manual of Mental Disorders, Fourth Edition.* Washington, DC: American Psychiatric Association.

American Psychological Association. 2004. "Teen Choices: Dating Abuse." Washington, DC: American Psychological Association.

Ammerman, R. T. 1991. "The Role of the Child in Physical Abuse: A Reappraisal." *Violence and Victims* 6: 87–101.

Ammons, L. L. 1999. "What's God Got to Do with It? Church and State Collaboration in the Subordination of Women and Domestic Violence." *Rutgers Law Review* 51: 1207–1288.

Anda, R. F., Felitti, V. J., Chapman, V. J., Croft, J. B., Williamson, D. F., Santelli, J., Dietz, P. M., and Marks, J. S. 2001. "Abused Boys, Battered Mothers, and Male Involvement in Teen Pregnancy." *Pediatrics* 107.

Anderson, D. G. 2000. "Coping Strategies and Burnout among Veteran Child Protection Workers." *Child Abuse and Neglect* 24: 839–848.

Anderson, K. L. 2002. "Perpetrator or Victim? Relationships between Intimate Partner Violence and Well-Being." *Journal of Marriage and Family* 64: 851–863.

———. 2003. "Courting Disaster: Intimate Stalking, Culture, and Criminal Justice." *Gender and Society* 17: 646–647.

Andrews, B. 1997. "Bodily Shame in Relation to Abuse in Childhood and Bulimia: A Preliminary Investigation." *British Journal of Clinical Psychology* 36: 41–49.

Antler, S. 1978. "Child Abuse: An Emerging Priority." *Social Work* 23: 58–61.

Appel, A. E., and Holden, G. W. 1998. "The Co-Occurrence of Spouse and Physical Child Abuse: A Review and Appraisal." *Journal of Family Psychology* 12: 578–599.

Arbuckle, J., Olson, L., Howard, M., Brillman, J., Anctil, C., and Sklar, D. 1996. "Safe at Home? Domestic Violence and Other Homicides among Women in New Mexico." *Annals of Emergency Medicine* 27: 210–215.

Archer, J. 2000. "Sex Differences in Physical Aggression to Partners: A Reply to Frieze (2000), O'Leary (2000), and White, Smith, Koss, and Figueredo (2000)." *Psychological Bulletin* 126: 697–702.

Ards, S., Chung, C., and Myers, S. L., Jr. 1998. "The Effects of Sample Selection Bias on Racial Differences in Child Abuse Reporting." *Child Abuse and Neglect* 22: 103–115.

———. 1999. Letter to the Editor. *Child Abuse and Neglect* 23: 1211–1215.

———. 2001. Letter to the Editor. "Sample Selection Bias and Racial Differences in Child Abuse Reporting: Once Again." *Child Abuse and Neglect* 25: 7–12.

Ards, S. D., Myers, S. L., Jr., Erin, A., and Zhou, L. 2003. "Racial Disproportionality in Reported and Substantiated Child Abuse and Neglect: An Examination of Systematic Bias." *Children and Youth Services Review* 25: 375–392.

Aries, P. 1962. Centuries of Childhood: A Social History of Family Life. New York: Knopf.

Arriaga, X. B., and Foshee, V. A. 2004. "Adolescent Dating Violence: Adolescents Follow in Their Friends' or Their Parents' Footsteps?" *Journal of Interpersonal Violence* 19: 162–184.

Ashton, V. 2001. "The Relationship between Attitudes toward Corporal Punishment and the Perception and Reporting of Child Maltreatment." *Child Abuse and Neglect* 25: 389–399.

Asser, S., and Swan, R. 1998. "Child Fatalities from Religion-Motivated Medical Neglect." *Pediatrics* 101: 625–629.

Atkinson, L., and Butler, S. 1996. "Court-Ordered Assessment: Impact of Maternal Non-Compliance in Child Maltreatment Cases." *Child Abuse and Neglect* 20: 185–190.

Ayoub, C., and Milner, J. S. 1985. "Failure to Thrive: Parental Indicators, Types and Out-comes." *Child Abuse and Neglect* 9: 491–499.

Bachman, Ronet. 2000. "A Comparison of Annual Incidence Rates and Contextual Characteristics of Intimate-Partner Violence Against Women from the National Crime Victimization Survey (NCVS) and the National Violence Against Women Survey (NVAWS). *Violence against Women* 6: 839–867.

Bagley, C., Rodberg, G., Wellings, D., Moose-Mitha, M., and Young, L. 1995. "Sexual and Physical Child Abuse and the Development of Dissociative Personality Traits." *Child Abuse Review* 4: 99–113.

Bailey, S., and Whittle, N. 2004. "Young People: Victims of Violence." *Current Opinion in Psychiatry* 17: 263–268.

Bakan, D. 1971. Slaughter of the Innocents. San Francisco: Jossey-Bass.

Baker, A. J. L., Piotrkowski, C. S., and Brooks-Gunn, J. 1999. "The Home Instruction Program for Preschool Youngsters (HIPPY)." *The Future of Children* 9 (1): 116–133.

Baldwin, P. C. 2002. "Nocturnal Habits and Dark Wisdom: The American Response to Children in the Streets at Night, 1880–1930." *Journal of Social History* 35: 593–612.

Ballif-Spanvill, B., Clayton, C. J., and Hendrix, S. B. 2003. "Gender, Types of Conflict, and Individual Differences in the Use of Violent and Peaceful Strategies among Children Who Have and Have Not Witnessed Interparental Violence." *American Journal of Orthopsychiatry* 73: 141–153.

Bandura, A. 1973. Aggression: A Social Learning Analysis. Englewood Cliffs, N.J.: Prentice-Hall.

———. 1977. Social Learning Theory. Englewood Cliffs, N.J.: Prentice-Hall.

Barata, Paula, and Senn, Charlene Y. 2003. "When Two Fields Collide: An Examination of the Assumptions of Social Science Research and Law within the Domain of Domestic Violence." *Trauma, Violence, and Abuse* 4: 3–21.

Bardis, P. 1964. "Family Forms and Variations Historically Considered." In Handbook of Marriage and the Family, edited by H. Christensen, 403–461. Chicago: Rand McNally.

Barmeyer, G. H., Anderson, L. R., and Cox, W. B. 1951. "Traumatic Periostitis in Young Children." *Journal of Pediatrics* 38: 184–190.

Barnett, D., Vondra, J. I., and Shonk, S. M. 1996. "Self-Perceptions, Motivations, and School Functioning of Low-Income Maltreated and Comparison Children." *Child Abuse and Neglect* 20: 397–410.

Barnett, Ola W. 2000. "Why Battered Women Do Not Leave, Part 1: External Inhibiting Factors Within Society." *Trauma, Violence, and Abuse* 1: 343–372.

———. 2001. "Why Battered Women Do Not Leave, Part 2: External Inhibiting Factors, Social Support and Internal Inhibiting Factors." *Trauma, Violence, and Abuse* 2: 3–35.

Barydon, R. M., Deitrich-MacLean, G., Dietrich, M. S., Sherod, K. B., and Altemeier, W. A. 1995. "Evidence for Specific Effects of Childhood Sexual Abuse on Mental Well-Being and Physical Self-Esteem." *Child Abuse and Neglect* 19: 1255–1262.

Bath, H. I., and Haapala, D. A. 1993. "Intensive Family Preservation Services with Abused and Neglected Children: An Examination of Group Differences." *Child Abuse and Neglect* 17: 213–225.

Baumrind, D. 1994. "The Social Context of Child Maltreatment." *Family Relations* 43: 360–368.

———. 1996. "The Discipline Controversy Revisited." *Family Relations* 45: 405–414.

Bauserman, R., and Rind, B. 1997. "Psychological Correlates of Male Child and Adolescent Sexual Experiences with Adults: A Review of the Nonclinical Literature." *Archives of Sexual Behavior* 26: 105–141.

Beach, S. R. H., Kim, S., Cercone-Keeney, J., Gupta, M., Arias, I., and Brody, G. H. 2004. "Physical Aggression and Depressive Symptoms: Gender Asymmetry in Effects?" *Journal of Social and Personal Relationships* 21: 341–360.

Bearup, R. S., and Palusci, V. J. 1999. "Improving Child Welfare Through a Children's Ombudsman." *Child Abuse and Neglect* 23: 449–457.

Beeman, S. K. 1997. "Reconceptualizing Social Support and Its Relationship to Child Neglect." *Social Service Review* 37: 421–440.

Behl, L. E., Conyngham, H. A., and May, P. F. 2001. "Trends in Child Maltreatment Literature." *Child Abuse and Neglect* 27: 215–229.

Bellingham, B. 1988. "The History of Childhood since the 'Invention of Childhood': Some Issues in the Eighties." *Journal of Family History* 113: 347–358.

Belsky, J. 1993. "Etiology of Maltreatment: A Developmental Ecological Analysis." *Psychological Bulletin* 114: 413–434.

Benedict, M. I., Zuravin, S., Brandt, D., and Abbey, H. 1994. "Types and Frequency of Child Maltreatment by Family Foster Care Providers in an Urban Population." *Child Abuse and Neglect* 18: 577–585.

Benedict, M. I., Zuravin, S., Somerfield, M., and Brandt, D. 1996. "The Reported Health and Functioning of Children Maltreated While in Family Foster Care." *Child Abuse and Neglect* 20: 561–571.

Benjet, C., and Kazdin, A. E. 2003. "Spanking Children: The Controversies, Findings, and New Directions." *Clinical Psychological Review* 23: 197–224.

Benoit, J. L., and Kennedy, W. L. 1992. "The Abuse History of Male Adolescent Sex Offenders." *Journal of Interpersonal Violence* 7: 543–548.

Bensley, L., Ruggles, D., Simmons, K. W., Harris, C., Williams, K., Putvin, T., and Allen, M. 2004. "General Population Norms about Child Abuse and Neglect and Associations with Childhood Experiences." *Child Abuse and Neglect* 28: 1321–1337.

Bergen, Raquel Kennedy. 1996. Wife Rape: Understanding the Response of Survivors and Service Providers. Thousand Oaks, Calif.: Sage Publications.

———. 2001. "Marital Rape: A United States Study." Washington, DC: U.S. Department of Justice.

Berger, A. M., Knutson, J. F., Mehm, J. G., and Perkins, K. A. 1988. "The Self-Report of Punitive Childhood Experiences of Young Adults and Adolescents." *Child Abuse and Neglect* 12: 251–262.

Berger, L. M. 2004. "Income, Family Structure, and Child Maltreatment Risk." *Children and Youth Services Review* 26: 725–748.

Bergman, L. 1992. "Dating Violence among High School Students." *Social Work* 37: 21–27.

Berkeley Planning Associates. 1978. Evaluation of Child Abuse and Neglect Demonstration Projects: 1974–1977, Vols. 1 and 2. Washington, DC: U.S. Department of Health, Education, and Welfare.

Berliner, L., and Loftus, E. 1992. "Sexual Abuse Accusations: Desperately Seeking Reconciliation." *Journal of Interpersonal Violence* 7: 570–578.

Berman, Greg, and Feinblatt, John. 2005. Good Courts: The Case for Problem-Solving Justice. New York: The New Press.

Berman, Helene. 2000. "The Relevance of Narrative Research with Children Who Witness War and Children Who Witness Woman Abuse." *Journal of Aggression, Maltreatment and Trauma* 3: 107–125.

Berns, Nancy. 2004. Framing the Victim: Domestic Violence Media and Social Problems. Hawthorne, N.Y.: Aldine de Gruyter.

Besharov, D. J. 1990. "Gaining Control over Child Abuse Reports." *Public Welfare* 48: 34–40, 46–47.

———. 1998. "Commentary." *The Future of Children* 8 (1): 120–123.

Best, Joel. 1990. Threatened Children: Rhetoric and Concern about Child Victims. Chicago: University of Chicago Press.

———. 2001. Damned Lies and Statistics: Untangling Numbers from the Media, Politicians, and Activists. Berkeley: University of California Press.

———. 2005. More Damned Lies and Statistics: How Numbers Confuse Public Issues. Berkeley: University of California Press.

Bevan, E., and Higgins, D. J. 2002. "Is Domestic Violence Learned? The Contribution of Five Forms of Child Maltreatment to Men's Violence and Adjustment." *Journal of Family Violence* 17: 223–245.

Billingham, R. E., Bland, R., and Leary, A. 1999. "Dating Violence at Three Time Periods: 1976, 1992, and 1996." *Psychological Reports* 85: 574–578.

Bird, G. W., Stith, S. M., and Schladale, J. 1991. "Psychological Resources, Coping Strategies, and Negotiation Styles as Discriminators of Violence in Dating Relationships." *Family Relations* 40: 45–50.

Birkbeck, C., and Lafree, G. 1993. "The Situational Analysis of Crime and Deviance." *Annual Review of Sociology* 19: 113–137.

Bishop, S. J., and Leadbeater, B. J. 1999. "Maternal Social Support Patterns and Child Maltreatment: Comparison of Maltreating and Nonmaltreating Mothers." *American Journal of Orthopsychiatry* 69: 172–181.

Bjorklund, D. F. 2000. False-Memory Creation in Children and Adults: Theory, Research, and Implications. Mahwah, N.J.: Lawrence Erlbaum Associates.

Black, B. M., and Weisz, A. N. 2003. "Dating Violence: Help-Seeking Behaviors of African American Middle Schoolers." *Violence against Women* 9: 187–206.

Black, M. M., Hess, C. R., and Berenson-Howard, J. 2000. "Toddlers from Low-Income Families Have Below Normal Mental, Motor, and Behavior Scores on the Revised Bayley Scales." *Journal of Applied Developmental Psychology* 21: 655–666.

Blau, G. M., Whewell, M. C., Gullotta, T. P., and Bloom, M. 1994. "The Prevention and Treatment of Child Abuse in Households of Substance Abusers: A Research Demonstration Progress Report." *Child Welfare* 73: 69–81.

Block, Carolyn Rebecca. 2003. "How Can Practitioners Help an Abused Women Lower Her Risk of Death?" *NIJ Journal* 250: 4–7.

Bloom, S. L. 1995. "When Good People Do Bad Things: Meditations on the 'Backlash.'" *Journal of Psychohistory* 22: 273–303.

Boat, B. W., and Everson, M. D. 1994. "Exploration of Anatomical Dolls by Non-referred Preschool-Aged Children: Comparisons by Age, Gender, Race and Socio-Economic Status." *Child Abuse and Neglect* 18: 139–153.

———. 1996. "Concerning Practices of Interviewers When Using Anatomical Dolls in Child Protective Services Investigations." *Child Maltreatment* 1: 96–104.

Bond, J. B., Cuddy, R., Dixon, G. L., Duncan, K. A., and Smith, D. L. 1999. "The Financial Abuse of Mentally Incompetent Adults: A Canadian Study." *Journal of Elder Abuse and Neglect* 11: 23–38.

Boris, N. W., Heller, S. S., Sheperd, and Zeanah, C. H. 2002. "Partner Violence among Homeless Young Adults: Measurement Issues and Associations." *Journal of Adolescent Health* 30: 355–363.

Borzekowski, D. L. G., and Rickert, V. I. 2001. "Adolescent Cybersurfing for Health Information: A New Resource that Crosses Barriers." *Archives of Pediatrics and Adolescent Medicine* 155: 813–817.

Bowen, K. 2000. "Child Abuse and Domestic Violence in Families of Children Seen for Suspected Sexual Abuse." *Clinical Pediatrics* 39: 33–40.

Bower, M. E., and Knutson, J. F. 1996 "Attitudes toward Physical Discipline as a Function of Disciplinary History and Self-Labeling as Physically Abused." *Child Abuse and Neglect* 20: 689–699.

Bower-Russa, M. E., Knutson, J. F., and Weinbarger, A. 2001. "Disciplinary History, Adult Disciplinary Attitudes, and Risk for Abusive Parenting." *Journal of Community Psychology* 29: 219–240.

Bracher, P. B. 1996. "Mandatory Arrest for Domestic Violence: The City of Cincinnati's Simple Solution to a Complex Problem." *University of Cincinnati Law Review* 65: 155–182.

Brantingham, Paul J., and Brantingham, Pat. 2001. "The Implications of the Criminal Event Model for Crime Prevention." In The Process and Structure of Crime: Criminal Events and Crime Analysis, edited by Robert F. Meier, Leslie W. Kennedy, and Vincent F. Sacco, 277–303. New Brunswick, N.J.: Transaction Publishers.

Brecklin, L. R., and Ullman, S. E. 2002. "The Roles of Victim and Offender Alcohol Use in Sexual Assaults: Results from the National Violence Against Women Survey." *Journal of Studies on Alcohol* 63: 57–63.

Brendgen, M., Vitaro, F., Tremblay, R. E., and Wanner, B. 2002. "Parent and Peer Effects on Delinquency-Related Violence and Dating Violence: A Test of Two Mediational Models." *Social Development* 11: 225–244.

Briere, J., and Conte, J. 1993. "Self-Reported Amnesia for Abuse in Adults Molested as Children." *Journal of Traumatic Stress* 6: 21–31.

Briere, J., and Eliott, D. M. 2003. "Prevalence and Psychological Sequelae of Self-Reported Childhood Physical and Sexual Abuse in a General Population Sample of Men and Women." *Child Abuse and Neglect* 27: 1205–1222.

Briere, J., and Gil, El. 1998. "Self-Mutilation in Clinical and General Population Samples: Prevalence, Correlates, and Functions." *American Journal of Orthopsychiatry* 68: 609–620.

Briere, J., Henschel, D., and Smiljanich, K. 1992. "Attitudes toward Sexual Abuse: Sex Differences and Construct Validity." *Journal of Research in Personality* 26: 398–406.

Briere, J., Johnson, K., Bissada, A., Damon, L., Crouch, J., Gil, E., Hanson, R., and Ernst, V. 2001. "The Trauma Symptom Checklist for Young Children (TSCYC): Reliability and Association with Abuse Exposure in a Multi-Site Study." *Child Abuse and Neglect* 25: 1001–1014.

Briggs, L., and Joyce, P. R. 1997. "What Determines Post-Traumatic Stress Disorder Symptomatology for Survivors of Childhood Sexual Abuse?" *Child Abuse and Neglect* 21: 575–582.

Brilleslijper-Kater, S. M., Friedrich, W. N., and Corwin, D. L. 2004. "Sexual Knowledge and Emotional Reaction as Indicators of Sexual Abuse in Young Children: Theory and Research Challenges." *Child Abuse and Neglect* 28: 1007–1017.

Brinig, M. E. 2002. "Empirical Work in Family Law." *University of Illinois Law Review* 2002: 1083–1110.

Brinig, M. E., Jogerst, G. J., Daly, J. M., Schmuch, G. A., and Dawson, J. D. 2004. "Public Choice and Domestic Abuse Law." *Journal of Legal Studies* 33: 517–549.

Britner, P. A., and Mossler, D. G. 2002. "Professionals' Decision-Making about Out-of-Home Placements Following Instances of Child Abuse." *Child Abuse and Neglect* 26: 317–332.

Brock, Kathleen J., and Mintz, Laurie B. 1997. "Differences among Sexually Abused and Nonabused Women from Functional and Dysfunctional Families." *Journal of Counseling Psychology* 44: 425–432.

Brook, J. S., Whiteman, M., and Zheng, L. 2002. "Intergenerational Transmission of Risks for Problem Behavior." *Journal of Abnormal Child Psychology* 30: 65–76.

Brooks, C., and James, S. 2003. "Willingness to Adopt Black Foster Children: Implications for Child Welfare Policy and Recruitment of Adoptive Families." *Children and Youth Services Review* 25: 463–489.

Brooks, C. M., Perry, N. W., Starr, S. D., and Teply, L. L. 1994. "Child Abuse and Neglect Reporting Laws: Understanding Interests, Understanding Policy." *Behavioral Sciences and the Law* 12: 49–64.

Brooks, S. L. 1999. "Therapeutic Jurisprudence and Preventive Law in Child Welfare Proceedings: A Family Systems Approach." *Psychology, Public Policy, and Law* 5: 951–965.

Brosig, C., and Kalichman, S. 1992. "Child Reporting Decisions: Effects of Statutory Wording of Reporting Requirements." *Professional Psychology: Research and Practice* 23: 486–492.

Browning, C. R. 2002. "The Span of Collective Efficacy: Extending Social Disorganization Theory to Partner Violence." *Journal of Marriage and Family* 64: 833–850.

Browning, C. R., and Laumann, E. O. 1997. "Sexual Contact between Children and Adults: A Life Course Perspective." *American Sociological Review* 62: 540–60.

Brownridge, Douglas A. 2004. "Understanding Women's Heightened Risk of Violence in Common-Law Unions: Revisiting the Selection and Relationship Hypothesis." *Violence against Women* 10: 626–651.

Brownridge, D. A., and Halli, S. S. 1999. "Measuring Family Violence: The Conceptualization and Utilization of Prevalence and Incidence Rates." *Journal of Family Violence* 14: 333–350.

———. 2000. "'Living in Sin' and Sinful Living: Toward Filling a Gap in the Explanation of Violence against Women." *Aggression and Violent Behavior* 5: 565–583.

Bruck, M., Ceci, S. J., and Hembrooke, H. 1998. "Reliability and Credibility of Young Children's Reports: From Research to Policy and Practice." *American Psychologist* 53: 136–151.

Brush, Lisa D. 1990. "Violent Acts and Injurious Outcomes in Married Couples: Methodological Issues in the National Survey of Families and Households." *Gender and Society* 4: 56–67.

Bryant, S. L., and Range, L. M. 1995. "Suicidality in College Women Who Were Sexually Abused and Physically Punished by Parents." *Violence and Victims* 10: 195–201.

Buel, Sarah M. 2002. "Why Juvenile Courts Should Address Family Violence: Promising Practices to Improve Intervention Outcomes." *Juvenile and Family Court Journal* 2002: 1–16.

Bullough, V. L. 1990. "History in Adult Human Sexual Behavior with Children and Adolescents in Western Societies." In Pedophilia: Biosocial Dimensions, edited by Fierman, 69–90. New York: Springer-Verlag.

Bumby, K. M., and Hansen, D. J. 1997. "Intimacy Deficits, Fear of Intimacy, and Lone-Lines among Sexual Offenders." Criminal Justice and Behavior 24: 315–331.

Buntain-Ricklefs, J. J., Kemper, K. J., Bell, M., and Babonis, T. 1994. "Punishments: What Predicts Adult Approval?" Child Abuse and Neglect 18: 945–955.

Burch, R. L., and Gallup, G. G. 2000. "Perceptions of Paternal Resemblance Predict Family Violence." Evolution and Human Behavior 21: 429–435.

———. 2004. "Pregnancy as a Stimulus for Domestic Violence." Journal of Family Violence 19: 243–247.

Burgess-Proctor, Amanda. 2003. "Evaluating the Efficacy of Protection Orders for Victims of Domestic Violence." Women and Criminal Justice 15: 33–54.

Burton, D. L., Miller, D. L., and Shill, C. T. 2002. "A Social Learning Theory Comparison of the Sexual Victimization of Adolescent Sexual Offenders and Nonsexual Offending Male Delinquents." Child Abuse and Neglect 26: 893–907.

Bush, D. M. 1992. "Women's Movements and State Policy Reform Aimed at Domestic Violence against Women: A Comparison of the Consequences of Movement Mobilization in the United States and India." Gender and Society 6: 587–608.

Bush, Jack, Glick, Barry, and Taymans, Juliana. 2001. Thinking for a Change: Facilitator Training: Lesson Plans. National Institute of Corrections Academy. Washington, DC: National Institute of Corrections.

Caetano, R., Schafer, J., and Cunradi, C. B. 2001. "Alcohol-Related Intimate Partner Violence among White, Black, and Hispanic Couples in the United States." Alcohol Research and Health 25: 58–65.

Caffey, J. 1946. "Multiple Fractures in the Long Bones of Infants Suffering from Chronic Subdural Hematoma." American Journal of Roentgenology 56: 163–173.

———. 1957. "Some Traumatic Lesions in Growing Bones Other Than Fractures and Dislocations: Clinical and Radiological Features." British Journal of Radiology 30: 225–228.

Caliso, J. A., and Milner, J. S. 1994. "Childhood Physical Abuse, Childhood Social Support, and Adult Child Abuse Potential." Journal of Interpersonal Violence 9: 27–44.

Calkins, C. A., and Millar, M. 1999. "The Effectiveness of Court Appointed Special Advocates to Assist in Permanency Planning." Child and Adolescent Social Work Journal 16: 37–45.

Campbell, J. C., Coben, J. H., McLoughlin, E., Dearwater, S., Nah, G., Glass, N., Lee, D., and Durborow, N. 2001. "An Evaluation of a System-Change Training Model to Improve Emergency Department Response to Battered Women." Academic Emergency Medicine 8: 131–138.

Campbell, Jacquelyn C., Webster, Daniel, Koziol-McLain, Jane, Block, Carolyn Rebecca, Campbell, Doris, Curry, Mary Ann, Gary, Faye, McFarlane, Judith, Sachs, Carolyn, Sharps, Phyllis, Ulrich, Yvonne, and Wilt, Susan A. 2003. "Assessing Risk Factors for Intimate Partner Homicide." National Institute of Justice Journal 250: 14–19.

Capaldi, D. M., and Clark, S. 1998. "Prospective Family Predictors of Aggression toward Female Partners for At-Risk Young Men." *Developmental Psychology* 34: 1175–1188.

Capaldi, D. M., Pears, K. C., Patterson, G. R., and Owen, L. D. 2003. "Continuity of Parenting Practices across Generations in an At-Risk Sample: A Prospective Comparison of Direct and Mediated Associations." *Journal of Abnormal Child Psychology* 31: 127–142.

Carey, T. A. 1994. "Spare the Rod and Spoil the Child: Is This a Sensible Justification for the Use of Punishment in Child Rearing?" *Child Abuse and Neglect* 18: 1005–1010.

Carlin, A. S., Kemper, K., Ward, N. G., Sowell, H., Gustafson, B., and Stevens, N. 1994. "The Effect of Differences in Objective and Subjective Definitions of Childhood Physical Abuse on Estimates of Its Incidence and Relationship to Psychopathology." *Child Abuse and Neglect* 18: 393–399.

Carlson, B. E., McNutt, L. A., Choi, D. Y., and Rose, I. M. 2002. "Intimate Partner Abuse and Mental Health: The Role of Social Support and Other Protective Factors." *Violence against Women* 8: 720–745.

Caron, S. L., and Moskey, E. G. 2002. "Changes over Time in Teenage Sexual Relationships: Comparing the High School Class of 1950, 1975, and 2000." *Adolescence* 37: 515–526.

Carp, E. W. 1998. Family Matters: Secrecy and Disclosure in the History of Adoption. Cambridge, Mass.: Harvard University Press.

Carr, J. L., and VanDeusen, K. M. 2002. "The Relationship between Family of Origin Violence and Dating Violence in College Men." *Journal of Interpersonal Violence* 17: 630–646.

Cascardi, M., Avery-Leaf, S., O'Leary, K. D., and Slep, A. M. S. 1999. "Factor Structure and Convergent Validity of the Conflict Tactics Scale in High School Students." *Psychological Assessment* 11: 546–555.

Ceci, S. J., and Bruck, M. 1993. "Suggestibility of the Child Witness: A Historical Review and Synthesis." *Psychological Bulletin* 113: 403–419.

Centers for Disease Control. 1988. "Guidelines for Evaluating Surveillance Systems." *Morbidity and Mortality Weekly Report* 37: 1–18.

Chaffin, M. 2004. "Is It Time to Rethink Healthy Start/Healthy Families?" *Child Abuse and Neglect* 28: 589–595.

Chaffin, M., Bonner, B. L., and Hill, R. F. 2001. "Family Preservation and Family Support Programs: Child Maltreatment Outcomes across Client Risk Levels and Program Types." *Child Abuse and Neglect* 25: 1269–1289.

Chaffin, M., Kelleher, K., and Hollenberg, J. 1996. "Onset of Physical Abuse and Neglect: Psychiatric, Substance Abuse, and Social Risk Factors from Prospective Community Data." *Child Abuse and Neglect* 20: 191–203.

Chaffin, M., and Valle, L. A. 2003. "Dynamic Prediction Characteristics of the Child Abuse Potential Inventory." *Child Abuse and Neglect* 27: 463–481.

Chaffin, M., Wherry, J. N., and Dykman, R. 1997. "School Age Children's Coping with Sexual Abuse: Abuse Stresses and Symptoms Associated with Four Coping Strategies." *Child Abuse and Neglect* 21: 227–240.

Chasnoff, I. J., and Lowder, L. E. 1999. "Prenatal Alcohol and Drug Use and Risk for Child Maltreatment: A Timely Approach to Intervention." In Neglected Children: Research, Practice, and Policy, edited by H. Dubowitz, 132–155. Thousand Oaks, Calif.: Sage Publications.

Chen, Z., and Kaplan, H. B. 2001. "Intergenerational Transmission of Constructive Parenting." *Journal of Marriage and Family* 63: 17–31.

Child Abuse Prevention and Treatment Act. 1974. Public Law 93-247. Signed into law January 31, 1974.

Child Welfare League of America. 1984. Implementing Adoption Assistance and Child Welfare Act of 1980, P. L. 96-272. New York: Child Welfare League of America.

Choi, N. G., Kulick, D. B., and Mayer, J. 1999. "Financial Exploitation of Elders: Analysis of Risk Factors Based on County Adult Protective Services Data." *Journal of Elder Abuse and Neglect* 10: 39–62.

Choi, N. G., and Mayer, J. 2000. "Elder Abuse, Neglect, and Exploitation: Risk Factors and Prevention Strategies." *Journal of Gerontological Social Work* 33: 5–25.

Choice, P., Lamke, L. K., and Pittman, J. F. 1995. "Conflict Resolution Strategies and Marital Distress and Mediating Factors in the Link Between Witnessing Inter Parental Violence and Wife Battering." *Violence and Victims* 10: 107–131.

Christensen, H. T., ed. 1964. Handbook of Marriage and the Family. Chicago: Rand McNally and Company.

Christenson, L. 1970. The Christian Family. Minneapolis, Minn.: Bethany House.

Cicchetti, D., and Carlson, V., eds. Child Maltreatment: Theory and Research on the Causes and Consequences of Child Abuse and Neglect. New York: Cambridge University Press.

Claussen, A., and Crittenden, P. 1991. "Physical and Psychological Maltreatment: Relations among Types of Maltreatment." *Child Abuse and Neglect* 15: 5–18.

Cleveland, H. H., Herrera, V. M., and Stuewig, J. 2003. "Abusive Males and Abused Females in Adolescent Relationships: Risk Factor Similarity and Dissimilarity and the Role of Relationship Seriousness." *Journal of Family Violence* 18: 325–339.

Cohen, J. A., Mannarino, A. P., and Rogal, S. 2001. "Treatment Practices for Childhood Post-Traumatic Stress Disorder." *Child Abuse and Neglect* 25: 123–135.

Coker, A. L., Davis, K. E., Arias, I., Desai, S., Sanderson, M., Brandt, H. M., and Smith, P. H. 2002. "Physical and Mental Health Effects of Intimate Partner Violence for Men and Women." *American Journal of Preventive Medicine* 23: 260–268.

Coker, D. 1999. "Enhancing Autonomy for Battered Women: Lessons from Navajo Peacemaking." *UCLA Law Review* 47(1): 1–111.

Collins, M. E. 2004. "Enhancing Services to Youths Leaving Foster Care: Analysis of Recent Legislation and Its Potential Impact." *Children and Youth Services Review* 26: 1051–1065.

Collins, M. E., Stevens, J. W., and Lane, T. S. 2000. "Teenage Parents and Welfare Reform: Findings from a Survey of Teenagers Affected by Living Requirements." *Social Work* 45: 327–338.

Colman, R. A., and Widom, C. S. 2004. "Childhood Abuse and Neglect and Adult Intimate Relationships: A Prospective Study." *Child Abuse and Neglect* 28: 1133–1151.

Conger, R. D., Neppl, T., Kim, K. J., and Scaramella, L. 2003. "Angry and Aggressive Behavior across Three Generations: A Prospective, Longitudinal Study of Parents and Children." *Journal of Abnormal Child Psychology* 31: 143–170.

Conrad, P., and Schneider, J. W. 1982. Deviance and Medicalization: From Badness to Sickness. St. Louis: C. W. Mosby.

Constantino, J. N., Hashemi, N., Soliss, E., Alon, T., Haley, S., McClure, S., Nordlicht, N., Constantino, M. A., Elmen, J., and Carlson, V. K. 2001. "Supplementation of Urban Home Visitation with a Series of Group Meetings for Parents and Infants: Results of a 'Real-World' Randomized, Controlled Trial." *Child Abuse and Neglect* 25: 1572–1581.

Conway, M., Mendelson, M., Giannopoulos, C., Csank, P. A. R., and Holm, S. L. 2004. "Childhood and Adult Sexual Abuse, Rumination on Sadness, and Dysphoria." *Child Abuse and Neglect* 28: 393–410.

Coohey, C. 1996. "Child Maltreatment: Testing the Social Isolation Hypothesis." *Child Abuse and Neglect* 20: 241–154.

———. 2003. "Making Judgments about Risk in Substantiated Cases of Supervisory Neglect." *Child Abuse and Neglect* 27: 821–840.

Cook-Fong, S. K. 2000. "The Adult Well-Being of Individuals Reared in Family Foster Care Placements." *Child and Youth Care Forum* 29: 7–25.

Cooney, C., and Mortimer, A. 1995. "Elder Abuse and Dementia: A Pilot Study." *International Journal of Social Psychiatry* 41: 276–283.

Corbett, J. I. 1964. "A Psychiatrist Reviews the Battered Child Syndrome and Mandatory Reporting Legislation." *Northwest Medicine* 63: 920–922.

Corvo, K., and Carpenter, E. H. 2000. "Effects of Parental Substance Abuse on Current Levels of Domestic Violence: A Possible Elaboration of Intergenerational Transmission Processes." *Journal of Family Violence* 15: 123–135.

Costello, D. O. 2004. "Judging in a Therapeutic Key: Therapeutic Jurisprudence and the Courts." *Judicature* 87: 302.

Costin, L. B., Karger, H. J., and Stoesz, D. 1996. The Politics of Child Abuse in America. New York: Oxford University Press.

Coulton, C. J., Korbin, J. E., and Su, M. 1999. "Neighborhoods and Child Maltreatment: A Multi-Level Study." *Child Abuse and Neglect* 23: 1019–1040.

Courtney, M. E., and Barth, R. P. 1996. "Pathways of Older Adolescents out of Foster Care: Implications for Independent Living Services." *Social Work* 41: 75–83.

Cowan, A. B. 2004. "New Strategies to Promote the Adoption of Older Children out of Foster Care." *Children and Youth Services Review* 26: 1007–1020.

Cox, C., Kotch, J., and Everson, M. 2003. "A Longitudinal Study of Modifying Influences in the Relationship between Domestic Violence and Child Maltreatment." *Journal of Family Violence* 18: 5–17.

Coyne, A. C., Reichman, W. E., and Berbig, L. J. 1993. "The Relationship between Dementia and Elder Abuse." *American Journal of Psychiatry* 150: 643–646.

Craissati, J., Clurg, G., and Browne, K. 2002. "The Parental Bonding Experiences of Sex Offenders: A Comparison between Child Molesters and Rapists." *Child Abuse and Neglect* 26: 909–921.

Crenshaw, W. B. 2004. Treating Families and Children in the Child Protection System. New York: Brunner Routledge.

Crenshaw, W. B., Crenshaw, L. M., and Lichtenberg, J. W. 1995. "When Educators Confront Child Abuse: An Analysis of the Decision to Report." *Child Abuse and Neglect* 19: 1095–1113.

Crittenden, P. M. 1999. "Child Neglect: Causes and Contributors." In Neglected Children: Research, Practice, and Policy, edited by H. Dubowitz, 47–68. Thousand Oaks, Calif.: Sage Publications.

Crouch, J. L., and Milner, J. S. 1993. "Effects of Child Neglect on Children." *Criminal Justice and Behavior* 20: 49–65.

Crouch, J. L., Milner, J. S., and Thomsen, C. 2001. "Childhood Physical Abuse, Early Social Support, and Risk for Maltreatment: Current Social Support as a Mediator of Risk for Child Physical Abuse." *Child Abuse and Neglect* 25: 93–107.

Czumbil, M. R., and Hyman, I. A. 1997. "What Happens When Corporal Punishment Is Legal?" *Journal of Interpersonal Violence* 12: 300–315.

Dagenais, C., Begin, J., Bouchard, C., and Fortin, D. 2004. "Impact of Intensive Family Support Programs: A Synthesis of Evaluation Studies." *Children and Youth Services Review* 26: 249–263.

Dallam, S. J., Gleaves, D. H., Cepeda-Benito, A., Silberg, J. L., Kraemer, H. C., and Spiegel, D. 2001. "The Effects of Child Sexual Abuse: Comment on Rind, Tromovitch, and Bauserman (1998)." *Psychological Bulletin* 127: 715–733.

Daly, J. A., Jogerst, G. J., et al. 2003. "Mandatory Reporting: Relationship of APS Statute Language on State Reported Elder Abuse." *Journal of Elder Abuse and Neglect* 15(2): 1–21.

Danso, H., Hunsberger, B., and Pratt, M. 1997. "The Role of Parental Religious Fundamentalism and Right-Wing Authoritarianism in Child-Rearing Goals and Practices." *Journal for the Scientific Study of Religion* 36: 496–512.

Daro, D. 1988. Confronting Child Abuse: Research for Effective Program Design. New York: Free Press.

Daro, Deborah, Edleson, Jeffrey L., and Pinderhughes, Howard. 2004. "Finding Common Ground in the Study of Child Maltreatment, Youth Violence, and Adult Domestic Violence." *Journal of Interpersonal Violence* 19: 282–298.

Daro, D., McCurdy, K., Falconnier, L., and Stojanovic, D. 2003. "Sustaining New Parents in Home Visitation Services: Key Participant and Program Factors." *Child Abuse and Neglect* 27: 1101–1125.

Darwish, D., Esquivel, G. B., Houtz, J. C., and Alfonso, V. C. 2001. "Plan and Social Skills in Maltreated and Non-Maltreated Preschoolers during Peer Interactions." *Child Abuse and Neglect* 25: 13–31.

Das Dasgupta, S. 2002. "A Framework for Understanding Women's Use of Nonlethal Violence in Intimate Heterosexual Relationships." *Violence against Women* 8: 1364–1389.

Davidson, H. 2003. "The Impact of HIPPA on Child Abuse and Neglect Cases." *Child Law Practice* 22(1): 11–13.

Davidson, H. A., Horowitz, R. M., Marvell, T. B., and Ketcham, O. W. 1981. Child Abuse and Neglect Litigation: A Manual for Judges. Washington, DC: The National Center on Child Abuse and Neglect.

Davies, S. L., Glaser, D., and Kossoff, R. 2000. "Children's Sexual Play and Behavior in Pre-School Settings: Staff's Perceptions, Reports, and Responses." *Child Abuse and Neglect* 24: 1329–1343.

Davis, Keith E., and Frieze, Irene Hanson. 2000. "Research on Stalking: What Do We Know? Where Do We Go?" *Violence and Victims* 15: 473–487.

Davis, P. W., Chandler, J. L., and LaRoosa, R. 2004. "'I've Tried the Switch but He Laughs through the Tears': The Use and Conceptualization of Corporal Punishment during the Machine Age, 1924–1939." *Child Abuse and Neglect* 28: 1291–1310.

Dawson, B., Geddie, L., and Wagner, W. 1996. "Low-Income Preschoolers' Behavior with Anatomically Detailed Dolls." *Journal of Family Violence* 11: 363–378.

Day, R. D., Peterson, G. W., and McCracken, C. 1998. "Predicting Spanking of Younger and Older Children by Mothers and Fathers." *Journal of Marriage and the Family* 60: 79–94.

De Bellis, M. D., Broussard, E. R., Herring, D. J., Wexler, S., Moritz, G., and Benitez, J. G. 2001. "Psychiatric Co-Morbidity in Caregivers and Children Involved in Maltreatment: A Pilot Research Study with Policy Implications." *Child Abuse and Neglect* 25: 923–944.

Deblinger, E., Hathaway, C. R., Lippmann, J., and Steer, R. 1993. "Psychosocial Characteristics and Correlates of Symptom Distress in Non-Offending Mothers of Sexually Abused Children." *Journal of Interpersonal Violence* 8: 155–168.

De Francis, V. 1963. Child Abuse: Preview of a Nationwide Survey. Denver, Colo.: Children's Division, The American Humane Association.

———. 1972. "Protecting the Abused Child: A Coordinated Approach." In A National Symposium on Child Abuse, 6–14. Denver, Colo.: American Humane Association.

DeKeseredy, W. S., and MacLeod, L. 1997. Woman Abuse: A Sociological Story. Toronto: Harcourt Brace.

DeKeseredy, W. S., Saunders, D. G., Schwartz, M. D., and Alvi, S. 1997. "The Meanings and Motives for Women's Use of Violence in Canadian College Dating Relationships: Results from a National Survey." *Sociological Spectrum* 17: 199–222.

DeKeseredy, W. S., and Schwartz, M. D. 2001. Definitional Issues. Sourcebook on Violence against Women, edited by C. M. Renzetti, Jeffrey Edelson, and Raquel Kennedy Bergen, 23–34. Thousand Oaks, Calif.: Sage Publications.

Delaronde, S., King, S., Bendell, R., and Reece, R. 2000. "Opinions among Mandated Reporters toward Child Maltreatment Reporting Policies." *Child Abuse and Neglect* 24: 901–910.

De Loache, J., and Gottlieb, A., eds. 2000. A World of Babies: Imagined Childcare Guides for Seven Societies. New York: Cambridge University Press.

Del Sol, C., and Margolin, G. 2004. "The Role of Family-of-Origin Violence in Men's Marital Violence Perpetration." *Clinical Psychology Review* 24: 99–122.

Del Sol, C., Margolin, G., and John, R. S. 2003. "A Typology of Maritally Violent Men and Correlates of Violence in a Community Sample." *Journal of Marriage and the Family* 65: 635–651.

DeMaris, A., Benson, M. L., Fox, G. L., Hill, T., and Van Wyk, J. 2002. "Distal and Proximal Factors in Domestic Violence: A Test of an Integrated Model." *Journal of Marriage and Family* 64: 652–667.

deMause, L. 1974. The History of Childhood. New York: Psychohistory Press.

———. 1991. "The Universality of Incest." *Journal of Psychohistory* 19: 123–164.

Dembo, R., Williams, L., Wothke, W., Schmeidler, J., and Brown, C. H. 1992. "The Role of Family Factors, Physical Abuse, and Sexual Victimization in High-Risk Youths' Alcohol and Other Drug Use and Delinquency: A Longitudinal Model." *Violence and Victims* 7: 245–266.

Demos, J. 1970. A Little Commonwealth: Family Life in Plymouth Colony. New York: Oxford University Press.

———. 1986. Past, Present, and Personal. New York. Oxford University Press.

DePanfilis, D. 1996. "Social Isolation of Neglectful Families: A Review of Social Support Assessment and Intervention Models." *Child Maltreatment* 1: 37–60.

———. 1999. "Intervening with Families When Children Are Neglected." In Neglected Children: Research, Practice, and Policy, edited by H. Dubowitz, 211–236. Thousand Oaks, Calif.: Sage Publications.

DePanfilis, D., and Scannapieco, M. 1994. "Assessing the Safety of Children at Risk Maltreatment Decision Making Models." *Child Welfare* 73: 229–245.

DePanfilis, D., and Zuravin, S. J. 1998. "Rates, Patterns, and Frequency of Child Maltreatment Recurrences among Families." *Child Maltreatment* 3: 27–42.

———. 1999. "Predicting Child Maltreatment Recurrences during Treatment." *Child Abuse and Neglect* 23: 729–743.

———. "The Effect of Services on the Recurrence of Child Maltreatment." *Child Abuse and Neglect* 26: 187–205.

Derr, M. K., and Taylor, M. J. 2004. "The Link between Childhood and Adult Abuse among Long-Term Welfare Recipients." *Children and Youth Services Review* 26: 173–184.

Desai, Sujata, and Saltzman, Linda E. 2001. "Measurement Issues for Violence against Women." In Sourcebook on Violence against Women, edited by Claire M. Renzetti, Jeffrey Edelson, and Raquel Kennedy Bergen, 35–52. Thousand Oaks, Calif.: Sage Publications.

Dietz, Tracy L., and Jasinski, Jana L. Forthcoming. "Item Order and Disclosure Rates of Intimate Partner Violence: A Quasi Experimental Model." *Social Science Research*.

Dimah, A., and Dimah, K. P. 2002. "Gender Differences among Abused Older African American Abusers in an Elder Abuse Provider Agency." *Journal of Black Studies* 32: 557–573.

Dobash, R. E., and Dobash, R. 1979. Violence against Wives. New York: Free Press.

———. 1992. Women, Violence, and Social Change. London: Routledge.

———. 2000. "The Politics and Policies of Responding to Violence against Women." In Home Truths about Domestic Violence: Feminist Influence on Policy and

Practice: A Reader, edited by Jalna Hanmer and Catherine Itzin with Sheila Quaid and Debra Wigglesworth, 187–204. London: Routledge.

Dobash, R. P., Dobash, R. E., Wilson, M., and Daly, M. 1992. "The Myth of Sexual Symmetry in Marital Violence." *Social Problems* 39: 71–91.

Dobson, J. 1970. Dare to Discipline. Wheaton, Ill.: Living Books/Tyndale House.

———. 1987. Parenting Isn't for Cowards. Dallas, Tex.: Word Press.

Dodge, K. A., Pettit, G. S., and Bates, J. E. 1994. "Effects of Physical Maltreatment on the Development of Peer Relations." *Development and Psychopathology* 6: 43–55.

Dodson, D. 1985. The Legal Framework for Ending Foster Care Drift: A Guide to Evaluating and Improving State Laws, Regulations, and Court Rules. Washington, DC: American Bar Association.

Doezema, Jo. 1999. "Loose Women or Lost Women? The Re-Emergence of the Myth of White Slavery in Contemporary Discourses of Trafficking in Women." *Gender Issues* 18: 23–50.

Dolz, L., Cerezo, M. A., and Milner, J. S. 1997. "Mother-Child Interactional Patterns in High and Low-Risk Mothers." *Child Abuse and Neglect* 21: 1149–1158.

Dong, M., Anda, R. F., Felitti, V. J., Dube, S. R., Williamson, D. F., Thompson, T. J., Loo, C. M., and Giles, W. H. 2004. "The Interrelatedness of Multiple Forms of Childhood Abuse, Neglect, and Household Dysfunction." *Child Abuse and Neglect* 28: 771–784.

Donzelot, J. 1977. The Policing of Families. New York: Random House.

Dore, M. M., and Alexander, L. B. 1996. "Preserving Families at Risk of Child Abuse and Neglect: The Role of the Helping Alliance." *Child Abuse and Neglect* 20: 349–361.

Dore, M. M., and Lee, J. M. 1999. "The Role of Parent Training with Abusive and Neglectful Parents." *Family Relations* 48: 313–325.

Doueck, H. J., Levine, M., and Bronson, D. E. 1993. "Risk Assessment in Child Protective Services: An Evaluation of the Child at Risks Field System." *Journal of Interpersonal Violence* 8: 446–467.

Downs, D. A. 1996. More than Victims: Battered Women, The Syndrome Society, and the Law. Chicago: University of Chicago Press.

Drake, B. 1996. "Harassment Reports to Child Protective Services: An Empirical Examination." *Journal of Social Service Research* 21: 1–18.

Drake, B., and Pandey, S. 1996. "Understanding the Relationship between Neighborhood Poverty and Specific Types of Maltreatment." *Child Abuse and Neglect* 20: 1003–1018.

Drake, B., and Zuravin, S. 1998. "Bias in Child Maltreatment Reporting: Revisiting the Myth of Classlessness." *American Journal of Orthopsychiatry* 65: 295–304.

Dube, S. R., Anda, R. F., Felitti, V. J., Croft, J. B., Edwards, V. J., and Giles, W. H. 2001. "Growing Up with Parental Alcohol Abuse: Exposure to Childhood Abuse, Neglect, and Household Dysfunction." *Child Abuse and Neglect* 25: 1627–1640.

Dube, S. R., Williamson, D. F., Thompson, T., Felitti, V. J., and Anda, R. F. 2004. "Assessing the Reliability of Retrospective Reports of Adverse Childhood Experiences among Adult HMO Members Attending a Primary Care Clinic." *Child Abuse and Neglect* 28: 729–737.

Dubow, E. F., Huesmann, L. R., and Boxer, P. 2003. "Theoretical and Methodological Considerations in Cross-Generational Research on Parenting and Child Aggressive Behavior." *Journal of Abnormal Child Psychology* 31: 185–192.

Dubowitz, H. 1999. Neglected Children: Research, Practice, and Policy. Thousand Oaks, Calif.: Sage Publications.

Dubowitz, H., Klockner, A., Starr, R. H., and Black, M. M. 1998. "Community and Professional Definitions of Child Neglect." *Child Maltreatment* 3: 235–243.

Dugan, A. K., McFarlane, E. C., Windham, A. M., Rohde, C. A., Salkever, D. S., Fuddy, L., Rosenberg, L. A., Buchbinder, S. B., and Sia, C. C. J. 1999. "Evaluation of Hawaii's Healthy Start Program." *The Future of Children* 9 (1): 66–90.

Dugan, Laura, Nagin, Daniel S., and Rosenfeld, Richard. 2003. "Do Domestic Violence Services Save Lives?" *NIJ Journal* 250: 20–25.

Duggan, A., McFarlane, E., Fuddy, L., Burrell, L., Higman, S. M., Windham, A., and Sia, C. 2004. "Randomized Trial of a Statewide Home Visiting Program: Impact in Preventing Child Abuse and Neglect." *Child Abuse and Neglect* 28: 597–622.

Dunne, M. P., Purdie, D. M., Cook, M. D., Boyle, F. M., and Najman, J. M. 2003. "Is Child Sexual Abuse Declining? Evidence from a Population-Based Survey of Men and Women in Australia." *Child Abuse and Neglect* 27: 141–152.

Durrant, J. E. 1999. "Evaluating the Success of Sweden's Corporal Punishment Ban." *Child Abuse and Neglect* 23: 435–448.

———. 2000. "Trends in Youth Crime and Well-Being Since the Abolition of Corporal Punishment in Sweden." *Youth and Society* 31: 437–455.

Dutton, M. A., and Goodman, L. A. 1994. "Post-Traumatic Stress Disorder among Battered Women: Analysis of Legal Implications." *Behavioral Sciences and the Law* 12: 215–234.

Dyer, C. B., Pavlik, V. N., Murphy, K. P., and Hyman, D. J. 2000. "The High Prevalence of Depression and Dementia in Elder Abuse or Neglect." *Journal of the American Geriatrics Society* 48: 205–208.

Eamon, M. K. 2001. "Antecedents and Socioemotional Consequences of Physical Punishment on Children in Two-Parent Families." *Child Abuse and Neglect* 25: 787–802.

Earle, A. M. 1926. Child Life in Colonial Days. New York: Macmillan.

Eckenrode, J., Ganzel, B., Henderson, C. R., Smith, E., Olds, D. L., Powers, J., Cole, R., Kitzman, H., and Sidora, K. 2000. "Preventing Child Abuse and Neglect with a Program of Nurse Home Visitation: The Limiting Effects of Domestic Violence." *Journal of the American Medical Association* 284: 1385–1391.

Eckenrode, J., Laird, M., and Doris, J. 1993. "School Performance and Disciplinary Problems among Abused and Neglected Children." *Developmental Psychology* 29: 53–62.

Eckhardt, C., Jamison, T. R., and Watts, K. 2002. "Anger Experience and Expression among Male Dating Violence Perpetrators during Anger Arousal." *Journal of Interpersonal Violence* 17: 1102–1114.

Edna McConnell Clark Foundation. 1985. Keeping Families Together: The Case for Family Preservation. New York: Edna McConnell Clark Foundation.

Edwards, J., and Alexander, P. C. 1992. "The Contribution of Family Background to the Long-Term Adjustment of Women Sexually Abused as Children." *Journal of Interpersonal Violence* 7: 306–320.

Ehrenreich, R., and English, D. 1978. For Her Own Good: 150 Years of the Experts' Advice to Women. New York: Doubleday.

Ehrensaft, M. K., Cohen, P., Brown, J., Smailes, E., Chen, H. N., and Johnson, J. G. 2003. "Intergenerational Transmission of Partner Violence: A 20-Year Prospective Study." *Journal of Consulting and Clinical Psychology* 71: 741–753.

EKOS, Research Associates, Inc. 2002. "Public Attitudes towards Family Violence: A Syndicated Study. Final Report." Ottawa: EKOS Research Associates.

Elders, M. J. 1999. "The Call to Action." *Child Abuse and Neglect* 23: 1003–1009.

Elliott, A. N., O'Donahue, W. T., and Nickerson, M. A. 1993. "The Use of Sexually Anatomically Detailed Dolls in the Assessment of Sexual Abuse." *Clinical Psychology Review* 13: 207–221.

Elliott, D. M. 1994. "The Impact of Christian Faith on the Prevalence and Sequelae of Sexual Abuse." *Journal of Interpersonal Violence* 9: 95–108.

Ellis, D. 1989. "Male Abuse of a Married or Cohabiting Partner: The Application of Sociological Theory to Research Findings." *Violence and Victims* 4: 235–255.

Ellison, C. G., and Sherkat, D. E. 1993. "Conservative Protestantism and Support for Corporal Punishment." *American Sociological Review* 58: 131–144.

Elmer, E. 1977. Fragile Families, Troubled Children. Pittsburgh, Pa.: University of Pittsburgh Press.

———. 1981. "Traumatized Children, Chronic Illness, and Poverty." In The Social Context of Child Abuse and Neglect, edited by L. H. Pelton. New York: Human Sciences Press.

England, P., Budig, M., et al. 2002. "Wages of Virtue: The Relative Pay of Care Work." *Social Problems* 49(4): 455–473.

English, D. J., and Pecora, P. J. 1994. "Risk Assessment as a Practice Method in Child Protective Services." *Child Welfare* 73: 451–473.

English, D. J., Wingard, T., Marshall, D., Orme, M., and Orme, A. 2000. "Alternative Responses to Child Protective Services: Emerging Issues and Concerns." *Child Abuse and Neglect* 24: 375–388.

Epstein, Deborah. 1999. "Rethinking the Role of Prosecutors, Judges, and the Court System. *Yale Journal of Law and Feminism* 11: 3-50.

Epstein, J. N., Saunders, B. E., Kilpatrick, D. G., and Resnick, H. S. 1998. "PTSD as a Mediator between Childhood Rape and Alcohol Use in Adult Women." *Child Abuse and Neglect* 22: 223–234.

Ethier, L. S., Lacharite, C., and Couture, G. 1995. "Childhood Adversity, Parental Stress, and Depression of Negligent Mothers." *Child Abuse and Neglect* 19: 619–632.

———. 2004. "Risk Factors Associated with the Chronicity of High Potential for Child Abuse and Neglect." *Journal of Family Violence* 19: 13–24.

Ethier, L. S., Lemelin, J., and Lacharite, C. 2004. "A Longitudinal Study of the Effects of Chronic Maltreatment on Children's Behavioral and Emotional Problems." *Child Abuse and Neglect* 28: 1265–1278.

Everill, J., and Waller, G. 1995. "Disclosure of Sexual Abuse and Psychological Adjustment in Female Undergraduates." *Child Abuse and Neglect* 19: 93–100.

Everson, M. D., and Boat, B. W. 1994. "Putting the Anatomical Doll Controversy in Perspective: An Examination of the Major Uses and Criticisms of the Dolls in Child Sexual Abuse Evaluations." *Child Abuse and Neglect* 18: 113–129.

Ezzell, C. E., Wenson, C. C., and Brondino, M. J. 2000. "The Relationship of Social Support to Physically Abused Children's Adjustment." *Child Abuse and Neglect* 24: 641–651.

Fagan, A. A. 2003. "The Short- and Long-Term Effects of Adolescent Violent Victimization Experienced within the Family and Community." *Violence and Victims* 18: 445–459.

Fagan, J. A., Stewart, D. K., and Hansen, K. V. 1983. "Violent Men or Violent Husbands? Background Factors and Situational Correlates." In The Dark Side of Families, edited by R. G. Gelles, D. Finkelhor, and G. T. Hotaling, 49–68. Beverly Hills, Calif.: Sage Publications.

Farmer, A., and Tiefenthaler, J. 1997. "An Economic Analysis of Domestic Violence." *Review of Social Economy* 55: 337–358.

Featherstone, B. 1997. "What Has Gender Got to Do with It? Exploring Physically Abusive Behaviour towards Children." *British Journal of Social Work* 27: 419–433.

Feierman, J. R., ed. 1990. Pedophilia: Biosocial Dimensions. New York: Springer-Verlag.

Feiring, C., Taska, L., and Lewis, M. 1996. "A Process Model for Understanding Adaptation to Sexual Abuse: The Role of Shame in Defining Stigmatization." *Child Abuse and Neglect* 20: 767–782.

Feldman, M. D., and Brown, R. M. A. 2002. "Munchausen by Proxy in an International Context." *Child Abuse and Neglect* 26: 509–524.

Felson, R. B., Ackerman, J., and Yeon, S. 2002. "The Infrequency of Family Violence." *Journal of Marriage and Family* 64: 622–634.

Fennema-Notestine, C., Stein, M. B., Kennedy, C. M., Archibald, S. L., and Jernigan, T. L. 2002. "Brain Morphometry in Female Victims of Intimate Partner Violence with and Without Post-Traumatic Stress Disorder." *Biological Psychiatry* 52: 1089–1101.

Ferrari, A. M. 2002. "The Impact of Culture Upon Child Rearing Practices and Definitions of Maltreatment." *Child Abuse and Neglect* 26: 793–813.

Ferraro, K. J., and Johnson, J. M. 1983. "How Women Experience Battering: The Process of Victimization." *Social Problems* 30: 325–339.

Ferris, L. E., Norton, P. G., et al. 1997. "Guidelines for Managing Domestic Abuse When Male and Female Partners Are Patients of the Same Physician." *Journal of the American Medical Association* 278(10): 851–857.

Fetsch, R. J., Schultz, C. J., and Wahler, J. J. 1999. "A Preliminary Evaluation of the Colorado Rethink Parenting and Anger Management Program." *Child Abuse and Neglect* 23: 353–360.

Field, C. A., and Caetano, R. 2003. "Longitudinal Model Predicting Partner Violence among White, Black, and Hispanic Couples in the United States." *Alcoholism: Clinical and Experimental Research* 27: 1451–1458.

Fiene, R. 2002. "Improving Child Care Quality Through an Infant Caregiver Mentoring Project." *Child and Youth Care Forum* 31: 79–87.

Finch, E. 2002. "Stalking the Perfect Stalking Law: An Evaluation of the Efficacy of the Protection from Harassment Act 1997." *Criminal Law Review* 703–718.

Fine, Gary Alan. 2004. "Adolescence as Cultural Toolkit: High School Debates and the Repertoires of Childhood and Adulthood." *Sociological Quarterly* 45:1– 20.

Fineran, S., and Bennett, L. 1999. "Gender and Power Issues of Peer Sexual Harassment among Teenagers." *Journal of Interpersonal Violence* 14:626–641.

Finkelhor, D. 1994a. "Current Information on the Scope and Nature of Child Sexual Abuse." *The Future of Children* 4 (2): 31–53.

———. 1994b. "The International Epidemiology of Child Sexual Abuse." *Child Abuse and Neglect* 18: 409–417.

Finkelhor, D., and Araji, S. 1986. "Explanations of Pedophilia: A Four Factor Model." *Journal of Sex Research* 2: 145–161.

Finkelhor, D., and Jones, L. M. 2004. "Explanations for the Decline in Child Sexual Abuse Cases." *Juvenile Justice Bulletin*, January. U.S. Department of Justice. www.ojp.usdoj/ojjdp

Finkelhor, D., Moore, D., Hamby, S., and Straus, M. 1997. "Sexually Abused Children in a National Survey of Parents: Methodological Issues." *Child Abuse and Neglect* 21: 1–9.

Finkelhor, D., and Wells, M. 2003. "Improving Data Systems about Juvenille Victimization in the United States." *Child Abuse and Neglect* 27: 77–102.

Finkelhor, D. and Yllo, Kirsti. 1985. License to Rape: Sexual Abuse of Wives. New York: Holt, Rinehart, and Winston.

———. 1995. "Types of Marital Rape." In Rape and Society: Readings on the Problem of Sexual Assault, edited by Patricia and Berger Searles. Boulder, Colo.: Westview Press.

Finn, M. A., Blackwell, Stalans, L. J., Studdard, S., and Dugan, L. 2004. "Dual Arrest Decisions in Domestic Violence Cases: The Influence of Departmental Policies." *Crime and Delinquency* 50: 565–589.

Fisher, D. G., and McDonald, W. L. 1998. "Characteristics of Intrafamilial and Extra-Familial Child Sexual Abuse." *Child Abuse and Neglect* 22: 915–929.

Fisher, W. 1987. Human Communication as Narration: Toward a Philosophy of Reason, Value, and Action. Columbia: University of South Carolina Press.

Fluke, J. D., Yuan, Y. T., and Edwards, M. 1999. "Recurrence of Maltreatment: An Application of the National Child Abuse and Neglect Data System (NCANDS)." *Child Abuse and Neglect* 23: 633–650.

Fluke, J. D., Yuan, Y. T., Hedderson, J., and Curtis, P. A. 2003. "Disproportionate Representation of Race and Ethnicity in Child Maltreatment: Investigation and Victimization." *Children and Youth Services Review* 25: 359–373.

Flynn, C. P. 1994. "Regional Differences in Attitudes toward Corporal Punishment." *Journal of Marriage and Family* 56: 314–324.

———. 1996. "Regional Differences in Spanking Experiences and Attitudes: A Comparison of Northeastern and Southern College Students." *Journal of Family Violence* 11: 59–80.

———. 1998. "To Spank or Not to Spank: The Effect of Situation and Age of Child on Support for Corporal Punishment." *Journal of Family Violence* 113: 21–37.

———. 1999. "Exploring the Link Between Corporal Punishment and Children's Cruelty to Animals." *Journal of Marriage and Family* 61: 971–981.

Fontana, V. J. 1968. "Further Reflections on Maltreatment of Children." *New York Journal of Medicine* 68: 2214–2215.

Forbat, Liz. 2002. "'Tinged with Bitterness': Representing Stress in Family Care." *Disability and Society* 17: 759–768.

Ford, David A. 2003. "Coercing Victim Participation in Domestic Violence Prosecutions." *Journal of Interpersonal Violence* 18: 669–684.

Ford, David A., Bachman, Ronet, Friend, Monika, and Meloy, Michelle. 2002. "NIJ Brief on Violence against Women Research. Controlling Violence against Women: A Research Perspective on the 1994 VAWA's Criminal Justice Impacts. The Convergence of Advocacy, Research, and Law." In NIJ Brief, edited by Office of Justice Programs. Washington, DC: U.S. Department of Justice, National Institute of Justice.

Ford, J., Rompf, E. L., Faragher, T., and Weisenfluh, S. 1995. "Case Outcomes in Domestic Violence Court: Influence of Judges." *Psychological Reports* 77: 587–594.

Fortune, Marie M. 2001. "Religious Issues and Violence against Women." In Sourcebook on Violence against Women, edited by Claire M. Renzetti, Jeffrey Edelson, and Raquel Kennedy Bergen, 371–385. Thousand Oaks, Calif.: Sage Publications.

Foshee, V. A., Bauman, K. E., Greene, W. F., Koch, G. G., Linder, G. F., and MacDougall, J. E. 2000. "The Safe Dates Program: One-Year Follow-Up Results." *American Journal of Public Health* 90: 1619–1622.

Foshee, V. A., Bauman, K. E., and Linder, G. F. 1999. "Family Violence and the Perpetration of Adolescent Dating Violence: Examining Social Learning and Social Control Processes." *Journal of Marriage and Family* 61: 331–342.

Foshee, V. A., Linder, F., MacDougall, J. E., and Bangdiwala, S. 2001. "Gender Differences in the Longitudinal Predictors of Adolescent Dating Violence." *Preventive Medicine* 32: 128–141.

Fox, G. L., Benson, M. L., DeMaris, A. A., and Van Wyk, J. 2002. "Economic Distress and Intimate Violence: Testing Stress and Resources Theories." *Journal of Marriage and Family* 64: 793–807.

Fox, James Alan, and Zawitz, Marianne W. 2004. "Homicide Trends in the United States: 2002 Update (NCJ 204885)." In Bureau of Justice Statistics Crime Data Briefs, 4. Washington, DC: U.S. Department of Justice, Office of Justice Programs.

Frensch, K. M., and Cameron, G. 2002. "Treatment of Choice or a Last Resort? A Review of Residential Mental Health Placements for Children and Youth." *Child and Youth Care Forum* 31: 313–345.

Freundlich, M., and Avery, R. J. 2005. "Planning for Permanency for Youth in Congregate Care." *Children and Youth Services Review* 27: 115–134.

Friedrich, W. N. 1991. "Mothers of Sexually Abused Children: An MMPI Study." *Journal of Clinical Psychology* 47: 778–783.

Friedrich, W. N., and Baoriskin, J. A. 1976. "The Role of the Child in Abuse: A Review of the Literature." *American Journal of Orthopsychiatry* 46: 580–590.

Fromuth, M. E., and Burkhart, B. R. 1987. "Childhood Sexual Victimization among College Men: Definitional and Methodological Issues." *Violence and Victims* 2: 241–253.

Fromuth, M. E., Burkhart, B. R., and Jones, C. W. 1991. "Hidden Child Molestation: An Investigation of Adolescent Perpetrators in a Nonclinical Sample." *Journal of Interpersonal Violence* 6: 376–384.

Frude, N. 1982. "The Sexual Nature of Sexual Abuse: A Review of the Literature." *Child Abuse and Neglect* 6: 221–223.

Fry, A. R. 1974. "The Children's Migration." *American Heritage Magazine* (December): 4–10, 79–81.

Gagne, P. 1996. "Identity, Strategy, and Feminist Politics: Clemency for Battered Women Who Kill." *Social Problems* 43: 77–93.

Gagne, Marie Helene, and Bouchard, Camil. 2004. "Family Dynamics Associated with the Use of Psychologically Violent Parental Practices." *Journal of Family Violence* 19: 117–130.

Garbarino, J. 2001. "An Ecological Perspective on the Effects of Violence on Children." *Journal of Community Psychology* 29: 361–378.

Garbarino, J., and Collins, C. C. 1999. "Child Neglect: The Family with a Hole in the Middle." In Neglected Children: Research, Practice, and Policy, edited by H. Dubowitz, 1–23. Thousand Oaks, Calif.: Sage Publications.

Garbarino, J., Kostelny, K., and Dubrow, N. 1991. No Place to Be a Child: Growing Up in a War Zone. Lexington, Mass.: Lexington Books.

Garland, David. 2001. The Culture of Control: Crime and Social Order in Contemporary Society. Chicago: University of Chicago Press.

Garner, J., Fagan, J., and Maxwell, C. 1995. "Published Findings from the Spouse Assault Replication Program: A Critical Review." *Journal of Quantitative Criminology* 11: 3–28.

Gaudin, J. M., Jr. 1999. "Child Neglect: Short-Term and Long-Term Outcomes." In Neglected Children: Research, Practice, and Policy, edited by H. Dubowitz, 89–108. Thousand Oaks, Calif.: Sage Publications.

Gaudin, J. M., Jr., Polansky, N. A., Kilpatrick, A. C., and Shilton, P. 1993. "Loneliness, Depression, Stress, and Social Supports in Neglectful Families." *American Journal of Orthopsychiatry* 63: 597–605.

Geen, R., Boots, S. W., and Tumlin, K. C. 1999. The Cost of Protecting Vulnerable Children: Understanding Federal, State, and Local Child Welfare Spending. Washington, DC: Urban Institute.

Gelles, R. J. 1973. "Child Abuse as Psychopathology: A Sociological Critique and Reformulation." *American Journal of Orthopsychiatry* 43: 611–621.

———. 1983. "Toward a Theory of Intra-Familial Violence: An Exchange/Social Control Theory." In The Dark Side of Families: Current Family Violence Research, edited by D. Finkelhor, R. J. Gelles, G. Hotaling, and M. A. Straus, 151–165. Beverly Hills, Calif.: Sage Publications.

———. 1992. "Methodological Issues in the Study of Family Violence." In Physical Violence in American Families: Risk Factors and Adaptations to Violence in 8,145 Families, edited by M. A. Straus, R. J. Gelles, and (with the assistance of) C. Smith, 17–28. New Brunswick, N.J.: Transaction.

———. 1996. The Book of David: How Preserving Families Can Cost Children's Lives. New York: Basic Books.

———. 2000. "Estimating the Incidence and Prevalence of Violence against Women: National Data Systems and Sources." Violence against Women 6: 784–804.

———. 2003. "Violence in the Family." In International Handbook of Violence Research, edited by Wilhelm and Hagan Heitmeyer and John Dordrecht, 837–862. The Netherlands: Kluwer Academic Publishers.

Gelles, Richard J., and Loseke, Donileen R. 1993. Current Controversies on Family Violence. Thousand Oaks, Calif.: Sage Publications.

Gelles, Richard J., Loseke, Donileen R., and Cavanaugh, Mary M. 2004. Current Controversies on Family Violence, 2nd ed. Thousand Oaks, Calif.: Sage Publications.

Gelles, Richard J., and Straus, Murray A. 1979. "Violence in the American Family." Journal of Social Issues 35: 15–39.

Gembeck, M. 1999. "Stability, Change and Individual Differences in Involvement with Friends and Romantic Partners among Adolescent Females." Journal of Youth and Adolescence 28: 419–438.

General Accounting Office. 2003. "HHS Could Play a Greater Role in Helping Child Welfare Agencies Recruit and Retain Staff." www.gao.gov/cgi–bin/getrpt?gao–03–357.

George, C., and Main, M. 1979. "Social Interactions of Young Abused Children: Approach, Avoidance, and Aggression." Child Development 50: 306–318.

Gerbner, G., Ross, C. J., and Zigler, E. 1980. Child Abuse: An Agenda for Action. New York: Oxford University Press.

Gershoff, E. T., Miller, P. C., and Holden, G. W. 1999. "Parenting Influence from the Pulpit: Religious Affiliation as a Determinant of Parental Corporal Punishment." Journal of Family Psychology 3: 307–320.

Gibbs, N. 1990. "Shameful Bequests to the Next Generation." Time 136 (October 8): 42–46.

Gibson, R. L., and Hartshorne, T. S. 1996. "Childhood Sexual Abuse and Adult Loneliness and Network Orientation." Child Abuse and Neglect 20: 1087–1093.

Gil, D. 1970. Violence against Children: Physical Child Abuse in the United States. Cambridge, Mass.: Harvard University Press.

Gil, D., ed. 1979. Child Abuse and Violence. New York: AMS Press.

Giorgi-Guarnieri, D. 2003. "Surviving Stalking." Journal of the American Academy of Psychiatry and the Law 31: 400–400.

Giovannoni, J. M. 1991. "Unsubstantiated Reports: Perspectives of Child Protection Workers." *Child and Youth Services* 15: 51–62.

Giovannoni, J. M., and Becerra, R. M. 1979. Defining Child Abuse. New York: Free Press.

Giovannoni, J. M., and Billingsley, A. 1970. "Child Neglect among the Poor: A Study of Parental Adequacy in Families of Three Ethnic Groups." *Child Welfare* 40: 196–204.

Gish, C. 1999. "Rescuing the 'Waifs and Strays' of the City: The Western Emigration Program of the Children's Aid Society." *Journal of Social History* 33: 121–141.

Gladstone, G., Parker, G., Wilhelm, K., Mitchell, D., and Austin, M. 1999. "Characteristics of Depressed Patients Who Report Childhood Sexual Abuse." *American Journal of Psychiatry* 156: 431–437.

Glaser, D. 2002. "Emotional Maltreatment and Neglect (Psychological Maltreatment): A Conceptual Framework." *Child Abuse and Neglect* 26: 697–714.

Gleaves, D. H. 1966. "The Evidence for 'Repression': An Examination of Holmes (1990) and the Implications for the Recovered Memory Controversy." *Journal of Child Sexual Abuse* 5: 1–19.

Gleick, E. 1996. "The Children's Crusade." *Time* 147 (June 3): 31–35.

Goebel, G., and Lapp, M. 2003. "Stalking with Fatal Outcome: Five Fatal and Nonfatal Assaults against Women by Their Ex-Partners." *Kriminalistik* 57: 369–377.

Goetting, A. 1994. "Do Americans Really Like Children?" *Journal of Primary Prevention* 15.

Golden, J. 2002. "An Argument that Goes Back to the Womb: The Demedicalization of Fetal Alcohol Syndrome." *Journal of Social History* 33: 269–299.

Goldman, J., Graves, L. M., Ward, M., Albanese, I., Sorensen, E., and Chamberlain, C. 1993. "Self-Report of Guardians Ad Litem: Provision of Information to Judges in Child Abuse and Neglect Cases." *Child Abuse and Neglect* 17: 227–232.

Goldstein, E. 1997. "False Memory Syndrome: Why Would They Believe Such Terrible Things If They Weren't True?" *American Journal of Family Therapy* 25: 307–317.

Goldstein, J., Freud, A., and Solnit, A. J. 1979. Before the Best Interests of the Child. New York: Free Press.

Gomby, D. S. 1999. "Understanding Evaluations of Home Visitation Programs." *The Future of Children* 9 (1): 27–43.

Gomby, D. S., Cubross, P. L., and Behrman, R. E. 1999. "Home Visiting: Recent Program Evaluations, Analysis and Recommendations." *The Future of Children* 9 (1): 4–26.

Gomby, D. S., Larner, M. B., Stevenson, C. S., Lewit, E. M., and Behrman, R. E. 1995. "Long-Term Outcomes of Early Childhood Programs: Analysis and Recommendations." *The Future of Children* 5 (3): 6–24.

Gondolf, E. W., Heckert, D. A., and Kimmel, C. M. 2002. "Nonphysical Abuse among Batterer Program Participants." *Journal of Family Violence* 17: 293–314.

Goode, E. 2004. "Courting Disaster: Intimate Stalking, Culture, and Criminal Justice." *Symbolic Interaction* 27: 119–122.

Goode, W. J. 1963. World Revolution and Family Patterns. New York: Free Press.

Goodman, L. A., Dutton, M. A., and Bennett, L. 2000. "Predicting Repeat Abuse among Arrested Batterers: Use of the Danger Assessment Scale in the Criminal Justice System." *Journal of Interpersonal Violence* 15: 63–74.

Goodman-Brown, T. B., Edelstein, R. S., Goodman, G. S., Jones, D. P. H., and Gordon, D. S. 2003. "Why Children Tell: A Model of Children's Disclosure of Sexual Abuse." *Child Abuse and Neglect* 27: 525–540.

Goodmark, Leigh, and Klein, Catherine F. 2004. "Case Studies from American Universities: Deconstructing Teresa O'Brien, a Role Play for Domestic Violence Clinics." *Saint Louis University Public Law Review* 23: 253–288.

Goodson, B. D., Layzer, J. I., St. Pierre, R. G., and Bernstein, L. S. 2000. "Good Intentions Are Not Enough: A Response to Gilliam, Ripple, Zigler, and Leiter." *Early Childhood Research Quarterly* 15: 61–66.

Gordon, K. C., Burton, S., and Porter, L. 2004. "Predicting the Intentions of Women in Domestic Violence Shelters to Return to Partners: Does Forgiveness Play a Role?" *Journal of Family Psychology* 18: 331–338.

Gordon, Malcolm. 2000. "Definitional Issues in Violence against Women: Surveillance and Research from a Violence Research Perspective." *Violence against Women* 6: 747–783.

Gorey, K. M., and Leslie, D. R. 1997. "The Prevalence of Child Sexual Abuse: Integrative Review Adjustment for Potential Response and Measurement Bias." *Child Abuse and Neglect* 21: 391–398.

Gough, B., and Reavey, P. 1997. "Parental Account Regarding the Physical Punishment of Children: Discourses of Empowerment." *Child Abuse and Neglect* 21: 417–430.

Gough, D. 1996. "Defining the Problem." *Child Abuse and Neglect* 11: 993–1002.

Gover, A. R. 2004. "Risky Lifestyles and Dating Violence: A Theoretical Test of Violent Victimization." *Journal of Criminal Justice* 32: 171–180.

Graham-Bermann, S. A., and Brescoll, V. 2000. "Gender, Power, and Violence: Assessing the Family Stereotypes of the Children of Batterers." *Journal of Family Psychology* 14: 600–612.

Graham-Kevan, N., and Archer, J. 2003. "Intimate Terrorism and Common Couple Violence: A Test of Johnson's Predictions in Four British Samples." *Journal of Interpersonal Violence* 18: 1247–1270.

Grasmick, H. G., Bursik, R. J., Jr., and Kimpel, M. 1991. "Protestant Fundamentalism and Attitudes toward Corporal Punishment of Children." *Violence and Victims* 6: 282–298.

Gray, J., Spurway, P., and McClatchy, J. 2001. "Lay Therapy Intervention with Families at Risk for Parenting Difficulties: The Kempe Community Caring Program." *Child Abuse and Neglect* 25: 641–655.

Green, A. H. 1993. "Child Sexual Abuse: Immediate and Long-Term Effects and Interventions." *Journal of the American Academy of Child and Adolescent Psychiatry* 32: 890–902.

Greene, K., and Bogo, M. 2002. "The Different Faces of Intimate Violence: Implications for Assessment and Treatment." *Journal of Marital and Family Therapy* 28: 455–466.

Gregoire, T. K. 1994. "Assessing the Benefits and Increasing the Utility of Addiction Training for Public Child Welfare Workers: A Pilot Study." *Child Welfare* 73: 69–81.

Greven, P. J., Jr. 1970. Four Generations: Population, Land, and Family in Colonial Andover, Massachusetts. Ithaca, N.Y.: Cornell University Press.

———. 1977. The Protestant Temperament: Patterns of Child-Rearing, Religious Experience, and Self in Early America. New York: Knopf.

Gully, K. J. 2003. "Expectations Test: Trauma Scales for Sexual Abuse, Physical Abuse, Exposure to Family Violence, and Post-Traumatic Stress." *Child Maltreatment* 8: 218–229.

Gurdin, J. B. 2003. "Stalking and Violence: New Patterns of Trauma and Obsession." *International Journal of Offender Therapy and Comparative Criminology* 47: 608–609.

Guterman, H. A., Beavers, W. R., et al. 1995. "A Model for the Classification and Diagnosis of Relational Disorders." *Psychiatric Services* 46: 926–931.

Guterman, N. A. 1999. "Enrollment Strategies in Early Home Visitation to Prevent Physical Child Abuse and Neglect and the 'Universal versus Targeted' Debate: A Meta-Analysis of Population-Based and Screening-Based Programs." *Child Abuse and Neglect* 23: 863–890.

Guterman, N. B. 2002. "The Role of Research in Defining a 'Practiceable' Problem for Social Work: The Parallax of Community and Family Violence Exposure among Children and Youths." *Social Work Education* 21: 313–322.

Hadley, J., and Holahan, J. 2004. "The Cost of Care for the Uninsured: What Do We Spend, Who Pays, and What Would Full Coverage Add to Medical Spending?" Issue Update. The Kaiser Commission on Medicaid and the Uninsured.

Hagan, J., and Foster, H. 2001. "Youth Violence and the End of Adolescence." *American Sociological Review* 66: 874–899.

Halliday-Boykins, C. A., and Graham, S. 2001. "At Both Ends of the Gun: Testing the Relationship between Community Violence Exposure and Youth Violent Behavior." *Journal of Abnormal Child Psychology* 29: 383–402.

Halpern, C. T., Oslak, S. G., Young, M. L., Martin, S. L., and Kupper, L. L. 2001. "Partner Violence among Adolescents in Opposite-Sex Romantic Relationships: Findings from the National Longitudinal Study of Adolescent Health." *American Journal of Public Health* 91: 1679–1685.

Hamberger, L. K., and Guse, C. E. 2002. "Men's and Women's Use of Intimate Partner Violence in Clinical Samples." *Violence against Women* 8: 1 301–1331.

Hanawalt, B. A. 1992. "Historical Descriptions and Prescriptions for Adolescence." *Journal of Family History* 17: 341–351.

Hanna, C. 1996. "No Right to Choose: Mandated Victim Participation in Domestic Violence Prosecutions." *Harvard Law Review* 109: 1849–1910.

Hanson, R. F., Lipovsky, J. A., and Saunders, B. E. 1994. "Characteristics of Fathers in Incest Families." *Journal of Interpersonal Violence* 9: 155–169.

Haraven, Tamara K. 1982. Family Time and Industrial Time: The Relationship Between the Family and Work in a New England Industrial Community. New York: Cambridge University Press.

Hardesty, J. L. 2002. "Separation Assault in the Context of Postdivorce Parenting: An Integrative Review of the Literature." *Violence against Women* 8: 597–625.

Hardin, M., ed. 1983. Foster Children in the Courts. Washington, DC: American Bar Association.

Harris, M. S., and Courtney, M. E. 2003. "The Interaction of Race, Ethnicity, and Family Structure with Respect to the Timing of Family Reunification." *Children and Youth Services Review* 25: 409–429.

Hartley, C. C. 2003. "A Therapeutic Jurisprudence Approach to the Trial Process in Domestic Violence Felony Trials." *Violence against Women* 9: 410–437.

———. 2004. "Severe Domestic Violence and Child Maltreatment: Considering Child Physical Abuse, Neglect, and Failure to Protect." *Children and Youth Services Review* 26: 373–392.

Hartman, G. L., Karlson, H., and Hibbard, R. A. 1994. "Attorney Attitudes Regarding Behaviors Associated with Child Sexual Abuse." *Child Abuse and Neglect* 18: 657–662.

Hasday, Jill Elaine. 2000. "Contest and Consent: A Legal History of Marital Rape." *California Law Review* 88: 1373–1505.

Haskett, M. E., and Kistner, J. A. 1991. "Social Interactions and Peer Perceptions of Young Physically Abused Children." *Child Development* 62: 979–990.

Haugaard, J. J., and Emery, R. E. 1989. "Methodological Issues in Child Sexual Abuse Research." *Child Abuse and Neglect* 13: 89–100.

Hays, Sharon. 2003. Flat Broke with Children: Women in the Age of Welfare Reform. New York: Oxford University Press.

Hazzard, A., Celano, M., Gould, J., Lawry, S., and Webb, C. 1995. "Predicting Symptomatology and Self-Blame among Child Sex Abuse Victims." *Child Abuse and Neglect* 19: 707–714.

Hazzard, A., and Rupp, G. 1986. "A Note on the Knowledge and Attitudes of Professional Groups toward Child Abuse." *Journal of Community Psychology* 14: 219–223.

Hegarty, K., Sheehan, M., and Schonfeld, C. 1999. "A Multidimensional Definition of Partner Abuse: Development and Preliminary Validation of the Composite Abuse Scale." *Journal of Family Violence* 14: 399–415.

Heiman, J. R., and Meston, C. M. 1998. "Empirically Validated Treatment of Sexual Dysfunction." In Empirically Supported Therapies: Best Practices in Professional Psychology, edited by Keith S. Dobson and Kenneth D. Craig, 259–303. Thousand Oaks, Calif.: Sage Publications.

Heisler, C. J., and Quinn, M. J. 1995. "A Legal Perspective." *Journal of Elder Abuse and Neglect* 7: 131–156.

Heisler, C. J., and Stiegel, L. A. 2002. "Enhancing the Justice System's Response to Elder Abuse: Discussions and Recommendations of the 'Improving Prosecution' Working Group of the National Policy Summit on Elder Abuse." *Journal of Elder Abuse and Neglect* 14: 31–54.

Helfer, R. E., and Kempe, C. H., eds. 1968. The Battered Child. Chicago: University of Chicago Press.

Heller, S. S., Larrieu, J. A., D'Imperio, R., and Boris, N. W. 1999. "Research on Resilience to Child Maltreatment: Empirical Considerations." *Child Abuse and Neglect* 23: 321–338.

Hench, David. 2003. "Two Face Charges in Thefts of Rings in Nursing Home." *Portland Press Herald (Maine)*. July 17, 2003: 9B.

Hendy, H. M., Weiner, K., Bakerofskie, J., Eggen, D., Gustitus, C., and McLeod, K. C. 2003. "Comparison of Six Models for Violent Romantic Relationships in College Men and Women." *Journal of Interpersonal Violence* 18: 645–665.

Henning, K., and Feder, L. 2004. "A Comparison of Men and Women Arrested for Domestic Violence: Who Presents the Greater Threat?" *Journal of Family Violence* 19: 69–80.

Henry, D. R. 1978. "The Psychological Aspects of Child Abuse." In Maltreatment of Children, edited by Smith, 205–219. Baltimore, Md.: University Park Press.

Herman-Giddens, M. E., Brown, G., Verbiest, S., Carlson, P. J., Hooten, E. G., Howell, E., and Butts, J. D. 1999. "Unascertainment of Child Abuse Mortality in the United States." *Journal of the American Medical Association* 282: 463–467.

Herrenkohl, E. C., Herrenkohl, R. C., Egolf, B. P., and Russo, M. J. 1998. "The Relationship between Early Maltreatment and Teenage Parenthood." *Journal of Adolescence* 21: 291–303.

Herrenkohl, E. C., Herrenkohl, R. C., Toedter, L., and Yanushefski, A. M. 1984. "Parent-Child Interactions in Abusive and Nonabusive Families." *Journal of the American Academy of Child Psychiatry* 23: 641–648.

Herrenkohl, R. C., and Herrenkohl, E. C. 1981. "Some Antecedents and Developmental Consequences of Child Maltreatment." In Developmental Perspectives on Child Maltreatment, edited by R. Rizley and D. Cicchetti, 57–76. San Francisco: Jossey-Bass.

Herrenkohl, T. I., Mason, W. A., Kosterman, R., Lengua, L. J., Hawkins, J. D., and Abbott, R. D. 2004. "Pathways from Physical Childhood Abuse to Partner Violence in Young Adulthood." *Violence and Victims* 19: 123–136.

Hetherton, J. 1999. "The Idealization of Women: Its Role in the Minimization of Child Sexual Abuse by Females." *Child Abuse and Neglect* 23: 161–174.

Hewlett, S. A. 1991. When the Bough Breaks: The Costs of Neglecting Our Children. New York: Basic Books.

Heyman, R. E., and Slep, A. M. S. 2002. "Do Child Abuse and Interparental Violence Lead to Adulthood Family Violence?" *Journal of Marriage and Family* 64: 864–870.

Hiatt, S. W., Michalek, P., Younge, P., Miyoshi, T., and Fryer, E. 200. "Characteristics of Volunteers and Families in a Neonatal Home Visitation Project: The Kempe Community Caring Program." *Child Abuse and Neglect* 24: 85–97.

Hiatt, S. W., Sampson, D., and Baird, D. 1997. "Paraprofessional Home Visitation: Conceptual and Pragmatic Considerations." *Journal of Community Psychology* 25: 77–93.

Higgins, D. J., and McCabe, M. P. 2001. "Multiple Forms of Child Abuse and Neglect: Adult Retrospective Reports." *Aggression and Violent Behavior* 6: 547–578.

Hildyard, K. L., and Wolfe, D. A. 2002. "Child Neglect: Developmental Issues and Outcomes." *Child Abuse and Neglect* 26: 679–695.

Hillis, S. D., Anda, R. F., Dube, S. R., Felitti, V. J., Marchbanks, P. A., and Marks, J. S. 2004. "The Association between Adverse Childhood Experiences and Adolescent Pregnancy, Long-Term Psychosocial Consequences, and Fetal Death." *Pediatrics* 113: 320–327.

Himelein, M. J., and McElrath, J. A. 1996. "Resilient Child Sexual Abuse Survivors: Cognitive Coping and Illusion." *Child Abuse and Neglect* 20: 747–758.

Hines, A. M., Lemon, K., Wyatt, P., and Merdinger, J. 2004. "Factors Related to the Dis-Proportionate Involvement of Children of Color in the Child Welfare System: A Review and Emerging Themes." *Children and Youth Services Review* 26: 507–527.

Hines, Denise A., and Malley-Morrison, Kathleen. 2005. Family Violence in the United States: Defining, Understanding, and Combating Abuse. Thousand Oaks, Calif.: Sage Publications.

Hines, Denise A., and Saudina, Kimberly J. 2002. "Intergenerational Transmission of Intimate Partner Violence: A Behavioral Genetic Perspective." *Trauma, Violence, and Abuse* 3: 210–225.

Hirschel, D., and Buzawa, E. 2002. "Understanding the Context of Dual Arrest with Directions for Future Research." *Violence against Women* 8: 1449–1473.

Hirschel, D., and Hutchison, I. W. 2003. "The Voices of Domestic Violence Victims: Predictors of Victim Preference for Arrest and the Relationship between Preference for Arrest and Revictimization." *Crime and Delinquency* 49: 313–336.

Hoctor, M. M. 1997. "Domestic Violence as a Crime against the State: The Need for Mandatory Arrest in California." *California Law Review* 85: 643–700.

Hoffman, K. L., and Edwards, J. N. 2004. "An Integrated Theoretical Model of Sibling Violence and Abuse." *Journal of Family Violence* 19: 185–200.

Hohman, Melinda M., Shillington, Audrey, and Baxter, Heather Grigg. 2003. "A Comparison of Pregnant Women Presenting for Alcohol and Other Drug Treatment by CPS Status." *Child Abuse and Neglect* 27: 303–317.

Holden, G. W., Coleman, S. M., and Schmidt, K. L. 1995. "Why 3-Year-Old Children Get Spanked: Parent and Child Determinants as Reported by College-Educated Mothers." *Merrill-Palmer Quarterly* 41: 431–452.

Holmes, W. C., and Slap, G. C. 1998. "Sexual Abuse of Boys: Definition, Prevalence, Correlates, Sequelae, and Management." *Journal of the American Medical Association* 280: 1855–1862.

Holton, J. K., and Oshana, D. 2004. "Overview of Child Neglect: Theory, Research, and Practice." *Perspectives on Youth* (Summer/Fall). www.perspectivesonyouth.org.

Hops, H., Davis, B., Leve, C., and Sheeber, L. 2003. "Cross-Generational Transmission of Aggressive Parent Behavior: A Prospective, Mediational Examination." *Journal of Abnormal Child Psychology* 31: 161–169.

Hora, P. F., and Schma, W. G. 1998. "Therapeutic Jurisprudence." *Judicature* 82: 8–12.

Horn, I. B., Joseph, J. G., and Cheng, T. L. 2004. "Nonabusive Physical Punishment and Child Behavior among African American Children: A Systematic Review." *Journal of the National Medical Association* 96: 1162–1168.

Horner, T. M., Guyer, M. J., and Kalter, N. M. 1993. "Clinical Expertise and the Assessment of Child Sexual Abuse." *Journal of the American Academy of Child and Adolescent Psychiatry* 32: 925–933.

Horvath, L. S., Logan, T. K., et al. 2002. "Child Custody Cases: A Content Analysis of Evaluations in Practice." *Professional Psychology: Research and Practice* 33(6): 557–565.

Houry, D., Sachs, C. J., Feldhaus, K. M., and Linden, J. 2002. "Violence-Inflicted Injuries: Reporting Laws in the Fifty States." *Annals of Emergency Medicine* 39: 56–60.

Hunt, D. 1972. Parents and Children in History. New York: Harper and Row.

Hunter, J. A., Jr., and Figueredo, A. J. 2000. "The Influence of Personality and History of Victimization in the Prediction of Juvenile Perpetrated Child Molestation." *Behavior Modification* 24: 241–263.

Hyman, I. E., Jr., and Loftus, E. L. 1998. "Errors in Autobiographical Memory." *Clinical Psychology Review* 18: 933–947.

Illick, J. E. 1974. "Child-Rearing in Seventeenth-Century England and America." In The History of Childhood, edited by L. deMause, 303–350. New York: Psychohistory Press.

Imbrogno, A. R., and Imbrogno, S. 2000. "Mediation in Court Cases of Domestic Violence." *Families in Society: The Journal of Contemporary Human Services* 81: 392–401.

Institute of Judicial Administration, American Bar Association. 1977. Standards Relating to Abuse and Neglect. Cambridge, Mass.: Ballinger.

Irwin, K. 2004. "The Violence of Adolescent Life: Experiencing and Managing Every-Day Threats." *Youth and Society* 35: 452–479.

Jackson, M. 2002. Infanticide: Historical Perspectives on Child Murder and Concealment. Burlington, Vt.: Ashgate.

Jackson, S., Thompson, R. A., Christiansen, E. H., Colman, R. A., Wyatt, J., Buckendahl, C. W., Wilcox, B. L., and Peterson, R. 1999. "Predicting Abuse-Prone Parental Attitudes and Discipline Practices in a Nationally Representative Sample." *Child Abuse and Neglect* 23: 15–29.

Jagannathan, R., and Camasso, M. J. 1996. "Risk Assessment in Child Protective Services: A Canonical Analysis of the Case Management Function." *Child Abuse and Neglect* 20: 599–612.

James, D. V., and Farnham, F. R. 2003. "Stalking and Serious Violence." *Journal of the American Academy of Psychiatry and the Law* 31: 432–439.

James, S., and Mennen, F. 2001. "Treatment Outcomes Research: How Effective are Treatments for Abused Children?" *Child and Adolescent Social Work Journal* 18: 73–95.

Jasinski, J. L., and Dietz, T. L. 2003. "Domestic Violence and Stalking among Older Adults: An Assessment of Risk Markers." *Journal of Elder Abuse and Neglect* 15: 3–18.

Jaudes, P. K., Ekwo, E., and Voorhis, J. V. 1995. "Association of Drug Abuse and Child Abuse." *Child Abuse and Neglect* 19: 1065–1075.

Jellen, Linda K., McCarroll, James E., and Thayer, Laurie E. 2001. "Child Emotional Maltreatment: A 2-Year Study of U.S. Army Cases." *Child Abuse and Neglect* 25: 623–639.

Jenkins, Philip. 1995. "Clergy Sexual Abuse: The Symbolic Politics of a Social Problem." In Images of Issues, Typifying Contemporary Social Problems, 2nd ed., edited by Joel Best, 105–130. Hawthorne, N.Y.: Aldine de Gruyter.

Jenness, Valerie, and Grattet, Ryken. 2001. Making Hate a Crime: From Social Movement to Law Enforcement. New York: Russell Sage Foundation.

Jenson, J., and Sineau, M. 2001. Who Cares? Women's Work, Child Care, and Welfare State Redesign. Toronto: University of Toronto Press.

Johnson, I. M., and Sigler, R. G. 2000. "Public Perceptions: The Stability of the Public's Endorsements of the Definition and Criminalization of the Abuse of Women." *Journal of Criminal Justice* 28: 165–179.

———. 1996. "Public Perceptions of Interpersonal Violence." *Journal of Criminal Justice* 24: 419–430.

Johnson, J. D., Adams, M. S., and Ashburn, L. 1995. "Differential Gender Effects of Exposure to Rap Music on African American Adolescents' Acceptance of Teen Dating Violence." *Sex Roles* 33: 597–605.

Johnson, John M. 1995. "Horror Stories and the Construction of Child Abuse." In Images of Issues: Typifying Contemporary Social Problems, 2nd ed., edited by Joel Best, 17–31. Hawthorne, N.Y.: Aldine de Gruyter.

Johnson, Michael P. 2004. "Conflict and Control: Gender Symmetry and Asymmetry in Domestic Violence." In *Couples in Conflict*, ed. Booth, Crouter, and Clements, 95–104. Mahwah, N.J.: Laurence Erlbaum.

Johnson, M. P., and Ferraro, Kathleen. 2000. "Research on Domestic Violence in the 1990s: Making Distinctions." *Journal of Marriage and Family* 62: 948–963.

Jones, Ann M., and Keilitz, Susan. 2002. "Domestic Violence Cases and the State Courts." National Center for State Courts.

Jones, Loring, Hughes, Margaret, and Unterstaller, Ulrike. 2001. "Post-Traumatic Stress Disorder (PTSD) in Victims of Domestic Violence: A Review of the Research." *Trauma, Violence, and Abuse* 2: 99–119.

Jones, N. T., Ji, P., Beck, M., and Beck, N. 2002. "The Reliability and Validity of the Revised Conflict Tactics Scale (CTS 2) in a Female Incarcerated Population." *Journal of Family Issues* 23: 441–457.

Jones, W. P., and Emerson, S. 1994. "Sexual Abuse and Binge Eating in a Nonclinical Population." *Journal of Sex Education and Therapy* 20: 47–55.

Joseph, D. I. 2004. "Surviving Stalking." *Journal of Clinical Psychiatry* 65: 449–449.

Julian, T. W., and McKenry, P. C. 1993. "Mediators of Male Violence toward Female Intimates." *Journal of Family Violence* 8, no. 1 (Mar): 39–56.

Jurik, Nancy C. 2004. "Imagining Justice: Challenging the Privatization of Public Life." *Social Problems* 51(1): 1–15.

Kahn, F. S., and Paris, B. E. C. 2003. "Why Elder Abuse Continues to Elude the Health Care System." *Mount Sinai Journal of Medicine* 70: 62–68.

Kalichman, S. C., and Brosig, C. L. 1993. "Practicing Psychologists' Interpretations of and Compliance with Child Abuse Reporting Laws." *Law and Human Behavior* 17: 83–93.

Kalichman, S. C., Craig, M. E., and Follingstad, D. R. 1988. "Mental Health Professionals and Suspected Cases of Child Abuse: An Investigation of Factors Influencing Reporting." *Community Mental Health Journal* 24: 43–51.

Kammerman, S. B., and Gatenio, S. 2003. "Overview of the Current Policy Context." In Early Childhood Education and Care in the USA, edited by D. Cryer and R. M. Clifford. Baltimore, Md.: Paul H. Brookes Publishing Co.

Kammerman, S. B., and Kahn, A. J. 1993. "If CPS Is Driving Child Welfare, Where Do We Go from Here?" *Public Welfare* 51 (1): 41–43.

———. 2001. "Child and Family Policies in an Era of Social Policy Retrenchment and Restructuring." In Child Well-Being, Child Poverty, and Child Policy in Modern Nations, edited by Vleminckx and Smeeding, 501–525. Bristol, UK: Policy Press.

Karan, A., Keilitz, S., and Denaro, S. 1999. "Domestic Violence Courts: What Are They and How Should We Manage Them?" *Juvenile and Family Court Journal* 50: 75–86.

Kaufman, J., Jones, B., Stieglitz, E., Vitulano, L., and Mannarino, A. P. 1994. "The Use of Multiple Informants to Assess Children's Maltreatment Experiences." *Journal of Family Violence* 9: 227–248.

Kaufman, Joan, and Zigler, Edward F. 1987. "Do Abused Children Become Abusive Parents?" *American Journal of Orthopsychiatry* 57: 186–202.

Kaufman Kantor, G., and Little, L. 2003. "Defining the Boundaries of Child Neglect: When Does Domestic Violence Equate with Parental Failure to Protect?" *Journal of Interpersonal Violence* 18: 338–355.

Kaukinen, C. 2004. "Status Compatibility, Physical Violence, and Emotional Abuse in Intimate Relationships." *Journal of Marriage and the Family* 66: 452–471.

Kaura, S. A., and Allen, C. M. 2004. "Dissatisfaction with Relationship Power and Dating Violence Perpetration by Men and Women." *Journal of Interpersonal Violence* 19: 576–588.

Keilitz, Susan L., Hannaford, Paula L., and Efkerman, Hillery S. 1996. "Civil Protection Orders: The Benefits and Limitations for Victims of Domestic Violence." *State Court Journal* 20: 17.

Kelley, S. A., and Jennings, K. D. 2003. "Putting the Pieces Together: Maternal Depression, Maternal Behavior, and Toddler Helplessness." *Infant Mental Health Journal* 24: 74–90.

Kellogg, N. D., and Hoffman, T. J. 1995. "Unwanted and Illegal Sexual Experiences in Childhood and Adolescence." *Child Abuse and Neglect* 19: 1457–1468.

Kelly, K. A. 2003. Domestic Violence and the Politics of Privacy. Ithaca, N.Y.: Cornell University Press.

———. 2004. "Working Together to Stop Domestic Violence: State-Community Partnerships and the Changing Meaning of Public and Private." *Journal of Sociology and Social Welfare* 31(1): 27–47.

Kempe, C. H., Silverman, F. N., Steele, B. F., Droegenmueller, W., and Silver, H. K. 1962. "The Battered-Child Syndrome." *Journal of the American Medical Association* 181 (July): 17–24.

Kempe, R. S., and Kempe, C. H. 1978. Child Abuse. Cambridge, Mass.: Harvard University Press.

Kendall-Tackett, K. 2002. "The Health Effects of Childhood Abuse: Four Pathways by which Abuse Can Influence Health." *Child Abuse and Neglect* 26: 715–729.

———. 2003. Treating the Lifetime Health Effects of Childhood Victimization. Kingston, N.J.: Civic Research Institute.

Kendall-Tackett, K., and Becker-Blease, K. 2004. "The Importance of Retrospective Findings in Child Maltreatment Research." *Child Abuse and Neglect* 28: 723–727.

Kendall-Tackett, K., and Eckenrode, J. 1996. "The Effects of Neglect on Academic Achievement and Disciplinary Problems: A Developmental Perspective." *Child Abuse and Neglect* 20: 161–169.

Kenniston, K. 1970. "Do Americans REALLY Like Children?" In Child Abuse and Violence, edited by Gil, 274–285. New York: AMS Press.

Kenny, M. C. 2001. "Child Abuse Reporting: Teachers' Perceived Deterrents." *Child Abuse and Neglect* 25: 81–92.

———. 2004. " Teachers' Attitudes toward and Knowledge of Child Maltreatment." *Child Abuse and Neglect* 28: 1311–1319.

Kilpatrick, Dean G., Best, C. C., Saunders, B. E., and Vernon, L. J. 1988. "Rape in Marriage and Dating Relationships: How Bad Is It for Mental Health?" *Annals of the New York Academy of Sciences* 528: 335–344.

Kilpatrick, Dean G., Edmunds, C. M., and Seymour, A. K. 1992. "Rape in America: A Report to the Nation." Arlington, Va.: National Victim Center.

Kimmel, Michael S. 2002. "'Gender Symmetry' in Domestic Violence." *Violence against Women* 8: 1332–1363.

Kinard. E. M. 2001. "Perceived and Actual Academic Competence in Maltreated Children." *Child Abuse and Neglect* 25: 33–45.

———. 2004. "Methodological Issues in Assessing the Effects of Maltreatment Characteristics on Behavioral Adjustment in Maltreated Children." *Journal of Family Violence* 19: 303–325.

King, G., Reece, R., Bendel, R., and Patel, V. 1998. "The Effects of Socio-Demographic Variables, Training and Attitudes on the Lifetime Reporting Practices of Mandated Reporters." *Child Maltreatment* 3: 276–283.

Klein, Ethel, Soler, Esta, Ghez, Marissa, and Campbell, Jacquelyn C. 1997. Ending Domestic Violence: Changing Public Perceptions, Halting the Epidemic. Thousand Oaks, Calif.: Sage Publications.

Knitzer, J., Allen, M. L., and McGowan, B. 1978. Children Without Homes: An Examination of Public Responsibility to Children in Out-of-Home Care. Washington, DC: Children's Defense Fund.

Knudsen, D. D. 1988. Child Protective Services: Discretion, Decisions, Dilemmas. Springfield, Ill.: Charles C. Thomas.

Knudsen, Dean. D., and Miller, JoAnn L. 1991. Abused and Battered: Social and Legal Responses to Family Violence. New York: Walter de Gruyter, Inc.

Knutson, J. F., and Selner, M. B. 1994. "Punitive Childhood Experiences Reported by Young Adults over a 10-Year Period." *Child Abuse and Neglect* 18: 155–166.

Kolko, D. J. 1996. "Clinical Monitoring of Treatment Course in Child Physical Abuse: Psychometric Characteristics and Treatment Comparisons." *Child Abuse and Neglect* 20: 23–43.

———. 1998. "CPS Operational and Risk Assessment in Child Abuse Cases Receiving Services: Initial Findings from the Pittsburgh Service Delivery Study." *Child Maltreatment* 3: 262–275.

Kolko, J. R., Blakely, E. J., and Engleman, D. 1996. "Children Who Witness Domestic Violence: A Review of Empirical Literature." *Journal of Interpersonal Violence* 11: 281–293.

Korbin, J. 2002. "Culture and Child Maltreatment: Cultural Competence and Beyond." *Child Abuse and Neglect* 26: 637–644.

Korbin, J. E., Coulton, C. J., Lindstrom-Ufuti, H., and Spilsbury, J. 2000. "Neighborhood Views on the Definition and Etiology of Child Maltreatment." *Child Abuse and Neglect* 24: 1509–1527.

Koss, M. P. 2000. "Blame, Shame, and Community: Justice Responses to Violence against Women." *American Psychologist* 55: 1332–1343.

Kotch, J. B., Browne, D. C., Ringwalt, P. W., Stewart, P. W., Ruina, E., Holt, K., Lowman, B., and Jung, J. 1995. "Risk of Child Abuse or Neglect in a Cohort of Low-Income Children." *Child Abuse and Neglect* 19: 1115–1130.

Kotlowitz, A. 1991. There Are No Children Here: The Story of Two Boys Growing Up in the Other America. New York: Doubleday.

Kovera, M., Borgida, E., Gresham, A. W., Swim, J., and Gray, E. 1993. "Do Child Sexual Abuse Experts Hold Pro-Child Beliefs? A Survey of the International Society for Traumatic Stress Studies." *Journal of Traumatic Stress* 6: 383–404.

Kruttschnitt, C., McLeod, J. D., and Dornfeld, M. 1994. "The Economic Environment of Child Abuse." *Social Problems* 41: 299–315.

Kuper, A. 2002. "Incest, Cousin Marriage, and the Origin of the Human Sciences in Nineteenth-Century England." *Past and Present* 174: 158–183.

Kurtz, P. D., Gaudin, J. M., Howling, P. T., and Wodarski. 1993. "The Consequences of Physical Abuse and Neglect on the School-Age Child: Mediating Factors." *Children and Youth Services Review* 15: 85–104.

Kurz, D. 1989. "Social Science Perspectives on Wife Abuse: Current Debates and Future Directions." *Gender and Society* 3: 489–505.

———. 1996. " Separation, Divorce, and Woman Abuse." *Violence against Women* 2: 63–81.

Kwong, M. J., Bartholomew, K., Henderson, A. J. Z., and Trinke, S. J. 2003. "The Intergenerational Transmission of Relationship Violence." *Journal of Family Psychology* 17: 288–301.

Kydd, J. W. 2003. "Preventing Child Maltreatment: An Integrated, Multisectoral Approach." *Health and Human Rights* 6: 34–63.

LaHaye, B. 1977. How to Develop Your Child's Temperament. Eugene, Ore.: Harvest House.

Lamb, M. E., Hershkowitz, I., Sternberg, K. J., Boat, B., and Everson, M. D. 1996. "Investigative Interviews of Alleged Sexual Abuse Victims with and without Anatomical Dolls." *Child Abuse and Neglect* 20: 1251–1259.

Lamb, S., and Coakley, M. 1993. "'Normal' Childhood Sexual Play and Games: Differentiating Play from Abuse." *Child Abuse and Neglect* 17: 515–528.

Langhinrichsen-Rohling, Hankla, J., M., and Stormberg, C. D. 2004. "The Relationship Behavior Networks of Young Adults: A Test of the Intergenerational Transmission of Violence Hypothesis." *Journal of Family Violence* 19: 139–151.

Lantz, H., Schultz, M., and O'Hara, M. 1977. "The Changing American Family from the Preindustrial to the Industrial Period: A Final Report." *American Sociological Review* 42: 406–421.

Lareau, A. 2002. "Invisible Inequality: Social Class and Childbearing in Black Families and White Families." *American Sociological Review* 67: 747–776.

Larzelere, R. E. 1996. "A Review of the Outcomes of Parental Use of Nonabusive or Customary Physical Punishment." *Pediatrics* 98: 824–828.

———. 2000. "Child Outcomes of Nonabusive and Customary Physical Punishment by Parents: An Updated Literature Review." *Clinical Child and Family Psychology Review* 3: 199–221.

Larzelere, R. E., Sather, P. R., Schneider, W. N., Larson, D. B., and Pike, P. L. 1998. "Punishment Enhances Reasoning's Effectiveness as a Disciplinary Response to Toddlers." *Journal of Marriage and the Family* 60: 388–403.

LasCaratos, J., and Poulakou-Rebalakou, E. 2000. "Child Sexual Abuse: Historical Cases in the Byzantine Empire (324–1453 A.D.)." *Child Abuse and Neglect* 24: 1085–1090.

Laslett, P., and Wall, R. 1972. Household and Family in Past Time. New York: Cambridge University Press.

Lauder, W., Anderson, I., and Barclay, A. 2002. "Sociological and Psychological Theories of Self-Neglect." *Journal of Advanced Nursing* 40: 331–338.

Lawrence-Webb, C. 1997. "African American Children in the Modern Child Welfare System: A Legacy of the Flemming Rule." *Child Welfare* 74: 9–30.

Layzer, J. I., Goodson, B. D., Bernstein, L., and Price, C. 2001 (April). National Evaluation of Family Support Programs, Final Report. Volume A: Meta-Analysis. Washington, DC: U.S. Department of Health and Human Services. aspe.hhs.gov/hsp/evalfampres94.

Lazoritz, S., and Shelman, E. A. 1996. "Before Mary Ellen." *Child Abuse and Neglect* 20: 235–237.

Lee, J. K. P., Jackson, H. J., Pattison, P., and Ward, T. 2002. "Developmental Risk Factors for Sexual Offending." *Child Abuse and Neglect* 26: 73–92.

Lee, R. K., Thompson, V. L. S., and Mechanic, M. B. 2002. "Intimate Partner Violence and Women of Color: A Call for Innovations." *American Journal of Public Health* 92: 530–534.

Leiter, J., and Johnson, M. C. 1994. "Child Maltreatment and School Performance." *American Journal of Education* 102: 154–189.

———. 1997. "Child Maltreatment and School Performance Declines: An Event-History Analysis." *American Educational Research Journal* 34: 563–589.

Lemon, Nancy K. D. 2001. Domestic Violence Law. St. Paul, Minn.: West Group.

———. 2006. Domestic Violence Law, 2nd ed. St. Paul, Minn.: Thomson / West.

Leone, J. M., Johnson, M. P., Cohan, C. L., and Lloyd, S. E. 2004. "Consequences of Male Partner Violence for Low-Income Minority Women." *Journal of Marriage and the Family* 66: 472–490.

Levendosky, A. A., Huth-Bocks, A., and Semel, M. A. 2002. "Adolescent Peer Relationships and Mental Health Functioning in Families with Domestic Violence." *Journal of Clinical Child and Adolescent Psychology* 31: 206–218.

Levine, Jeffrey M. 2003. "Elder Neglect and Abuse: A Primer for Primary Care Physicians." *Geriatrics* 58: 37–44.

Levy, H. B., Markovic, J., Chaudhry, U., Ahart, S., and Torres, H. 1995. "Reabuse Rates in a Sample of Children Followed for Five Years After Discharge from a Child Abuse Inpatient Assessment Program." *Child Abuse and Neglect* 19: 1363–1377.

Levy, H. B., Markovic, J., Kalinowski, M. N., Ahart, S., and Torres, H. 1995. "Child Sexual Abuse Interviews: The Use of Anatomic Dolls and the Reliability of Information." *Journal of Interpersonal Violence* 10: 334–353.

Lewis, N. K. 2003. "Balancing the Dictates of Law and Ethical Practice: Empowerment of Female Survivors of Domestic Violence in the Presence of Overlapping Child Abuse." *Ethics and Behavior* 13(4): 353–366.

Lewis, S. F., and Fremouw, W. 2001. "Dating Violence: A Critical Review of the Literature." *Clinical Psychology Review* 21: 105–127.

Liem, J. H., James, J. B., O'Toole, J. G., and Boudewyn, A. C. 1997. "Assessing Resilience in Adults with Histories of Childhood Sexual Abuse." *American Journal of Orthopsychiatry* 67: 594–606.

Light, R. J. 1973. "Abused and Neglected Children in America: A Study of Alternative Policies." *Harvard Educational Review* 43: 556–598.

Lindsay, D. S., and Briere, J. 1997. "The Controversy Regarding Recovered Memories of Childhood Sexual Abuse: Pitfalls, Bridges, and Future Directions." *Journal of Interpersonal Violence* 12: 631–647.

Lindsey, D. 2004. The Welfare of Children. New York: Oxford University Press.

Lindsey, D., and Schwartz, I. M. 2004. "Advances in Child Welfare: Innovations in Child Protection, Adoptions, and Foster Care." *Children and Youth Services Review* 26: 999–1005.

Lingler, J. H. 2003. "Ethical Issues in Distinguishing Sexual Activity from Sexual Maltreatment among Women with Dementia." *Journal of Elder Abuse and Neglect* 15(2): 85–102.

Lipien, L., and Forthofer, M. S. 2004. "An Event History Analysis of Recurrent Child Maltreatment Reports in Florida." *Child Abuse and Neglect* 28: 947–966.

Littell, J. H., and Schuerman, J. R. 1999. "Innovations in Child Welfare: Preventing Out-of-Home Placement of Abused and Neglected Children." In Innovations in Practice and Service Delivery across the Lifespan, edited by D. E. Biegel and A. Blum, 102–123. New York: Oxford University Press.

Litty, C. G., Kowalski, R., and Minor, S. 1996. "Moderating Effects of Physical Abuse and Perceived Social Support on the Potential to Abuse." *Child Abuse and Neglect* 20: 305–314.

Loftus, E., and Ketcham, K. 1994. The Myth of Repressed Memory. New York: St. Martin's Griffin.

Logan, T. K., Walker, R., and Leukefeld, C. G. 2001. "Rural, Urban Influenced, and Urban Differences among Domestic Violence Arrestees." *Journal of Interpersonal Violence* 16: 266–283.

Logan, T. K., Walker, R., Horvath, L. S., and Leukefeld, C. 2003. "Divorce, Custody, and Spousal Violence: A Random Sample of Circuit Court Docket Records." *Journal of Family Violence* 18: 269–279.

Lombardi, J. 2003. "Looking Back: Child Care in the United States in the Twentieth Century." In A Time to Care: Redesigning Child Care to Promote Education, Support Families, and Build Communities, 29–53. Philadelphia: Temple University Press.

Long, P. J., and Jackson, J. L. 1994. "Childhood Sexual Abuse: An Examination of Family Functioning." *Journal of Interpersonal Violence* 9: 270–277.

Loos, M. E., and Alexander, P. C. 1997. "Differential Effects Associated with Self-Reported Histories of Abuse and Neglect in a College Sample." *Journal of Inter-Personal Violence* 12: 340–360.

Lu, Y. E., Landsverk, J., Ellis-Macleod, E., Newton, R., Ganger, W., and Johnson, I. 2004. "Race, Ethnicity, and Case Outcomes in Child Protective Services." *Children and Youth Services Review* 26: 447–461.

Luster, T., and Small, S. A. 1997. "Sexual Abuse History and Problems in Adolescence: Exploring the Effects of Moderating Variables." *Journal of Marriage and the Family* 59: 131–142.

Lynch, M. 1985. "Child Abuse before Kempe: An Historical Literature Review." *Child Abuse and Neglect* 9: 7–15.

Lynskey, M. R., and Fergusson, D. M. 1997. "Factors Protecting against the Development of Adjustment Difficulties in Young Adults Exposed to Childhood Sexual Abuse." *Child Abuse and Neglect* 21: 1177–1190.

Lyons, P., Doueck, H. J., and Wodarski, J. S. 1996. "Risk Assessment for Child Protective Services: A Review of the Empirical Literature on Instrument Performance." *Social Work Research* 20: 143–152.

Maan, C. 1991. "Assessment of Sexually Abused Children with Anatomically Detailed Dolls: A Critical Review." *Behavioral Sciences and the Law* 9: 43–51.

MacLeod, L., Montero, D., and Speer, A. 1999. "America's Changing Attitudes toward Welfare and Welfare Recipients, 1938–1995." *Journal of Sociology and Social Welfare* 26: 175–185.

MacMillan, H. L., Jamieson, E., and Walsh, C. A. "Reported Contact with Child Protection Services among Those Reporting Child Physical and Sexual Abuse: Results from a Community Survey." *Child Abuse and Neglect* 27: 1397–1408.

Macmillan, Ross, and Gartner, Rosemary. 1999. "When She Brings Home the Bacon: Labor-Force Participation and the Risk of Spousal Violence against Women." *Journal of Marriage and the Family* 61: 947–958.

Macmillan, R., McMorris, B. J., and Kruttschnitt, C. 2004. "Linked Lives: Stability and Change in Maternal Circumstances and Trajectories of Antisocial Behavior in Children." *Child Development* 75: 205–220.

Madden, R. G., and Wayne, R. H. 2003. "Social Work and the Law: A Therapeutic Jurisprudence Perspective." *Social Work* 48: 338–347.

Magura, S., and Moses, B. S. 1987. The Child Well-Being Scales. Washington, DC: Child Welfare League of America, Inc.

Mahlstedt, D., and Keeny, L. 1993. "Female Survivors of Dating Violence and Their Social Networks." Feminism and Psychology 3: 319–333.

Mahoney, Patricia, and Williams, Linda M. 1998. "Sexual Assault in Marriage: Prevalence, Consequences, and Treatment of Wife Rape." In Partner Violence: A Comprehensive Review of 20 Years of Research, edited by Jana Jasinski and Linda M. Williams. Thousand Oaks, Calif.: Sage Publications.

Mahoney, Patricia, Williams, Linda M., and West, Carolyn M. 2001. "Violence Against Women by Intimate Partners." In Sourcebook on Violence Against Women, edited by Claire M. Renzetti, Jeffrey L. Edleson, and Raquel Kennedy Bergen, 143–178. Thousand Oaks, Calif.: Sage Publications.

Maker, A. H., Kemmelmeier, M., and Peterson, C. 1999. "Parental Sociopathy as a Predictor of Childhood Sexual Abuse." Journal of Family Violence 14: 47.

Making Reasonable Efforts: Steps for Keeping Families Together. 1987. Reno, Nev.: National Council of Juvenile and Family Court Judges, Child Welfare League of American, Youth Law Center, National Center for Youth Law.

Maletzky, Barry M., and Steinhauser, Cynthia. 2002. "A 25-Year Follow-Up of Cognitive/Behavioral Therapy with 7,275 Sexual Offenders." Behavior Modification 26: 123–147.

Margolin, G., and Gordis, E. B. 2000. "The Effects of Family and Community Violence on Children." Annual Review of Psychology 51: 445–479.

———. 2003. "Co-Occurrence between Marital Aggression and Parents' Child Abuse Potential: The Impact of Cumulative Stress." Violence and Victims 18: 243–258.

Margolin, G., Gordis, E. B., Medina, A. M., and Oliver, P. H. 2003. "The Co-Occurrence of Husband-to-Wife Aggression, Family-of-Origin Aggression, and Child Abuse Potential in a Community Sample: Implications for Parenting." Journal of Interpersonal Violence 18: 413–440.

Markowitz, F. E. 2001. "Attitudes and Family Violence: Linking Intergenerational and Cultural Theories." Journal of Family Violence 16: 205–218.

Marshall, C. E., Benton, D., and Brazier, J. M. 2000. "Elder Abuse: Using Clinical Tools to Identify Clues of Maltreatment." Geriatrics 55: 42–49.

Marshall, W. L., Anderson, D., and Champagne, F. 1996. "Self-Esteem and Its Relationship to Sexual Offending." Psychology, Crime and Law 3: 81–106.

Marshall, W. L., Champagne, F., Brown, C., and Miller, S. 1997. "Empathy, Intimacy, Loneliness, and Self-Esteem in Non-Familial Child Molesters." Journal of Child Sexual Abuse 6: 87–97.

Marshall, W. L., Cripps, E., Anderson, D., and Cortoni, F. A. 1999. "Self-Esteem and Coping Strategies in Child Molesters." Journal of Interpersonal Violence 9: 955–962.

Martin, G., Bergen, H., Richardson, A. S., Roeger, L., and Allison, A. 2004. "Sexual Abuse and Suicidality: Gender Differences in a Large Community Sample of Adolescents." Child Abuse and Neglect 28: 491–503.

Martone, M., Jaudes, P. K., Cavins, M. K. 1996. "Criminal Prosecution of Child Sexual Abuse Cases." Child Abuse and Neglect 20: 457–464.

Maxwell, C., Garner, J., and Fagan, J. 2001. "The Effects of Arrest on Intimate Partner Violence: New Evidence from the Spouse Assault Replication Program." In Research in Brief. Washington, DC: U.S. Department of Justice.

Mayer, G. R. 2002. "Behavioral Strategies to Reduce School Violence." *Child and Family Behavior Therapy* 24: 83–100.

Maynard, C., and Wiederman, M. 1997. "Undergraduate Students' Perceptions of Child Sexual Abuse: Effects of Age, Sex, and Gender Role Attitudes." *Child Abuse and Neglect* 21: 833–844.

Mays, W. 2002. "Elder Abuse and Mental Health." *Journal of Elder Abuse and Neglect* 14: 21–29.

McClellan, D. S., Farabee, D., and Crouch, B. M. 1997. "Early Victimization, Drug Use, and Criminality: A Comparison of Male and Female Prisoners." *Criminal Justice and Behavior* 24: 455–476.

McCloskey, L. A., and Lichter, E. L. 2003. "The Contribution of Marital Violence to Adolescent Aggression across Different Relationships." *Journal of Interpersonal Violence* 18: 390–412.

McCloskey, L. A., Treviso, M., Scionti, T., and dal Pozzo, G. 2002. "A Comparative Study of Battered Women and Their Children in Italy and the United States." *Journal of Family Violence* 17: 53–74.

McDaniel, A. 1994. "Historical Racial Arrangements in Living Arrangements of Children." *Journal of Family History* 19: 57–77.

McDaniel, M., and Slack, K. S. 2005. "Major Life Events and the Risk of a Child Maltreatment Investigation." *Children and Youth Services Review* 27: 171–195.

McFarlane, J., Malecha, A., Gist, J., Watson, K., Batten, E., Hall, I., and Smith, S. 2004. "Protection Orders and Intimate Partner Violence: An 18-Month Study of 150 Black, Hispanic, and White Women." *American Journal of Public Health* 94: 613–618.

McGee, R. A., Wolfe, D. A., Yuen, S. A., Wilson, S. K., and Carnochan, J. 1995. "The Measurement of Maltreatment: A Comparison of Approaches." *Child Abuse and Neglect* 19: 233–249.

McGloin, J. M., and Widom, C. S. 2001. "Resilience among Abused and Neglected Children Grown Up." *Development and Psychopathology* 13: 1021–1038.

McGuigan, W. M., Katzev, A. R., and Pratt, C. C. 2003. "Multi-Level Determinants of Retention in a Home-Visiting Child Abuse Prevention Program." *Child Abuse and Neglect* 27: 363–380.

McGuire, J. 2004. "Commentary: Promising Answers, and the Next Generation of Questions." *Psychology Crime and Law* 10: 335–345.

McKay, M. M., Chapman, J. W., and Long, N. R. 1996. "Causal Attributions for Criminal Offending and Sexual Arousal: Comparison of Child Sex Offenders with Other Offenders." *British Journal of Clinical Psychology* 35: 63–75.

McKenzie, R. B. 2003. "The Impact of Orphanages on the Alumni's Lives and Assessments of Their Childhoods." *Children and Youth Services Review* 25: 703–753.

McLoughlin, W. G. 1975. " Evangelical Child-Rearing in the Age of Jackson." *Journal of Social History* 9: 20–39.

McLoyd, V. C. 1990. "The Impact of Economic Hardship on Black Families and Children: Psychological Distress, Parenting, and Socioemotional Development." *Child Development* 61: 311–346.

Mead, M., and Wolfenstein, M., eds. 1955. Childhood in Contemporary Cultures. Chicago: University of Chicago Press.

Meier, Robert F., Kennedy, Leslie W., and Sacco, Vincent F., eds. 2001. The Process and Structure of Crime: Criminal Events and Crime Analysis. New Brunswick, N.J.: Transaction Publishers.

Melzer, S. A. 2002. "Gender, Work, and Intimate Violence: Men's Occupational Violence Spillover and Compensatory Violence." *Journal of Marriage and Family* 64: 820–832.

Merton, D. E. 1996. "Going-With: The Role of Social Form in Early Romance." *Journal of Contemporary Ethnography* 24: 462–484.

Messman-Moore, T. L., and Brown, A. L. 2004. "Child Maltreatment and Perceived Family Environment as Risk Factors for Adult Rape: Is Child Sexual Abuse the Most Salient Experience?" *Child Abuse and Neglect* 28: 1019–1034.

Migliaccio, Todd A. 2002. "Abused Husbands: A Narrative Analysis." *Journal of Family Issues* 23: 26–52.

Mignon, S. I., and Holmes, W. M. 1995. "Police Response to Mandatory Arrest Laws." *Crime and Delinquency* 41: 430–442.

Mignon, S. I., Larson, C. J., and Holmes, W. M. 2002. Family Abuse: Consequences, Theories, and Responses. Boston: Allyn and Bacon.

Miller, B. C., Monson, B. H., and Norton, M. C. 1995. "The Effects of Forced Sexual Intercourse on White Female Adolescents." *Child Abuse and Neglect* 19: 1289–1301.

Miller, B. V., Fox, B. R., and Garcia-Beckwith, L. 1999. "Intervening in Severe Physical Child Abuse Cases: Mental Health, Legal, and Social Services." *Child Abuse and Neglect* 23: 905–914.

Miller, D. R., and Swanson, G. E. 1958. The Changing American Parent. New York: John Wiley and Sons.

Miller, JoAnn. 2002. "Convicted Batterers' Accounts for Their Anger and Violence." Unpublished Manuscript, 1–52. West Lafayette, Ind.

———. 2003. "An Arresting Experiment: Domestic Violence Victim Experiences and Perceptions." *Journal of Interpersonal Violence* 18: 695–716.

Miller, JoAnn Langley, and Knudsen, Dean D. 1999. "Family Abuse and Violence." In Handbook of Marriage and the Family, 2nd ed., edited by M. B. Sussman, S. K. Steinmetz, and G. W. Peterson, 705–741. New York: Plenum Press.

Miller, Jody, and White, Norman A. 2003. "Gender and Adolescent Relationship Violence: A Contextual Examination." *Criminology* 41: 1207–1248.

Miller, T., Cohen, M., and Wiersema, B. 1996. "The Extent and Costs of Crime Victimization: A New Look (NCJ 155281)." Washington, DC: U.S. Department of Justice, National Institute of Justice.

Mills, L. G. 1998. "Mandatory Arrest and Prosecution Policies for Domestic Violence: A Critical Literature Review and the Case for More Research to Test Victim Empowerment Approaches." *Criminal Justice and Behavior* 25: 306–319.

———. 1999. "Killing Her Softly: Intimate Abuse and the Violence of State Intervention." *Harvard Law Review* 113: 550–613.

———. 2003. Insult to Injury: Rethinking Our Responses to Intimate Abuse. Princeton: Princeton University Press.

Milner, J. S. 1989. "Additional Cross-Validation of the Child Abuse Potential Inventory." *Psychological Assessment* 1: 219–223.

———. 1994. "Assessing Physical Child Abuse Risk: The Child Abuse Potential Inventory." *Clinical Psychology Review* 14: 547–583.

Milner, J. S., Gold, R. G., Ayobb, C., and Jacevitz, M. M. 1984. "Predictive Validity of the Child Abuse Potential Inventory." *Journal of Consulting and Clinical Psychology* 52: 879–884.

Mintz, S., and Kellogg, S. 1988. Domestic Relations: A Social History of American Family Life. New York: Free Press.

Mitterauer, M., and Sieder, R. 1982. The European Family: Patriarchy to Partnership from the Middle Ages to the Present. Translated by K. Oosterveen and M. Horzinger. Chicago: University of Chicago Press.

Moffitt, T. E., and Caspi, A. 1998. "Annotation: Implications of Violence between Intimate Partners for Child Psychologists and Psychiatrists." *Journal of Child Psychology and Psychiatry* 39: 137–144.

Mollen, C. J., Fein, J. A., Vu, T. N., Shofer, F. S., and Datner, E. M. 2003. "Characterization of Nonfatal Events and Injuries Resulting from Youth Violence in Patients Presenting to an Emergency Department." *Pediatric Emergency Care* 19: 379–384.

Moore, E., Armsden, G., and Gogerty, P. L. 1998. "A Twelve-Year Follow-Up of Maltreated and At-Risk Children Who Received Early Therapeutic Child Care." *Child Maltreatment* 3: 3–16.

Moran, P. B., Vuchinich, S., and Hall, N. K. 2004. "Associations between Types of Maltreatment and Substance Use during Adolescence." *Child Abuse and Neglect* 28: 565–574.

Mordini, N. M. 2004. "Note: Mandatory State Interventions for Domestic Abuse Cases: An Examination of the Effects on Victim Safety and Autonomy." *Drake Law Review* 52: 295–329.

Morgan, S., Nackerud, L., and Yegidis, B. 1998. "Domestic Violence Gun Ban: An Analysis of Interest-Group Conflict." *Affilia: Journal of Women and Social Work* 13: 474–486.

Morton, M. J. 2000. "Institutional Inequalities: Black Children and Child Welfare in Cleveland, 1859–1940." *Journal of Social History* 34: 141–163.

Morton, T. D. 1999. Letter to the Editor. *Child Abuse and Neglect* 23: 1209.

Mullen, P. E. 2003. "Stalking Crimes and Victim Protection: Prevention, Intervention, Threat Assessment, and Case Management." *Journal of Forensic Psychiatry and Psychology* 14: 452–454.

Muller, R. T., Hunter, J. E., and Stollak, G. 1995. "The Intergenerational Transmission of Corporal Punishment: A Comparison of Social Learning and Temperament Models." *Child Abuse and Neglect* 19: 1323–1335.

Muller, R. W., Goebel-Fabbri, A. E., Diamond, E., and Dinklage, D. 2000. "Social Support and the Relationship between Family and Community Violence Exposure and Psychopathology among High Risk Adolescents." *Child Abuse and Neglect* 24: 449–464.

Munro, E. 1996. "Avoidable and Unavoidable Mistakes in Child Protection Work." *British Journal of Social Work* 26: 793–808.

Muram, D. 2003. "The Medical Evaluation of Sexually Abused Children." *Journal of Pediatric and Adolescent Gynecology* 16: 5–114.

Musick, J. S. 1994. "The Special Role of Parenting in the Context of Poverty: The Case of Adolescent Motherhood." In Threats to Optimal Development: Integrating Biological, Psychological and Social Risk Factors, edited by C. A. Nelson, 179–218. Hillsdale, N.J.: Lawrence Erlbaum Associates.

Myers, J. E. B. 2004. A History of Child Protection in America. New York: Xlibris.

Myers, J. E. B., Diedrich, S., Lee, D., Fincher, K. M., and Stern, R. 1999. "Professional Writing on Child Sexual Abuse from 1900 to 1975: Dominant Themes and Impact on Prosecution." *Child Maltreatment* 4: 201–216.

National Center on Child Abuse and Neglect. 1978. Interdisciplinary Glossary on Child Abuse and Neglect: Legal, Medical, Social Work Terms. Washington, DC: U.S. Department of Health, Education, and Welfare.

———. 1997. Child Maltreatment 1995: Reports from the States to the National Child Abuse and Neglect Data System. Washington, DC: U.S. Department of Health and Human Services.

Nayak, M. B., and Milner, J. S. 1998. "Neuropsychological Functioning: Comparison of Mothers at High- and Low-Risk for Child Physical Abuse." *Child Abuse and Neglect* 22: 687–703.

Needell, B., Brookhart, M. A., and Lee, S. 2003. "Black Children and Foster Care Placement in California." *Children and Youth Services Review* 25: 393–408.

Neidigh, L., and Krop, H. 1992. "Cognitive Distortions among Child Sexual Offenders." *Journal of Sex Education and Therapy* 18: 208–215.

Nelson, B. 1984. Making an Issue of Child Abuse: Political Agenda Setting for Social Problems. Chicago: University of Chicago Press.

Nelson, K. E., Saunders, E. J., and Landsman, M. J. 1993. "Chronic Child Neglect in Perspective." *Social Work* 38: 661–671.

Newcomb, M. D., and Locke, T. F. 2001. "Intergenerational Cycle of Maltreatment: A Popular Concept Obscured by Methodological Limitations." *Child Abuse and Neglect* 25: 1219–1240.

NICHD Early Child Care Research Network. 1997. "Child Care in the First Year of Life." *Merrill-Palmer Quarterly* 43: 340–360.

Nimkoff, M. F., ed. 1965. Comparative Family Systems. Boston: Houghton Mifflin.

Nolan, James L., Jr. 2001. Reinventing Justice: The American Drug Court Movement. Princeton: Princeton University Press.

———. 2003. "Redefining Criminal Courts: Problem-Solving and the Meaning of Justice." *American Criminal Law Review* 40: 1541–1565.

Noland, V. J., Liller, K. D., McDermott, R. J., Coulter, M. L., and Seraphine, A. E. 2004. "Is Adolescent Sibling Violence a Precursor to College Dating Violence?" *American Journal of Health Behavior* 28: S13–S23.

Nunno, J. A., and Motz, J. K. 1988. "The Development of an Effective Response to the Abuse of Children in Out-of-Home Care." *Child Abuse and Neglect* 12: 521–528.

Oates, R. K., and Bross, D. C. 1995. " What Have We Learned about Treating Child Physical Abuse: A Literature Review of the Last Decade." *Child Abuse and Neglect* 19: 463–473.

O'Connor, M., and Rosenfeld, B. 2004. "Introduction to the Special Issue on Stalking: Finding and Filling the Empirical Gaps." *Criminal Justice and Behavior* 31: 3–8.

O'Connor, S. 2001. Orphan Trains: The Story of Charles Loring Brace and the Children He Saved and Failed. Boston: Houghton Mifflin.

O'Donohue, W. T., Elliott, A. N., Nickerson, M., and Valentine, S. 1992. "Perceived Credibility of Children's Sexual Abuse Allegations: Effects of Gender and Sexual Attitudes." *Violence and Victims* 7: 147–155.

Ofshe, R. 1994. "Making Grossly Damaging but Avoidable Errors: The Pitfalls of the Olio/Cornell Thesis." *Journal of Child Sexual Abuse* 3: 95–108.

Okami, P., and Goldberg, A. 1992. "Personality Correlates of Pedophilia: Are They Reliable Indicators?" *Journal of Sex Research* 29: 297–328.

O'Keefe, M. 1998. "Factors Mediating the Link between Witnessing Interparental Violence and Dating Violence." *Journal of Family Violence* 13: 39–57.

Olds, D. L., Henderson, C. R., Jr., Kitzman, H. J., Echenrode, J. J., Cole, R. E., and Tatelbaum, R. C. 1999. "Prenatal and Infancy Home Visitation by Nurses: Recent Findings." *The Future of Children* 9 (1): 44–65.

Olds, D. L., and Kitzman, H. 1993. "Review of Research on Home Visiting for Pregnant Women and Parents of Young Children." *The Future of Children* 3 (3): 53–92.

Oliver, J. E. 1993. "Intergenerational Transmission of Child Abuse: Rates, Research, and Clinical Implications." *American Journal of Psychiatry* 150: 1315–1324.

Ondersma, S. J., Chaffin, M., Berliner, L., Cordon, I., Goodman, G. S., and Barnett, D. 2001. "Sex with Children Is Abuse: Comment on Rind, Tromovitch, and Bauserman (1998)." *Psychological Bulletin* 127: 707–714.

Orbach, Y., and Lamb, M. E. 1999. "Assessing the Accuracy of a Child's Account of Sexual Abuse: A Case Study." *Child Abuse and Neglect* 23: 91–98.

Osofsky, J. E., ed. 1997. Children in a Violent Society. New York: Guilford Press.

Overmier, J. B. 2002. "On Learned Helplessness." *Integrative Physiological and Behavioral Science* 37: 4–8.

Palker-Corell, A., and Marcus, D. K. 2004. "Partner Abuse, Learned Helplessness, and Trauma Symptoms." *Journal of Social and Clinical Psychology* 23: 445–462.

Paolucci, E. O., and Violato, C. 2004. "A Meta-Analysis of the Published Research on the Affective, Cognitive, and Behavioral Effects of Corporal Punishment." *Journal of Psychology* 138: 197–221.

Parrott, D. J., Drobes, D. J., Saladin, M. E., Coffey, S. F., and Dansky, B. S. 2003. "Perpetration of Partner Violence: Effects of Cocaine and Alcohol Dependence and Post-Traumatic Stress Disorder." *Addictive Behaviors* 28: 1587–1602.

Parton, N. 1985. The Politics of Child Abuse. New York: St. Martin's Press.

Pate, Antony M., and Hamilton, Edwin E. 1992. "Formal and Informal Deterrents to Domestic Violence: The Dade County Spouse Assault Experiment." *American Sociological Review* 57: 691.

Payne, B. K. 2002. "An Integrated Understanding of Elder Abuse and Neglect." *Journal of Criminal Justice* 30: 535–547.

Pearce, L. D., and Axinn, W. G. 1998. "The Impact of Family Religious Life on the Quality of Mother-Child Relations." *American Sociological Review* 63: 810–828.

Pears, K. C., and Capaldi, D. M. 2001. "Intergenerational Transmission of Abuse: A Two-Generational Prospective Study of an At-Risk Sample." *Child Abuse and Neglect* 25: 1439–1461.

Pelcovitz, D., Kaplan, S., Goldenberg, B., Mandel, F., Lehane, J., and Guarrera, J. 1994. "Post-Traumatic Stress Disorder in Physically Abused Adolescents." *Journal of the American Academy of Child and Adolescent Psychiatry* 33: 305–312.

Pelton, L. H. 1978. "Child Abuse and Neglect: The Myth of Classlessness." *American Journal of Orthopsychiatry* 48: 608–617.

———. 1981. The Social Context of Child Abuse and Neglect. New York: Human Sciences Press.

———. 1991. "Poverty and Child Protection." *Protecting Children* 7: 3–5.

———. 1997. "Child Welfare Policy and Practice: The Myth of Family Preservation." *American Journal of Orthopsychiatry* 67: 545–553.

———. 1998. "Commentary." *The Future of Children* 8: 126–129.

Pendergrast, M. 1995. Victims of Memory: Incest Accusations and Shattered Lives. Hinesbury, Vt.: Upper Access, Inc.

Perez, C., and Widom, C. S. 1994. "Childhood Victimization and Long-Term Intellectual and Academic Outcomes." *Child Abuse and Neglect* 18: 617–633.

Perkins, D. F., and Luster, T. 1999. "The Relationship between Sexual Abuse and Purging: Findings from Community-Wide Surveys of Female Adolescents." *Child Abuse and Neglect* 23: 371–382.

Peters, D. F. 2001. "Examining Child Sexual Abuse Evaluations: The Types of Information Affecting Expert Judgment." *Child Abuse and Neglect* 25: 149–178.

Pfohl, S. 1977. "The 'Discovery' of Child Abuse." *Social Problems* 24: 310–323.

Phipps, S. 2001. "Values, Policies and the Well-Being of Young Children in Canada, Norway, and the United States." In Child Well-Being, Child Poverty, and Child Policy in Modern Nations, edited by K. Vleminckx and T. M. Smeeding, 79–98. Bristol, UK: Policy Press.

Pilkington, B., and Kremer, J. 1995a. "A Review of the Epidemiological Research on Child Sexual Abuse: Community and College Student Samples." *Child Abuse Review* 4: 84–94.

———. 1995b. "A Review of the Epidemiological Research on Child Sexual Abuse: Clinical Samples." *Child Abuse Review* 4: 191–205.

Pillemer, K., and McCartney, K., eds. 1991. Parent-Child Relations Throughout Life. Hillsdale, N.J.: Lawrence Erlbaum Associates.

Pittaway, E. D., Westhues, A., and Peressini, T. 1995. "Risk-Factors for Abuse and Neglect among Older Adults." *Canadian Journal on Aging, Revue Canadienne Du Vieillissement* 14: 20–44.

Pittman, J. F., and Lee, C. S. 2004. "Comparing Different Types of Child Abuse and Spouse Abuse Offenders." *Violence and Victims* 19: 137–156.

Pleck, E. 1987. Domestic Tyranny: The Making of American Social Policy against Family Violence from Colonial Times to the Present. New York: Oxford University Press.

———. 1989. "Criminal Approaches to Family Violence, 1640–1980." In Family Violence, edited by L. Ohlin and M. Tonry, 19–57. Chicago: University of Chicago Press.

Plichta, S. B., and Falik, M. 2001. "Prevalence of Violence and Its Implications for Women's Health." *Women's Health Issues* 11: 244–258.

Polansky, N. A., and Chalmers, M. A. 1978. "Assessing Adequacy of Child Caring: An Urban Scale." *Child Welfare* 57: 439–449.

Pollock, L. A. 1983. Forgotten Children: Parent-Child Relations from 1500 to 1900. New York: Cambridge University Press.

Portwood, S. G. 1999. "Coming to Terms with a Consensual Definition of Child Maltreatment." *Child Maltreatment* 4: 56–68.

Portwood, S. G., Grady, M. T., and Dutton, S. E. 2000. "Enhancing Law Enforcement Identification and Investigation of Child Maltreatment." *Child Abuse and Neglect* 24: 195–207.

Postman, N. 1982. The Disappearance of Childhood. New York: Delacorte Press.

Prescott, A., Bank, L., Reid, J. B., Knutson, J. F., Burraston, B. O., and Eddy, J. M. 2000. "The Veridicality of Retrospective Reports of Punitive Childhood Experiences." *Child Abuse and Neglect* 24: 411–423.

Prevent Child Abuse America. 2001. "Total Annual Cost of Child Abuse and Neglect." The Edna McConnell Clark Foundation.

Price, J. M., and Glad, K. 2003. "Hostile Attributional Tendencies in Maltreated Children." *Journal of Abnormal Child Psychology* 31: 329–343.

Purcell, R., Pathe, M., and Mullen, P. E. 2004. "Stalking: Defining and Prosecuting a New Category of Offending." *International Journal of Law and Psychiatry* 27: 157–169.

Queen, S. A., Habenstein, R. W., and Quadagno, J. S., eds. 1985. The Family in Various Cultures. New York: Harper and Row.

Quinn, M. J. 2000. "Undoing Undue Influence." *Journal of Elder Abuse and Neglect* 12: 9–17.

Radbill, S. X. 1968. "A History of Child Abuse and Infanticide." In The Battered Child, edited by M. Helfer and R. Kempe, 3–17. Chicago: University of Chicago Press.

Rainwater, L., Smeeding, T. M., and Coder, J. 2001. "Poverty across States, Nations, and Continents." In Child Well-Being, Child Poverty, and Child Policy in Modern Nations, edited by K. Vleminckx, et al., 33–74. Bristol, UK: Policy Press.

Rand, M. R., and Saltzman, L. E. 2003. "The Nature and Extent of Recurring Intimate Partner Violence against Women in the United States." *Journal of Comparative Family Studies* 34: 137–149.

Reed, R. S., and Kenning, M. K. 1987. "The Prevalence of Child Sexual Abuse among a Midwestern College Population." Presented at the Family Violence Conference. Durham: University of New Hampshire.

Reese, D. 2000. "A Parenting Manual, with Words of Advice for Puritan Mothers." In A World of Babies: Imagined Childcare Guides for Seven Societies, edited by J. DeLoache and A. Gottlieb, 29–54. New York: Cambridge University Press.

Regalado, M., Sareen, H., Inkelas, M., Wissow, L. S., and Halfon, N. 2004. "Parents' Discipline of Young Children: Results from the National Survey of Early Childhood Health." *Pediatrics* 113: 1952–1958.

Renzetti, Claire M. 1992. *Violent Betrayal: Partner Abuse in Lesbian Relationships.* Newbury Park, Calif.: Sage Publications.

Reynolds, A. J., ed. 2004. "Promoting Well Being in Children and Youth: Findings from the Chicago Longitudinal Study." *Children and Youth Services Review* 26: 1–119 (Entire Issue).

Rhodes, K. V., Lauderdale, D. S., He, T., Howes, D. S., and Levinson, W. 2002. "'Between Me and the Computer': Increased Detection of Intimate Partner Violence Using a Computer Questionnaire." *Annals of Emergency Medicine* 40: 476–484.

Richie, Beth E. 2000. "A Black Feminist Reflection on the Antiviolence Movement." *Signs: Journal of Women in Culture and Society* 25: 1113–1137.

Riger, Stephanie, Raja, Sheela, and Camacho, Jennifer. 2002. "The Radiating Impact of Intimate Partner Violence." *Journal of Interpersonal Violence* 17: 184–205.

Rind, B., and Tromovitch, P. 1994. "A Meta-Analytic Review of Findings from National Samples on Psychological Correlates of Child Sexual Abuse." *Journal of Sex Research* 34: 237–255.

Robbins, A. D. 1998. "False Memories or Hidden Agendas?" *Journal of Psycho-History* 22: 305–311.

Roberts, T. A., and Klein, J. 2003. "Intimate Partner Abuse and High-Risk Behavior in Adolescents." *Archives of Pediatrics and Adolescent Medicine* 157: 375–380.

Roberts, T. A., Klein, J. D., and Fisher, S. 2003. "Longitudinal Effect of Intimate Partner Abuse on High-Risk Behavior among Adolescents." *Archives of Pediatrics and Adolescent Medicine* 157: 875–881.

Robertson, S. 2002. "Age of Consent Law and the Making of Modern Childhood in New York City, 1886–1921." *Journal of Social History* 36: 781–799.

Rodriguez, C. M., and Price, B. L. 2004. "Attributions and Discipline History as Predictors of Child Abuse Potential and Future Discipline Practices." *Child Abuse and Neglect* 28: 845–861.

Romano, E., and De Luca, R. V. 1997. "Exploring the Relationship between Childhood Sexual Abuse and Adult Sexual Perpetration." *Journal of Family Violence* 12: 85–98.

Ronfeldt, H. M., Kimerling, R., and Arias, I. 1998. "Satisfaction with Relationship Power and the Perpetration of Dating Violence." *Journal of Marriage and the Family* 60: 70–78.

Roosa, M., Reyes, L., Reinholta, C., and Angelini, P. J. 1998. "Measurement of Women's Child Sexual Abuse Experiences: An Empirical Demonstration of the Impact of Choice of Measure on Estimates of Incidence Rates and Relationships with Pathology." *Journal of Sex Research* 35: 225–233.

Rose, S. J., and Meezan, W. 1996. "Variations in Perceptions of Child Neglect." *Child Welfare* 75: 139–151.

Rosen, K. H., Bartle-Haring, S., and Stith, S. M. 2001. "Using Bowen Theory to Enhance Understanding of the Intergenerational Transmission of Dating Violence." *Journal of Family Issues* 22: 124–142.

Rosenfeld, B. 2004. "Violence Risk Factors in Stalking and Obsessional Harassment: A Review and Preliminary Meta-Analysis." *Criminal Justice and Behavior* 31: 9–36.

Ross, C. J. 1980. "The Lessons of the Past: Defining and Controlling Child Abuse in the United States." In Child Abuse: An Agenda for Action, edited by G. Gerbner et al., 63–81. New York: Oxford University Press.

Rossi, Peter H., and Berk, Richard A. 1997. Just Punishments: Federal Guidelines and Public Views Compared. Hawthorne, N.Y.: Aldine de Gruyter.

Rossi, Peter H., and Nock, Steven, eds. 1983. Measuring Social Judgments: The Factorial Survey Approach. Beverly Hills, Calif.: Sage Publications.

Rossi, Peter H., Schuerman, J., and Budde, S. 1999. "Understanding Decisions about Child Maltreatment Evaluation Review." *Journal of Applied Social Research* 23: 579–598.

Rotenberg, K. J., Shewchuk, V. A., and Kimberley, T. 2001. "Loneliness, Sex, Romantic Jealousy, and Powerlessness." *Journal of Social and Personal Relationships* 18: 55–79.

Rothenberg, B. 2002. "The Success of the Battered Woman Syndrome: An Analysis of How Cultural Arguments Succeed." *Sociological Forum* 17(1): 81–103.

———. 2003. "'We Don't Have Time for Social Change': Cultural Compromise and the Battered Woman Syndrome." *Gender and Society* 17: 771–787.

Rowe, E., and Eckenrode, J. 1999. "The Timing of Academic Difficulties among Maltreated and Nonmaltreated Children." *Child Abuse and Neglect* 23: 813–832.

Roy, K. (2004). "Three-Block Fathers: Spatial Perceptions and Kin-Work in Low-Income African American Neighborhoods." *Social Problems* 51(4): 528–548.

Rudd, J. M., and Herzberger, S. D. 1999. "Brother-Sister-Father-Daughter Incest: A Comparison of Characteristics and Consequences." *Child Abuse and Neglect* 23: 915–928.

Rumm, P. D., Cummings, P., Krauss, M. R., Bell, M. A., and Rivara, F. P. 2000. "Identified Spouse Abuse as a Risk Factor for Child Abuse." *Child Abuse and Neglect* 24: 1375–1381.

Russell, Diana E. H. 1990. Rape in Marriage. New York: Macmillan Press.

———. 1998. "The Making of a Whore." In Issues in Intimate Violence, edited by Raquel Kennedy Bergen, 65–77. Thousand Oaks, Calif.: Sage Publications.

Rutter, M. 1998. "Some Research Considerations on Intergenerational Continuities and Discontinuities: Comment on the Special Section." *Developmental Psychology* 34: 1269–1273.

Ryan, G. 2002. "Victims Who Go On to Victimize Others: No Simple Explanations." *Child Abuse and Neglect* 26: 891–892.

Ryan, S., Wiles, D., Cash, S., and Siebert, C. 2005. "Risk Assessments: Empirically Supported or Values Driven?" *Children and Youth Services Review* 27: 213–225.

Salazar, L. F., Baker, C. K., Price, A. W., and Carlin, K. 2003. "Moving Beyond the Individual: Examining the Effects of Domestic Violence Policies on Social Norms." *American Journal of Community Psychology* 32: 253–264.

Sanderson, M., Coker, A. L., Roberts, R. E., Tortolero, S. R., and Reininger, B. M. 2004. "Acculturation, Ethnic Identity, and Dating Violence Among Latino Ninth-Grade Students." *Preventive Medicine* 39: 373–383.

Sappington, A. A. 2000. "Childhood Abuse as a Possible Locus for Early Intervention into Problems of Violence and Psychopathology." *Aggression and Violent Behavior* 5: 255–266.

Schene, P. A. 1998. "Past, Present, and Future Roles of Child Protective Services." *The Future of Children* 8 (1): 23–38.

Scher, C. D., Forde, D. R., McQuaid, J. R., and Stein, M. B. 2004. "Prevalence and Demographic Correlates of Childhood Maltreatment in an Adult Community Sample." *Child Abuse and Neglect* 28: 167–180.

Schmitt, F. E., and Martin, P. Y. 1999. "Unobtrusive Mobilization by an Institutionalized Rape Crisis Center: 'All We Do Comes from Victims.'" *Gender and Society* 13: 364–384.

Scholle, S. H., Rost, K. M., and Golding, J. M. 1998. "Physical Abuse among Depressed Women." *Journal of General Internal Medicine* 13: 607–613.

Schorr, Lisbeth B. 1988. Within Our Reach: Breaking the Cycle of Disadvantage. New York: Doubleday.

Schorsch, A. 1979. Images of Childhood. New York: Mayflower Books.

Schwartz, L. L., and Isser, N. K. 2000. Endangered Children: Neonaticide, Infanticide, and Filicide. New York: CRC Press.

Schwartzberg, B. 2004. "'Lots of Them Did That': Desertion, Bigamy, and Marital Fluidity in Late Nineteenth-Century America." *Journal of Social History* 37: 573–601.

Scott, C. 2004. "Judging in a Therapeutic Key: Therapeutic Jurisprudence and the Courts." *Journal of Legal Medicine* 25: 377–388.

Scott, D. M., and Wishy, B., eds. 1982. America's Families: A Documentary History. New York: Harper and Row.

Sears, R. R., Maccoaby, E. C., and Levin, H. 1957. Patterns of Child Rearing. Evanston, Ill.: Row, Peterson.

Sedlak, A. J., and Broadhurst, D. D. 1996. Third National Incidence Study of Child Abuse and Neglect. Final Report. Washington, DC: U.S. Department of Health and Human Services.

Serin, R. C., Malcolm, P. B., Khanna, A., and Barbaree, H. E. 1994. "Psychopathy and Deviant Sexual Arousal in Incarcerated Sexual Offenders." *Journal of Interpersonal Violence* 9: 3–11.

Serra, P. 1993. "Physical Violence in the Couple Relationship: A Contribution toward the Analysis of the Context." *Family Process* 32(1): 21–33.

Seva, A. 2003. "Surviving Stalking." *European Journal of Psychiatry* 17: 251–251.

Sherman, Lawrence W., Schmidt, Janell D., Rogan, Dennis P., Gartin, Patrick R., Cohn, Ellen G., Collins, Dean J., and Bacich, Anthony R. 1991. "From Initial Deterrence to Long-Term Escalation: Short Custody Arrest for Poverty Ghetto Domestic Violence." *Criminology* 29: 821–850.

Sherman, Lawrence W., and Smith, Douglas A. 1992. "Crime, Punishment, and Stake in Conformity: Legal and Informal Control of Domestic Violence." *American Sociological Review* 57: 680–690.

Shorter, E. 1975. The Making of the Modern Family. New York: Basic Books.

Sidebotham, P., Golding, J., and The ALSPAC Study Team. 2001. "Child Maltreatment in the 'Children of the Nineties': A Longitudinal Study of Parental Risk Factors." *Child Abuse and Neglect* 25: 1177–1200.

Silver, L. B., Dublin, C. C., and Lourie, R. S. 1969. "Does Violence Breed Violence? Contributions from a Study of the Child Abuse Syndrome." *American Journal of Psychiatry* 126: 404–407.

Silverman, A., Reinherz, H. Z., and Giaconia, R. M. 1996. "The Long-Term Sequelae of Child and Adolescent Abuse: A Longitudinal Community Study." *Child Abuse and Neglect* 20: 709–723.

Silverman, F. N. 1953. "The Roentgen Manifestations of Unrecognized Skeletal Trauma in Infants." *American Journal of Roentgenology, Radium Therapy and Nuclear Medicine* 69: 413–427.

Silverman, J. G., Raj, A., Mucci, L. A., and Hathaway, J. E. 2001. "Dating Violence against Adolescent Girls and Associated Substance Use, Unhealthy Weight Control, Sexual Risk Behavior, Pregnancy, and Suicidality." *Jama: Journal of the American Medical Association* 286: 572–579.

Simkins, L., and Renier, A. 1996. "An Analytic Review of the Empirical Literature on Children's Play with Anatomically Detailed Dolls." *Journal of Child Sexual Abuse* 5: 21–45.

Simon, L. M. J. 1995. "A Therapeutic Jurisprudence Approach to the Legal Processing of Domestic Violence Cases." *Psychology, Public Policy, and Law* 1: 43–79.

Simon, L. M. J., Sales, B., Kaszniak, A., and Kahn, M. 1992. "Characteristics of Child Molesters: Implications for the Fixated-Regressed Dichotomy." *Journal of Interpersonal Violence* 7: 211–225.

Simonelli, C. J., Mullis, T., Elliott, A. N., and Pierce, T. W. 2002. "Abuse by Siblings and Subsequent Experiences of Violence within the Dating Relationship." *Journal of Interpersonal Violence* 17: 103–121.

Simonich, H., Wonderlich, S., Crosby, R., Smyth, J. M., Thompson, K., Redlin, J., Mitchell, J., and Haseltine, B. 2004. "The Use of Ecological Momentary Assessment Approaches in the Study of Sexually Abused Children." *Child Abuse and Neglect* 28: 803–809.

Simons, R. L., Johnson, C., Beaman, J., and Conger, R. D. 1993. "Explaining Women's Double Jeopardy: Factors that Mediate the Association between Harsh Treatment as a Child and Violence by a Husband." *Journal of Marriage and the Family* 55: 713–723.

Simons, R. L., Johnson, C., and Conger, R. D. 1994. "Harsh Corporal Punishment Versus Quality of Parental Involvement as an Explanation of Adolescent Maladjustment." *Journal of Marriage and the Family* 56: 591–607.

Simons, R. L., Lin, K. H., and Gordon, L. C. 1998. "Socialization in the Family of Origin and Male Dating Violence: A Prospective Study." *Journal of Marriage and the Family* 60: 467–478.

Simons, R. L., Wu, C., Johnson, C., and Conger, R. D. 1995. "A Test of Various Perspectives on the Intergenerational Transmission of Domestic Violence." *Criminology* 33: 141–171.

Sinden, P. G., and Stephens, B. J. 1999. "Police Perceptions of Domestic Violence: The Nexus of Victim, Perpetrator, Event, Self and Law." *Policing: An International Journal of Police Strategies and Management* 22: 313–326.

Sipe, R., Jensen, E. L., and Everett, R. S. 1998. "Adolescent Sexual Offenders Grown Up: Recidivism in Young Adulthood." *Criminal Justice and Behavior* 25: 109–124.

Slee, P. T. 2002. Child, Adolescent and Family Development, 2nd ed. New York: Cambridge University Press.

Smith, A. 2004. "What Doctors and Policymakers Should Know: Battered Women's Views about Mandatory Medical Reporting Laws." *Journal of Criminal Justice* 32: 207–221.

Smith, A. L., Sullivan, Q. E., and Cohen, A. J. 1995. "Factors Associated with the Indication of Child Abuse Reports." *Journal of Social Service Research* 21: 15–34.

Smith, A. M., ed. 1978. The Maltreatment of Children. Baltimore, Md.: University Park Press.

Smith, Brenda D., and Testa, Mark F. 2002. "The Risk of Subsequent Maltreatment Allegations in Families with Substance Exposed Infants." *Child Abuse and Neglect* 26: 97–114.

Smith, C., and Thornberry, T. P. 1995. "The Relationship between Childhood Maltreatment and Adolescent Involvement in Delinquency." *Criminology* 33: 451–481.

Smith, D., Letourneau, E. J., Saunders, B. E., Kilpatrick, D. G., Resnick, H. S., and Best, C. L. 2000. "Delay in Disclosure of Childhood Rape: Results from a National Survey." *Child Abuse and Neglect* 24: 273–287.

Smith, J. P., and Williams, J. G. 1992. "From Abusive Household to Dating Violence." *Journal of Family Violence* 7: 153–165.

Sniderman, Paul M., and Grob, Douglas B. 1996. "Innovation in Experimental Design in Attitude Surveys." *Annual Review of Sociology* 22: 377–399.

Sokoloff, B. Z. 1993. "Antecedents of American Adoption." *The Future of Children* 3: 17–25.

Spencer, G. A., and Bryant, S. A. 2000. "Dating Violence: A Comparison of Rural, Suburban, and Urban Teens." *Journal of Adolescent Health* 27: 302–305.

Spitz, M. A. L. 2003. "Stalking: Terrorism at Our Doors, How Social Workers Can Help Victims Fight Back." *Social Work* 48: 504–512.

Stalans, Loretta J. 1996. "Family Harmony or Individual Protection? Public Recommendations about How Police Can Handle Domestic Violence Situations." *American Behavioral Scientist* 39: 433–448.

Starr, R. H., Jr., ed. 1982a. Child Abuse Prediction: Policy Implications. Cambridge, Mass.: Ballinger Publishing Company.

Starr, R. H., Jr. 1982b. "A Research-Based Approach to the Prediction of Child Abuse." In Child Abuse Prediction: Policy Implications, edited by R. H. Starr, Jr., 105–134. Cambridge, Mass.: Ballinger Publishing Company.

Staudt, M. M., Scheuler-Whitaker, L., and Hinterlong, J. 2001. "The Role of Family Preservation Therapists in Facilitating Use of Aftercare Services." *Child Abuse and Neglect* 25: 803–817.

Steel, J., Sanna, L., Hammond, B., Whipple, J., and Cross, H. 2004. "Psychological Sequelae of Childhood Sexual Abuse: Abuse-Related Characteristics, Coping Strategies, and Attributional Style." *Child Abuse and Neglect* 28: 785–801.

Steele, B. F., and Pollock, C. B. 1968. "A Psychiatric Study of Parents Who Abuse Infants and Small Children." In *The Battered Child*, edited by M.E. Helfer and R. S. Kempe, 103–147. Chicago: University of Chicago Press.

Steinberg, K. L., Levine, J. D., and Doueck, H. J. 1997. "Effects of Legally Mandated Child-Abuse Reports on the Therapeutic Relationship: A Survey of Psychotherapists." *American Journal of Orthopsychiatry* 67: 112–122.

Steinberg, S. R., and Kincheloe, J., eds. 1997. Kinderculture: The Corporate Construction of Childhood. Boulder, Colo.: Westview Press.

Stephan, A. 2002. "Symposium: Therapeutic Jurisprudence and Children: Introduction." *University of Cincinnati Law Review* 71: 13–18.

Stets, J. 1999. "Cohabiting and Marital Aggression: The Role of Social Isolation." *Journal of Marriage and the Family* 53: 669–680.

Stevens, Patricia E., and Richards, Deborah J. 1998. "Narrative Case Analysis of HIV Infection in a Battered Woman." *Health Care for Women International* 19: 9–22.

Stevens-Simon, C., Nelligan, D., and Kelly, L. 2001a. "Adolescents at Risk for Mistreating Their Children, Part I: Prenatal Identification." *Child Abuse and Neglect* 25: 737–751.

———. 2001b. "Adolescents at Risk for Mistreating Their Children, Part II: A Home- and Clinic-Based Prevention Program." *Child Abuse and Neglect* 25: 753–769.

Stith, S., Rosen, M., Middleton, K., Busch, A. L., Lundeberg, K., and Carlton, R. P. 2000. "The Intergenerational Transmission of Spouse Abuse: A Meta-Analysis." *Journal of Marriage and the Family* 62: 640–654.

Stone, L. 1977. The Family, Sex, and Marriage in England: 1500–1800. New York: Harper and Row.

St. Pierre, R. G., and Layzer, J. I. 1999. "Using Home Visits for Multiple Purposes: The Comprehensive Child Development Program." *The Future of Children* 9 (1): 134–151.

Straus, Murray A. 1990. "The National Family Violence Surveys." In Physical Violence in American Families: Risk Factors and Adaptations to Violence in 8,145 Families, edited by M. A. Straus, R. J. Gelles, and (with the assistance of) C. Smith, 3–16. New Brunswick, N.J.: Transaction.

———. 1991. "Discipline and Deviance: Physical Punishment of Children and Violence and Other Crime in Adulthood." *Social Problems* 38: 101–123.

———. 1994. Beating the Devil Out of Them: Corporal Punishment in American Families. New York: Lexington Books.

Straus, Murray A., and Gelles, Richard A. 1986. "Societal Change and Change in Family Violence from 1975 to 1985 as Revealed in Two National Surveys." *Journal of Marriage and the Family* 48.

Straus, Murray A., Hamby, S. L., Finkelhor, D., Moore, D. W., and Runyan, D. 1998. "Identification of Child Maltreatment with the Parent-Child Conflict Tactics Scales: Development and Psychometric Data for a National Sample of American Parents." *Child Abuse and Neglect* 22: 249–270.

Straus, Murray A., and Mathur, A. 1996. "Social Change and Change in Approval of Corporal Punishment by Parents from 1968 to 1994." In Family Violence against Children: A Challenge for Society, edited by D. Frehsee et al., 91–105. New York: de Gruyter.

Straus, Murray A., and Yodanis, C. L. 1996. "Corporal Punishment in Adolescence and Physical Assaults on Spouses in Later Life: What Accounts for the Link?" *Journal of Marriage and the Family* 58: 825–841.

Sullivan, J. M. 2004. HIPAA: A Practical Guide to the Privacy and Security of Health Data. Chicago: American Bar Association.

Sundell, K. 1997. "Child-Care Personnel's Failure to Report Child Maltreatment: Some Swedish Evidence." *Child Abuse and Neglect* 21: 93–105.

Sunley, R. 1955. " Early Nineteenth-Century American Literature on Child Rearing." In Childhood in Contemporary Cultures, edited by M. Mead and M. Wolfenstein, 150–167. Chicago: University of Chicago Press.

Swanston, H. Y., Plunkett, A. M., O'Toole, B. I., Shrimpton, S., Parkinson, P. N., and Oates, R. K. 2003. "Nine Years after Child Sexual Abuse." *Child Abuse and Neglect* 27: 967–984.

Swinford, S. P., DeMaris, A., Cernkovich, S. A., and Giordano, P. C. 2000. "Harsh Physical Discipline in Childhood and Violence in Later Romantic Involvements: The Mediating Role of Problem Behaviors." *Journal of Marriage and the Family* 62: 508–519.

Synott, A. 1983. "Little Angels, Little Devils: A Sociology of Children." *Canadian Review of Sociology and Anthropology* 20: 79–95.

Taylor, Cissy. 2000. "Resolution in Murder Case May Provide Some Comfort to Family: Unsolved Deaths in New Hampshire since 1970." *Manchester Union Leader*. January 4, 2000: A2.

Tein, J., Roosa, M., and Michaels, M. 1994. "Agreement between Parent and Child Report on Parental Behaviors." *Journal of Marriage and the Family* 56: 341–355.

Terling-Watt, Toni. 2000. "A Communitarian Critique of the Child Protective System." *Journal of Sociology and Social Welfare* 27: 3–23.

Testa, M. 2004. "Then Children Cannot Return Home: Adoption and Guardianship." *The Future of Children* 14 (Winter): 115–129.

Thomas, G. 1995. "Travels in the Trench between Child Welfare Theory and Practice: A Case Study of Failed Promises and Prospects for Renewal." *Child and Youth Services* 17: 1–250.

Thompson, K. M., Wonderlich, S. A., Crosby, R. D., and Mitchell, J. E. 2001. "Sexual Violence and Weight Control Techniques among Adolescent Girls." *International Journal of Eating Disorders* 29: 166–176.

Thornberry, T. P., Freeman-Gallant, A., Lizotte, A. J., Krohn, M. D., and Smith, C. A. 2003. "Linked Lives: The Intergenerational Transmission of Antisocial Behavior." *Journal of Abnormal Child Psychology* 31: 171–185.

Tite, R. 1993. "How Teachers Define and Respond to Child Abuse: The Distinction between Theoretical and Reportable Cases." *Child Abuse and Neglect* 17: 591–603.

Tjaden, P., and Thoennes, N. 1999. "Violence and Threats of Violence against Women and Men in the United States, 1994–1996." In ICPSR Version. Denver: Center for Policy Research (Producer). Ann Arbor, Mich.: Inter-University Consortium for Political and Social Research (Distributor).

———. 2000a. "Full Report of the Prevalence, Incidence, and Consequences of Violence against Women: Findings from the National Violence Against Women

Survey." Washington, DC: U.S. Department of Justice, Office of Justice Programs.

———. 2000b. "Prevalence and Consequences of Male-to-Female and Female-to-Male Intimate Partner Violence as Measured by the National Violence Against Women Survey." Washington, DC: U.S. Department of Justice and Centers for Disease Control.

Tjaden, P., Thoennes, N., and Allison, Christine J. 2000. Comparing Stalking Victimization from Legal and Victim Perspectives." *Violence and Victims* 15: 7–22.

Tremblay, C., Hebert, M., and Piche, C. 1999. "Coping Strategies and Social Support as Mediators of Consequences in Child Sexual Abuse Victims." *Child Abuse and Neglect* 23: 929–945.

Tribe, L. H. 2004. "*Lawrence v. Texas*: The 'Fundamental' Right that Dare Not Speak Its Name." *Harvard Law Review* 117: 1893–1955.

Tricket, P. K., and McBride-Chang, C. 1995. "The Developmental Impacts of Different Forms of Child Abuse and Neglect." *Developmental Review* 15: 311–337.

Tsai, Betsy. 2000. "Note: The Trend Toward Specialized Domestic Violence Courts, Improvements on an Effective Innovation." *Fordham Law Review* 68: 1285–1327.

Turner, H. A., and Finkelhor, D. 1996. "Corporal Punishment as a Stressor among Youth." *Journal of Marriage and the Family* 58: 155–166.

Turner, H. A., and Muller, P. A. 2004. "Long-Term Effects of Child Corporal Punishment on Depressive Symptoms in Young Adults: Potential Moderators and Mediators." *Journal of Family Issues* 25: 761–782.

U.S. Department of Health and Human Services. Child Abuse Prevention and Treatment Act. Including Adoption Opportunities and the Abandoned Infants Assistance Act. As Amended by the Keeping Children and Families Safe Act of 2003. Washington, DC: Administration for Children, Youth, and Families. Children's Bureau. Office on Child Abuse and Neglect.

———. 1995. A Nation's Shame: Fatal Child Abuse and Neglect in the United States. A Report of the U.S. Advisory Board on Child Abuse and Neglect. Washington, DC: U.S. Department of Health and Human Services.

———. 2004a. Child Welfare Outcomes 2001: Annual Report. www.acf.hhs.gov/programs/cb/Publications/cwo01.

———. 2004b. Child Maltreatment 2002. www.acf.hhs.gov/programs/cb/Publications/cm02.

U.S. Department of Health and Human Services. 1998 (September). The National Elder Abuse Incidence Study: Final Report. Washington, DC: U.S. Government Printing Office.

U.S. Department of Justice. 2004. When Violence Hits Home: How Economics and Neighborhood Play a Role. Research in Brief. Washington, DC: National Institute of Justice.

U.S. General Accounting Office. 1996. Cycle of Sexual Abuse: Research Inconclusive about Whether Child Victims Become Adult Abusers (GGD-96-178).

Valentine, L., and Feinauer, L. L. 1993. "Resilience Factors Associated with Female Survivors of Childhood Sexual Abuse." *American Journal of Family Therapy* 21: 216–224.

Vandivere, S., Tout, K., Capizzano, J., and Zaslow, M. 2003. "Left Unsupervised: A Look at the Most Vulnerable Children." *Child Trends: Research Brief.* Publication 2003–05. www.childtrends.org.

Van Haeringen, A. R., Dadds, M., and Armstrong, K. L. 1998. "The Child Lottery: Will the Doctor Suspect and Report? Physician Attitudes towards and Reporting of Suspected Child Abuse and Neglect." *Child Abuse and Neglect* 22: 159–169.

Van Hasselt, V. B., Morrison, R. L., Bellack, A. S., and Herson, M., eds. 1987. Handbook of Family Violence. New York: Plenum Press.

Van Wormer, K. 1997. Social Welfare: A World View. Chicago: Nelson-Hall.

Van Wyk, J. A., Benson, M. L., Fox, G. L., and DeMaris, A. 2003. "Detangling Individual-, Partner-, and Community-Level Correlates of Partner Violence." *Crime and Delinquency* 49: 412–438.

Vleminckx, K., and Smeeding, T. M., eds. 2001. "Child Well-Being, Child Poverty and Child Policy in Modern Nations: What Do We Know?" Bristol, UK: Policy Press.

Vulliamy, A. P., and Sullivan, R. 2000. "Reporting Child Abuse: Pediatricians' Experiences with the Child Protection System." *Child Abuse and Neglect* 24: 1461–1470.

Wagner, M. M., and Clayton, S. L. 1999. "The Parents as Teachers Program: Results from Two Demonstrations." *The Future of Children* 9 (1): 91–115.

Wald, M. S. 1975. "State Intervention on Behalf of 'Neglected' Children: A Search for Realistic Standards." *Stanford Law Review* 27: 985–1040.

———. 1976. "State Intervention on Behalf of 'Neglected' Children: Standards for Removal of Children from Their Homes, Monitoring the Status of Children in Foster Care and Termination of Parental Rights." *Stanford Law Review* 28: 673–706.

Walker, Robert, Logan, T. K., Jordan, Carol E., and Campbell, Jacquelyn C. 2004. "An Integrative Review of Separation in the Context of Victimization: Consequences and Implications for Women." *Trauma, Violence, and Abuse* 5: 143–193.

Walrath, C., Ybarra, M., Holden E. W., Liao, Q., Santiago, R., and Leaf, P. 2003. "Children with Reported Histories of Sexual Abuse: Utilizing Multiple Perspectives to Understand Clinical and Psychosocial Profiles." *Child Abuse and Neglect* 27: 509–524.

Walsh, J. F., and Foshee, V. 1998. "Self-Efficacy, Self-Determination and Victim Blaming as Predictors of Adolescent Sexual Victimization." *Health Education Research* 13: 139–144.

Walton, E. 1997. "Enhancing Investigative Decisions in Child Welfare: An Exploratory Use of Intensive Family Preservation Services." *Child Welfare* 76: 447–461.

Wanless, M. 1996. "Mandatory Arrest: A Step toward Eradicating Domestic Violence, but Is It Enough?" *University of Illinois Law Review* 533–587.

Ward, T., and Keenan, T. 1999. "Child Molesters' Implicit Theories." *Journal of Interpersonal Violence* 14: 821–838.

Warner, J., and Griller, R. 2003. "My Papa Is Out, and My Mama Is Asleep: Minors, Their Routine Activities, and Interpersonal Violence in an Early Modern Town, 1653–1781." *Journal of Social History* 36: 561–585.

Warner, J., and Lunny, A. 2003. "Marital Violence in a Martial Town: Husbands and Wives in Early Modern Portsmouth, 1652–1781." *Journal of Family History* 28: 258–276.

Warr, Mark, and Ellison, Christopher G. 2000. "Rethinking Social Reactions to Crime: Personal and Altruistic Fear in Family Households." *American Journal of Sociology* 106: 551–578.

Wasik, B. H., and Roberts, R. N. 1994. "Survey of Home Visiting Programs for Abused and Neglected Children and Their Families." *Child Abuse and Neglect* 18: 271–283.

Watkins, B., and Bentovim, A. 1992. "The Sexual Abuse of Male Children and Adolescents: A Review of Current Research." *Journal of Child Psychology and Psychiatry* 33: 197–248.

Watkins, S. A. 1990. "The Mary Ellen Myth: Correcting Child Welfare History." *Social Work* 35: 500–503.

Wattendorf, Daniel J., and Muenke, Maximilian. 2005. "Fetal Alcohol Spectrum Disorders." *American Family Physician* 72: 279–283.

Wayland, Francis [A Plain Man]. 1831. "A Case of Conviction." *American Baptist Magazine* (October): 35–38. Reprinted in America's Families: A Documentary History, edited by D. Scott and B. Wishy. New York: Harper.

Webster, Stephen W. 1991. "Variations in Defining Family Maltreatment: A Community Survey." In Abused and Battered: Social and Legal Responses to Family Violence, edited by Dean D. Knudsen and JoAnn L. Miller, 49–62. Hawthorne, N.Y.: Aldine deGruyter.

Wekerle, C., Wolfe, D. A., Hawkins, D. L., Pittman, A. L., Glickman, S., and Lovald, B. E. 2001. "Childhood Maltreatment, Post-Traumatic Stress Symptomatology, and Adolescent Dating Violence: Considering the Value of Adolescent Perceptions of Abuse and a Trauma Mediational Model." *Development and Psychopathology* 13: 847–871.

Welden, S. Laurel. 2002. Protest, Policy, and the Problem of Violence Against Women: A Cross-National Comparison. Pittsburgh, Pa.: University of Pittsburgh Press.

Wellman, M. M. 1993. "Child Sexual Abuse and Gender Differences: Attitudes and Prevalence." *Child Abuse and Neglect* 17: 539–547.

Wells, R., McCann, J., Adams, J., Voris, J., and Dahl, B. 1997. "A Validational Study of the Structured Interview of Symptoms Associated with Sexual Abuse (SASA) Using Three Samples of Sexually Abused, Allegedly Abused, and Nonabused Boys." *Child Abuse and Neglect* 21: 1159–1167.

Wells, S. J. 1985. "Decision-Making in Child Protective Service Intake and Investigation." *Protecting Children* 2: 3–8.

Wells, S. J., Stein, T. J., Fluke, J., and Downing, J. 1989. "Screening in Child Protective Services." *Social Work* 34: 45–47.

West, Carolyn M. 1998. "Lifting the 'Political Gag Order': Breaking the Silence around Partner Violence in Ethnic Minority Families." In Partner Violence: A Comprehensive Review of 20 Years of Research. Thousand Oaks, Calif.: Sage Publications.

West, M. M. 1998. "Meta-Analysis of Studies Assessing the Efficacy of Projective Techniques in Discriminating Child Sexual Abuse." *Child Abuse and Neglect* 22: 1151–1161.

Whealin, J. M. 2002. "Women's Report of Unwanted Sexual Attention during Childhood." *Journal of Child Sexual Abuse* 11: 75– 88.

Wheeler, K. H. 1997. "Infanticide in Nineteenth-Century Ohio." *Journal of Social History* 31: 407–418.

Whiffen, V. E., and Clark, S. E. 1997. "Does Victimization Account for Sex Differences in Depressive Symptoms?" *British Journal of Clinical Psychology* 36: 185–193.

Whipple, E. E., and Richey, C. A. 1997. "Crossing the Line from Physical Discipline to Child Abuse: How Much Is Too Much?" *Child Abuse and Neglect* 21: 431–444.

White, H. R., and Widom, C. S. 2003. "Intimate Partner Violence among Abused and Neglected Children in Young Adulthood: The Mediating Effects of Early Aggression, Antisocial Personality, Hostility and Alcohol Problems." *Aggressive Behavior* 29: 332–345.

Whittaker, J. K., Kinney, J., Tracy, E. M., and Booth, C. 1990. Reaching High-Risk Families: Intensive Family Preservation in Human Services. Hawthorne, N.Y.: Aldine de Gruyter.

Widom, Cathy Spatz. 1989a. "Does Violence Beget Violence: A Critical Examination of the Literature." *Psychological Bulletin* 106: 3–28.

———. 1989b. "The Cycle of Violence." *Science* 244: 160–166.

———. 1999. "Post-Traumatic Stress Disorder in Abused and Neglected Children Grown Up." *American Journal of Psychiatry* 156: 1223–1229.

———. 2003. "Understanding Child Maltreatment and Juvenile Delinquency: the Research." In Understanding Child Maltreatment and Juvenile Delinquency: From Research to Effective Program, Practice, and Systemic Solutions, 1–10. Washington, DC: Child Welfare League of America.

Widom, C. S., Ireland, T., and Glynn, P. T. 1995. "Alcohol Abuse in Abused and Neglected Children Followed-Up: Are They at Increased Risk?" *Journal of Studies on Alcohol* 56: 207–217.

Widom, C. S., and Kuhns, J. B. 1996. "Childhood Victimization and Subsequent Risk for Promiscuity, Prostitution, and Teenage Pregnancy." *American Journal of Public Health* 86: 1607–1612.

Widom, C. S., and Maxfield, M. G. 2001. "An Update on the 'Cycle of Violence.'" *National Institute of Justice Research in Brief* (February). Washington, DC: U.S. Department of Justice.

Widom, C. S., Raphael, K. G., and DuMont, K. A. 2004. "The Case for Prospective Longitudinal Studies in Child Maltreatment Research: Commentary on Dube, Williamson, Thompson, Felitti, and Anda (2004)." *Child Abuse and Neglect* 28: 715–722.

Wilcox, W. G. 1998. "Conservative Protestant Childrearing: Authoritarian or Authoritative?" *American Sociological Review* 63: 796–809.

Wilkes, G. 2002. "Abused Child to Nonabusive Parent: Resilience and Conceptual Change." *Journal of Clinical Psychology* 58: 261–276.

Williams, L., and Finkelhor, D. 1995. "Paternal Caregiving and Incest: Test of a Biosocial Model." *American Journal of Orthopsychiatry* 65: 101–113.

Wingood, G. M., DiClemente, R. J., McCree, D. H., Harrington, K., and Davies, S. L. 2001. "Dating Violence and the Sexual Health of Black Adolescent Females." *Pediatrics* 107: 1363–1368.

Winn, M. 1983. Children Without Childhood. New York: Random House.

Wishy, B. 1968. The Child and the Republic: The Dawn of American Child Nurture. Philadelphia: University of Pennsylvania Press.

Wolak, J., Mitchell, K., and Finkelhor, D. 2003. "Internet Sex Crimes against Minors: The Response of Law Enforcement." National Center for Missing and Exploited Children.

Wolcott, D. 2001. "The Cop Will Get You: The Police and Discretionary Juvenile Justice, 1890–1940." *Journal of Social History* 35: 349–372.

Wolf, K. A., and Foshee, V. A. 2003. "Family Violence, Anger Expression Styles, and Adolescent Dating Violence." *Journal of Family Violence* 18: 309–316.

Wolfe, Charles. 2003. "Court Says Domestic Violence Order Not Meant for 'Boyfriend/Girlfriend' Cases." Frankfort, Ky.: *Courier Journal*.

Wolfe, D. A. 1987. Child Abuse: Implications for Child Development and Psychopathology. Newbury Park, Calif.: Sage Publications.

———. 1985. "Child-Abusive Parents: An Empirical Review and Analysis." *Psychological Bulletin* 97: 462–482.

Wolfe, D.A., and Wekerle, C. 1993. "Treatment Strategies for Child Physical Abuse and Neglect: A Critical Progress Report." *Clinical Psychology Review* 13: 473–500.

Wolfenstein, M. 1951. "The Emergence of Fun Morality." *Journal of Social Issues* 7 (4): 15–25.

Wolock, L., and Horowitz, B. 1984. "Child Maltreatment as a Social Problem: The Neglect of Neglect." *American Journal of Orthopsychiatry* 58: 91–103.

Wood, Julia T. 2001. "The Normalization of Violence in Heterosexual Romantic Relationships: Women's Narratives of Love and Violence." *Journal of Social and Personal Relationships* 18: 239–261.

Wrigley, Julia, and Dreby, Joanna. 2005. "Fatalities and the Organization of Child Care in the United States: 1985–2003." *American Sociological Review* 70: 729–757.

Wu, S. S., Ma, C., Carter, R. L., Ariet, M. M., Feaver, E. A., Resnick, M. B., and Roth, J. 2004. "Risk Factors for Infant Maltreatment: A Population-Based Study." *Child Abuse and Neglect* 28: 1253–1264.

Wulczyn, F. 2003. "Closing the Gap: Are Changing Exit Patterns Reducing the Time African American Children Spend in Foster Care Relative to Caucasian Children?" *Children and Youth Services Review* 25: 431–462.

Wurtele, S. K., and Miller, C. L. 1987. "Children's Conceptions of Sexual Abuse." *Journal of Clinical Child Psychology* 16: 184–191.

Wyatt, G. E., Loeb, T. B., Solis, B., and Carmona, J. V. 1999. "The Prevalence and Circumstances of Child Sexual Abuse: Changes across a Decade." *Child Abuse and Neglect* 23: 45–60.

Zahn, Margaret A. 2003. "Intimate Partner Homicide: An Overview." *National Institute of Justice Journal* 250: 2–3.

Zelenko, M., Lock, J., Kraemer, H. C., and Steiner, H. 2000. "Perinatal Complications and Child Abuse in a Poverty Sample." *Child Abuse and Neglect* 24: 939–950.

Zelenko, M. A., Huffman, L. C., Brown, B. W., Jr., Daniels, K., Lock, J., Kennedy, A., and Steiner, H. 2001. "The Child Abuse Potential Inventory and Pregnancy Outcome in Expectant Adolescent Mothers." *Child Abuse and Neglect* 25: 1481–1495.

Zelizer, V. 1985. Pricing the Priceless Child. New York: Basic Books.

Zellman, G. L., 1990. "Child Abuse Reporting and Failure to Report among Mandated Reporters." *Journal of Interpersonal Violence* 5: 3–22.

Zellman G. L., and Antler, S. 1990. "Mandated Reporters and CPS: A Study in Frustration." *Public Welfare* 48: 30–37, 46.

Zigler, E., and Hall, N. 1989. "Physical Child Abuse in America: Past, Present, and Future." In Child Maltreatment: Theory and Research on the Causes and Consequences of Child Abuse and Neglect, edited by Cicchetti and Carlson, 38–75. New York: Cambridge University Press.

Zigler, E. F., Kagan, S. L., and Hall, N. W., eds. 1996. Children, Families and Government: Preparing for the Twenty-First Century. New York: Cambridge University Press.

Zivi, Karen D. 2000. "Who Is the Guilty Party? Rights, Motherhood, and the Problem of Prenatal Drug Exposure." *Law and Society Review* 34: 237–258.

Zola, S. M. 1998. "Memory, Amnesia, and the Issue of Recovered Memory: Neuro-Biological Aspects." *Clinical Psychology Review* 19: 915–932.

Zun, L. S., Downey, L. V., and Rosen, J. 2003. "Violence Prevention in the ED: Linkage of the ED to a Social Service Agency." *American Journal of Emergency Medicine* 21: 454–457.

Zuravin, S. J. 1999. "Child Neglect: A Review of Definitions and Measurement Research." In Neglected Children: Research, Practice, and Policy, edited by H. Dubowitz, 24–46. Thousand Oaks, Calif.: Sage Publications.

Zuravin, S. J., Benedict, M., and Somerfield, M. 1993. "Child Maltreatment in Family Foster Care." *American Journal of Orthopsychiatry* 63: 589–596.

Zuravin, S. J., and DiBlasio, F. A. 1996. "The Correlates of Child Physical Abuse and Neglect by Adolescent Mothers." *Journal of Family Violence* 11: 149–166.

Index

About the Authors

JoAnn Miller is associate professor of sociology and an affiliated member of the Women's Studies faculty at Purdue University. She holds graduate degrees from the College of William and Mary and the University of Massachusetts, Amherst. She was a research associate at the National Center for State Courts, a visiting professor at the University of Hamburg and the University of Indonesia, and a liberal arts fellow at the Harvard Law School. With Robert Perrucci she was the editor of *Contemporary Sociology* and she was the associate editor of *Social Problems*. Most of her family abuse and violence work is published in the *Journal of Interpersonal Violence, Violence Against Women*, the *Handbook of Marriage and the Family*, and *Abused and Battered: Social and Legal Responses to Family Violence*. She teaches in the fields of sociology of law and social problems.

Dean D. Knudsen is professor emeritus of sociology at Purdue University where he taught for thirty-five years. He holds graduate degrees from the University of Minnesota and the University of North Carolina, Chapel Hill, and was an NIH Fellow at the Family Violence Program at the University of New Hampshire. He is the author or coauthor of several books, including *Child Protective Services; Abused and Battered: Social and Legal Responses to Family Violence* (with JoAnn Miller); and *Child Maltreatment: Emerging Perspectives*.